D1129956

Nixon's War at Home

Justice, Power, and Politics

COEDITORS
Heather Ann Thompson
Rhonda Y. Williams

EDITORIAL ADVISORY BOARD
Peniel E. Joseph
Daryl Maeda
Barbara Ransby
Vicki L. Ruiz
Marc Stein

The Justice, Power, and Politics series publishes new works in history that explore the myriad struggles for justice, battles for power, and shifts in politics that have shaped the United States over time. Through the lenses of justice, power, and politics, the series seeks to broaden scholarly debates about America's past as well as to inform public discussions about its future.

More information on the series, including a complete list of books published, is available at http://justicepowerandpolitics.com/.

Nixon's War at Home

The FBI, Leftist Guerrillas, and the
Origins of Counterterrorism

· ·

DANIEL S. CHARD

The University of North Carolina Press Chapel Hill

© 2021 The University of North Carolina Press
All rights reserved
Set in Charis by Westchester Publishing Services
Manufactured in the United States of America

The University of North Carolina Press has been a member
of the Green Press Initiative since 2003.

Library of Congress Cataloging-in-Publication Data
Names: Chard, Daniel S., author.
Title: Nixon's war at home : the FBI, leftist guerrillas, and the origins
    of counterterrorism / Daniel S. Chard.
Other titles: Justice, power, and politics.
Description: Chapel Hill : University of North Carolina Press, [2021] |
    Series: Justice, power, and politics | Includes bibliographical references
    and index.
Identifiers: LCCN 2021000641 | ISBN 9781469664507 (cloth ; alk. paper) |
    ISBN 9781469664514 (ebook)
Subjects: LCSH: Nixon, Richard M. (Richard Milhous), 1913–1994. |
    United States. Federal Bureau of Investigation—History—20th century. |
    Terrorism—Prevention—History—20th century. | Terrorism—
    Government policy—United States—History—20th century. |
    Left-wing extremists—Government policy—United States. |
    Domestic intelligence—United States—History—20th century. |
    United States—Politics and government—1969–1974.
Classification: LCC HV8144.F43 C4267 2021 | DDC 363.325/
    16097309047—dc23
LC record available at https://lccn.loc.gov/2021000641

Cover illustration: Detail from a People's Assembly to Impeach Nixon flyer.

For L. and A.

The social revolution . . . cannot draw its poetry from the past, but only from the future. It cannot begin with itself, before it has stripped off all superstition in regard to the past.

—Karl Marx

Contents

Illustrations

Introduction

The Making of American Counterterrorism

• •

These people are called what? These people who are doing these bombings on campuses, these anti-Vietnam War people, people that are trying to overthrow our Government and get rid of the Capitalist system. They're called, well, militants . . . revolutionaries, radicals, Commies, Pinkos, weirdos, beatniks . . . I mean there's all sorts of terms.

In the early 1970s, the word terrorism creeps into our vocabulary. . . . All of a sudden . . . these people are all sort of lumped into the word terrorism.

—FBI special agent William E. Dyson

Insurgent violence, carried out by rebels with political grievances against state authorities, has come and gone throughout history. But in the late twentieth century it transformed into something new. It was not until the 1970s that police agencies and state officials began to explicitly frame some forms of insurgent violence—particularly bombing, airplane hijacking, and hostage taking—as something called "terrorism." As leftist guerrilla insurgents raged in the United States and throughout the globe, police investigators, state officials, and policy experts *invented* the modern concept of terrorism as a problem distinct from other forms of violence, criminality, and political activity.[1]

Transforming insurgent violence into "terrorism" amounted to more than just giving a new name to an old tactic. The concept of terrorism enabled U.S. state officials such as Federal Bureau of Investigation (FBI) director J. Edgar Hoover and President Richard M. Nixon to revive and legitimize intrusive mass surveillance tactics previously used against Communists. Framing insurgent violence as terrorism also helped authorities develop new strategies, institutions, and policies to counter what they defined as a distinct, urgent threat to U.S. national security.

By the late 1970s, such state efforts had a name of their own: "counterterrorism." The term refers to active police operations designed to *preempt* terrorism—that is, detect violent attacks and stop them before they happen. Such operations are sometimes contrasted with defensive antiterrorism measures intended to identify terrorists at borders, ports, and airports. In addition to obtaining intelligence that can give officials advance warning of terrorist attacks, counterterrorism operatives seek to neutralize organizations' capacity to engage in political violence, and ultimately to destroy them altogether.[2]

Preemption was and is central to counterterrorism. Those who lived through the 9/11 attacks and the presidency of George W. Bush may recall that preemption was the underlying principle of the Bush Doctrine used to justify America's 2003 military invasion of Iraq. Preemption was also the goal behind the mass electronic surveillance established by the National Security Agency (NSA) and other U.S. intelligence agencies after passage of the PATRIOT Act of 2001. Today counterterrorism is a major industry, with counterterrorism units embedded in more than 1,000 federal government organizations, as well as in state and municipal police departments and roughly 2,000 private companies.[3]

Though America's counterterrorism apparatus ballooned after 9/11, U.S. counterterrorism first emerged in the 1970s in response to homegrown leftist guerrillas. Its development was deeply influenced by the Weather Underground and the Black Liberation Army (BLA), clandestine armed organizations that splintered off from the New Left and the Black Power movement, respectively, of the late 1960s and early 1970s. Violent conflicts between the United States and these political dissidents—over issues of global power, racism, and economic inequality—were the crucible in which the tactics, doctrine, and sprawling bureaucratic structures of counterterrorism were forged.

Guerrillas and the State

The pages that follow will trace the origins of counterterrorism to violent conflicts in the Cold War era. This history will show how the U.S. war in Vietnam and police brutality—particularly directed against African American communities and political activists—motivated a small number of American leftist radicals to import strategies of clandestine urban guerrilla warfare from revolutionary anti-imperialist movements in Asia, Africa, and Latin America. It will also illustrate how U.S. leaders neglected to build lasting alternatives to the state violence, racism, and poverty that many liberals, leftists, and social scientists of the late 1960s identified as root causes of violent social conflict.

For U.S. officials, the response to civil disorder and insurgency was to surveil, police, and incarcerate the crisis.[4] American politics, already deeply punitive, grew even more so with President Richard Nixon's 1968 election on a "law and order" platform. The Nixon administration went on to lay much of the groundwork for the rise of mass incarceration that during the 1980s and 1990s made the United States one of the greatest jailers of its own people.[5] FBI and White House officials developed what would become counterterrorism in the context of Nixon's law-and-order crackdown on the Black Power movement, the antiwar movement, and other social movements of the era.

Counterterrorism and guerrilla insurgency were intimately connected from the start. Agents of the state and leftists influenced one another and studied one another. The sources that inform this book—including thousands of pages of declassified FBI documents and other government materials, Nixon White House tape recordings, and memoirs and oral histories of leftists and FBI personnel alike—are filled with their claims and conspiracy theories.[6] To be clear, this book does not argue that militant leftists were responsible for the rise of counterterrorism. Nor does it conclude that U.S. officials concocted counterterrorism as some sort of state conspiracy. Instead, it seeks to trace the ways that insurgents and state agents unintentionally goaded each other forward—how the state's preemptive tactics amplified leftist paranoia, just as guerrilla violence informed and sometimes helped legitimize the FBI and Nixon administration's frequently extralegal programs.

During the Nixon years, from 1969 to 1974, young radicals detonated over 600 bombs inside the United States.[7] (Some government estimates put the number of bombings much higher, into the thousands.) Teaching themselves explosives manufacturing from any number of how-to guides then circulating within the radical Left, militants used bombs as a way of protesting the war in Vietnam and police violence in Black communities. Many, if not most, hoped their actions would ignite a broader revolutionary uprising, bringing the violence of racism, imperialism, patriarchy, and capitalist exploitation to an end once and for all.

A small number of young radicals took their commitment to revolutionary struggle further. Beginning in 1969, militant factions within Students for a Democratic Society (SDS) and the Black Panther Party initiated plans to form what would become the Weather Underground and the BLA, the United States' first clandestine revolutionary urban guerrilla organizations.[8]

Taking inspiration from Latin American theorists Ernesto "Ché" Guevara and Carlos Marighella, they believed that spectacular armed actions carried out by small *focos* of highly disciplined guerrillas could spark popular revolutionary uprisings, rendering unnecessary traditional leftist strategies of building working-class constituencies through labor unions, community organizations, and socialist political parties. Loosely modeling themselves after Uruguay's Tupamaros and other Latin American guerrilla organizations, they established a revolutionary "underground," building an infrastructure of "safe houses" throughout the country and taking on assumed names and forged IDs. They trained themselves in the use of firearms and bomb making and launched attacks on America's corporations, military, and police.[9]

And they were not alone. These organizations were part of a larger trend within the international Left—in Brazil, Italy, Japan, West Germany, and elsewhere—in which radicals adopted clandestine urban guerrilla warfare as a strategy for overthrowing the state and creating a socialist society.[10]

In the United States, the sparks of revolution never caught fire. Leftist guerrillas were revolutionary in their ideologies, identities, and aspirations, but at no point in the 1960s or 1970s was the United States in a "revolutionary situation." Though groups like the Black Panthers attracted widespread media coverage, inspiring significant revolutionary sentiment, the Left in this period did not build broad, organized power among working-class Americans of any race or ethnicity. Leftists lacked the capacity to lead workers' strikes and halt industrial production, inspire mutinies in domestic police agencies, or prevent state officials from following through with their daily executive decisions.[11]

Instead, America's homegrown guerrillas faced a fearsome backlash. Though responsible for only a fraction of the revolutionary violence carried out in the United States during the Nixon years, the Weather Underground and BLA attracted a disproportionate amount of police attention. These guerrilla organizations had a particularly strong influence on the FBI, the primary federal agency dedicated to protecting America's "internal security."

The Weather Underground, known originally as Weatherman, and then the Weatherman Underground, first emerged as a clandestine urban guerrilla organization in 1970, a year before the BLA. Most frustrating to the FBI was the group's clandestinity—its ability to elude capture while carrying out bombings throughout the country and taking credit for them in widely publicized communiqués. FBI officials were quick to discover that many of their traditional tactics were of little use for fighting clandestine guerrillas.

The FBI's expansive surveillance network of informants in and around radical political groups was unable to gather intelligence on members of the Weather Underground, and covert counterintelligence operations were of little use against a group that special agents were unable to locate. The Weather Underground also incited Nixon and his White House staff, who personally and repeatedly implored FBI director J. Edgar Hoover to suppress America's guerrilla insurgency. Initiated in 1970, the FBI's Weather Underground investigation (code-named WEATHFUG) was the bureau's largest investigation since the Charles Lindbergh kidnapping case of 1932–34. Though the FBI captured a few of the Weather Underground's dozens of members, the group carried out over twenty-five bombings throughout the United States, hitting the Capitol, the Pentagon, and the State Department, among other targets before disbanding in 1976.[12]

The Weather Underground's self-fashioned explosives mainly targeted empty buildings, and the group never killed anyone in the bomb attacks it took credit for. The FBI suspected Weather Underground involvement in a handful of unclaimed bombings that did result in deaths or serious injury, however. Moreover, while preparing to go underground in early 1970, three Weatherpeople accidentally blew themselves up as they constructed nail bombs that were very much intended to kill and maim. The deaths of its own members prompted major soul-searching within Weatherman, and over the next several months the organization changed its initial strategy of targeting police and other human beings to one focused on symbolic acts of property destruction.[13] The FBI remained skeptical of Weatherman's renunciation of murder as a revolutionary tactic in later communiqués, however, and continued to treat it as a lethal threat.

Formed amid the suppression and decline of the Black Panther Party, the BLA also attracted massive, nationwide FBI investigations, many of them coordinated with those of local police agencies. Seeking to retaliate for police violence against Black communities and build an armed revolutionary movement inside the United States, the BLA assassinated police officers, broke comrades out of jail, and robbed banks to fund its underground activities. From 1971 to 1974, BLA guerrillas killed at least eight police officers in New York, San Francisco, Atlanta, and New Jersey and wounded more than a dozen. The BLA's wave of assaults did not last as long as the Weather Underground's because the group engaged in riskier, more lethal actions that exposed its members to police capture and bullets. As Black people, the BLA's underground guerrillas drew greater suspicion (and harsher treatment) from racially biased law enforcement. By the time Nixon resigned from office on August 9, 1974, police had sent most BLA members to prison or the grave.[14]

Many have written about America's leftist insurgency of the late 1960s and early 1970s. The topic has inspired a slew of memoirs, journalistic histories, scholarly studies, and documentary films—works that give us a good sense of the factors that drove some young radicals to take up arms.[15] Missing, however, is an adequate explanation of how such violence influenced U.S. police agencies and American politics beyond the radical Left.[16] *Nixon's War at Home* seeks to fill this gap, revealing how guerrilla insurgency influenced a critical shift from the anticommunism of the early Cold War to antiterrorist concerns that would become the central pillar of the twenty-first-century national security state.

This shift encompassed the whole career of a crucial, paradoxical figure who stood at the center of Nixon's war with leftist guerrillas. Hoover directed the FBI from 1924 until his death on May 2, 1972, at age seventy-seven.[17] Americans today tend to associate Hoover with a host of nefarious covert operations against his perceived political enemies, including inside the U.S. government. But during the late 1960s Hoover was, in fact, highly reluctant to expand surveillance of American leftists. Throughout his career as director, Hoover had carefully crafted the FBI's public image as trusted crime fighter and defender of national security, knowing that this image was critical to maintaining the bureau's powerful institutional autonomy from Congress and the White House.[18] As dissident activists and politicians began to challenge the FBI's authority in the mid-1960s, Hoover worried that leaked information detailing illegal spy practices could raise alarms over civil liberties violations. Calls for congressional oversight, he feared, could undermine the bureau's reputation and power. So, between 1965 and 1967, Hoover restricted the FBI's use of teenaged informants, mail opening, warrantless wiretapping, and break-ins, tactics the bureau had used widely against the Communist Party over the previous decade.[19]

But Hoover did not ban all unlawful FBI operations. Shortly after he rolled back the FBI's use of illegal surveillance tactics, Hoover increased his use of top-secret counterintelligence programs (COINTELPROs), designed "to expose, disrupt, misdirect, discredit, or otherwise neutralize" the Black Panther Party, SDS, and other radical organizations.[20] COINTELPRO tactics included mailing anonymous, inflammatory materials intended to sow distrust and discord within organizations; providing true or falsified derogatory information on radical groups to the news media; informing local police about leftists' criminal or civil violations; and notifying employers of targeted individuals' political affiliations.[21]

The FBI's COINTELPROs loom large in the scholarship and lore of the 1960s-era radical Left, but misconceptions abound. Writers have frequently neglected to distinguish between the bureau's counterintelligence and domestic surveillance programs, and have portrayed both one-dimensionally, as products of officials' paranoia, anticommunist hatred, racism, or hunger for power, without also examining how the FBI changed over time or considering how state actors understood and responded to insurgent violence.[22] Journalist Betty Medsger, for example, has argued that the FBI carried out its secret operations throughout the 1950s, 1960s, and early 1970s merely to "silence people whose political opinions the director [Hoover] opposed."[23] The literature has also tended to blur key distinctions in police activity: between FBI activities and those of other police and intelligence agencies; between officially sanctioned and informal FBI actions; and between undercover agents and informants.[24]

In many cases, writers have cast the state as all-powerful, as if no dissident movement ever had a chance of creating change in the United States so long as the FBI stood in the way. Take sociologist David Cunningham's generalization that "the FBI has gone beyond the passive monitoring of dissidents [and instituted disruptive counterintelligence programs] whenever threats to the status quo have intensified."[25] The most influential proponents of such a perspective are Ward Churchill and Jim Vander Wall, who remain widely cited despite being discredited as reliable scholars. According to Churchill and Vander Wall, the core lesson to be learned from the history of the FBI and the U.S. Left is that "to the extent that you become effective at advocating and organizing around your agenda, you will be targeted by the FBI for systematic undermining and discrediting, harassment, and—ultimately—outright elimination by counterintelligence operatives."[26]

Yes, the FBI was powerful, and it was no friend of the American Left. Yet in the 1960s, Hoover initiated domestic counterintelligence operations not simply because he despised leftists in particular but because he hoped to preemptively destroy organizations the FBI deemed prone to revolutionary violence. Hoover focused the FBI's COINTELPROs on a range of groups and individuals who vocally encouraged armed insurrection or other forms of civil disorder, including right-wing organizations like the Ku Klux Klan. The results of these programs were mixed. By encouraging existing factional disputes within the Black Panthers, for example, the FBI's COINTELPRO against the organization surely contributed to its disintegration, limiting the group's capacity for violence. At the same time, however, amid federal and state indictments of prominent radicals and violent police attacks on Black Panthers throughout the country, the FBI's disruptive covert operations helped radicalize the U.S. Left, pushing many Panthers, SDS militants, and other radicals down the road to armed resistance.

The FBI's development of what would become counterterrorism was improvisational, drawing from techniques used previously against the Communist Party while also inventing new tactics to address the problem of clandestine guerrilla violence. In 1970, after the young Jonathan Jackson's deadly armed raid on a California courtroom and a lethal bombing at the University of Wisconsin, the FBI began to revive restricted illegal surveillance tactics and expand surveillance of the Black Power movement and New Left in the name of fighting terrorism. The FBI also introduced a host of new policing practices dedicated to combating terrorism, including the bureau's first undercover agent program and contingency plans for hostage situations. The FBI implemented these changes under intense pressure from President Nixon, who repeatedly called on J. Edgar Hoover, and his successor Acting Director L. Patrick Gray, to preempt and defeat what he called "revolutionary terrorism."

While demanding that the FBI halt leftist violence, Nixon established the nation's first institutions explicitly dedicated to combatting terrorism. These included the short-lived Huston Plan of 1970 and the Cabinet Committee to Combat Terrorism, established in 1972. Such developments established the political, intellectual, tactical, and legal foundations of American counterterrorism. They occurred as part of a broader, global post–World War II history of states embracing the term "terrorism" in efforts to describe, delegitimize, and destroy their insurgent adversaries.

From Anticommunism to Antiterrorism

It is common for Americans to think of 9/11 as the starting point for today's battles with terrorism, and for good reason. When al-Qaeda militants slammed hijacked passenger jets into the Twin Towers of New York's World Trade Center and Washington's Pentagon on September 11, 2001, killing themselves and nearly 3,000 others, they ushered in an era marked by President George W. Bush's global war on terrorism, U.S.-led invasions of Afghanistan and Iraq, U.S. drone wars across Africa and the Middle East, mass electronic surveillance, and the emergence of a new international terrorist organization, the so-called Islamic State in Iraq and Syria.[27] But terrorism and counterterrorism have a longer history.[28]

Nixon's war at home is part of a larger, international history of how insurgent violence became "terrorism." After World War II, as the United States kicked off a nuclear arms race with the Soviet Union, American leaders warned that Communism was the greatest threat to national security. The specter of Communism had eclipsed anarchism, which had been U.S. authorities' main bogeyman from the 1886 Chicago Haymarket riot until the national Red Scare that followed World War I.[29] In the eyes of American leaders, Communism was not a political ideology that oppressed people would reasonably embrace because of its promise of social and economic equality; it was an evil, irrational global conspiracy that threatened the foundations of American democracy, Christianity, and Western civilization. According to the State Department's top-secret 1950 National Security Document 68, a key document informing America's Cold War military and intelligence buildup, the Soviet Union was a Communist "slave-state" motivated by a "fundamental design . . . to retain and solidify . . . absolute power." The authors of this document warned President Harry S. Truman that the nuclear-armed Soviet Union threatened "the destruction not only of [the United States] but of civilization itself."[30]

In the name of anticommunism, the United States established a massive national security state. The National Security Act of 1947 reorganized America's military and established the National Security Council and the Central Intelligence Agency (CIA), highly secretive and undemocratic institutions that operated with minimal congressional oversight. Presidents Harry S. Truman, Dwight D. Eisenhower, John F. Kennedy, and Lyndon B. Johnson poured millions of tax dollars into the development of nuclear missiles and other weaponry, the expansion of foreign military bases, and the strengthening of the FBI, CIA, and NSA.[31] At home, Hoover's FBI fed intelligence on thousands of suspected American Communists to the House Un-American Activities Committee and others in the federal government, fueling a second national Red Scare that ravaged the multi-racial organized Left that had helped build the New Deal.[32] Overseas, the United States backed coups in Iran (1953), Guatemala (1954), and beyond; colluded in the killing of the Congo's first elected prime minister Patrice Lumumba (1961); and bankrolled France's war to recolonize Indochina (1946–54) before launching its own war in Vietnam shortly thereafter.

America's Cold War state violence inspired resistance throughout the world. Newly independent regimes of the so-called Third World initially forged alliances through the United Nations in hopes of securing a path of development independent from both the United States and the Soviet Union. But by the mid-1960s the Non-Aligned Movement crumbled beneath the weight of U.S. intervention, Soviet disinterest, capitalist underdevelopment, and a host of local problems related to these global trends. In this context, revolutionaries reevaluated their strategies, and many turned to violence. As Vietnam's outgunned Communist rebels took on the U.S. war machine, more and more Third World revolutionaries embraced guerrilla warfare as a strategy for socialist and anticolonial revolution.[33] It was in this context that state powers began to frame guerrilla insurgencies as terrorist in nature, spawning the contemporary definition of terrorism in law and cultural understanding.

A shared understanding of this new definition of terrorism proved crucial. Decades earlier, the 1937 Convention on the Prevention and Punishment of Terrorism failed precisely because member states could not agree on a legal definition of terrorism.[34] But in the decades after World War II, a number of states passed antiterrorist laws to delegitimize their guerrilla adversaries. In 1948, the newly formed state of Israel passed the Prevention of Terror Ordinance No. 43 to criminalize armed groups of both Palestinian nationalists and Zionist extremists.[35] Apartheid South Africa's Terrorism Act of 1967 proscribed indefinite detention for members of Umkhonto we Sizwe and other multiracial guerrilla organizations seeking to liberate the country's indigenous Black majority from racist white minority rule.[36] During the 1960s, U.S. military documents frequently described Vietnamese guerrilla actions as "terrorist," but they used the word interchangeably with terms such as "guerrilla" and "insurgent." At this point the concept of international terrorism did not yet exist. In Southeast Asia and Latin America, U.S. officials used "terrorist" to describe military tactics rather than categorize people and responded to regional insurgencies by providing funding and training for police and military operations known as counterinsurgency.[37]

States institutionalized antiterrorism with growing frequency in the early 1970s amid a global uptick in urban guerrilla warfare. Following a rash of hostage-taking incidents in Latin America, the Organization of American States adopted a convention on terrorism in 1971 with protocols for extraditing individuals involved in such attacks.[38] Israel instituted a series of new antiterrorism measures after Palestinian nationalists gained world attention by hijacking international commercial airline flights.[39]

A crucial turning point in international terrorism discourse occurred in September 1972 at the Olympic Games in Munich, West Germany, when commandos from the Palestinian nationalist Black September Organization launched an attack on the Israeli team that resulted in the deaths of eleven Israeli athletes and three Palestinian guerrillas. After Munich, the United Nations (UN) General Assembly began a series of debates over the definition of terrorism and international efforts to prevent it. Like the League of Nations forty years earlier, the UN was unable to reach an international antiterrorism agreement because of objections from newly independent nations in Africa and Asia whose people had recently taken up arms against European colonial powers.[40] Palestinian leader Yasser Arafat spoke to anticolonial concerns when he told the UN General Assembly, "The difference between the revolutionary and the terrorist lies in the reasons for which each fight. For whoever stands by a just cause and fights for the freedom and liberation of his land from invaders, the settlers and the colonialists, cannot possibly be called a terrorist."[41]

In the absence of a UN accord, individual countries moved ahead with their own antiterrorism initiatives. The United Kingdom passed the Prevention of Terrorism Act of 1973 in response to Irish nationalist violence, outlawing the Irish Republican Army and other armed groups and delineating special punishments for members and supporters.[42] Following a wave of attacks by Québécois separatists, Canada's government tasked the national Royal Canadian Mounted Police Security Service with preventing terrorism in 1975 ahead of the 1976 Montreal Olympics.[43] In 1976, West Germany went after homegrown leftist guerrillas by updating its Criminal Code with measures outlawing "terrorist associations" and making support for terrorist groups punishable regardless of foreknowledge of violent attacks.[44]

It was in this context, in June 1970, that President Nixon approved plans for America's first institution devoted to fighting terrorism. The so-called Huston Plan never got off the ground, however. J. Edgar Hoover sabotaged it as part of his bureaucratic conflict with the White House. Nixon signed off on a plan to combat "revolutionary terrorism" drafted by his young staffer Tom Huston and disgruntled FBI assistant director William Sullivan in response to the Weather Underground and other leftist bombers. The proposal sought to bring all federal intelligence under the command of the White House and reinstitute domestic break-ins, mail opening, and warrantless wiretapping in order to coordinate and obtain preventive intelligence on potential terrorists.[45] Though the Huston Plan never went into effect, it was an important antecedent to the PATRIOT Act of 2001 and the Department of Homeland Security Act of 2002, post-9/11 bills that vastly broadened the executive branch's surveillance capacity.

In the absence of the Huston Plan, America's first lasting antiterrorism institution was Nixon's Cabinet Committee to Combat Terrorism (CCCT), founded shortly after Director Hoover's death. But the CCCT lacked the consolidation of executive branch surveillance powers outlined in the Huston Plan. Instead, the Cabinet Committee functioned primarily as a source of funding for terrorism research. The CCCT met only once, but its working group convened regularly over the next several years. Members of the CCCT working group produced monthly reports on worldwide insurgent political violence for federal agencies and hosted a series of international conferences pivotal to the creation of counterterrorism and the academic field of terrorism studies.[46] Yet, as critical as the CCCT was to the development of counterterrorism, it lacked policing powers, leaving the federal government without institutions to guide U.S. intelligence agencies' counterterrorism operations until the early 1980s.

Counterterrorism and Watergate

Given Nixon's long-standing fixation on insurgent attacks and his persistent efforts to broaden the use of extralegal intelligence tactics through the Huston plan, the failure to consolidate counterterrorism actions after Hoover's death is notable. One possible explanation for this delay was, in a word, Watergate. The Watergate scandal began on June 17, 1972, when police arrested a group of mysterious operatives burglarizing the Democratic National Committee Headquarters in Washington's Watergate apartment complex. The scandal gathered momentum over the next two years as investigators uncovered more and more evidence linking the burglars to the White House. It is likely that Nixon did not reinstitute the Huston Plan in October 1972 because in the midst of the FBI's growing Watergate investigation, the president did not want to implicate his cabinet in further illegal activities. After Nixon's resignation on August 9, 1974, the scandal would continue to rattle the American political system, further stalling the development of formal counterterrorism initiatives in Congress and the executive branch.

But there is also a more complex explanation for why Nixon did not consolidate American counterterrorism operations: the histories of American counterterrorism and Watergate are, in fact, intertwined. Ironically, the very same conflict that *inspired* the development of U.S. counterterrorism also helped fuel a political scandal that *delayed* the development of U.S. counterterrorism. As this book will show, when Hoover torpedoed the Huston Plan, a full-blown institutional conflict ensued. The Nixon administration eventually responded by establishing its own unit of covert operatives, the so-called Plumbers who carried out the Watergate burglary and other secret operations against the president's political adversaries. In addition to explaining the origins of American counterterrorism, this book reveals for the first time how institutional conflict over how to combat terrorism led to Watergate.[47]

The Nixon-Hoover conflict was not only about leftist violence. It was also about leaks of government sources exposing Nixon's escalation of the war in Vietnam, about Nixon's authoritarian drive to neutralize his political "enemies," and about a power struggle among Hoover's deputies within the FBI. After Hoover's death, this conflict and these leaks continued through the actions of a secret informant known as Deep Throat, later revealed to be FBI associate director W. Mark Felt, whose leaks to the press were manifestations of the power struggle between the FBI and the Nixon White House over extralegal surveillance techniques, jurisdiction, and counterterrorism policy.

The final chapters of this book unpack a paradox inherent in these tactics. Felt exposed the Nixon administration's use of illegal break-ins, even while authorizing the very same sorts of break-ins during the FBI's Weather Underground investigation. Felt was both a Hoover loyalist and firm advocate of preventive action against those the FBI considered terrorists. Felt had no problem with illegal break-ins for the purpose of countering terrorists and foreign spies, but he resented Nixon's efforts to exert control over the FBI by installing bureau outsider L. Patrick Gray as acting director of the FBI after Hoover's death. Felt also opposed the Nixon administration's use of break-ins for purely partisan objectives. Using his position as the second most powerful figure in the FBI, Felt sought to undermine both men.

At the same time, Felt authorized break-ins in FBI terrorism investigations because agents had already been carrying out such operations since August 1970 in response to Hoover's unofficial orders. With the support of assistant director Edward Miller, Felt established a formal procedure for authorizing break-ins in order to restore morale among FBI field agents, who sought assurance that headquarters would support them if ever they were caught participating in such illegal acts. Under Felt, the FBI carried out break-ins against alleged Weather Underground supporters as well as lesser known break-ins targeting Arabs suspected of planning a Munich-style attack in the United States. The latter break-ins were part of a wider FBI campaign harassing Arab and Arab Americans that I refer to as America's first "Arab scare," a precedent to U.S. intelligence agencies' widespread targeting of Arabs and Muslims after 9/11.[48]

Like Hoover's mass surveillance of American dissidents in 1970, Felt's secret wars backfired, leading to outcomes that clashed with his objectives. His leaks enflamed the Watergate scandal and helped bring down Nixon and Gray but also ended his own career as well. And instead of leading to the capture of Weather Underground fugitives, the FBI's break-ins landed Felt a 1980 federal felony conviction. In the process, the FBI's popular legitimacy plummeted. It has yet to fully recover.

The FBI's war with American guerrillas was no mere sideshow to the larger political dramas of the 1960s and 1970s. On the contrary, Nixon's war at home and the development of counterterrorism intersected with all of the period's major political conflicts and changes: the Vietnam War, the New Left, the Black Power movement, the women's movement, Watergate, controversies over mass surveillance and covert operations, and the rise of mass incarceration. Today, amid a revival of leftist social movements, heightened fears of political violence, and the aftermath of a Trump administration embroiled in scandal, this history is more important than ever.

1 Nixon, Hoover, and America's Homegrown Insurgency

· ·

Before sunrise on January 20, 1969, four young white radicals bundled up in winter coats, hats, and gloves and came down from the mountain. Leaving the cabin they shared in snowy Idaho Springs, Colorado, Cameron David Bishop, Linda Goebel, Steven Knowles, and Susan Parker drove the steep grade of the Rocky Mountains' eastern slope. In their car, they transported a homemade bomb.

Over the past few days, members of the group had built the bomb with dynamite and other materials stolen from a local mine. Their target was one of the hundreds of colossal steel towers that held up the Public Service Company of Colorado's sprawling electricity grid servicing the Denver metropolitan area. These lines powered one facility in particular: the massive Coors Porcelain Plant in the Denver suburb of Golden. Lugging the device to the base of the tower, they set the timer and fled the scene.

The explosion destroyed the tower, knocking out electricity at the Coors factory and surrounding areas of Jefferson County for several hours. During the blackout, Coors workers were forced to halt construction of two of the Coors Company's most lucrative products: nose cones for Sidewinder missiles and armored plates for military helicopters. These were essential components of weaponry the U.S. military used in Vietnam, where America's ongoing war had killed over 30,000 Americans and 2 million Vietnamese since 1964.[1] The bombing was a success as far as temporarily slowing the war machine was concerned—even more important, however, was the timing.

More than 1,500 miles away, President Richard Nixon was delivering an inaugural speech espousing peace, urging Americans to move on from the domestic turmoil of the Johnson administration.[2] Arrayed against him were thousands of nonviolent protesters who had descended on Washington for the day's "counterinaugural" events, as well as several hundred members of a rowdy faction of Students for a Democratic Society (SDS) who hurled stones, bottles, smoke bombs, firecrackers, and paint-filled lightbulbs. Police met violence with more violence, clubbing protesters with their batons and making 119 arrests, in what the *New York Times* called "the first at an inaugural ceremony in the 180 years of the Presidency." Nixon also made history as the first American president to give an inaugural speech behind a barrier of bullet-proof glass.[3] Meanwhile in Colorado, Cameron Bishop and his crew sent Nixon a message by greeting his presidency with an exploding bomb.

· · · · · ·

Nixon had narrowly won the 1968 election on a campaign to end the war in Vietnam and restore law and order to American society. The latter pledge appealed to a large constituency of working and middle-class white Americans—a group Nixon soon referred to as the "Silent Majority"—who felt threatened by increasing Black radicalism, white youth counterculture, rising crime rates, and violent civil disorder on America's college campuses and city streets. Despite the peaceful rhetoric in his inaugural address, Nixon had no intentions of eliminating the root causes of violent social conflict, problems that social scientists of the day and peace activists such as the late Martin Luther King Jr. had identified as racism, economic inequality, and militarism.[4] Instead, the new president sought repression.

Suppressing America's domestic insurgency would not come easy. As a matter of fact, Nixon's election seemed to inspire increased militant resistance. During the fall of 1968, membership of the Black Panther Party (BPP) mushroomed from only a handful of chapters to over forty in cities throughout the country.[5] The BPP stood out from other protesters for both its visibility and its advocacy of armed revolution. The group's black-leather-clad African American male leaders were staples of international television news, and the *Black Panther* newspaper reached tens of thousands with its calls for retaliatory violence against police and other state figures. Amid its sudden growth, the BPP also attracted heavy police violence. As Nixon entered office, Panther cofounder Huey P. Newton awaited trial behind bars on murder charges for the 1967 death of an Oakland cop, and fellow Panther leader Eldridge Cleaver was in socialist Algeria, where he had fled to escape separate felony charges. During the first half of 1969, local police staged at least ten armed raids on BPP offices and homes throughout the country and arrested hundreds of the group's members.[6] In multiple instances, Panthers responded to police violence with violence of their own, injuring officers in the process. SDS members stepped up their confrontational tactics as well, clashing violently with police on several occasions in the months after the counterinaugural melee.[7]

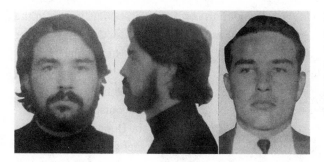

FBI mugshots of Cameron David Bishop, the first leftist radical to appear on the bureau's list of Ten Most Wanted Fugitives. FBI.gov.

Bombings also became increasingly popular. Just a week after the inauguration, on January 28, Cameron Bishop and company were already planting more bombs in the Denver area. These bombings targeted powerlines servicing the Martin-Marietta Corporation and Dow Chemical Company, two other companies with factories that manufactured weapons for the U.S. military.[8] And they weren't the only ones.

A small number of young radicals had first adopted bombing as a political tactic in 1968. Over fifty bombs were set by the end of the year, and as Nixon escalated the U.S. air war on Vietnam and police amplified attacks on radicals in 1969, incidents of revolutionary violence surged. Between January 1969 and April 1970, leftist militants carried out over 400 bombings and acts of arson in the United States.[9]

Nixon's reaction to militant resistance was to use the tools of law and order, issuing federal felony indictments against activists. On March 20, 1969, just a few weeks after his inauguration, Attorney General John Mitchell indicted a group of radicals known as the Chicago Eight on a slew of felony charges, including conspiracy to cross state lines with intent to incite a riot. Mitchell accused the men—peace activist David Dellinger, SDS leaders Tom Hayden and Rennie Davis, Yippie leaders Jerry Rubin and Abbie Hoffman, antiwar activist professors Lee Weiner and John Froines, and Black Panther chairman Bobby Seale—of orchestrating the massive antiwar protests that disrupted the 1968 Democratic National Convention.[10] The Justice Department lodged at least a half dozen other federal conspiracy indictments against leftist radicals during Nixon's first term.[11] Such high-profile, politically motivated indictments were characteristic of the style of law-and-order policing and prosecution Nixon encouraged.[12]

Yet the *first* American radical the Nixon administration indicted was accused Colorado bomber Cameron Bishop. On February 14, 1969, less than a month into Nixon's presidency, Attorney General Mitchell charged the twenty-six-year-old radical under an obscure antisabotage law from the World War I era. When Bishop went into hiding, Director J. Edgar Hoover put him on the FBI's list of Ten Most Wanted Fugitives. He was the first leftist radical to earn such a distinction.

The president hoped to go further, pressuring Hoover to intensify FBI surveillance of American dissidents. Nixon had been an outspoken anticommunist since the late 1940s, when his leadership of the House Un-American Activities Committee's (HUAC) investigation of Soviet spy Alger Hiss elevated his status to that of the Republican Party's most prominent figure.[13] As a member of HUAC, Nixon worked closely with Hoover, developing a lasting professional relationship.[14] Two decades later, Nixon found it almost impossible to believe that American radicals' increased proclivities for mass protest and bombings were purely homegrown. Nixon insisted that foreign Communist governments must be funding SDS, the Panthers, and other radical groups and demanded that Hoover escalate his tactics in response.

The problem, however, was that Nixon and Hoover disagreed over what tactics to use. They also feared that leaked disclosures of secret state actions could result in political fallout that would damage their careers. For this reason, both men were reluctant to authorize illegal intelligence activities in writing. Nixon and Hoover agreed on the need to combat leftist violence with militaristic, law-and-order strategies of preemptive surveillance, covert operations, and criminal prosecution. But how to carry out these tasks led to a power struggle with outsize consequences.

Law and Order

The rise of counterterrorism and law-and-order politics was not inevitable. The late 1960s was a period in which mainstream political figures openly discussed addressing the root causes of violent social conflict. In the spring of 1968, the National Advisory Commission on Civil Disorders (better known as the Kerner Commission) issued a 511-page report commissioned by the Johnson administration following the devastating 1967 riots in Newark, Detroit, and dozens of other cities. This document called for robust federal spending on programs to eliminate the economic and racial inequality that gave rise to violent unrest. Doing so, the report argued, could help America realize "common opportunities for all within a single society."[15] The *Kerner Report*'s recommendations echoed Martin Luther King Jr.'s appeal the previous year to end the war in Vietnam and guarantee jobs, education, health care, and economic security for all Americans. The United States, King declared, required a nonviolent "radical revolution of values" to eliminate the "triple evils of racism, economic exploitation, and militarism."[16] In other words, people like King and the authors of the *Kerner Report* sought not merely to suppress insurgent violence but to reduce all forms of violence, including the police and military violence that inspired most insurgent violence.[17]

But instead of addressing the roots of violence, Nixon pursued law and order, a deliberate appeal to both racism and fear of increasing violent crime.[18] The racist white vote had been much less of a consideration during Nixon's earlier political career, when he represented California in the House and the Senate and served as vice president under President Dwight D. Eisenhower. Back in the late 1940s and 1950s, segregation was a given. Both political parties made modest overtures to northern Black voters, but Democrats ruled the "solid South," where under the Jim Crow system of legalized racial segregation, white Democrats and the Ku Klux Klan used local laws and vigilante violence to maintain political, social, and economic dominance over African Americans. The Democratic Party's voter base was a paradoxical coalition of southern "Dixiecrats," farmers, and northern white and African American workers stitched together during President Franklin Roosevelt's New Deal of the 1930s. The Republican voter base consisted of small-town and middle-class whites throughout the North and West. Liberals dominated the Democratic Party and maintained important influence among Republicans. Despite racial and gender inequality that seems obvious in retrospect, white male intellectuals spoke of a Cold War political "consensus" that united Americans in a commitment to upholding New Deal economic regulations and social programs, fighting Soviet-backed Communism at home and abroad, and maintaining America's post–World War II dominance of global affairs.

The civil rights movement and white backlash reshuffled this system from top to bottom. Conflicts over racial equality in the 1960s forged the greatest overhaul of America's political parties since the Civil War.

Nixon's 1968 presidential campaign had been a critical part of this transformation. Nixon campaigned with a calculated "Southern strategy," calling for law and order in an effort to break up the Democratic Party's New Deal coalition. Nixon specifically courted white voters in the South and in industrial cities in the North, playing on their fears that a rise in African Americans' status would diminish their own social standing. As his close advisor John Ehrlichman put it, "That subliminal appeal to the anti-black voter was always present in Nixon's statements and speeches."[19] An example of this appeared in Nixon's "Failure of Leadership" television ad, which featured film footage of young Black rioters and white antiwar protesters clashing with police along with eerie music punctuated by gun blasts. In his voiceover, Nixon assured implicitly white "forgotten Americans" that they were "not racist or sick" or "guilty of the crime that plagues the land." America's "non-shouters" and "non-demonstrators," Nixon asserted, "were good people, decent people," who deserved to live free from "domestic violence."[20]

Nixon's law-and-order rhetoric was loaded with bias. His campaign rarely mentioned the violence of racist vigilantes, police, and the U.S. military. In fact, Nixon's narrow emphasis on violence carried out by African Americans and political radicals helped *legitimize* violence targeting these groups. Nixon's strategy helped him eke out a slim victory over his Democratic rival, incumbent vice president Hubert Humphrey, and over Alabama's former segregationist governor George Wallace, who earned over 13 percent of the popular vote on an independent law-and-order campaign that compelled Nixon to ramp up his own rhetoric.[21]

Two individuals who helped build critical electoral support for Nixon among white conservatives would later become important figures in the development of U.S. counterterrorism. Tom Huston was a twenty-eight-year-old attorney who described himself as a "conservative hard-liner." While completing his law degree at Indiana University in 1966 and 1967, he served as president of the conservative student organization Young Americans for Freedom. In 1968, Huston campaigned for Nixon while working at the Pentagon as an analyst for the army's Defense Intelligence Agency. He rallied crucial support for Nixon among movement conservatives who had backed Barry Goldwater's nomination as the GOP presidential candidate in 1964.[22] As a White House aide, Huston would later help draft the so-called Huston Plan, a short-lived secret proposal early in Nixon's first term that sought to amplify federal surveillance capabilities in the name of fighting terrorism.[23]

Senator Strom Thurmond (SC) was instrumental in helping Nixon win southern white votes. Since running an independent presidential campaign under the States Rights Democratic Party in 1948, Thurmond had gained national renown for his outspoken anticommunism and support for racial segregation. As a Democratic senator, he staged a record-breaking twenty-four-hour filibuster in opposition to the Civil Rights Act of 1957. His opposition to the Civil Rights Act of 1964 later motivated him to change his membership to the Republican Party and support the Goldwater campaign. In 1968, Thurmond campaigned for Nixon in the South, warning white voters that a vote for George Wallace would only benefit Hubert Humphrey. As the first prominent southern politician to switch political parties in the 1960s, Thurmond built momentum for a broader, long-term shift in white southern voting preferences from Democrat to Republican.[24] Indeed, Thurmond's aide Henry Dent was the key architect of Nixon's "Southern Strategy."[25]

Nearly forgotten is Thurmond's critical role in the development of counterterrorism. From 1969 to 1977, Thurmond revitalized the Senate Subcommittee on Internal Security—long discredited as a relic of the postwar anticommunist Red Scare—with a focus on investigating left-wing violence. By framing such violence as terrorism and emphasizing the supposed threat it posed to U.S. national security, Thurmond pushed back against efforts by Congress and the Justice Department to impose legal limitations on FBI operations.[26] In 1981, after the Republicans gained control of the Senate on the coattails of Ronald Reagan's sweeping presidential election victory, Thurmond rose to the chair of the Senate Judiciary Committee. In this capacity he founded the Subcommittee on Security and Terrorism, which was essentially a reincarnation of the Internal Security Subcommittee. In the decades since, the subcommittee has played a central role in the development of U.S. counterterrorism policy.[27]

Nixon's 1968 election marked a critical shift in American politics away from the limited social democracy of the New Deal and Johnson's Great Society toward the gradual elimination of social programming and the rise of law-and-order policing, counterterrorism, and mass incarceration. Between 1970 and 2000, America's prison population swelled from around 300,000 to over 2 million, with Blacks and Latinos accounting for over half of those behind bars. This was an unprecedented prison boom, one that devastated working-class communities of color as municipal, state, and federal authorities transferred men and women forsaken by the deindustrializing urban economy out of their communities and into cages.[28] The punitive turn in American politics started before Nixon, under President Johnson, who helped make local policing a concern of the federal government for the first time in U.S. history. As his priorities shifted from the War on Poverty to a War on Crime, Johnson signed the Law Enforcement Enhancement Act of 1965 and the Omnibus Crime Control and Safe Streets Act of 1968. The latter bill established the Law Enforcement Assistance Administration (LEAA), which offered block grants to municipal police departments for the funding of new personnel, training, buildings, computer technology, vehicles, weapons, and other equipment. Nixon dramatically expanded on Johnson's efforts, however. Under Nixon, LEAA's annual budget grew from $400 million in 1968 to $850 million in 1973.[29]

Across both administrations, J. Edgar Hoover was one of America's most influential advocates of law-and-order policing. Hoover lobbied relentlessly behind the scenes to ensure crime legislation allocated funding to the FBI. The Omnibus Crime Control Act of 1968, for example, earmarked $5,110,000 for the bureau to train municipal police at the FBI National Academy during fiscal year 1969, and expanded the number of officers involved in such programming from 200 to 2,000.[30] Following Hoover's November 1970 testimony before members of the Senate Appropriations Committee, the federal government allocated $14 million in supplemental funding for the FBI's efforts to combat guerrilla bombings and airplane hijackings.[31]

During the Johnson administration, Hoover had pressured a reluctant president to expand federal policing measures in response to the era's urban riots. When Nixon came to office, Hoover found himself working for a longtime friend who held common views on law-and-order policing. Nonetheless, Hoover and Nixon would find themselves at odds as they argued about tactics for dealing with a left-wing insurgency.

"State of Emergency"

Cameron Bishop's inauguration day bombing gained little publicity outside of Colorado, but it did not go unnoticed in Washington. Bishop had a long history with SDS before shifting toward his later, more explosive tactics. He had joined the organization during the early 1960s as an undergraduate at Pennsylvania State University. There he and other student activists participated in a picketing campaign to desegregate a white-owned barbershop in the town of College Park that refused service to African Americans.[32] After he graduated, Bishop immersed himself in political activism in Colorado. A couple months before the powerline bombing, Bishop and a group of protesters had barricaded themselves in an upper floor of Colorado State University's Agricultural Building to protest campus recruitment by the Dow Chemical Company, manufacturer of the chemical weapon napalm used by the air force to burn the flesh of its victims in Vietnam.[33] He was arrested alongside fourteen others by Fort Collins police, but remained undeterred in his activism.

Bishop's politics grew exceedingly radical. Even among the SDS's militant "action faction," whose members would go on to form Weatherman, Bishop was known as a "crazy": someone whose advocacy of violent tactics was seen as insanely irresponsible and dangerous.[34] Despite this reputation, there were limits to how far he was willing to go. Of the multiple bombings he masterminded, not one physically harmed anyone.

Given the pressure the FBI was under to root out the bomber, it was only a matter of time before Bishop was found out. Shortly after the Colorado transmission tower explosions, Denver-based FBI agents discovered stolen dynamite and blasting caps similar to those used in the bombings in a mine tunnel near the cabin where Bishop lived with his three accomplices. The agents detained Bishop, questioning him for five and a half hours, but released him after determining they lacked sufficient evidence to press charges. Almost immediately after leaving FBI custody, Bishop went into hiding.[35]

Because Bishop's FBI file remains classified today, it is impossible to determine exactly how FBI and White House officials felt about the Denver bombing suspect's flight from federal authorities. But Bishop's escape must have been embarrassing to Hoover, who placed a high premium on the FBI's reputation for always capturing its suspects.

The White House made its feelings clear when Attorney General Mitchell charged Bishop under an amendment to the Federal Sabotage Act of 1918 that made it a crime to sabotage "war utilities . . . when the United States is at war, or in times of national emergency as declared by the President."[36] It was only the second such indictment since World War II. Two months earlier, President Johnson's outgoing attorney general Ramsey Clark issued the first one against Michael Siskind, a twenty-one-year-old SDS member who firebombed an ROTC building on the St. Louis campus of Washington University in December 1968. Siskind pleaded guilty on February 10, 1969, four days before Mitchell indicted Bishop.[37]

It is unclear what legal basis determined the "state of emergency" cited in the Bishop indictment.[38] Eight years later, in 1977, as the nation continued to reel from the Watergate scandal and Nixon's resignation, a federal judge dismissed the charges against Bishop after determining that the indictment's "state of emergency" had no legal standing.[39] In the meantime, however, the Bishop indictment conveyed the Nixon administration's view on domestic revolutionary bombings: America was at war not only in Vietnam but also at home.

Soon after the Justice Department's indictment, Hoover publicly signaled that the FBI too was committed to thwarting leftist bombings. On April 15, 1969, the director added Bishop to the FBI's list of Ten Most Wanted Fugitives. Hoover's decision to include a leftist revolutionary on the list for the first time in its history indicated an important change in FBI priorities.[40]

Over the course of 1969, Nixon officials would continue to demand the FBI accelerate its efforts to prevent revolutionary bombings as well as civil disturbances and leaks of classified state secrets. The FBI had a long history of surveillance operations and covert counterintelligence programs aimed at preempting perceived threats to U.S. national security. The reasons behind Hoover's reluctance to accede to Nixon's orders to expand FBI surveillance can be found in the longer history of FBI preemptive action.

J. Edgar Hoover and Preemptive Action

After his inauguration, Nixon had every reason to believe that his long-standing friendship with J. Edgar Hoover would carry over into his presidency. The pair shared political views, especially on policing, radicalism, and race. Hoover also wielded incredible power as gatekeeper of the FBI's vast catalog of information on thousands of Americans—including the personal secrets of U.S. political leaders. Hoover had proved a steadfast ally to Nixon's liberal predecessor, directing his agents to tap the phones and hotel rooms of Martin Luther King and other civil rights leaders during the 1964 Democratic National Convention at President Johnson's request, in the event that any protests might derail the incumbent president's expected nomination.[41] Shortly before Nixon took office, Johnson advised him that Hoover was "a pillar of strength in a city of weak men." "You will rely on him time and time again to maintain security," Johnson said; "He's the only one you can put your complete trust in."[42] Nixon fully expected the director to employ the bureau's surveillance capacities in the service of his administration's law-and-order domestic security agenda.

But America's political climate had changed dramatically over the five turbulent years of Johnson's presidency. As Nixon took over at the White House, Hoover was just as concerned with protecting the FBI's autonomous policing powers and his own personal reputation as he was with upholding America's national security.

Hoover's FBI had established its capacity for the sorts of preventive intelligence measures that would later undergird counterterrorism during the World War II era. In 1939, President Roosevelt issued a wartime directive granting the bureau exclusive jurisdiction over domestic "espionage, counterespionage, and sabotage matters."[43] Hoover used Roosevelt's directive as a license to establish the FBI as an autonomous police institution with minimal government oversight, and to carry out a range of secret operations unknown to presidents, lawmakers, or the American public.[44] The

FBI built up extensive surveillance files on African American activists and other leftists, as well as on suspected German spies and American anti-interventionists.[45] After the war, as the Cold War set in alongside a wave of anticommunist paranoia, the FBI focused its domestic security efforts on those associated with the Communist Party (CPUSA). The ostensible purpose of this surveillance was to investigate espionage and prevent Soviet-backed radicals from "subverting" the U.S. labor and civil rights movements and organizing a Communist revolution.

In the name of fighting Communism, Director Hoover oversaw the creation of the FBI's Security Index, a secret list containing the names of thousands of Americans with suspected Communist sympathies to be rounded up and detained in a "time of war or national emergency."[46] The FBI gathered intelligence on suspected Communists with the help of thousands of paid informants and "confidential sources," including bankers, landlords, and telephone operators.[47] The FBI also targeted CPUSA with a range of illegal surveillance tactics, including break-ins (known in bureau parlance as "surreptitious entries" or "black bag jobs"), safe breaking, "mail covers" (surveillance of addresses on the envelopes of a target's mail), mail opening, "trash covers" (surveillance of a target's curbside garbage bins), warrantless electronic telephone wiretaps, and hidden microphones (also known as "bugs").[48]

During the early 1950s, Hoover's FBI was central to the postwar Red Scare typically associated with the notorious anticommunist crusader Senator Joe McCarthy (R-WI). Hoover's FBI provided intelligence on American leftists to the anticommunist HUAC and Senate Internal Security Committee, and gathered evidence used to convict Eugene Dennis, Gus Hall, Henry Winston, and other CPUSA leaders on shaky conspiracy charges.[49] Hoover's FBI also gathered evidence used to wrongfully try, convict, and execute CPUSA members Julius and Ethel Rosenberg.[50]

In addition to engaging in preventive surveillance of suspected Communists and gathering intelligence to prosecute prominent members of CPUSA, the FBI carried out covert counterintelligence programs (COINTELPROs) designed to destroy radical organizations. The FBI first developed counterintelligence tactics during World War II as a means to undermine German, Japanese, and Soviet spies operating inside the United States. In 1956, after the Supreme Court curtailed the government's ability to prosecute suspected Communists, Hoover began directing counterintelligence operations against domestic radicals.[51]

The FBI's first such program targeted the Communist Party and was codenamed COINTELPRO-CPUSA. CPUSA's membership had already dwindled from an all-time high of around 75,000 at the close of World War II to only a few thousand, many of them FBI informants. But this did not faze Hoover, who regularly exaggerated the threat Communists posed to U.S. national security in order to attract congressional funding and expand the FBI's power. COINTELPRO-CPUSA tactics included mailing anonymous, inflammatory materials intended to sow distrust and discord within the party; providing true or falsified derogatory information about the organization to the news media; informing local police about members' criminal or civil violations; and notifying employers of individuals' membership in the group.[52] By 1971, the FBI had carried out 1,388 separate COINTELPRO operations against the CPUSA.[53] In the early 1960s, the FBI also initiated smaller COINTELPROs against the Socialist Workers Party (SWP) and the Puerto Rican independence movement.[54] In one of the FBI's most notorious counterintelligence operations, carried out independently of the latter programs, the bureau mailed an anonymous letter to Martin Luther King Jr. in November 1964, urging the civil rights leader to commit suicide or else the sender would leak tape recordings of his extramarital affairs to the press.[55]

Two changes in the FBI's operations against the U.S. Left during the Johnson years set the stage for the bureau's Nixon-era war with leftist guerrillas and the emergence of counterterrorism. First, amid the decline of the CPUSA and the growing problem of urban riots and disruptive antiwar demonstrations, the FBI's Domestic Security Division shifted many of its investigative priorities from preventing Communist "subversion" to preventing violent "civil disorder." Between 1964 and 1967, urban riots resulted in a severe crisis for President Johnson, who repeatedly implored Hoover to investigate and contain violent civil disturbances. In response, the FBI expanded its surveillance of African Americans. Its aim: to detect urban riots in advance.

The bureau initially focused its preventive surveillance on Black activists. Agents tapped the phones of prominent Black Nationalist leaders Malcolm X, Elijah Muhammad, and Maxwell Stanford and maintained surveillance notes on thousands of civil rights demonstrations.[56] After the Newark and Detroit riots of 1967, however, the FBI widened surveillance beyond Black radicals to entire African American communities. In other words, the FBI cast its gaze on all of urban Black America as a suspect community. Through the Ghetto Informant Program (GIP), white male FBI agents developed thousands of informants in African American neighborhoods who provided information used to gauge the potential for violent civil disturbance.[57] The program was wildly ineffective. As former special agent Jack Ryan remembered, Hoover's weekly GIP quota drove agents in many field offices to fill their reports with falsified intelligence attributed to fake "paper informants."[58] There is no evidence that intelligence gathered through the GIP ever enabled the FBI to stop a riot in advance.

The FBI also expanded surveillance of the antiwar movement under the rubric of violence prevention. Though he provided no specific evidence of impending violence, in 1966 Hoover ordered his agents to develop "awareness and alertness" of antiwar demonstrations in order to gain foreknowledge of "potentialities for violence outbreaks."[59] "I want to stress to you," he wrote, "that the emphasis in these matters must be on *advance detection*. . . . We are an intelligence agency and as such are expected to know what is going to or is likely to happen. National, state, and local authorities rely upon us to obtain this information so they can take appropriate action to avert disastrous outbreaks."[60]

The second significant Johnson-era change in FBI domestic security operations was Hoover's decision to rein in the bureau's use of illegal surveillance techniques. Throughout his four-decade career as director, Hoover had carefully crafted the FBI's public image as an organization of trusted crime fighters and defenders of national security. Hoover also promoted the FBI as apolitical—as an intelligence agency that operated in accordance with the law and outside partisan concerns. Hoover understood that such public imagery was necessary in order for the bureau to legitimize its independent power, autonomous from Congress and the White House.[61]

During the mid-1960s, however, dissident activists and politicians began to challenge U.S. intelligence agencies' authority. A Senate subcommittee's investigation of IRS surveillance in 1965 and 1966, for example, caused Hoover to worry that legislators would launch a similar investigation of FBI practices. From 1965 to 1967, Attorneys General Nicholas Katzenbach and Ramsey Clark implemented formal restrictions on the bureau's wiretapping and microphone surveillance powers.[62] Hoover also turned seventy in 1965, the FBI's mandatory retirement age. President Johnson could have forced Hoover to retire, but he recognized Hoover's status as one of the most powerful men in Washington. Instead, Johnson maintained the director's status as an ally and passed an executive order allowing him to keep his position.[63]

These developments made Hoover nervous. Between 1965 and 1967, amid growing political dissent and public scrutiny of his age, the director grew ever more preoccupied with defending the FBI from outside interference, worrying that leaks of information detailing bureau involvement in unlawful activities could lead to calls for government oversight. Accordingly, he made several moves intended to safeguard the FBI's institutional autonomy, restricting the bureau's use of break-ins, mail opening, warrantless wiretapping, and teenaged informants.[64] After 1965, the FBI also cut back its surveillance and counterintelligence operations against Martin Luther King and other civil rights leaders.[65]

But Hoover did not restrict all of the FBI's illegal operations. Striving to meet Johnson's repeated demands that the FBI prevent violence, the director established new top-secret COINTELPROs. The first one, code-named COINTELPRO-White Hate Groups, targeted the Ku Klux Klan and other violent right-wing organizations. Before establishing this program, the FBI had done little to combat deadly white supremacist violence. Hoover, after all, had come of age as a white man in segregated Washington, D.C. As a conservative supporter of federalism and "states rights," he had tacitly supported Klan violence for decades. In Hoover's view, the Klan was a problem to be solved by local authorities—the very same southern white leaders who maintained the racist Jim Crow regime in collaboration with the deadly vigilante organization.

Increased public scrutiny of Klan violence, however, compelled the FBI to act. The June 1964 disappearance of three young civil rights workers in Neshoba County, Mississippi, was particularly influential in this regard. Johnson faced an international outcry over the incident and ordered Hoover to take down the Klan with haste. Flooding the organization with paid informants and utilizing covert tactics similar to those employed against the Communist Party, the FBI succeeded within five years in destroying the Ku Klux Klan as a functional national organization.[66]

Toward the end of Johnson's term, Hoover launched COINTELPROs targeting the Black Power movement and the student New Left. The director established both of these COINTELPROs in an effort to preempt violent civil disorders. The FBI initiated COINTELPRO-Black Nationalist-Hate Groups (COINTELPRO-BNHG) after the Newark and Detroit riots of 1967, modeling the program after both COINTELPRO-CPUSA and COINTELPRO-White Hate Groups. According to Hoover's classified memo founding the program, the purpose of COINTELPRO-BNHG was "to expose, disrupt, misdirect, discredit, or otherwise neutralize" Black freedom organizations that allegedly threatened America's "internal security" owing to their "propensity for violence and civil disorder."[67] Hoover inaccurately characterized a wide spectrum of African American groups as "black nationalist, hate-type organizations," including Martin Luther King Jr.'s nonviolent Southern Christian Leadership Conference (SCLC), Elijah Muhammad's separatist Nation of

Islam (NOI), and a number of groups advocating philosophies of Black Power and armed self-defense: Student Nonviolent Coordinating Committee (SNCC), Congress for Racial Equality (CORE), Revolutionary Action Movement (RAM), and Deacons for Defense and Justice.[68]

Most scholars have interpreted Hoover's sweeping characterization of disparate Black freedom organizations as evidence of his racism, misunderstanding of African American politics, and personal desire to crush the Black Power movement. While there is truth in these interpretations, it must be understood that Hoover's stated reason for targeting the Black Power movement in 1967 was to monitor and preempt its potential for violence—a preoccupation that would inform many of his decisions in the years to come.

On March 4, 1968, Hoover expanded COINTELPRO-BNHG from twenty-three of the FBI's fifty-one field offices to forty-one. The primary goal, Hoover explained, was to "prevent violence on the part of black nationalist groups."[69] In a reference to the previous decade's armed Kenyan revolt against British colonial rule, Hoover called on agents to preempt a "'Mau Mau' in America." He directed his men to prevent a "coalition of militant black nationalist groups" and "the rise of a 'messiah' who could unify . . . the black nationalist movement," in part, by "pinpoint[ing] potential trouble-makers and neutraliz[ing] them before they exercise their potential for violence."[70] Hoover's reference to the "Mau Mau" and a "black messiah" have been widely quoted and corroborate Hoover's undeniable racism. But violence prevention remained the FBI's core aim. In regard to King, Hoover warned of the possibility that the civil rights leader might "abandon his supposed 'obedience' to 'white liberal doctrines' (nonviolence) and embrace black nationalism."[71]

Before Nixon's election, COINTELPRO-BNHG focused primarily on SNCC, whose leaders Stokely Carmichael and H. Rap Brown had become the Black Power movement's most visible spokesmen and critics of nonviolence. But this activity was limited. Beginning in the fall of 1968, COINTELPRO-BNHG would shift its focus to a group Hoover did not mention in the program's initial memorandum: the Black Panther Party.

Violence prevention also informed the FBI's COINTELPRO against the New Left. Hoover authorized COINTELPRO-New Left in April 1968 after a disruptive weeklong student strike at Columbia University gained international media coverage, including images of university administrators' offices ransacked by student protesters. Officials in the FBI's Domestic Security Division explained that the objective of the new COINTELPRO was to "expose, disrupt, or otherwise neutralize" the vaguely defined "New Left."

The program focused on SDS, seeking to prevent its members from engaging in "violent and illegal activities."[72] Like COINTELPRO-BNHG, COINTELPRO-New Left sought to prevent disruptive civil disturbances by "neutralizing" leftist radicals and organizations whose members promoted militant protest tactics and violent revolution. The FBI was concerned about SDS's "subversive" potential as well. During the first year of COINTELPRO-New Left, beginning in the spring of 1968, the FBI sought to undermine the organization's ability to lead a national movement against capitalism, war, and racism. Antisubversion would become less of a priority for COINTELPRO-New Left after June 1969, however, following the emergence of the Weatherman faction.

The FBI's war on the Black Power movement and New Left was undeniably political. Though Hoover portrayed the bureau as a neutral intelligence agency operating outside of Washington's influence, to him, maintaining law and order meant granting police departments a license to use violent force with impunity. In both the 1967 riots and the 1968 Columbia University student strike, for example, police engaged in far more violence than did protesters. During the Detroit riots, police and National Guardsmen were responsible for the deaths of at least twenty-seven people, most of them African American.[73] In New York, police brutally beat student occupiers and professors while clearing out Columbia's administrative buildings.[74]

Yet throughout the 1960s—and throughout his forty-eight-year career as FBI director—Hoover disregarded the problem of police violence. He regularly dismissed African Americans' and student protesters' complaints of police brutality as "wild charges" or "false allegations" lodged to justify violent criminal activity.[75] He also routinely shirked his responsibilities to investigate police violence as required by the 1964 Civil Rights Act.[76] In 1966, after the Supreme Court's *Miranda* decision ruled that police officers had to inform detained criminal suspects of their rights to an attorney, Hoover complained to his colleagues about "Negroes" who "cry 'police brutality' on the slightest provocation."[77] African American Chicago police officer Howard Saffold observed that Hoover's stance communicated to local police that "it was open season"; officers would not "have to worry about the law" when inflicting violence on Blacks and political radicals.[78]

And, of course, Hoover raised no critiques of American leaders who violated international law by waging a war of aggression in Vietnam. On the contrary, FBI officials saw SDS's attempts to disrupt the U.S. war effort as one of the reasons the organization needed to be destroyed.[79] Through its biased, selective policing operations, the FBI helped uphold a consensus among America's political leadership and much of its population: U.S. state violence in urban communities of color and in Vietnam was normal.[80]

Yet Hoover knew his limits. He understood that perceived violations of the law and Americans' civil liberties could diminish the FBI's reputation and prompt calls for oversight and reform. This is why during the 1960s, at the same time that Hoover sought to prevent radicalism, heightened public scrutiny of U.S. political institutions compelled the director to curtail most of its illegal surveillance operations. After Nixon took office, Hoover struggled to balance his desire to safeguard the FBI's public image with increasing White House pressure to preempt bombers and other law-breaking dissidents.

The Nixon-Hoover Power Struggle

President Nixon inherited from past administrations several surveillance-reporting programs designed to inform him of perceived threats to U.S. national security. The FBI, for example, provided the White House with regular reports on the activities of dissident political organizations and leaders, and on Congress members' and congressional staffers' contacts with foreign embassies. The IRS also issued reports on tax investigations of select American activists, while the CIA reported on antiwar and civil rights activists' foreign contacts. The NSA, meanwhile, shared information gleaned from domestic dissidents' international telecommunications.[81]

U.S. intelligence agencies did not inform the president of all their activities, however. Hoover, for example, kept the existence of the FBI's COINTELPROs secret from Nixon, just as he had done with previous presidents. America's other federal intelligence agencies also implemented illegal domestic surveillance operations during the late 1960s that they kept secret from Nixon. From 1967 to 1974, the CIA's top-secret Operation CHAOS kept surveillance files on thousands of antiwar and Black Power activists and monitored the movements of Stokely Carmichael, Eldridge Cleaver, and others in Guinea, Tanzania, Algeria, and Vietnam, passing much of their intelligence on to the FBI.[82] During the same period, the NSA's Project MINARET intercepted domestic antiwar and Black Power activists' international phone calls and relayed its findings to the CIA and FBI.[83]

Yet the president and his staff were not satisfied with the quality of the intelligence they received from America's spy agencies. Nixon suspected that foreign Communist regimes like the USSR, China, and Cuba were secretly calling the shots behind the scenes of the Black Power and antiwar

President Richard Nixon and FBI director J. Edgar Hoover meeting in the White House with Attorney General John Mitchell (far left) and presidential advisor John Ehrlichman (far right), 1971. Photograph by Byron Schumaker. Courtesy of the Richard Nixon Presidential Library and Museum (National Archives and Records Administration).

movements. Like Johnson before him, Nixon was convinced that organized "subversive" groups were to blame for America's urban uprisings and campus rebellions. There was no evidence to support these conspiracy theories, but the president's anticommunist paranoia fueled his suspicions. Nixon's counsel John Ehrlichman was especially dissatisfied with the FBI's surveillance reports. "In general the FBI investigative work I saw was of poor quality," he complained.[84]

Though Nixon and his aides shared dissatisfaction with the FBI's intelligence reports, they differed in their feelings toward Hoover. Upon taking office, Nixon felt compelled to keep his longtime friend employed as FBI director. Ehrlichman and other cabinet members, on the other hand, resented the aging bureaucrat's power. They wished to see him replaced.[85] Though Hoover would keep his post, Nixon White House requests for FBI intelligence fueled a bureaucratic struggle between the president and the FBI director.

Nixon's Justice Department, like Johnson's, directed Hoover's FBI to obtain preventive intelligence to preempt civil disturbances. Immediately after taking office, Attorney General Mitchell strengthened the department's Interdivisional Information Unit (IDIU), a domestic intelligence clearinghouse that Attorney General Clark had established in order to coordinate reports from the FBI and other agencies. The IDIU's purpose was to obtain advance warning of urban riots.[86] Writing on behalf of the IDIU, Assistant Attorney General J. Walter Yeagley instructed Hoover on February 18, 1969, "to determine whether there is any underlying subversive group giving illegal directions and guidance to the numerous campus disorders throughout the country." A few weeks later, Yeagley asked the FBI for "the names of any individuals who appear at more than one campus either before, during, or after any active disorder or riot and the identities of those persons from outside the campus who might be instigators of these incidents."[87] In April 1969, at Nixon's request, John Ehrlichman ordered the FBI and other U.S. intelligence agencies to produce evidence tying domestic dissidents to foreign Communist governments.[88]

Besides seeking greater access to intelligence, Nixon also enlisted the FBI's assistance in investigating a series of leaks. On May 9, 1969, the *New York Times* published a front-page story announcing that the United States had secretly expanded its aerial bombing efforts from Vietnam to Cambodia. The article revealed a blatant contradiction of Nixon's campaign promise to end the war in Indochina, and claimed its information came from anonymous "Nixon Administration sources."[89] In reality Nixon had always intended to escalate the war. Documents declassified in 2007 revealed that Nixon staffers secretly instructed South Vietnamese president Nguyen Van Thieu not to sign the 1968 peace accord that President Johnson negotiated with North Vietnamese president Ho Chi Minh, promising that once elected Nixon would revive U.S. military backing for South Vietnam.[90] Long before this information came to light, however, the Cambodia leak exposed Nixon's secret war efforts in Indochina. This was the most serious of the more than a dozen leaks Nixon faced during his first year in office.[91]

Nixon's powerful national security advisor Henry Kissinger—architect of the U.S. war in Cambodia—concocted a plan to find the leakers by enlisting the FBI's assistance. At the requests of Kissinger, Attorney General Mitchell, and White House chief of staff H. R. Haldeman, the FBI established seventeen warrantless telephone wiretaps. Special agents targeted the phones of National Security Council staffers, news journalists, and personnel in the White House, Department of Defense, State Department, and Justice Department.[92] Later, after coming to light during the Watergate hearings, these illegal wiretaps would become known as the "Kissinger wiretaps."

Hoover did not passively comply with the Nixon administration's surveillance requests, however. Although he agreed with Nixon that revolutionary bombings, disruptive protests, and leaks of classified state secrets posed serious threats to national security, the director remained reluctant to authorize illegal FBI operations owing to his own worries about leaks.

So he resisted. Hoover complied with surveillance requests only when he could ensure that in the case of public exposure, the White House, rather than the FBI, would be held responsible for authorizing the measures. In March 1969, Hoover rejected Assistant Attorney General Yeagley's request for expanded FBI surveillance of campus radicals. Though he instructed his field offices to maintain "student informant coverage," Hoover insisted that "additional student informants cannot be developed."[93] Hoover also sought to protect the FBI by acquiring White House approval for the seventeen Kissinger wiretaps. Though Nixon wanted no written record of the wiretaps, Hoover maintained logs of the secret recordings and obtained Attorney General Mitchell's written authorization for the operations. The director kept these records hidden outside of the FBI's normal filing system in the top-secret "Official and Confidential" files he kept inside his personal inner office.[94] Meanwhile, the FBI's reports to the Nixon administration consistently demonstrated that New Left and Black Power radicalism grew largely from domestic conditions; there was little, if any, evidence that foreign Communist governments were directly supporting America's new generation of leftists.[95]

Unbeknownst to Nixon, Hoover continued to authorize the FBI's COINTELPROs against the dwindling Communist Party, the SWP, the Ku Klux Klan, the Black Power movement, and the New Left. Hoover was serious about defending the nation's status quo from foreign and domestic revolutionary movements, even if the threats posed by such movements were remote and the FBI's actions violated law-abiding Americans' civil liberties. But he was determined to go about this on his own terms, regardless of who was in control of the White House.

· · · · · ·

When they ignited their bombs in Colorado, Cameron Bishop and his friends had no way of knowing the consequences of their actions. They couldn't have guessed that they would spark a secret feud between Nixon and Hoover, or that an increase in similar bombings over the next few years would lead to the invention of something called counterterrorism. Aside from earning distinction as the first leftist on the FBI's Most Wanted list, however, Bishop did not contribute much more to these developments. He spent the next six years in hiding, eluding an FBI manhunt while living quietly in Canada's Yukon Territory, on Staten Island, and on a farm in southern Maine.

Bishop turned up in April 1975 in East Greenwich, Rhode Island. Police arrested him along with a young Vietnam veteran from Maine named Raymond Luc Levasseur as they sat in a car parked outside a Dunkin Donuts where they were casing a bank across the street. When police searched the car, they found sixteen firearms.[96] Authorities dragged Bishop back to Colorado, where he finally faced the Nixon Justice Department's charges for the transmission tower bombings. His old accomplices Susan Parker and Linda Goebel testified against him at trial in exchange for immunity, but the judge dismissed the indictment based on the now-disgraced Nixon administration's questionable "national emergency" claims.[97]

Much had changed while Bishop was underground. Just before Nixon's election, the FBI set its sights on the BPP, and the bureau escalated its war on the Panthers throughout 1969. Though the FBI sought to neutralize the BPP's capacity for violence, police repression yielded ironic consequences, inspiring some Panthers to embrace urban guerrilla warfare. Instead of solving the problem of insurgent violence, the FBI's actions would ultimately open a new phase in the bureau's war with the radical Left.

2 Off the Pigs!

· ·

The year 1969 was supposed to be the "YEAR OF THE PANTHER." That's what the *Black Panther* newspaper proclaimed in capital letters and bold font on the cover of its January 4, 1969, edition. The large headline was dwarfed by an image created by the paper's art director, Emory Douglas. Filling the broadsheet's lower portion, the illustration depicted a Black man in a black beret, brow furrowed, mouth open, teeth bared, shouting. Above the fold, the man's right arm extended upward. In his fist, running parallel to the paper's nameplate, the man clenched a hefty black assault rifle.[1]

A large-print passage in the middle of the newspaper's centerfold offered an explanation for the headline: "The undeniable truth of the statement that '1969 is the year of the Panther' can be seen by reviewing the dynamic rise of the Black Panther Party despite the despotic attempts of the establishment to suppress the Party's move to liberate Black people."[2]

Ringing the centerfold's statement were twelve images of previous *Black Panther* covers. Nine of these covers displayed one of the following: cartoons of police caricatured as pigs, headlines referring to police officers as pigs, images of Panthers or other Black people bearing guns, drawings of Panthers attacking pigs in police uniforms, or some combination thereof. Two covers bore photographs of Minister of Information Huey Newton, then incarcerated while awaiting trial on murder charges for the October 1967 shooting death of Oakland police officer John Frey. The remaining cover featured a large photograph of Minister of Information Eldridge Cleaver, who had gone into exile in Algeria to escape charges of attempted murder after a January 1968 shootout with Oakland police.

Published a week before President Richard Nixon's inauguration, these images left no doubt about the Black Panthers' understanding of their relationship with American police agencies. They were revolutionaries, cops were counterrevolutionaries, and if it took violence to deal with cops, the Panthers were ready to oblige.

While students at Oakland's Merritt College in 1966, Huey Newton and Bobby Seale had founded the Black Panthers in response to widespread police discrimination and brutality in their community and in urban African

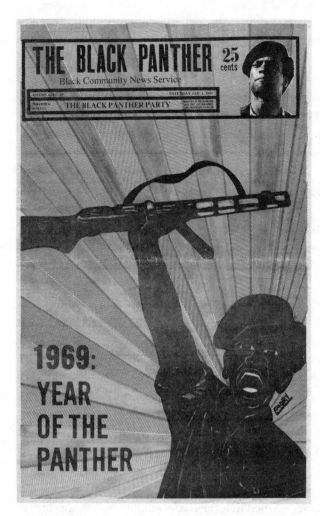

Cover of *Black Panther* newspaper, January 4, 1969. The BPP's newspaper regularly extolled revolutionary violence. © 2020 Emory Douglas / Artists Rights Society (ARS), New York. Courtesy of Bloom Alternative Press Collection, Amherst College Archives and Special Collections.

American communities throughout the country. Analyzing the nation's political landscape through an anti-imperialist lens, Newton popularized the notion that America's Black ghettos were "internal colonies" where predominantly white police forces occupied segregated African American neighborhoods at gunpoint, similar to how the U.S. military occupied South Vietnam.[3]

Extending this analogy, Newton believed that liberating America's internal colonies would ultimately require an armed revolution similar to those of national liberation struggles in Africa, Asia, and Latin America. For young Blacks in America's segregated and often impoverished urban ghettos, police were the primary face of the state, whose daily surveillance and violence upheld institutional racism and economic inequality. To make a successful revolution, Newton believed, revolutionaries would need to use violence to defeat the police. In order to "stigmatize" police officers, Newton and the Panthers deliberately popularized the term "pigs." The goal, according to Newton, was to give cops a "label other than that fear image they carried in the [Black] community."[4]

The Panthers promoted guns not only as a means of self-defense but also as means for Black people to liberate themselves through armed revolution. In addition to the cover and centerfold, the twenty-four pages of the *Black Panther*'s January 4, 1969, issue featured no less than ten graphics of Black revolutionaries shooting, stabbing, or choking pigs in police uniforms, as well as nine other images promoting guns.[5] A popular Panther slogan, often chanted as members of the group marched in military formation, was a call-and-response about killing the police: "Revolution has come! *Off the pigs!* Time to pick up the gun! *Off the pigs!*"[6]

Articles in the *Black Panther* elaborated on these positions, making clear that the Panthers viewed armed struggle as a means to overcome police violence. And that police violence was very real. In a matter of weeks local police departments had raided BPP offices in Indianapolis, Denver, and De Moines, and a bomb had badly damaged the BPP office in Newark.[7] But was it true, as the paper claimed, that escalating police attacks on the organization over the past year were part of a concerted state effort to undermine the organization's attempts to "liberate Black people"? Why did police organizations target the Black Panthers and other radical groups?

The Black Panthers asserted that they were under attack because the state saw them as a serious *political* threat. Throughout the first half of 1969, the *Black Panther* newspaper warned that the Nixon administration was bringing "fascism" to the United States, and attributed mounting police attacks on its members to the "pig power structure's" nationwide conspiracy to "suppress the will of the black community."[8] Years later, following the BPP's decline, Huey Newton and other former Panthers would point to the FBI's COINTELPROs as the primary cause of the organization's disintegration.[9] Sympathetic historians have made similar arguments about the motives, nature, and consequences of the FBI's COINTELPROs.[10]

But FBI internal documents of the period tell a different story.

To judge from the FBI's own correspondence, J. Edgar Hoover and his men did not work to destroy the Black Panthers with their COINTELPROs simply because they disagreed with the organization's political views. Nor did they see the BPP as a credible threat to America's political system. The

FBI took such actions because Hoover and other top bureau officials took seriously the Panthers' calls for violent attacks on police officers.

Consider the secret memo FBI headquarters issued on September 27, 1968, directing field offices to make the BPP the main target of COINTELPRO-Black Nationalist-Hate Groups. In this document, Domestic Security Division official G. C. Moore described the BPP as "the most violence-prone organization of all the extremist groups now operating in the United States." The BPP, he stressed, "puts particular emphasis on not only verbal attacks but also physical attacks on police."[11] "More violence can be expected from this organization in the immediate future," he warned. With Hoover's official authorization, Moore ordered agents to accelerate investigations of the BPP, cultivate informants within the organization, and launch counterintelligence operations that "may bring about results which could lead to prosecution of these violence-prone leaders and active members, thereby thwarting their efforts to perpetrate violence in the United States."[12]

COINTELPRO-BNHG certainly may have contributed to the Panthers' decline. It is well documented that the FBI's COINTELPRO operations encouraged factional disputes within the Panthers, as well as between the Panthers, other political organizations, and local street gangs.[13] But to blame the party's collapse on the state is to disregard the centrality of violence itself in tearing the organization apart. A close examination of FBI documents from the summer of 1968, when the bureau first began targeting the organization with COINTELPRO-BNHG, reveals that a great deal of internecine conflict bordering on violence was well under way when the bureau stepped in with covert activities designed to fan the flames. To attribute the BPP's downfall to COINTELPRO is to vastly overstate the power and competence of the state, and to greatly diminish the agency of the Panthers themselves.

This is not to deny or downplay the existence of Hoover's covert counterintelligence operations against the Black Panthers and SDS, the fact that the Nixon administration and various state officials pressed charges against radicals throughout the country, or the reality that local police engaged in dozens of violent attacks on Black Panthers and other leftists, sometimes with the help of FBI intelligence, and always with impunity. The point here is that although these repressive state activities were related, they were not part of a single, nationally coordinated campaign, and they were not simply motivated by disagreement with paramilitary leftists' political viewpoints. Much as Nixon may have wished otherwise, there was no centralized state conspiracy to eliminate political dissent in America.[14]

Still, the Panthers' analysis of state repression was not completely off base. State attacks on their organization were indeed political and racially biased. The BPP had formed to confront racist policing, and its armed confrontational tactics quickly escalated tensions with local police, while at the same time drawing sensational media coverage and new members. It *felt* like a nationally coordinated campaign of state violence, and it was easy to misconstrue police repression as evidence of the Panthers' political effectiveness. Over the course of 1968, the party grew rapidly into a national organization, and conflict with police engulfed nearly every local chapter.

Under Nixon, the thread that linked various state agencies' repressive activities was not a centrally directed master plan—it was law-and-order politics. Both Nixon and Hoover gained political capital by decrying Black Panther violence, but in most cases, they either ignored or tacitly encouraged local police violence against political radicals and in communities of color. While Hoover's FBI and the Nixon White House clashed with one another over how the federal government should respond to leftist violence, they granted impunity to local police. By working to eliminate insurgent violence, they facilitated the expansion of state violence. And it was this escalation of police violence, alongside the FBI's counterintelligence operations against the Panthers and SDS, federal and state indictments of leftist radicals, and Nixon's escalation of the war in Vietnam, that fueled further insurgent violence and violent Panther rhetoric.

From September 1968 until April 1971, the stated goal of COINTELPRO-BNHG was to preemptively eliminate the BPP's capacity for violence. In reality, however, if the FBI's counterintelligence operations had any impact, it was in redirecting Panther violence. Most of this violence was diverted inward, toward the Panthers themselves or toward others in their communities.

But COINTELPRO-BNHG would come back to haunt local police departments. The FBI's covert operations pushed some Panthers to intensify their commitment to antipolice violence, shaping the formation of the BPP's clandestine guerrilla unit. Along with members' personal experiences with racism and state violence, Black Nationalist critiques of nonviolence popularized by Malcolm X, and a growing embrace of guerrilla warfare within the international Left, repressive state responses to the Black Panthers also contributed to the building of a Black revolutionary guerrilla underground. In their efforts to crush Panther militancy, Hoover, Nixon, and local police only nourished the seeds of the Black Liberation Army (BLA).

Cult of the Gun

The Panthers' views on politics and violence were informed by direct personal experiences with racist state violence. Huey Newton, Emory Douglas, Eldridge Cleaver, and other original members of the Oakland Panthers had all grown up coping with segregation, poverty, inadequate public schools, and incarcerated stints in California Youth Authority (CYA) penal facilities. Douglas remembered white guards taunting him with the n-word and telling him to "go back to Africa." Oakland Panther Raymond Johnson endured beatings by CYA guards and once spent a night there chained to a wall in a tiny, rat-infested cell.[15] New York Panther Kuwasi Balagoon, who grew up in Maryland and would later become a soldier in the BLA, was radicalized at age fourteen when police arrested his older sister's boyfriend, Jimmy, on accusations that he had sexually assaulted a white girl. Balagoon later recalled authorities bringing Jimmy to Marlboro County Jail, "a chamber of horrors where a black man could get whipped half or all the way to death for breaking the cold, concrete silence, replying to a question or statement with any sign of resentment, or for having the wrong tone in his voice." He went on to recall his anguish after the trial, in which white witnesses gave conflicting testimony in a racially segregated courtroom, and an all-white jury took fifteen minutes of deliberation to find Jimmy guilty. The white judge then sentenced the young man, whom Balagoon looked up to "like a big brother," to life in prison.[16] Similar stories dot the pages of the memoirs and oral histories of Black Panthers who lived to tell the tale.[17]

In addition to their personal experiences, a Black Nationalist critique of nonviolence in the civil rights movement, and an embrace of guerrilla warfare among many in the international Left helped nudge some of the organization's members toward forming a guerrilla underground.

The Black Panthers viewed themselves as heirs of Malcolm X, the era's most influential Black Nationalist political figure and the Black freedom movement's most visible critic of nonviolence. Born Malcolm Little in Omaha, Nebraska, in 1925, Malcolm X gained prominence during the late 1950s and early 1960s as a spokesperson for the Nation of Islam (NOI), a Black separatist religious sect led by Elijah Muhammad. In 1964, amid a fallout with Muhammad and his growing interest in Black Nationalism and Pan-African socialism, Malcolm X parted NOI to found the Organization for Afro-American Unity.[18] Malcolm X spoke before audiences throughout the United States, critiquing nonviolence on both moral and practical grounds. He affirmed African Americans' right to self-defense, calling on Blacks to form rifle clubs to protect themselves from racist white vigilantes, while presciently warning that growing numbers of Black youth would embrace armed revolt if denied the opportunity to gain self-determination for their communities through the electoral process. "Just as guerrilla warfare is prevailing in Asia and in parts of Africa and in parts of Latin America," he declared before a Cleveland audience on April 3, 1964, "you've got to be mighty naïve, or you've got to play the black man cheap, if you don't think that some day he's going to wake up and find that it's got to be the ballot or the bullet."[19] Malcolm X again predicted the coming of guerrilla warfare six days later in New York. Referring to a recent incident in which Black youth in Jacksonville, Florida, fought police with homemade gasoline bombs, Malcolm X observed, "There's a new strategy coming in. It'll be Molotov cocktails this month, hand grenades next month, and something else the next month." "You should not feel that I am inciting someone to violence," he explained. "I'm only warning of a powder keg situation."[20]

Meanwhile, a lesser-known militant named Robert F. Williams had a profound influence on those who would go on to form the BLA. As leader of the Monroe, North Carolina, chapter of the National Association for the Advancement of Colored People (NAACP), Williams gained international notoriety as an advocate for armed self-defense after his group used gunfire to fend off an attack by local Klansmen in October 1957.[21] Later, as a political exile in Cuba and China, Williams gained attention as an apostle of armed revolution after fleeing an FBI manhunt predicated on false kidnapping charges. In the spring 1964 issue of his newsletter, the *Crusader*, Williams published an article titled "The USA: The Potential of a Minority Revolution." The tract insisted that nonviolence was ineffective, and asserted that Black Americans "must prepare to wage an urban guerrilla war of self-defense."[22] He called on "Afroamerican freedom fighters" to learn the art of building Molotov cocktails, homemade acid bombs, and booby traps for use against racist police" and to clandestinely purchase "hand grenades, bazookas, light mortars, rocket launchers, machine guns and ammunition" from American servicemen.[23]

Williams's outlook differed from that of Malcolm X, who before his death at the hands of NOI gunmen on February 21, 1965, maintained openness to the possibility that African Americans could gain self-determination by voting Black political leaders into office.[24] Chased into exile by the Ku Klux Klan, North Carolina police, and the FBI, Williams believed that America's racist whites were responding to the civil rights movement with an organized effort to physically exterminate Black people. "The fascist elements are arming," he argued, "not to liberate our brutally oppressed people, but to liquidate us." In Williams's view, the rise of American fascism precluded the possibility of African American electoral organizing and necessitated guerrilla warfare. "What is integration," he asked, "when the law says yes and the police and howling mob say no? Our only logical and successful answer is to meet organized and massive violence with organized and massive violence." Williams argued that African American guerrilla violence was a form of self-defense because its aim was to eliminate "the source of evil and terror."[25] Armed revolution, in other words, would be the war to end all wars.

When they sought to implement Malcolm X's ideas on Black self-determination, Newton, Seale, and their recruits had no way of knowing that within a couple years they would be leaders of a burgeoning national organization. Initially, their main activity consisted of driving around on Friday and Saturday nights to patrol the Oakland police. When officers stopped African American motorists, Black Panthers would emerge from their vehicles displaying loaded guns, cameras, and law books, boldly announcing their intent to lawfully observe police behavior and ensure that the officers were not violating the rights of community members. These exchanges were often heated, with police attempting to confiscate the guns, and with Newton and other Panthers shouting back epithets of "pig" and "motherfucker." In some instances, Panthers aimed their guns at police to defend themselves from illegal arrest and brutality.[26] Newton and Seale also drafted the group's influential Ten Point Program, an ideological hybrid of Black Nationalism, Third World Marxism, and social democratic liberalism that called for full employment, public housing, culturally relevant education, reparations, an end to police brutality, freedom for Black prisoners, and Black men's exemption from U.S. military service.[27]

As soon as they began to resist police violence with guns, however, the Panthers found themselves caught in a cycle of escalating violence with the state. Not long after the organization's founding, California governor Ronald Reagan signed the Mulford Act, a gun control bill intended to disarm the Black Panthers by outlawing the public display of firearms. The Black Panthers responded by staging a dramatic armed protest at California's State House. On May 2, 1967, thirty Panthers, armed with rifles and decked out in black berets and leather jackets, stormed the state capitol in Sacramento.

As the Panthers hoped, the specter of young Black men with guns attracted widespread television coverage and interest in their organization. Overnight, they became an international sensation.[28]

The Panthers' predilection for guns followed a larger, worldwide trend in the revolutionary Left. In addition to taking inspiration from African American intellectuals like Malcolm X and Robert Williams, the Black Panthers and other American leftist militants imported political strategies from revolutionary anticolonial movements in the global South.

Guerrilla warfare became increasingly popular among revolutionaries throughout the world following the January 1966 First Solidarity Conference of the Peoples of Africa, Asia, and Latin America (popularly known as the Tricontinental Conference) in Havana, Cuba. As historian Vijay Prashad has explained, the Tricontinental Conference inaugurated a period in which growing sectors of the international Left embraced the "cult of the gun." Militants revived armed struggle "not only as a tactic of anticolonialism but significantly *as a strategy in itself.*"[29] With the embrace of armed struggle as a revolutionary strategy, radicals could skip the difficult work of building power through labor unions and other grassroots organizations and instead leap straight toward armed revolutionary insurrection. At least that was the theory.

The Tricontinental Conference was one in a series of meetings of Third World leaders convened in the decades after World War II for the purpose of advancing anticolonial struggles for land, peace, and freedom among the peoples of Asia, Africa, and Latin America. Earlier meetings of the Non-Aligned Movement had emphasized cooperative efforts to promote political independence and nonviolent international relations within the United Nations. By 1966, however, the war in Vietnam had driven an ideological wedge into the Third World movement. While some leaders sought continued efforts to build UN institutions while maintaining peaceful coexistence with the United States and its allies, increasing numbers of revolutionaries drew inspiration from the Vietnamese people's success using guerrilla warfare to bog down the mighty U.S. military. Nguyen Van Tien of South Vietnam's National Liberation Front and Tran Danh Tuyen of the government of North Vietnam provided some of the Tricontinental's most popular presentations, while the conference's host President Fidel Castro hailed the Vietnamese guerrillas' efforts.[30]

The most influential statement on revolutionary violence to come out of the Tricontinental was from the Argentine hero of the 1959 Cuban revolution, Ernesto Ché Guevara. Guevara did not attend the conference in person but sent a letter to the delegates from Tanzania, where he had recently gone into hiding after retreating from a failed mission to spark revolutionary insurgency in the Congo. In his "Message to the Tricontinental," Guevara outlined a strategy for global socialist revolution centered on guerrilla warfare. He argued that defeat of U.S. imperialism in the Third World—manifested in military interventions, economic domination, and backing of dictators friendly toward American business interests—necessitated "two, three, many Vietnams." Guevara called on revolutionaries to pick up the gun, arguing that a proliferation of armed insurgencies across Africa, Asia, and Latin America would overextend U.S. military capacities, foment dissent and class struggle within the United States, and ultimately result in the overthrow of U.S. imperialism and the liberation of Third World nations.[31]

While a "people's army" was a model of anti-imperialist resistance in places like Vietnam and the Portuguese colonies of Africa, in countries where a mass movement was less developed, armed struggle, according to Guevara, could still play an important role in the form of the "*foco*." French Marxist Regis Debray further popularized Guevara's revolutionary strategy in his 1967 book, *Revolution in the Revolution?*, published the same year that he participated in Guevara's failed guerrilla campaign in Bolivia. Debray argued that *focos*—small, mobile cells of disciplined guerrillas—could quickly strike enemy targets with spectacular attacks before retreating into hiding. In the process, such bands could recruit and train other *focos* that could eventually unite as a people's army capable of bringing about general insurrection and the overthrow of capitalist regimes.[32]

Looking back, it is clear that Guevara's *foco* theory was tragically oversimplified (Debray later mocked his earlier views as "Leninism in a hurry").[33] But for many young radicals, sickened by state violence and frustrated by the slow pace of change, *foco* theory presented an attractive way to fully commit oneself to revolutionary struggle. This included young radicals in the United States who eagerly circulated the writings of Guevara and Debray, often reading them in conjunction with Mao Zedong's Little Red Book, Frantz Fanon's *Wretched of the Earth*, works by Vladimir Lenin and Karl Marx, and Robert F. Williams's writings on guerrilla warfare.[34]

During the BPP's early years, Huey Newton was a leading advocate of *foco*-style revolution in the United States. The chairman's essay "On the Correct Handling of a Revolution," published in the July 20, 1967, issue of the *Black Panther* newspaper, outlined his vision for a clandestine revolutionary guerrilla organization in the United States. Newton wrote his essay in response to the Newark uprising of July 12–17. Members of the city's Black community rose up in rebellion after a white police officer brutally beat a Black taxi driver whom he had pulled over for an alleged traffic violation. After five nights of protests, looting, burning, and Black youth clashing with police and the National Guard, twenty-seven people lay dead (one was a cop, the rest were community members). During the conflict and after, police and National Guard officials justified their firing of 13,326 rounds of ammunition as a necessary response to Black snipers. Community members protested the state's violence, however, and witnesses on all sides debated the extent of Black sniping.[35]

Huey Newton sought to harness the energy from spontaneous urban rebellions like those in Newark and use it to form an organized guerrilla insurgency. Conceiving the Black Panthers as a "vanguard party," he saw this as the organization's central task. "When the people learn that it is no longer advantageous for them to resist by going into the streets in large numbers; and when they see the advantage in the activities of the guerrilla warfare method, they will quickly follow this example," Newton wrote. "When the vanguard group destroys the machinery of the oppressor by dealing with him in small groups of three and four, and then escapes the might of the oppressor, the masses will be overjoyed and will adhere to this correct strategy."[36]

From the outset, Newton sought to build a secret armed wing of the BPP to carry out guerrilla activities and prepare for what he saw as the party's inevitable need to go underground. According to Newton, a "vanguard group always starts out aboveground and is driven underground by the aggressor," or the state.[37] It was only a matter of time until someone took Newton's essay to heart.

Don Cox and the Black Panther Underground

Among those inspired by the Panthers was a young African American father of two named Don Cox, who lived across the bay from the Oakland Panthers in San Francisco. Like other Panthers, Cox developed a political consciousness shaped by incidents of racist violence.

Cox's grandfather Joseph Cox had been born into slavery in Missouri in 1845 and later married a Swiss immigrant woman, Don's grandmother, Maria Müller. To Cox and others in his family, the fact that Grandpa Joe had married a white woman demonstrated his status as "a righteous uppity nigger." Cox also remembered, "it was always a source of great pride in the family that a hole in the wall of a store in Osceola, Missouri—put there by

a shotgun blast—bore testimony to Grandpa's objection to that appella-
tion."[38] Don Cox would continue a family legacy of armed resistance to
racism as an adult in California, where he relocated in 1953 after graduat-
ing from high school in Sedalia, Missouri. Cox had acquired a fascination
with guns as a boy hunting rabbits, squirrels, and quail in the fields behind
his family home, and he maintained a firearms collection in San Francisco.[39] However, Cox's embrace of armed struggle came about gradually,
as his political views developed in dialogue with the period's wave of anticolonial resistance and urban rebellion.

Cox's first involvement in organized politics came in 1963, after a Ku
Klux Klan bombing in Birmingham, Alabama, killed four Black girls at the
16th Street Baptist Church, where civil rights activists had organized much
of their campaign to integrate the city's workplaces and public facilities.
Stirred by this act of racist violence—which most would consider an act of
domestic terrorism by today's standards—Cox and a group of friends organized a benefit jazz concert that raised $1,300 for Martin Luther King's
Southern Christian Leadership Council.[40] A short time later, Cox joined the
San Francisco chapter of the Congress of Racial Equality (CORE), though
he did not last long. He volunteered as chairman of the public relations committee for about six months but quit in frustration at the intractability of
racist institutions. "In the struggle for integration I was seeing only token
results," he remembered.[41] Cox nonetheless kept up a steady reading habit,
taking in the texts of W. E. B. Du Bois, Malcolm X, James Baldwin, and
Frantz Fanon, and following news of the 1965 Watts Rebellion and other
clashes between police and African American rebels. He also supported his
two young children as a mail carrier, photographer, printer, and bus driver.[42]

The Black Panthers' armed protest in Sacramento was a turning point in
Cox's political evolution. He recalled his elation when a friend showed him
a newspaper article about the demonstration: "I couldn't believe my eyes.
I devoured the article and learned that the group called itself the Black
Panther Party for Self-Defense, and they were advocating that black people
should be allowed to arm themselves, specifically for self-defense against
racist police. I immediately thought of my arsenal at home. I started asking
around to see what I could learn about these Panthers."[43] A couple weeks
later, Cox traveled to a Black Power conference in Los Angeles, where he
encountered movement luminaries Stokely Carmichael, H. Rap Brown, Le-
Roi Jones, James Forman, and Ron Karenga. His imagination soared. "I heard
blacks talk of revolution, killing our oppressors, going back to Africa . . .
My mind was blown." Cox recalled that on his last day in LA, he bought a

copy of the *Black Panther* newspaper. "I read it so many times I knew it by heart."[44]

Back in San Francisco, Don Cox and his friends began to meet regularly to study Black history, political theory, and the use of firearms. Cox sold his camera equipment to buy "several Sears-brand bolt-action twelve-gauge shotguns" and taught others how to use them by hunting jackrabbits.[45]

The group carried out its first public activities in response to the police killing of a seventeen-year-old Black youth from the Fillmore District. Word on the street was that San Francisco police knew of the young man's plan to rob a motel, but instead of arresting him they gunned him down in an ambush broadcast live on local television networks. Cox and his friends wrote a leaflet to protest the killing and convince Black community members "of the need to arm themselves for self-defense." They distributed thousands of fliers throughout the neighborhood, in the process recruiting new participants in their weekly community meetings.[46]

But Cox was not satisfied. He too was moved by the Newark uprising, and a couple weeks later, an even larger rebellion erupted in Detroit after police raided an after-hours social club frequented by Black military veterans. Six nights of rioting in the Motor City resulted in forty-three deaths, most at the hands of police and Michigan National Guard troops, as well as more than 7,200 arrests.[47] Cox watched these developments as members of his group immersed themselves in revolutionary texts, including Huey Newton's recent essay on guerrilla *foco* theory. It seemed to Cox as if a world revolution was on the horizon, and he wanted to be part of it. "We were convinced that we were running behind and needed to catch up," he recalled. "We were eager to make contact with the Panthers in Oakland, but we didn't yet feel worthy to be in their presence. . . . So far, we had only talked and informed and armed ourselves, but we hadn't yet proved ourselves on the firing line."[48] He would change that soon enough.

Cox recruited two members of his study group into a nascent guerrilla cell. Keeping their activities secret from the larger group, the trio began to accumulate arms and practice nighttime attacks. As he later wrote, "We began to do small-risk actions, mainly arsons and burglaries. The spoils from the burglaries were always sold to the community at very low prices, and the receipts were used to buy arms and ammunition. . . . Later the group also began to sell weed to raise funds. . . . We also tried our hand at making small bombs with varying degrees of success. Fortunately, we never had an accident."[49] A short time later, in August 1967, Cox and his friends began planning their first "substantial action"—an attack on police to retaliate for the killing of Black youth Matthew Johnson by an officer the previous September, an event that had set off an urban rebellion in San Francisco's Hunter's Point neighborhood.[50]

Cox and his crew originally hoped to assassinate the officer responsible for Matthew Johnson's death, but since they could not find his name in the newspapers, they decided to attack any officer they could find at the Ingleside police station. On September 27, the anniversary of Johnson's death, under the darkness of night, Cox and his two comrades set up positions outside the station. Cox held a rifle steady against a log next to an adjacent parking lot, while his comrades waited nearby in a stolen car, the motor running. When a police car pulled up next to the station and an officer stepped out to approach the building, Cox fixed his sights on the policeman's head. He opened fire and then sped away before he could see the results.

Cox read about the attack in the paper the next morning. It turned out that the bullet had struck the officer in the thigh. But Cox still felt "a sense of exaltation. . . . I had proved to myself, through my action, that I really believed what I had been saying, that I wasn't just talk."[51]

Shortly after the Ingleside attack, Cox and his San Francisco crew made contact with Huey Newton and other leaders of the Oakland Panthers. During their first meeting, Newton openly discussed guerrilla resistance. "He suggested it was best to first rip off the necessary funds to get everything we needed in advance of launching a major effort," Cox recalled.[52] This was the inception of the BPP underground, though at this point the arrangement was informal. Cox and his San Francisco comrades were not yet living clandestinely. If anything, they were recruiting openly and actively in the community, "attending and participating in any and all functions relevant to black people."[53]

The Black Panthers' confrontations with police entered a new phase after October 27, 1967, when an attempt by Oakland police to arrest Huey Newton at a traffic light erupted into a shootout that left Officer John Frey dead and both Newton and another officer wounded. The arrest elevated Newton's status. Mass media attention on his case and efforts to battle murder charges and the death penalty buoyed national interest in the Panthers.[54] After recovering from his wounds, Newton would spend nearly three years in prison before being acquitted on a technicality.

In the meantime, the cycle of violence escalated rapidly. Three weeks after Newton's arrest, Cox and his San Francisco comrades carried out a "retaliatory" attack on the Hunters Point police station. The late-night hail of bullets they blasted through two of the station's windows killed thirty-three-year-old Officer Herman L. George as he typed reports at this desk. Another officer suffered serious wounds.[55]

Newton's imprisonment created an opening in the BPP's leadership. Into this void stepped Eldridge Cleaver, a former prisoner of the California prison system and author of *Soul on Ice* (1968), a bestselling memoir full of bravado and wild claims that would later become notorious for its assertion that rape was an insurrectionary act. Cleaver had gained prominence in Bay Area radical circles after taking a position as a writer for *Ramparts*, a magazine published by white New Leftists. As the Black Panthers' minister of communication, Cleaver edited and expanded production of the *Black Panther* newspaper and led the "Free Huey" campaign. He also became well known for his vocal calls for urban guerrilla warfare, assassination of police officers, and other violence. On at least one occasion, he publicly threatened to burn down the White House. In another highly publicized incident, Cleaver challenged "the punk" Governor Ronald Reagan to a duel, threatening to beat him to death with a marshmallow.[56]

The Black Panthers kept up their violent rhetoric as the organization rapidly expanded amid an international "Free Huey" campaign led by Cleaver. The party opened offices in more than forty cities across the country over the course of 1968 and 1969, while spin-off "Black Panther" organizations set up base around the world, from London to Israel to Australia and the South Pacific. In Sweden and other European countries, white radicals established Huey Newton solidarity groups.[57]

Throughout the United States, Panthers endured escalating and often deadly conflict with local police agencies. Police in the Bay Area, Los Angeles, Chicago, New York, and other cities regularly harassed Black Panthers and their supporters, sometimes arresting them on trumped-up charges. Rank-and-file Bay Area Panther Brenda Presley Violent recalled, "You would get pulled over. They'd surround the car. . . . A lot of times you'd be followed depending on what you were doing or who you were with."[58] The Panthers claimed that in 1968 and 1969, their membership of approximately 1,200 endured 739 arrests and paid $4,890,580 in bail.[59] In 1968, violent confrontations between police and Panthers included

- the February 25 Berkeley police raid on the home of Bobby Seale and his wife;
- the April 3 police raid on a Black Episcopal Church in West Oakland whose pastor loaned the Panthers space for community meetings;

- the April 6 shootout at a West Oakland house that resulted in the wounding of Eldridge Cleaver and two officers and the police killing of Black Panther "Li'l Bobby" Hutton as he attempted to surrender;
- the August 1 police beating of New York Panther Gordon Cooke;
- the August 5 gunfight at a traffic stop in Los Angeles that ended with the deaths of three Panthers and the wounding of two police officers;
- the shooting up of storefront windows at the Oakland Panther headquarters by two on-duty cops;
- the October 15 police shooting death of Seattle Panther Welton Armstead.[60]

The Panthers publicized most of these incidents as unprovoked police attacks. The reality was somewhat murkier—the Panthers' confrontational rhetoric and open displays of firearms were legal, but they were also all but guaranteed to prompt violent police reactions. Not only that, but the BPP intentionally worked to politicize recruits from what it called the "lumpenproletariat": young drug dealers, hustlers, and petty criminals who survived on the margins of the deindustrialized urban economy. As a consequence, there was often a gray area between some members' criminal activity and political activity.[61]

At times, incidents that were described as unprovoked police violence were in fact the consequence of Panthers striking first. The April 6 firefight in West Oakland that resulted in the police killing of seventeen-year-old Bobby Hutton was one example. The violence erupted after Eldridge Cleaver bungled plans to ambush a group of police officers. Cleaver's intention was to put his advocacy of guerrilla warfare into practice in hopes of establishing the BPP's position as the "vanguard" of America's coming revolution amid the nationwide urban riots that followed Martin Luther King's assassination. But Cleaver's attempted guerrilla attack was a hastily organized, slapdash affair. Don Cox, who had by now been promoted to the role of Black Panther field marshal, later recalled his incredulity when Cleaver told him about the action: "I couldn't believe my ears when he said the only plan was to go find some pigs. No organization, no rehearsal, nothing. Just a haphazard assemblage of niggers who were handed guns and told, 'Let's go.'"[62]

Cleaver's attack did not spark a revolutionary insurrection, but the Panther leader continued to advocate armed revolution after posting bail. Throughout the summer of 1968, while awaiting trial, Cleaver toured the

United States as a presidential candidate for the Peace and Freedom Party, a small antiwar political party founded the previous year by white radicals in California. In his speaking engagements, Cleaver popularized the incendiary slogan, "Free Huey or the Sky's the Limit," and coaxed audiences to join him in singing a song he wrote called "Fuck Ronald Reagan."[63]

Cleaver had no intention of facing his murder charges, however. In November 1968, Cleaver jumped bail and fled the country. He made his way to Cuba before surfacing in Algeria in July 1969, where his wife, Kathleen Cleaver, and several other Panthers joined him in establishing the BPP's "International Section" in a downtown Algiers "Panther embassy" provided by the country's socialist government. Two years after Cleaver surfaced in Algeria, and unknowingly cajoled by covert FBI operations, Huey Newton would expel the head of the International Section from the party, partly over the inescapable debate over whether the Panthers should pursue social change through the ballot box or the barrel of a gun. After the split, Cleaver would become the ideological leader of the militant Panther faction—based primarily in New York—that would ultimately produce the BLA.[64] Don Cox would also wind up joining Cleaver in Algiers. Same with New York Panthers Sekou Odinga and Michael "Cetewayo" Tabor, who would flee the country to escape conspiracy indictments but later return to fight with the BLA.

The turn to revolutionary guerrilla warfare held an appeal for a substantial group of white radicals as well. In the years leading up to Nixon's election, a large portion of SDS also came to embrace armed guerrilla struggle. This was a far cry from the principles outlined in the group's foundational 1962 Port Huron Statement. Drafted by Tom Hayden and inspired by the nonviolent civil rights movement, the Port Huron Statement had laid out an idealistic vision for "participatory democracy," in which Americans of all races would contribute equally and directly in the political processes that governed the nation and their everyday lives. During the mid-1960s, SDS chapters organized civil rights campaigns in solidarity with SNCC and the civil rights movement, a series of grassroots Economic Research and Action Project social justice initiatives in midwestern cities, and several large demonstrations against the U.S. war in Vietnam.[65]

By 1966, however, nonviolence was losing its appeal. Amid President Johnson's escalation of the war and ongoing police attacks on protesters, SDS joined the larger antiwar movement in moving "from protest to resistance."[66] To most antiwar activists, resistance meant draft refusal or other forms of nonviolent direct action. But in the fall of 1967, antiwar militants in Berkeley and New York resisted police batons and tear gas grenades with helmets, shields, sticks, bottles, and rocks.[67] During the Columbia University student strike in 1968, protests outside Chicago's Democratic National Convention, and other mass demonstrations, radicals engaged in vandalism and street fighting. All the while, SDS membership was surging from around five thousand in 1965 into the tens of thousands.

Manuals for manufacturing bombs and other homemade weapons were making the rounds through the militant Left. The November 16, 1968, issue of the *Black Panther*, for example, included the article "Grenades and Bombs: Anti-property and Anti-personnel." An English translation of the 1963 Cuban booklet "150 Questions for a Guerrilla" and U.S. Army field guides on guerrilla warfare and explosives manufacture circulated through the Revolutionary Action Movement (RAM), SNCC, the Black Panthers, and SDS. According to observers, copies of a bomb-making guide called "Mechanical Methods of Sabotage" "were scooped up with unabashed enthusiasm" at the October 1968 SDS national convention held in Boulder, Colorado—not far from where Cameron Bishop and his friends were in the process of refining their skills in the manufacture of explosives.[68] The New Left newspaper the *Berkeley Barb* reported that entreaties to "kill a white cop" drew enthusiastic applause at radical student gatherings.[69]

The cult of the gun had arrived. On July 23, 1968, a surprise armed attack on Cleveland police officers by a group calling itself the Black Nationalists of New Libya resulted in the deaths of three cops and four militants. Eldridge Cleaver praised the assault. It demonstrated "that psychologically blacks are not only prepared to die but kill."[70] During the fall of 1968, New Left radicals dynamited a CIA office in Ann Arbor and firebombed ROTC facilities at UC Berkeley, University of Delaware, Oregon State University, Texas State University, Washington University, and the University of Washington.[71] The Michigan-based White Panther Party, composed of working-class white radicals who emulated the Black Panthers, issued a statement: "Get a gun, brother, and learn how to use it. You'll need it pretty soon."[72]

In the meantime, amid the BPP's chaotic growth and violent clashes with local law enforcement, members of the organization continued to build a clandestine armed underground. The Central Committee made this official in October 1968, proclaiming the new rule that "no party member can join any other army force than the Black Liberation Army."[73]

So it was that when J. Edgar Hoover worked to destroy the Panthers and other radical organizations, he appeared to be less concerned about stifling their "politics" and more fixated on preempting their use of political violence.

COINTELPRO Revisited

In January 1969, when the *Black Panther* published its "YEAR OF THE PANTHER" issue and Nixon took his oath of office, the FBI's COINTELPRO against the BPP was less than six months old. The bureau had begun to direct COINTELPRO-BNHG operations against the Panthers in the summer of 1968, but FBI headquarters did not order agents to make the BPP the main focus of the program until September 27, 1968, six weeks before Nixon's election victory.[74] At this time, Hoover outlined the types of covert operations he hoped could destroy the BPP:

> Consideration should be given as to how factionalism can be created between local leaders as well as national leaders and how BPP organizational efforts can be neutralized. Give consideration to actions which will create suspicion among the leaders with respect to their financial sources, suspicion concerning their respective spouses, suspicion as to who may be cooperating with law enforcement and suspicion as to who may be attempting to gain complete control of the organization for his own private betterment. In addition, consideration should be given to the best method of exploiting foreign visits BPP members have made as well as the best method of creating opposition to this party on the part of the majority of the residents of the ghetto areas.[75]

Following these directives, the FBI would carry out more than 200 counterintelligence operations against the Panthers over the next two years.[76]

At the time that the FBI began targeting the Black Panthers in earnest in late September 1968, the party had already been active for two years; Huey Newton had been in prison for nearly one year; and the BPP had become nationally known, with chapters in New York, Los Angeles, Chicago, and Seattle. This prompts the question: Why didn't the FBI target the Panthers sooner? One explanation is that Charles Bates, special agent in charge (SAC) of the FBI's San Francisco office (which held jurisdiction over Oakland), was resistant to implementing the program. On several occasions, Hoover reprimanded Bates for his failure to develop effective COINTELPRO operations against the BPP.[77] According to former San Francisco special agent William Cohendet, the office was also unsuccessful in developing reliable informants within the Oakland Black Panthers.[78] Another reason could be that prior to the BPP's rapid growth in the summer of 1968, FBI authorities viewed the organization as a local problem under the jurisdiction of California law enforcement agencies. Whatever the case, the FBI's lack of urgency in undermining the Black Panthers is just one of many striking revelations that can be drawn from the pages of once-secret COINTELPRO-BNHG documents.

The conventional story of FBI counterintelligence has claimed that the FBI targeted the Black Panthers because of their overall political beliefs and effectiveness in challenging the "status quo," and that COINTELPRO operations were the primary cause of the party's internecine conflicts. In fact, the documents demonstrate that Hoover's FBI targeted the Panthers in an effort to preempt their capacity for political violence against state authorities, especially police officers. Moreover, bureau agents worked hard to exploit and exacerbate existing factional conflicts more often than creating new ones. Factional tensions trending toward violence predated the FBI's COINTELPRO against the BPP, particularly on the national level and in Los Angeles. In places like Chicago, however, where agents could not identify preexisting disputes, the FBI did seek to manufacture violent conflicts between the Black Panthers and other local groups. In working to undermine the BPP's popular support, rather than manufacturing outright misinformation, agents often used the Black Panthers' violent rhetoric against them, publicizing examples of party leaders' most violent statements along with allegations of Panther violence against members of their own communities.

By the time the BPP attracted Hoover's attention, the organization was already entangled in a near-violent conflict with leaders of SNCC. In an August 8, 1968, memo to headquarters, the FBI's New York office reported information, likely gleaned from informants inside the Panthers, that a "break between SNCC and the Black Panthers appears severe and perhaps final."[79] SNCC leaders Stokely Carmichael, H. Rap Brown, and James Forman had entered an alliance with the Panthers the previous February in an attempt to unite a national Black Power movement. The seasoned Black Power activists remained critical of the Panthers on several grounds, however, including their heavy reliance on whites for fund-raising and media access.[80] According to the New York FBI memo, Forman and Brown had "resigned their BPP membership because they find it difficult to go along with BPP violent schemes."[81] At the time the FBI issued this memo, agents noted that Forman had been "committed to the psychiatric ward of a NYC hospital."[82]

Agents saw the BPP-SNCC split as a vulnerable target for counterintelligence operations. "In order to increase the friction between SNCC and

BPP," the New York FBI office requested headquarters' approval to "make several pretext telephone calls to the office of SNCC and attempt to convey the impression to them, using a Negro dialect and ghetto language, the fact that the Black Panthers are 'out to get them.'"[83] By this point, such an operation was hardly necessary. Tensions between leaders of SNCC and the BPP had already come to the brink of violence a month earlier, when Forman resigned from the Panthers amid a series of contentious meetings in mid-July with California Panther leaders Eldridge Cleaver, Bobby Seale, David Hilliard, Don Cox, and Emory Douglas. Arguments hinged on the two organizations' political relationship and a failed effort to organize an audience for Black Panther leaders at the United Nations. Forman recalled in his memoir that heated relations between SNCC and the Panthers had "nearly involve[d] gunplay" and required "great diplomacy. . . . A slight spark could split it asunder." The SNCC leader also recalled his exhaustion in July amid traveling from Panther meetings in California back to New York to coordinate the UN meeting. "I was in no physical condition to continue working without rest, but I felt that I could exert myself a few more days to complete the assignment. . . . I was stretching my own capacity far beyond the limits of the human body." Such stress, amid an "extraordinary output of energy" and "tensions between SNCC and the Panthers . . . created by continuing distrust and suspicion of intentions," is likely what led Forman to seek recuperation in the hospital.[84]

The FBI capitalized on SNCC and BPP leaders' frayed relationship, casting its efforts as attempts to preempt both organizations' capacities for insurrectionary violence. The bureau pursued a campaign of "pretext calls" as its primary tactic. In several instances, FBI agents posing as Black Nationalists telephoned the homes of SNCC members to inform them that Panthers intended to kill them. One of these calls reached Stokely Carmichael's mother, May Charles Carmichael. In his report to FBI headquarters, New York's SAC noted, "Mrs. Carmichael appeared shocked upon hearing the news and stated she would tell Stokely when he came home."[85] In an October 10 memo, the New York field office informed Director Hoover that recent phone calls to SNCC and Panther offices had revealed that "SNCC is constantly guarding their premises against planned attacks by the BPP," and that the Brooklyn Panthers had planned an armed defense in response to rumors that SNCC members sought to dynamite their office. The memo also noted that the Brooklyn Panthers kept "two live snakes in the basement of their storefront . . . to attack people who might prowl around their headquarters at night."[86]

Another successful tactic involved the press. The FBI or another police agency was also probably the unnamed source behind an October 7, 1968, *New York Times* article claiming that during the previous July, around the time of the organization's aborted UN meeting, members of the Panthers walked into SNCC's New York office and threatened James Forman by shoving a gun into his mouth.[87] In his memoir, Forman denied that this incident happened, and recalled his immediate efforts to de-escalate tensions with the Black Panthers and the implied assailant, Eldridge Cleaver: "When I read that vicious lie . . . I immediately called Eldridge Cleaver in San Francisco. . . . It was obvious, I told Cleaver, that the federal government had decided to escalate the conflict between SNCC and the Panthers. . . . I believed the article was written to create a fratricidal situation between our two organizations."[88] It is unclear whether Cleaver's assault of Forman ever happened—some suggested that Forman denied the incident to protect himself from Panther reprisals—but Panther animosity toward SNCC leaders had indeed come close to boiling over.[89] Eldridge Cleaver later admitted that by then, some Panther leaders "were ready to snuff Stokely [Carmichael]."[90]

This story was effective in part because it exploited Stokely Carmichael's lingering doubts about the Black Panthers' strategy. The SNCC leader had been uneasy about working with the Panthers from the beginning of the alliance between the two organizations earlier that year. "There was the irresponsible adventurism; a rigid, politically confused ideological direction; and the strong-arm tactics . . . combined to suggest that the [BPP] might not be salvageable," he recounted. But the attack on Forman was the "final straw." "I mean if the Panthers could be *that* ignorant of history, so confused, and with so little respect as to bring that kind of thuggery to a man like Jim? . . . You knew it was time to move on."[91] Carmichael went to his grave believing that Cleaver or his "enforcers" had indeed assaulted Forman in July 1968. The near-deadly conflict had caused lasting damage to personal relationships, fatally undermining the country's strongest national Black Power organizations.

In Southern California, the FBI made sure that its COINTELPRO operations built on the fractious conflicts between the Los Angeles Black Panthers and local community groups. A September 25, 1968, memo from the Los Angeles FBI office reported "friction" between the LA BPP chapter and most of the city's other radical groups, including SNCC and the militant Chicano organization the Brown Berets. Tensions were especially high between the Panthers and Ron Karenga's cultural nationalist organization US, which led the Black Congress, a coalition of Los Angeles Black Power groups formed after the 1965 Watts uprising. The LA office noted that the BPP "has 'let out a contract' on Karenga because they feel that he has sold out to the establishment."[92] In other words, the Panthers wanted Karenga dead.

Such hostilities with other groups were a long-standing feature of the LA Black Panthers dating back to the group's inception. Alprentice "Bunchy" Carter, the former leader of the powerful Slauson street gang, organized the first BPP chapter outside of Oakland at the suggestion of his friend from Soledad Prison, Eldridge Cleaver. In January 1968, Carter announced the formation of the chapter while crashing a Black Congress poetry reading flanked by twenty gun-wielding, black-leather-clad Slauson recruits. After taking the microphone, Carter announced, "The pig can no longer attack and suppress our people, or send his occupying army to maraud and maim our communities, without suffering grave consequences. . . . From this point forward, Brothers and Sisters, if the pig moves on this community, the Black Panther Party will deal with him."[93]

Though friction with US and other LA Black Power groups was immediately evident, the LA Panthers nevertheless became the fastest-growing and most influential radical Black organization in Southern California in the weeks and months after the assassination of Martin Luther King on April 4, 1968. Violent conflict with Los Angeles police broke out on August 5, when officers pulled over a car full of armed Panther men. In the ensuing gun battle, two police officers were wounded and the young Panthers Stephen Kenna, Robert Lawrence, and Thomas Melvin were killed.[94]

The LA chapter of the BPP also had an armed, underground wing almost from its outset. Though purposely omitting names and key details to avoid implicating his old comrades, LA Panther Geronimo "ji jaga" Pratt confirmed the existence of the chapter's underground unit during interviews with historians and journalists in the 1990s. According to Pratt, Carter and Cleaver had discussed forming a "revolutionary black nationalist" organization with an "underground military wing" during their incarceration in Soledad. Upon founding the Southern California BPP a couple years later, Carter recruited former Slauson gang members to form a secret organization called the Wolves that carried out unspecified "underground activities."[95]

Throughout the party's existence, the FBI remained unaware of the Panther underground. However, after observing mounting "trouble between the BPP and other Negro groups," the Los Angeles FBI field office informed Director Hoover of its intention to "utilize every technique in an attempt to capitalize on this development." The FBI's COINTELPRO-BNHG units wasted no time. Los Angeles agents scrambled "to determine if these individuals can be prosecuted under State or Federal laws."[96] Agents surveyed Southern California Black Nationalist leaders' telephone calls and firearms purchases, combing their federal income tax, Selective Service, and arrest records for exploitable information.

After Hoover's order on September 27, 1968, to focus on the party, COINTELPRO agents hammered the Panthers with covert operations. In one example, special agents sent a fake letter intended to sow distrust between the LA Panthers and the Oakland-based Central Committee. The letter was to "give the BPP headquarters in Oakland the impression that a considerable amount of money was being collected in Los Angeles for [Huey] Newton but the money was not being forwarded to the defense fund but rather being pocketed by Los Angeles Panthers."[97] In mid-November, agents mailed a letter from a "Mr. X" to Kathleen Cleaver, lamenting her husband Eldridge's unfaithfulness, claiming that he had been hanging around with "a group of 13 and 14 year old girls." "Your friends used to think that you loved your husband very much but now, I'm afraid, they are beginning to feel sorry for you because you are married to such a bum."[98] Around the same time, COINTELPRO agents mailed Eldridge Cleaver an anonymous letter stating that others in the BPP intended to kill him.[99]

Other FBI efforts to divide the BPP capitalized on members' violent activities to amplify the organizational chaos. On November 19, 1968, Black Panther Willie Brent pulled a black van emblazoned with the party logo into a San Francisco gas station and robbed the attendant at gunpoint. Minutes later, when police pulled him over, Brent jumped out of the van and opened fire, wounding three officers. Frustrated by the bad publicity, the BPP's Central Committee issued a press release. Panther leaders condemned "roving gangs of bandits robbing service stations" and labeled Brent as "either a provocateur agent or an insane man."[100] San Francisco FBI agents noted party leadership's disavowal of Brent and moved quickly to stoke party leaders' suspicions with a COINTELPRO tactic known as "snitch-jacketing." Working through the San Francisco Police Department, agents sought to create the impression that Brent was a police informant. They arranged for him to have "special privileges at City Prison, such as more lenient visiting hours, and to have the guards show him 'extra' courtesy in front of other prisoners."[101] Even an unstrategic act of violence like Brent's robbery and shootout, once recast by the FBI as the work of police provocateurs, could be used to keep the party on edge.

The FBI also sought to undermine the BPP's support in local communities. The simplest way of achieving this was to publicize evidence of alleged Panther violence and examples of party leaders' violent rhetoric. In late October 1968, agents circulated a *New York Daily News* article about how Catherine Basie, wife of the famed jazz band leader Count Basie, had resigned from the leadership position of the South Jamaica Community Council after facing death threats from New York Panthers. The article described Catherine Basie "trembling with emotion" and "near tears" as she related her experience to a meeting of state lawmakers. "What do you do when 15 or 20 of these Black Panthers disrupt your meeting and threaten your board members, threaten their lives?" she asked. "One hundred years ago we feared the white man and now we fear our own people."[102]

With little regard for Basie and her political goals, FBI agents mailed photocopies of the article to 326 individuals in twenty-one cities with Black Panther chapters.[103] Recipients included "Negroes in high offices, Negro Ministers, responsible civil rights leaders, leaders of various youth organizations, people whose names have been found in possession of Black Panther members and other individuals who might be in a position to help destroy the BPP or who might be developed as a source of information on BPP activities."[104]

Using a similar tactic, in November 1968 COINTELPRO agents anonymously mailed out dozens of copies of the typed, twenty-three-page transcript of Eldridge Cleaver's recent profanity-laced speech at Sacramento College, in which he challenged California governor Ronald Reagan to a duel, advocated assassinating "pigs," and announced that "political power grows out of the lips of a pussy."[105] For this mailing, recipients included university administrators, parents, and alumni, as well as "local parent-teacher associations, members of local school boards, high school principals, college alumni officials, and officials of the Rotary, Lions, Kiwanis, Optimists, and similar groups."[106]

In cities where tensions between new BPP chapters and other local groups did not already exist, COINTELPRO agents sought to create deadly conflicts. In early December 1968, Chicago FBI agents observed, "The Chicago BPP continues in its process of organization and recruiting locally . . . and at present is not involved in any organizational struggle with other local black nationalist groups."[107] A couple weeks later, however, the FBI sent an anonymous letter to Jeff Fort, leader of Chicago's powerful Blackstone Rangers street gang, warning him that the city's new Black Panther chapter sought to take over his organization. In January 1969, Chicago's SAC reported on the success of his office's covert operations, informing Hoover that "the Rangers and BPP have not only not been able to form any alliance, but enmity and distrust have arisen, to the point where each have been ordered to stay out of the other's territory."[108] In an effort to escalate the situation, agents then sent a phony letter to Fort claiming the Panthers had "a hit out" on him. Agents hoped the letter would prompt Fort to "take reprisals against" Panther leaders.[109] Fortunately, such violence did not come to pass, largely because the Chicago BPP's charismatic young leader Fred Hampton grew suspicious that covert operatives were sabotaging relations between the two groups. Hampton instead met face-to-face with Jeff Fort in efforts to avoid bloodshed.[110]

Another way the FBI disrupted the Black Panther Party was by working through local police. In December 1968, the FBI's Denver field office informed headquarters of its coordination with the Denver Police Department, which arrested leaders of the city's new BPP chapter and helped "keep the membership down and the treasury depleted." "Due to harassment by the local Police Department," Denver's FBI field officer explained, "BPP members have become suspicious of each other. Recently, one member [name redacted] was suspended as an informant, when he was not an informant."[111]

Back in Los Angeles, FBI agents stoked a war between the BPP and US. Agents surreptitiously informed the Panther Central Committee that US members knew of the BPP's "contract" on Ron Karenga and that they planned to assassinate Eldridge Cleaver during a November 3 rally in Los Angeles. Using intelligence from an informant inside the LA BPP, FBI agents reported to headquarters that Panthers had averted the suspected assassination by removing US members from the rally at gunpoint.[112] In order to shield themselves from direct involvement in bloodshed, FBI headquarters instructed the LA field office to order its informant not to engage in violence.[113] However, FBI officials were happy to let Black radicals kill one another. LA's SAC told Director Hoover that his office "hoped this counterintelligence measure will result in an US and BPP vendetta."[114]

Agents fanned the flames of violence by mailing fake letters and cartoon drawings mocking leaders of the BPP and the US to the headquarters of both organizations.[115] On November 25, 1968, Hoover conveyed that "the struggle" between the BPP and US was "taking an aura of gang warfare with attendant threats of murders and reprisals."[116] A week later, Hoover informed fourteen FBI offices with active COINTELPRO-BNHG units of the bureau intention to "fully capitalize upon BPP and US differences as well as to exploit all avenues of creating further dissension in the ranks of the BPP." He ordered the offices to submit biweekly letters to bureau headquarters with updates and recommendations for "imaginative and hard-hitting counterintelligence measures aimed at crippling the BPP."[117]

It didn't take long for the FBI's covert operations to reap deadly results.

State-Incited Fratricide

Measuring the success of the FBI's COINTELPRO-BNHG operations is nearly impossible. But whether it was due to the FBI, local police attacks, or the BPP's own violence and sectarianism, by the time Nixon came into office, the rapidly growing BPP was riddled with conflict. Such tensions were evident on January 12, 1969—a week after the *Black Panther* newspaper's "Year of the Panther" issue hit the streets, and eight days before Nixon's inauguration—when Bobby Seale closed the BPP to new members. He did so out of fear that the organization's swift expansion was creating too many opportunities for infiltration by police informants. "We now have 45 [chapters]," he told the press. "We aren't taking in any new members for the next three to six months. . . . We are turning inward to tighten security, [to] get rid of agents and provocateurs and to promote political education among those who have joined the Panthers but still don't understand what we're all about."[118]

Around the same time, members of the Black Panthers' San Francisco chapter resigned en masse. They did so to protest Seale's violent efforts to impose control over their chapter through the party's newly formed internal police force, "the black guards."[119] Over the next six months, BPP leaders Seale and David Hilliard purged dozens of additional members from the organization—in Los Angeles, Oakland, Vallejo, New Haven, Chicago, New York, Boston, and Denver—on various accusations of collaboration with police forces.[120]

Along with tightening party security, Seale decided to make "survival programs" the prime focus of the organization's activities. Huey Newton conceived the Panthers' mutual aid services as a way to build community support for the impending revolution by meeting community members' unmet human needs. Services such as free breakfast programs for children, community medical clinics, and transportation for family members to visit loved ones in prison were immensely popular, instilling Panther volunteers with pride and purpose, and leaving lasting imprints on their communities.[121]

But still the violence continued. Five days after Seale's press conference, conflict between the LA Panthers and the US organization finally erupted. On January 17, on the University of California Los Angeles campus, a fire-fight between members of both groups resulted in the deaths of local Panther leaders John Huggins and Bunchy Carter and the wounding of US member Larry Watani-Stiner. Representatives of the Panthers and US had just participated in a contentious meeting over control of the university's Black Student Union. After the meeting, LA Panther Elaine Brown got into a conflict with US member Harold Jones-Tawala, which quickly escalated as Huggins and Carter joined the fray. Los Angeles police initially responded to the violence by arresting seventeen local Panthers while the US assailants went free.[122] Hundreds attended the funerals for Huggins and Carter, including Oakland Central Committee members Bobby Seale and Kathleen Cleaver, as well as novelist James Baldwin. The killings also inspired Hollywood actress Jean Seberg to donate thousands of dollars to the LA Panthers to fund their free breakfast programs and community health clinics.[123]

The *Black Panther* newspaper denounced the killings as a "political assassination."[124] However, the party provided no evidence to back its claims that US gunmen had targeted Carter and Huggins with premeditated murder or that the killings had been at the behest of the U.S. federal government. Years later, the declassification of FBI COINTELPRO-BNHG documents during the Church Committee hearings confirmed many Panthers' longstanding suspicions that the FBI had incited the US-BPP feud, but the documents also fueled conspiracy theories claiming that federal intelligence agencies had played a direct role in the killings.[125] One Panther who believed police agencies had planned the Carter-Huggins killings was Geronimo Pratt, whom police had detained with their mass arrest of LA Panthers after the UCLA gun battle, and who would go on to help build the BPP's armed underground after the violent deaths of his friends. Toward the end of his life, Pratt shared with an interviewer his belief that the CIA had helped orchestrate the murders by surreptitiously subjecting Elaine Brown to a "mind control program."[126]

There is no evidence directly tying the FBI to the Carter-Huggins killings. In fact, it is highly unlikely that Director Hoover would have approved of his agents' participation in a political assassination, since doing so would have posed a great risk to the bureau's public reputation and political power. FBI officials took care to avoid direct involvement in the US-BPP feud, as when they instructed their informant inside the LA Panthers not to engage in violence.

But COINTELPRO agents were happy to redirect Panther violence away from police officers and toward one another. Agents from the FBI's San Diego field office made this clear in their response to the killing of Black Panther Sylvester Bell, whom US members shot dead on August 15, 1969, while he was selling newspapers in a shopping center parking lot. San Diego's SAC acknowledged that "no specific counterintelligence action can be credited" to the "shootings, beatings, and a high degree of unrest" that characterized the "over-all situation" in "the ghetto area of southeast San Diego." However, the San Diego office reported with satisfaction that "a substantial amount of the unrest is directly attributable" to the FBI's COINTELPRO. To encourage further internecine violence, San Diego proposed a new cartoon for anonymous mailing to "assist in the continuance of the rift between BPP and US."[127]

Steeped in moral ambiguity, this grim chapter in radical history remains difficult to untangle, but it is still possible to discern core dynamics of the FBI's and BPP's rising conflict. Black Panther leaders' portrayal of the Carter-Huggins killings as a government-backed assassination inflated the FBI's power and gave Panther leaders a way to avoid reckoning with their own roles in violent conflicts. Yet given party members' incessant harassment by various police agencies, trauma from the assassinations of Malcom X and Martin Luther King Jr., and outrage over the Nixon administration's escalation of the U.S. war in Vietnam, it is understandable that some Panther militants already inclined toward viewing police attacks on radicals as part of a centralized government conspiracy would see the Carter-Huggins killings as yet another example of ongoing state repression. In the months that followed the bloodshed in Los Angeles, two major conspiracy indictments against Black Panthers in other cities fueled further speculation along these lines.

Conspiracies

In the spring of 1969, with Nixon still settling into the White House, police conducted high-profile arrests of Black Panthers in New York and New Haven. To police and their sympathizers, the mass arrests—on charges of conspiracy to carry out bombings and other attacks in New York, and for participating in the torture and murder of an alleged police informant in New Haven—confirmed that the BPP was indeed a violent organization that threatened public safety. To the Panthers and their supporters, however, the charges were the latest example of a growing government conspiracy to destroy the party and with it all resistance to American racism and imperialism. Further confirmation of this view came in August, when FBI agents in California arrested Panther leader Bobby Seale, who was already facing Attorney General John Mitchell's federal conspiracy charges as a member of the Chicago Eight. Agents shipped Seale to Connecticut to face the additional charges that he ordered the torture and murder of Alex Rackley in New Haven. With Huey Newton still behind bars, Eldridge Cleaver in exile, Cameron Bishop in hiding, and the Chicago Eight facing decades of imprisonment, leftist radicals mobilized to defend the New York "Panther Twenty-One" and the "New Haven Nine" as the latest innocent victims of illegitimate political repression.

Details of the New York Twenty-One and New Haven Nine cases remain bitterly contested. Nevertheless, it is clear that the arrests and surrounding events were part of an escalating, increasingly violent war between militant leftists and American police agencies in the opening months of the Nixon presidency. These mass arrests, imprisonments, and ensuing trials also contributed to growing divisions within the BPP and its supporters while helping convince some of the need to build clandestine revolutionary guerrilla organizations.

The story of the New York Twenty-One commenced with a round of police raids on April 2, 1969. Early in the morning, officers entered Black Panther members' apartments throughout New York City, arresting ten. Two additional suspects were already in police custody on robbery charges on the morning of the raids. A few others managed to dodge the cops, eventually joining Eldridge Cleaver in Algeria, while police caught up with the rest over the following weeks and months. Together, the captives were among twenty-one members of the New York BPP whom a state grand jury, using testimonies of three police officers who had gone undercover inside the New York BPP, had indicted for conspiring to assassinate police officers and bomb police precincts, department stores, railroad tracks, and the Bronx Botanical Garden. A judge set bail for each of the detained defendants at $100,000. The drama came to an end two years later—after an eight-month trial, then the longest in New York history—when a jury acquitted all members of the New York Twenty-One. The case had been a failure, though given that most of the defendants had remained incarcerated for the duration, New York authorities had at least succeeded in depriving the New York Panthers of their core leaders and organizers.[128]

The Black Panthers and their supporters portrayed the indictments as trumped-up charges similar to those that Nixon's Justice Department had lodged against the Chicago Eight a month earlier, part of a broader campaign of state repression that made no distinction between state agencies and denied any Panther involvement in illegal activity. The *Black Panther* newspaper called the New York police raids part of a "pig conspiracy" to "destroy the Panthers."[129] But New York prosecutors filed the indictment to thwart Panther violence. The main question that remains is whether authorities merely aimed to prevent an impending attack on New York police officers, or whether they sought more broadly to destroy the New York Panthers' capacity to launch violent attacks before they planned them.

The New York Twenty-One arrests were certainly preemptive. Undercover police officer Eugene Roberts had burrowed his way into the New York Black Panthers as the group was forming in the fall of 1968. Using his inside access to party members, he alerted his superiors that New York Panthers were planning coordinated attacks on department stores and other sites throughout the city for the upcoming Easter holiday.[130] The New York Panther Twenty-One arrests foreshadowed the subsequent evolution of American counterterrorism, which would include surveillance, arrest, and criminal conviction among its repertoire of "preemptive" actions designed to prevent terrorist attacks.[131]

However, even if the arrests were premature, not all of the prosecutors' charges were baseless. In fact, the State of New York's complicated list of charges included several related to an ambush on police officers on January 17, 1969, that some members of the New York Twenty-One had already participated in.[132] Prosecutors may have been unable to prove their case beyond reasonable doubt, but it is entirely plausible that at least some of the defendants planned additional guerrilla attacks. After all, the Oakland Panthers' promotion of revolutionary violence had been a central factor inspiring many of the young radicals who formed the New York BPP chapter in the spring of 1968 after Martin Luther King's assassination. New York Twenty-One defendant Kuwasi Balagoon (formerly Donald Weems), a tenants' rights organizer who had previously endured a police beating during a protest inside the House of Representatives, later recalled that one reason he joined the party was because he appreciated "that the cadre believed that political power stems from the barrel of a gun."[133] Fellow defendant Afeni Shakur similarly described joining the BPP after being impressed with the California Panthers' armed 1967 protest in Sacramento.[134] Both Balagoon and Shakur would later fight with the BLA.

Panthers and city police had participated in a series of violent exchanges since the BPP set up shop in New York City. In a protest outside the Brooklyn BPP office on August 1, 1968, twenty-year-old Panther Gordon Cooke used a bullhorn to deride police as "racist," "pigs," and "crackers." The demonstration ended with police severely beating and arresting Cooke and seventeen-year-old fellow Panther Darrell Baines.[135] The next morning two men wielding a shotgun ambushed two cops in Brooklyn's Crown Heights neighborhood, wounding the officers with birdshot. Despite New York BPP captain Joudon Ford's denial, some police blamed the Panthers.

A few weeks later, Brooklyn Panthers participated in a rebellion with other African American youths. Protesters attacked police and firefighters with projectiles, smashed shop windows, and looted stores. During the next day's arraignment for seven rebels arrested during the mayhem, 150 white men gathered in the sixth-floor lobby of the Brooklyn Criminal Court, among them several off-duty police officers wearing pins supporting white supremacist presidential candidate George Wallace. Members of the mob shouted racial epithets while beating a small group of New York Panthers and white SDS members. The following week, in the early-morning hours of September 12, gunmen carried out another police ambush near the site of the previous month's shotgun attack, wounding two officers with .308 rifle blasts fired through their patrol car window.[136]

The New York Panthers also probably had a clandestine unit before the April 1969 police raids. According to Geronimo Pratt, the New York BPP, like its counterpart in Los Angeles, established an armed underground wing from the outset of its organizing efforts.[137] New York's Panther underground may have included soon-to-be members of the New York Twenty-One, who amid escalating violence between the Panthers and the city's police studied the art of guerrilla combat. Former marine sergeant Kwando Kinshasa (formerly William King) authored a mimeographed guide titled "Urban Guerrilla Warfare." In addition to strategizing guerrilla attacks on police stations, the booklet justified firebombing civilians in subways and other areas as a form of "shock treatment" to undermine people's faith in police.[138] Police seized a copy of the handbook upon arresting fellow defendant Dhoruba bin Wahad (formerly Richard Moore), along with a map of the Bronx annotated with pencil marks indicating the locations of train stations. From the apartment of Curtis Powell, a research chemist, police seized bottles of hydrochloric and nitric acid in addition to a book titled *High Explosives and Propellants*. Police also confiscated five pistols, two rifles, and three shotguns during the New York Twenty-One raids.[139]

At least three members of the New York Twenty-One participated in the attacks of January 17, 1969. That night around nine o'clock, an explosion blew out windows of the Highbridge Forty-Fourth Precinct police station, located on a hill overlooking the Harlem River in the Bronx. The blast had been intended to be much worse, but undercover police officer Eugene Roberts had managed to get hold of the homemade bomb in advance, swapping the dynamite with fake explosives made of clay and oatmeal. Only a blasting cap actually ignited, causing a far smaller explosion. A similar device planted at the Twenty-Fourth Precinct in Manhattan failed to detonate. The one real stick of dynamite that simultaneously ignited in Queens blew a hole in the side of a school building but hurt no one.[140]

Minutes after the blast, across from the station on Harlem River Drive, two police officers approached a car parked with its lights out. They were met with a hail of gunfire. The officers saw two men firing at them with handguns, but by the time they approached the vehicle, the gunmen were gone. They left behind a long-range rifle that they had allegedly planned to use to snipe police officers fleeing the station after the bombing. The assailants would later turn out to be Kuwasi Balagoon and Sekou Odinga. But at the scene, the police found Joan Bird, a nineteen-year-old daughter of Jamaican immigrants who had been, until recently, a nursing student at Bronx Community College.[141]

Bird had gotten involved with the Black Panthers the previous summer after witnessing off-duty police officers attack party members in the Brooklyn Criminal Court. "This seemingly unprovoked beating of black people like myself so enraged me," she recalled, "that I felt compelled to participate in a more direct way in the movement for black freedom."[142] After her arrest near the Highbridge police station, Bird too endured a police beating. A photo circulated after her release from police custody revealed unmistakable dark bruises around her badly swollen left eye.[143] According to Bird, police officers beat, kicked, and threatened to shoot her in an effort to make her provide information about her fellow Black Panthers. In her mind, this amounted to torture. Bird later testified in court that before the police sent her to see chief interrogator Delmar Watson, an officer warned her, "If you claim any police brutality, we'll shove this gun up your cunt."[144] The New York State District Attorney's office used information provided by Bird as the basis for the New York Twenty-One indictment.

One of Bird's accomplices resisted police efforts to capture him and would return to guerrilla struggle at a later date. On the morning of the raids, Sekou Odinga was asleep in his upper-story apartment near Brooklyn's Prospect Park when he heard the footsteps of police in the stairwell and on the roof. Odinga scrambled to get dressed and dashed to the bathroom, where he squeezed through a small window and shimmied down a concrete drainpipe before dropping nearly thirty feet onto the roof of a garage. Though the fall almost knocked him unconscious, Odinga managed to descend a tree down to the sidewalk. Nearby he found a brownstone with an unlocked door. Police cordoned off the block and conducted a house-to-house search, but they somehow overlooked their suspect, who hid for the rest of the day behind an oil tank in the brownstone's basement. A year later, Odinga turned up in Algeria with Eldridge Cleaver, but he would slip back into the United States once more to join the BLA.[145]

Whether there was any truth to prosecutors' claims that members of the Panther Twenty-One were planning an Easter assault on police officers before their arrest may never be known. The extent of Panther involvement in other attacks on police, such as the December 1968 machine-gunning of a Newark police station, may likewise remain a mystery.[146] However, it is clear—and important to acknowledge—that violence flowed both ways between the Panthers and police, and that elements of each understandably saw the other as a threat to its existence. Though a third party, standing outside of this duel between Panthers and police, Hoover's FBI actively encouraged local police agencies' war on the Black Panthers while continuing to target the party with its own counterintelligence operations.

In New Haven, these police attacks took their toll. Paranoia about police informants climaxed in the gruesome torture and murder of nineteen-year-old Alex Rackley. One of the figures implicated in the killing was Ericka Huggins, a former Los Angeles Panther and wife of John Huggins, who moved to her late husband's hometown of New Haven after his violent death at the hands of US militants. Other participants included Huggins's lover, New Haven Panther Warren Kimbro, and West Coast Panthers George Sams and Lonnie McLucas, who had been sent to instill discipline in East Coast BPP chapters.

Before he was taken in by the BPP in New York, Rackley had been a drifter from Florida. Afterward, he sold Panther newspapers and used his skills as a karate black belt to teach Panther self-defense classes. In early May 1969, he came to New Haven with Sams and McLucas, joining them, Ericka Huggins, and other Panthers at Warren Kimbro's three-level townhouse in the Ethan Gardens apartment complex. Paranoia levels had shot through the roof since the New York Twenty-One case, and Panthers across the country were wary of undercover cops in their midst. Rackley couldn't have known what he was getting into.

Relations in the townhouse turned fractious, and then deadly. One day after Huggins and Rackley got into a dispute, Sams beat the young recruit with a wooden paddle he called the "Panther Stick," baselessly accused him of being an FBI informant, and dragged him to the cellar for a farcical "trial" that Huggins captured on a tape recorder. Over a three-day period, Sams led other Panthers in torturing Rackley with beatings, death threats, a coat-hanger twisted around his neck like a noose, and boiling water poured over his body. On May 20, Sams, Kimbro, and McLucas drove Rackley to the nearby town of Middletown, where they shot him to death and left his body in a swamp.[147]

Police recovered Rackley's corpse the next evening and arrested Kimbro, McLucas, Huggins, and four other local Panthers. On August 7, authorities extradited Sams from Canada, where he had been arrested on weapons charges while trying to start up a BPP chapter in Halifax, Nova Scotia.[148] Nineteen days later in Berkeley, FBI agents arrested Bobby Seale, who had been in New Haven at the time of Rackley's torture session. Speaking to a mostly white audience at Yale University, Seale had roused enthusiastic applause when he proclaimed, "Today's pigs are tomorrow's bacon!"[149] Almost immediately after his arrest, Sams told police that Seale had ordered Rackley's execution as part of his ongoing efforts to purge the party of suspected police infiltrators, and despite the lack of any corroborating evidence, Nixon's Justice Department formed a new special unit for the "purpose of instituting federal prosecution against the BPP and associated groups throughout the United States and any areas where sufficient evidence is available to support federal prosecution."[150] As the accused masterminds of the affair, Seale and Huggins faced capital punishment in the electric chair.[151]

The defendants became known as the New Haven Nine, and their May 1970 trial became a rallying point for a large number of supporters on the Left who doubted the accused could ever receive a fair hearing. Thousands of protesters gathered on the New Haven green during the trial, and a subset of militants clashed with the National Guard amid clouds of tear gas. Charges against Seale and Huggins were eventually dropped, though the case damaged the Panthers in other ways, as revelations of Panther involvement in torture and murder contributed to declining support for the party.[152]

As with the cases of the Los Angeles Huggins-Carter killings and the indictment of the New York Panther Twenty-One, details of covert state involvement in the case of the New Haven Nine remain difficult to parse and are likely to be debated for years to come. Panther sympathizers and some scholars have alleged that Rackley's torturer, George Sams, was a police informant and agent provocateur, though there is no documentary evidence to support this claim.[153] Even so, circumstantial evidence points to suspicious behavior on the part of the New Haven police. For example, the green Buick Riviera that Rackley's killers used to drive their captive to his place of execution had been loaned to George Sams by a local Panther volunteer named Kelly Moye, who actually *was* a paid police informant. When Sams called asking to borrow the vehicle, Moye first checked for approval with his handler Nick Pastore, chief of the intelligence division at the New Haven Police Department. New Haven police also had information about Rackley's abduction at the time—and police cruisers followed the green Buick partway to Middletown on the night of the murder—but they did not intervene in the case until after Rackley was dead.[154]

The Nixon administration and Hoover's FBI were also eager to capitalize on the case. FBI agents raided six different Black Panther offices around the country in the weeks following the Rackley murder. Both before Rackley's murder and throughout the following year of drawn-out legal proceedings, FBI agents supplied the New Haven police with information used to harass local party members while they targeted the New Haven Black Panthers with their own COINTELPRO operations publicizing violent Panther rhetoric in an effort to undermine the organization's support in the community.[155] The FBI also played a central role in establishing New Haven prosecutors' shaky case against Bobby Seale.

Though certain questions surrounding the case may never be definitively answered, what is clear is that the New Haven Panthers' torture and murder of Alex Rackley occurred as Hoover's FBI and the New Haven Police Department enflamed deadly factionalism within the BPP. And although there is no evidence that the FBI had any direct role in Rackley's killing, Hoover and his men continued to uphold a political status quo rooted in inequality and police violence. The power of the New Haven Police Department remained unchecked, as the FBI abstained from investigating the department's possible complicity in Alex Rackley's death.

Sidestepping the signs of spiraling fratricidal violence within the organization, BPP leaders and supporters pointed to the New York and New Haven indictments as evidence that police repression was getting worse. They claimed that with the authoritarian President Nixon in power, America was moving toward fascism. Bobby Seale asserted, "The government is trying to stop the Black Panther Party because we're exposing the racist, fascist system for what it is."[156] Headlines of the *Black Panther* newspaper's May 31, 1969, edition announced "FASCISM in America" and highlighted the New York and New Haven cases as prime examples.[157] In regard to the latter case, the editors wrote of a "pig conspiracy": "Most of the [New Haven] Party's leadership has been busted in the same manner that the New York Panther 21 was busted. What manner is that? Simple, it's the pig power structure's attempt to wipe out the Black Panther Party."[158]

Building on this premise, BPP leaders sought to build a multiracial coalition dedicated to fighting fascism. On a weekend in July 1969, thousands gathered for a United Front Against Fascism conference in Oakland, where they heard leaders of the Black Panthers, SDS, the Young Lords, and other organizations speak on the need to develop community control of police departments and improved legal support for political prisoners. Activists in several cities formed chapters of the National Committee to Combat Fascism after the conference, but such efforts were short-lived.[159]

The Black Panthers were not the first African Americans to understand American racism and European fascism as related forms of white supremacist rule. But the party's leaders' strategy for building a better world suffered from important gaps. If the United States was headed toward Nazi-style fascism, how could the party resist such efforts? How could it achieve its goals of socialism and Black liberation amid such a degree of fascist repression? The party's Central Committee did not offer viable answers to these questions. Instead, as Don Cox recalled, "the Panther party had become quite expert at identifying the problems and the real enemies, but in terms of analysis toward developing strategies, giving directions, and providing leadership to the struggle, zero. . . . Other than the few community programs, the only activity the Panthers were engaged in was the defense work for all the comrades behind bars."[160]

The Black Panthers seemed to be trapped by their own violent rhetoric. Guns had been pivotal to the Black Panthers' transformation from a group of neighborhood friends in Oakland into an international media sensation and national organization. Violent behavior and rhetoric had also attracted the attention of American police agencies and landed dozens of Panthers in jail. In 1969, Bobby Seale and the Oakland-based Central Committee sought to refocus the party's efforts on Breakfast for Children and other community programs. Yet in the *Black Panther* newspaper and in local communities, the Panthers continued to promote violence against police officers.

This was not lost on the FBI. Hoover continued to target the party with COINTELPRO operations not, as some have claimed, because he saw the Panthers' breakfast programs as a threat to America's political status quo, but because he continued to view the organization as a violent threat to

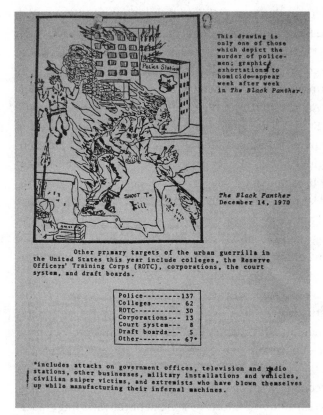

This drawing is only one of those which depict the murder of policemen; graphic exhortations to homicide—appear week after week in *The Black Panther*.

The Black Panther
December 14, 1970

Other primary targets of the urban guerrilla in the United States this year include colleges, the Reserve Officers' Training Corps (ROTC), corporations, the court system, and draft boards.

Police---------137
Colleges-------- 62
ROTC----------- 30
Corporations--- 13
Court system--- 8
Draft boards--- 5
Other---------- 67*

*includes attacks on government offices, television and radio stations, other businesses, military installations and vehicles, civilian sniper victims, and extremists who have blown themselves up while manufacturing their infernal machines.

Excerpt from FBI special report "1970: Year of the Urban Guerrilla." FBI domestic security agents underscored the *Black Panther* newspaper's promotion of antipolice violence to make their case for police targeting of the organization and its members. National Archives and Records Administration.

police. In a message to the San Francisco FBI office on May 27, 1969, Hoover excoriated the Black Panthers' breakfast programs as a means by which the party promoted the "insidious poison" of antipolice violence among children and the wider community. He provided an example from the *Black Panther* newspaper on a recent Panther wedding at an Oakland church that hosted BPP breakfast programs. During the festivities, Bobby Seale and other Panthers led children in a song with the refrain "We Want a Pork Chop Off the Pig."[161]

A couple months later, in mid-July, newspapers quoted Director Hoover saying that among Black Nationalist groups, "the Black Panther Party, without question, represents the greatest threat to the internal security of the country." This has since become Hoover's most famous quote about the party, and in Panther folklore, it is widely cited as evidence that the FBI sought to neutralize the organization because of its political ideals and effective organizing.[162] But Hoover was concerned about Panther guns taking aim at cops.

Central Committee member David Hilliard later reflected on the negative consequences of the Black Panthers' fixation on guns: "In retrospect, those guns were somewhat our nemesis. . . . The police, the media, used that. We got hung up into a confrontational thing with the police over those guns that we were never really able to live down."[163] Hilliard took over leadership of the party in August 1969 after police took Bobby Seale into custody. Inspired by Joseph Stalin's *The Foundations of Leninism*, Hilliard sought to consolidate control over the organization through force and intimidation. Members who questioned official party policy—which at this point was determined primarily by him—could face expulsion, beatings, or, worse, incarceration in a makeshift "jail" consisting of a large hole in the ground beneath Oakland's Panther headquarters.[164]

Instead of uniting the BPP, Hilliard's efforts created more distrust and internal conflict. One of the worst flare-ups of violence happened in Baltimore less than two months after Rackley's murder. On July 11, 1969, Black Panthers in Baltimore kidnapped Eugene Leroy Anderson, a twenty-year-old Panther sympathizer who had helped paint the row house at 1209 North Eden Street that the local chapter used as its headquarters. Accusing him of being a police informant, Baltimore Panthers dragged Anderson to a room on the third floor of the Eden Street house and tortured him for two days. Local news accounts based on witness testimonies later reported that eleven Panthers participated in the torture session, pistol-whipping Anderson, extinguishing cigarettes on his forehead, beating him with bed boards, slicing his body with a hot knife, and rubbing alcohol in his bloody wounds. On the night of July 12, Anderson was taken to nearby Leakin Park and executed with a single shotgun blast. His remains were not discovered until October, however, and by that time his body was so badly disintegrated that local media referred to the ordeal as the "bag of bones" case.[165]

Don Cox denied any involvement in the Anderson torture incident, but he remembered the circumstances well. He recalled dropping by the Baltimore Panther headquarters on his way from Washington, D.C., to New York while helping organize BPP chapters on the East Coast. Cox had come to pick up some comrades from New York, but when he hurried up the stairs at the Eden Street house, he was stopped outside the bedroom door. "Don't come in," he was told. There was a "pig in the closet." Cox recoiled and, according to his account, immediately left the premises and angrily sped off to New York. "I knew that soon there would be another conspiracy case," he recalled, "and that this time I would be included."[166]

His prediction turned out to be correct. The hammer came down after another violent incident the following April in Baltimore, when a group of Panthers ambushed white police officers Stanley Sierakowski and Donald W. Sager, killing the latter. Maryland authorities indicted Cox, a white attorney, and nineteen local Panthers on charges related to the "bag of bones" case.[167] As soon as he heard the news of his indictment, Cox booked a flight from San Francisco to London, making his way across the Atlantic in disguise with a phony passport. He eventually ended up in Algiers, where, along with Eldridge Cleaver, he would serve as a long-distance mentor to members of the BLA.[168]

· · · · · ·

Not until after the dissolution of the BPP outside of Oakland, with Cox in self-imposed exile in Algeria, would the Black Panthers' guerrilla army come to fruition. In May 1971, with a core membership including several acquitted members of the New York Twenty-One, the BLA would launch a wave of bloody attacks on police officers in New York City. All the police and FBI efforts to undermine the Panthers had coauthored a far more volatile entity.

There is little evidence that FBI COINTELPRO operations against the BPP succeeded in their objective of preventing leftist violence. G. C. Moore, a domestic security official at FBI headquarters, acknowledged this in his 1975 testimony before the Senate Church Committee's hearings on the bureau's covert operations: "It is not easy to measure effectiveness. . . . There were policemen killed in those days. There were bombs thrown. There were establishments burned with Molotov cocktails. . . . We can measure that damage. You cannot measure over on the other side, what lives were saved because . . . suspicion was sown on [someone's] leadership and this organization gradually declined . . . or this organization did not join with [that] organization as a result of a black power conference which was aimed towards consolidation efforts."[169] Moore acknowledged that the "ineptitude" of groups such as the Black Panthers and SDS could have been the main cause for their decline. But Moore also stated that he and other FBI personnel hoped that counterintelligence "did play a part" in undermining these organizations and their capacity to carry out political violence. "Maybe we just gave it a nudge."[170]

While it is unclear whether the FBI *prevented* leftist violence, the bureau clearly *fomented* deadly violence against members of the BPP. Citing COINTELPRO operations designed to enflame violent tensions with US in Southern

California and the Blackstone Rangers in Chicago, the Church Committee found that "some of the FBI's tactics against the BPP were clearly intended to foster violence, and many others could reasonably have been expected to cause violence."[171] Hoover's FBI also actively encouraged police attacks on radicals and collaborated with federal, state, and municipal efforts to criminally indict and arrest Bobby Seale and other leftist militants. These combined efforts, carried out amid Nixon's call for law and order, helped encourage the very sort of violence the FBI's COINTELPROs sought to prevent, as more and more leftists—unaware of growing tensions between Hoover and Nixon—felt the need to fight back against what they interpreted as a concerted government effort to repress the Black Power movement and the New Left.

Yet it would be disingenuous to attribute the militant Left's turn to violence to the state alone. The fact that the BPP cultivated an armed underground wing from its inception as a national organization shows that party leaders' exhortations to guerrilla warfare against police officers were far more than rhetoric. Local police and the FBI were not lying when they accused the Panthers of promulgating deadly violence against members of law enforcement. American radicals' decisions to embrace the "cult of the gun" were conscious and deliberate, part of an international revolutionary strategy.

During the second half of 1969, as Nixon expanded the U.S. war in Vietnam, violent conflict between the state and militant leftists would continue to escalate. In addition to deepening the BPP's factionalism, heightened violence increased divisions within SDS and pushed more white radicals down the path toward clandestine urban guerrilla warfare. The growing problem of leftist insurgency would also exacerbate rifts inside the FBI, and between J. Edgar Hoover and President Nixon.

3 Covert Operations and Clandestine Radicals

· ·

Two events—coincidentally occurring within days of one another—marked a decisive conjuncture in Nixon's war on American radicals. On Thursday, June 19, 1969, President Nixon's youthful aide Tom Huston took a fateful meeting in Washington with FBI officials William C. Sullivan and Charles D. Brennan. Two days later, Weatherman took over SDS during the organization's national convention in Chicago. The latter features prominently in many narratives of student radicalism; the former, however, is far less known.

As assistant director for domestic intelligence, William Sullivan was the third most powerful man in the FBI, beneath Director J. Edgar Hoover and his elderly deputy Clyde Tolson. Known among his colleagues for his wrinkled shirts and generally unkempt appearance, Sullivan was one of the few liberal Democrats in the heavily Republican FBI headquarters. He was also the only other person in the bureau besides Tolson whom Hoover addressed on a first-name basis—the director typically called him "Bill." Charles Brennan, the Domestic Security Division's internal security chief, was the second-ranking domestic security official under Sullivan, and a close ally to his supervisor. Sullivan had handpicked Brennan, helping him leap ahead from the rank of special agent in a mere two years, earning resentment from those who believed his position at the helm of the Domestic Security Division should have gone to someone with greater seniority and experience. As Brennan's successor Edward Miller later put it, "He was Sullivan's boy."[1]

Huston went to see Sullivan under orders from Nixon. The president remained paranoid about foreign Communist "subversion" of American social movements. The FBI had reiterated to White House counsel John Ehrlichman in April that there was no direct foreign influence on America's Black Power movement and New Left, but the president remained fixed in his beliefs, still convinced that the mass street protests and bombings sweeping the country had to be part of an international Communist conspiracy. When Ehrlichman and his assistant Egil "Bud" Krogh were unable to find evidence of such funding, Nixon turned to Ehrlichman and said, "Get Huston on this."[2]

Sullivan was quickly impressed with Huston. He recognized that the twenty-nine-year-old White House aide with dark-framed glasses and "an intellectual, thoughtful look to him" was a potential ally.

Sullivan's meeting with Huston came at a critical point in his career. A native of Bolton, Massachusetts, Sullivan had been working his way up the FBI hierarchy since 1941, when at the age of nineteen he joined the bureau as a special agent in the Milwaukee field office. He landed his promotion to assistant director of the Domestic Intelligence Division in 1961 after working a number of other positions and earning degrees at American University and George Washington University. As head of the largest of the FBI's five divisions, Sullivan oversaw the bureau's dirtiest covert operations: its COINTELPROs against American dissidents. Sullivan authored the bureau's notorious "suicide letter" to Martin Luther King.[3] He had also been the first to propose the FBI's COINTELPROs against the Black Power movement and the New Left. By 1969, Sullivan knew as well as anyone else in Washington that Hoover's remaining days as FBI director were limited. He aspired to one day serve as Hoover's successor, though he disapproved of his current agenda.

Sullivan believed that Hoover's fixation on an outdated threat of foreign Communist subversion had led him to devote inadequate resources to the main threat to U.S. internal security: homegrown leftist insurgents. Sullivan later recollected how he felt about the director's mid-1960s restrictions on illegal surveillance techniques: "Hoover in effect put the Domestic Intelligence Division of the FBI out of business. Our hands were tied. It became virtually impossible to do our job."[4]

To prevent leftist violence, Sullivan believed that the FBI needed to restore the far-reaching surveillance powers it had exercised against suspected Communists during the earlier part of the Cold War. He advocated returning to tactics like break-ins, mail opening, warrantless wiretapping, and use of teenaged informants.

Sullivan and Brennan used the occasion of their meeting with Huston to convince the Nixon staffer that leftist bombers and would-be guerrillas posed the primary threat to U.S. internal security. The three men met several more times over the next year to discuss strategies for combatting leftist bombings and guerrilla warfare. In their conversations, they began to construct "terrorism" as a new, urgent threat to U.S. national security. A year after the trio's first meeting, their proposal for the so-called Huston Plan would establish an intellectual basis for the development of American domestic counterterrorism. The meetings between Sullivan, Brennan, and

FBI assistant director William C. Sullivan testifies before the President's Commission on Campus Unrest, July 23, 1970. Charles Brennan, the bureau's domestic security chief, is seated to his right. AP Photo.

Huston also contributed to a growing conflict between Hoover and the Nixon administration over how best to combat leftist "terrorism."

As these government officials met and strategized, parallel debates over urban guerrilla warfare came to a head during the SDS National Convention. In Chicago, the Weatherman faction took over SDS and announced plans to build America's first revolutionary urban guerrilla army. Over the next six months, ongoing violence between leftist radicals and the state accelerated Weatherman's transition toward clandestine urban guerrilla warfare. Weatherman's militancy, in turn, reinforced the belief among Sullivan, Brennan, and Huston that the FBI was not adequately equipped to respond to leftist violence. Without realizing it, the FBI prodded Weatherman toward clandestinity just as Weatherman compelled the FBI to reevaluate its covert operations.

Weatherman

At SDS's annual meeting in Chicago, bitter sectarian debates were tearing the organization apart. Members argued over the best approaches for ending the war in Vietnam, challenging police attacks on the Black Panthers, and creating a revolutionary movement among America's youth. The 1969 National Convention brought about the collapse of SDS as a national organization capable of uniting student opposition to the war, but it gave birth to something new. Emerging from the wreckage came Weatherman. Over the next year, the Weatherman faction would transform itself into the Weather Underground, America's first clandestine urban guerrilla organization and major headache for both the FBI and the Nixon administration.

SDS met from June 19 to 21. By the third long day of agonizing debate, SDS had split into two rival factions. These factions' names and ideologies may seem tedious today, but understanding them is necessary for tracing the emergence of America's guerrilla insurgency. The faction that lost out at the national convention was the Worker-Student Alliance (WSA), a group of clean-cut Maoists associated with the earlier "action-praxis" faction and the doctrinaire Progressive Labor Party (PLP). Coming out on top was the Revolutionary Youth Movement (RYM), an outgrowth of the "action faction" that was itself made up of two subfactions united in their hatred of the PLP and their support for the BPP and Vietnam's National Liberation Front. Leading RYM was the Weatherman subfaction. The group took its name from the lengthy position paper members presented at the conference, "You Don't Need a Weatherman to Know Which Way the Wind Blows." The document's title came from a line in Bob Dylan's hit song "Subterranean Homesick Blues."[5]

Bernardine Dohrn read the Weatherman statement during the last day of the conference, flanked on both sides by fellow Weather militants who stood in pseudo-military formation. Dohrn was a sharp-witted, twenty-seven-year-old attorney from Wisconsin. She had organized legal support for arrested antiwar protesters with the National Lawyers Guild in New York before serving as SDS national secretary for the previous year. With long brown hair and magnetic charisma, her looks and confidence made many men weak in the knees. Weatherman Mark Rudd referred to Dohrn as "the most seductive person I have ever met in my whole life, without exception, and without even trying to be."[6]

Dohrn's life had changed in August 1968 after she led a delegation of thirty people to Budapest to meet with a delegation from North Vietnam. "The trip gave me a very strong sense that we had a unique role to play," she recalled, "and that our job was to mobilize the broadest possible opposition to this immoral, illegal, and genocidal war." Dohrn felt that history "was calling on us to act as our most aggressive moral selves to stop the slaughter" in Vietnam.[7] By the following summer, this conviction had led her and others in SDS down the road to guerrilla warfare. In Chicago, when members of the PLP faction booed her speech, Dohrn expelled them from the organization and led the Weatherman and RYM faction out of the meeting hall. This effectively spelled the end of SDS.

Weatherman's manifesto took inspiration from *foco* theory and the Black Panthers. Hailing the martyrdom of Ché Guevara, the statement called for the development of a revolutionary antiracist movement among America's working-class white youth. The authors sought to mold this movement into "one division of the International Peoples' Army" they hoped would "dismember and dispose of U.S. imperialism." Like the Black Panthers, Weatherman saw no possibilities for creating social change through nonviolent direct action or normal avenues of the U.S. political process. They were not entirely giving up on organizing social movements just yet, but they asserted that armed struggle would be necessary in the near future to counter an "inevitable" wave of "all-out military repression" carried out by the "pigs" on behalf of the "ruling class" and its "imperialist state."[8] Weatherman sought war: armed resistance to U.S. imperialism and Nixon's law-and-order crackdown. They framed armed resistance not only as necessary but as the only viable alternative to collaboration with racism and imperialism.

To draw this conclusion, however, Weatherman took a set of legitimate grievances and applied a distorted political analysis. It is true that police brutality remained a major problem in African American communities, and that local police frequently met civil rights and antiwar demonstrators with violent force. Weatherman's cynicism toward the American political system was understandable too, especially given the Democratic Party establishment's insistence on nominating Hubert Humphrey as its 1968 presidential nominee over Eugene McCarthy and other antiwar candidates. Dohrn and other Weatherpeople had also attended Panther funerals in California; they had experienced the emotional weight of political violence firsthand. But despite Nixon's election, America had not become a fascist dictatorship. Social movement organizing was difficult but still possible. Weatherman's analysis gave its members an excuse to deny this reality while railing against police repression that their own tactics relentlessly provoked.

Plans for *foco*-inspired clandestinity set Weatherman apart from Cameron Bishop and other late 1960s' radical bombers, including Sam Melville, who led a group that carried out a string of bombings in New York City during the summer and fall of 1969 before being captured by the FBI and New York police.[9] Weatherman was also distinct from anarchist insurgents of the late nineteenth and early twentieth centuries as well as the contemporary underground wing of the BPP. Previous revolutionary bombers, saboteurs, and assassins had maintained public activist lives while occasionally engaging in secretive acts of political violence. Weatherman, in contrast, set out to construct a clandestine underground infrastructure that would allow members to escape state surveillance completely.[10] From the underground, they hoped to launch a sustained campaign of urban guerrilla warfare, one that could divert the state's resources away from its attack on the Black Liberation movement, and, according to their interpretation of *foco* theory, ignite a broader revolutionary uprising among America's youth.

Over the six months following the June 1969 SDS convention, Weatherman began preparations for clandestine urban guerrilla warfare while also engaging in some final attempts at movement building. The group's members studied the texts of Guevara, Debray, and other revolutionaries and trained themselves in martial arts, firearms, and bomb making. They would fail miserably, however, in their efforts to recruit working-class white youth. If anything, their violent rhetoric and behavior would alienate far more than they would inspire.

COINTELPRO-New Left

The FBI was glad to help Weatherman discredit itself. Before the June 1969 National Convention, the bureau had worried that a revolutionary movement led by a united and powerful SDS could threaten America's "internal security." In other words, though the Columbia University strike and concerns over disruptive student unrest had been the impetus behind COINTELPRO-New Left, FBI officials also worried about SDS's potential for revolutionary "subversion." Because of this, the FBI's COINTELPRO-New Left sometimes devoted resources to supporting the nascent Weatherman faction as a way to weaken the organization as a whole. It was only after the SDS National Convention that COINTELPRO-New Left shifted to a nearly exclusive focus on undermining Weatherman.

In the view of FBI domestic security officials, the threat of New Left "subversion" was distinct from the supposed foreign-backed threat posed by the Communist Party. In November 1968, the Domestic Security Division's third-ranking official Robert L. Shackelford explained this distinction to his supervisors Charles Brennan and William Sullivan. "It appears the New Left is gravitating towards establishing a power base within the structure of higher education," he wrote. "It is well established the basic ideological difference between the New Left and the Communist Party, USA (CPUSA) rests on this point. The CPUSA believes revolution must come from the laboring class, the New Left believes from the intelligentsia."[11] Shackelford feared that America's New Left could gain the strength of student movements in places like Mexico and Uruguay, where campus radicals had thrown their countries into turmoil over the past year as the leaders of massive nationwide street mobilizations. "The Latin American version of universities being corrupted into power bases for revolution is well known," he warned. "The evolution of their universities, as sacrosanct places, off limits to their governments, is not something we can afford to sit by and see followed here.[12]

In the year leading up to the 1969 National Convention, the FBI carried out COINTELPRO operations against SDS intent on preventing both subversion and violence. Sometimes these objectives conflicted with one another. Shortly before the national convention, for example, the FBI saw the PLP's "praxis action" faction as a greater national security threat than the "action faction" that controlled the SDS National Office and would later become Weatherman. The SAC of the FBI's Cleveland field office warned headquarters that PLP could transform SDS from "a shapeless and fractionalized group into a militant and disciplined organization" capable of consolidating a revolutionary student movement.[13] These fears took immediate precedent over violence prevention.

The FBI undertook several COINTELPRO actions designed to prevent PLP from dominating SDS. In one instance, FBI officials directed their numerous informants inside SDS to vote for the National Office faction in the election for officers during the national convention. Unbeknownst to the FBI, conference staffers loyal to Weatherman/RYM had also helped achieve this outcome by tampering with delegates' votes.[14] The Cleveland field office later reported that although the "precise effect" of their initiative could not be measured, the FBI's preferred outcome materialized nonetheless: Weatherleaders Mark Rudd, Bernardine Dohrn, Bill Ayers, and Jeff Jones had assumed new positions as SDS national officers. "The SDS as the mainstay of the national New Left Movement is now seriously divided and, to this extent, weakened," SAC Cleveland reported. "The National Office faction is gradually being forced into a position of militant extremism," he noted, "which hopefully will isolate it from other elements of the libertarian [sic] community and eventuate its complete discrediting in the eyes of the American public."[15]

But after supporting SDS's most violence-prone faction, the FBI shifted course. As Weatherman pursued "militant extremism," the FBI immediately pivoted the focus of its New Left counterintelligence and surveillance operations toward the group. On July 25—less than a week since their meeting with Tom Huston and since Weatherman took over SDS—Charles Brennan warned William Sullivan about the faction's plans for clandestine guerrilla violence. Weatherman, he explained, sought to move SDS "into the position of a clandestine organization of Marxist-Leninist revolutionists which will support similar groups throughout the world and use force and violence to achieve their objectives in this country."[16] Ironically, Brennan and Sullivan now sought to prevent a group the FBI had just supported from carrying out lethal violence. The emergence of Weatherman also confirmed Sullivan and Brennan's view that leftist violence presented a new urgent threat to U.S. national security that the FBI was not fully prepared to confront.

Weatherman presented the FBI with a new challenge. The group's members openly announced their intentions to build a guerrilla army, but the bureau had no information about specific plans for violence. The bureau had also never investigated a clandestine guerrilla group before and had no strategy for doing so. In the absence of such a strategy, Brennan launched a counterintelligence operation focused on Weatherman that was similar to those the FBI had been directing against SDS since April 1968. With the aim of promoting "a wider split in this revolutionary youth group," Brennan recommended providing information on factionalism in SDS—which was now controlled by Weatherman—to "friendly news services."[17]

As with the BPP, the FBI endeavored to undermine Weatherman's capacity for violence by using surveillance and COINTELPROs to preemptively discredit the group. The FBI would carry out many COINTELPRO operations against Weatherman before the group's membership began to go underground in March 1970. By putting pressure on landlords, for example, special agents managed to get two Weatherman collectives kicked out of their apartments in Cambridge, Massachusetts.[18]

The FBI tracked Weatherman with growing alarm during the summer of 1969, a period of surging popular protest against the war in Vietnam. Gleaning information from informants and SDS publications such as *New Left Notes*, the FBI watched as Weatherman planned its "SDS National Action," otherwise known as the Days of Rage. Weatherman conceived the Days of Rage as a means to spark a white youth revolt against U.S. imperialism in the heart of America. The group sought to deliver tens of thousands of militant protesters to downtown Chicago from October 8 to October 11 to "bring the war home" and engage police in hand-to-hand combat.[19]

Extolling violence, organizers of the pre-planned riot pronounced their intentions to "tear up pig city" and "kick ass" in confrontations with the police as they attempted to recruit participants at high schools, community colleges, and youth hangouts.[20]

The Days of Rage riot was a failure, as participants would later admit. Years later, Weatherwoman Cathy Wilkerson observed that Weatherman's confrontational tactics made a kind of sense. They "gave voice to the frustration, anger, and growing abandon that so many young activists felt," Wilkerson wrote, and "seemed to electrify the imagination of a new constituency of young people, especially teenagers." But calling for violent insurrection was not an effective way to recruit new people into a movement capable of challenging America's prevailing political order. "Some of the leaders of Weatherman . . . mistook these youthful expressions of alienation for political consciousness," Wilkinson recalled. "Many wanted to be convinced" of the erroneous notion "that if a few threw up the barricades, hundreds of thousands would follow."[21]

While Weatherman's tactics gained few recruits for the "people's army," they attracted increased attention from the FBI. Upon observing an escalation in Weatherman's militant rhetoric and plans for violence, FBI field offices in Chicago and other cities shifted the "major thrust of [New Left] counterintelligence activity" toward the group.[22]

One way the FBI's COINTELPRO-New Left sought to undermine Weatherman was by discrediting it in the eyes of the public. Achieving this objective was not difficult given the group's nearly nonexistent popular support. To further tarnish Weatherman's image, the FBI simply helped publicize its leaders' outrageous violent rhetoric. In one August 1969 counterintelligence operation, for example, Cleveland agents tipped off a local television news station that SDS was holding a regional conference in the city and suggested reporters seek interviews with the organization's leaders. As a result, Station WJW televised an interview with Mark Rudd and two other Weather-leaders. According to the FBI, Rudd and company "exhibited an insolent, arrogant attitude and openly proclaimed their communistic philosophy and intent to 'smash' the United States Government." Cleveland's SAC reported with satisfaction that "Rudd's statements have served to alarm and alert citizens of this area and have convinced many who were previously indifferent to this problem posed by the SDS."[23]

In another instance, Chicago agents distributed among "moderate groups" a twenty-seven-page cartoon book designed to lampoon Weatherman's "revolutionary ideals" and advocacy of violent street fighting. According to

Chicago's SAC Marlin C. Johnson, the book "caused concern over SDS activities" and "appeared to be especially successful among high school students where SDS was attempting to organize."[24]

COINTELPRO-New Left also promoted fissures between Weatherman and other radical groups. FBI agents sought to sow divisions between the SDS National Office and the Chicago Black Panthers, deepen animosity between Weatherman and the PLP, and promote distrust between Weatherman and Revolutionay Youth Movement II, the anti-PLP faction that split from Weatherman after the SDS National Convention.[25] As with COINTELPRO operations against the Black Panthers, a common tactic was spreading rumors through informants and anonymously mailed letters. On May 21, 1969, FBI headquarters approved the Chicago field office's request to institute counterintelligence operations to disrupt "a tenuous working relationship" between SDS and the local Black Panther chapter. Chicago proposed "depicting the working relationship as an effort on the part of SDS to utilize the BPP as a mercenary group fighting a black war for white liberation."[26] In his approval memo, J. Edgar Hoover called on Chicago agents to instruct Panther informants to create a rift between the two groups. "These sources should be given different arguments so that this does not look like a plan," he wrote. "Your selection of the sources should be of those who are in a position to influence BPP thinking."[27]

After the June 1969 National Convention, factionalism ran so high in SDS that FBI operations were barely needed to undermine the crumbling organization. In August 1969, the SAC of the Cleveland FBI office observed that Weatherman had "expelled" several SDS members who "expressed opinions differing from the 'line' established by the current leaders." Given that Weatherman was doing such a good job isolating itself, SAC Cleveland advised headquarters that attempting to disrupt SDS through the use of paid informants was not worth the risk. "At present," he wrote, "it does not seem wise to risk valuable informants by engaging them in the delicate task of injecting disruptive opinions into SDS policy-making decisions."[28]

The emergence of Weatherman inaugurated not only a new phase in COINTELPRO-New Left but also a vast expansion in the FBI's surveillance of the American leftists. Between July 1969 and July 1972, the FBI increased new domestic surveillance by over 50 percent, as agents initiated over 1,000 new investigations of "subversives" and "extremists."[29] A 1976 federal government report on FBI practices attributed this development to "the increasing number of radical new left groups associated with militant demonstrations and either involved or suspected of involvement in arson, bombings, and destruction of Government property." According to the report, the FBI was especially concerned with Weatherman as well as "black militant groups, particularly the Black Panther Party."[30] Much of the FBI's surveillance increase would begin in the fall of 1970 in response to a series of deadly leftist attacks in different parts of the country. In the meantime, the FBI widened its surveillance of Weatherman.

The FBI modeled much of its Weatherman surveillance on programs it used to monitor the CPUSA, SNCC, and the Black Panthers. In July 1969, the bureau initiated a program to develop "top level informants" within SDS's National Office, which Weatherman now controlled. Bureau officials hoped such informants could provide daily reports on the activities of the organization's leadership. In a message to FBI headquarters, the Chicago field office affirmed its support for such efforts while also conveying frustration over the lack of informants inside the Weatherman faction. Agents described the group as "extremely security conscious permitting very few individuals, even though known members of the SDS, to visit the National Office."[31]

As they prepared themselves for the armed conflict they foresaw on the horizon, Weatherman members grew increasingly security conscious and paranoid. Having become radicalized amid a political counterculture in which activists were accustomed to police surveillance, harassment, and brutality, Weatherman militants correctly assumed that their phones were tapped and that police informants sought to infiltrate their meetings and organization.[32] Weatherman Robert Roth recalled the group experiencing what seemed like constant physical surveillance from the Chicago Police Department. In one incident, while Chicago Weather radicals were meeting in an apartment, police officers snuck in through the back stairs. One cornered two women in a bedroom while another picked up Roth by his ankles and dangled him upside down outside a window. "I could smell the liquor on his breath," Roth recalled.[33] The officer pulled Roth out of the window and left with his buddies without making an arrest. The event nevertheless reinforced Weather radicals' anxiety and rage.

FBI memos document both Weatherman's security precautions and the bureau's surveillance operations. An August 1969 Chicago FBI report observed that activists in the SDS National Office had adopted an "extreme concern for security" after Chicago police arrested five leaders on the premises the previous May. "Since then and particularly after the new [Weatherman] leadership took over the [National Office]," the report noted, "their security procedures increased to the extent that at the present no one not known personally to one of the three national secretaries may be admitted."[34] FBI agents reported that Weatherman volunteers maintained this security with a twenty-four-hour "guard watch" stationed outside the office's steel-plated door.[35]

The FBI conducted much of its surveillance in order to ascertain the group's plans for the Days of Rage and other potentially violent actions. The FBI started tapping the phones in SDS's Chicago National Office in May 1969, just before Weatherman coalesced at the organization's June National Convention.[36] With the attorney general's approval, the FBI also installed a hidden microphone in SDS's Chicago Regional Office in September 1969.[37] FBI headquarters wished to bug SDS's National Office as well, but Weatherman's security precautions prevented the Chicago agents from breaking into the office to install the microphone.[38]

William Dyson was one of four special agents who logged more than 160 hours per week listening in on SDS conversations as the organization's members considered the merits of guerrilla warfare. He later remembered the excitement he felt while monitoring SDS activities on a recording machine in the "Central Tesur Plant," a locked, windowless room located in "the bowels of the Chicago Office."[39] "I *watched* them become the Weathermen! I was *with* them when they became the Weathermen!" he recalled. "I knew more about these people than they knew about themselves."[40]

The FBI obtained a great deal of information through its electronic surveillance of Weatherman. Dyson and his colleagues compiled extensive notes during their eavesdropping sessions, taking particular interest in Weatherman members' travels to Cuba, conversations with Black Panthers, and communications with activists in local SDS chapters.[41] In a report to Director Hoover, Chicago field office chief Marlin Johnson wrote that the electronic surveillance had "furnished numerous identities of SDS leaders in other parts of the United States, plus information concerning aims and purposes and future plans as well as information concerning finances of SDS."[42]

But there were limits to the FBI's surveillance. The bureau's agents were unable to bypass Weatherman's effective countersurveillance tactics. The FBI did not know Weatherman's specific plans for violence on the streets of Chicago, so it was unable to prevent it. Weatherman failed to recruit the crowd it hoped for during the Days of Rage, but its violent clashes with Chicago police continued a cycle of escalation in which Weatherman militants psyched themselves up for guerrilla warfare while the FBI improvised its responses.

Along the way, FBI domestic security officials William Sullivan and Charles Brennan grew even more frustrated with Director Hoover.

Days of Rage

The Days of Rage fell far short of the urban insurrection Weatherman leaders had envisioned. Only a few hundred demonstrators showed up in Chicago, a fraction of the 15,000 that organizers had hoped for.[43] Although the FBI's counterintelligence efforts likely enhanced the alienating effects of the militants' factionalism and lurid rhetoric, Weatherman had largely turned off would-be recruits on its own. Decades later, Mark Rudd reflected with heavy self-criticism that Weatherman had "played into the hands of the FBI. . . . We might as well have been on their payroll."[44]

The FBI, however, was unable to prevent Weatherman violence on Chicago's streets. Instead, by disrupting the Black Panthers and New Left, and giving local police a green light to harass, arrest, and beat radical activists, the FBI unintentionally helped inspire Weatherman's turn to increasing levels of violence.

Weatherman carried out its first bombing on October 6 in an attempt to inspire militancy at the Days of Rage. The blast demolished a statue commemorating Chicago police killed during the 1886 Haymarket riots (radicals despised the monument because it neglected to memorialize the four anarchist labor activists authorities hanged in 1887 in retaliation for the officers' deaths).[45] Days later, Weatherman militants provoked clashes with the police and smashed hundreds of residential, shop, and car windows. Sixty-four police officers sustained injuries during the confrontations, as did many of the rioters, who suffered brutal police baton beatings. Police shot 6 protesters and arrested 287, utilizing FBI intelligence to identify Weathermen.[46] Chicago assistant corporation counsel Richard Elrod became paralyzed during the street fights after hitting his neck against a concrete wall while trying to tackle Weatherman Brian Flanagan.[47]

At one point, militants recognized a plainclothes cop in a space the radicals were using to organize their demonstrations. According to witnesses, the officer was taken into a room and "beaten to a pulp." The Weatherperson who led the attack immediately went underground, the first of the group to do so.[48]

The *Chicago Tribune* described the Days of Rage as a "carnival of mindless terror." This echoed the feelings of many Americans who watched footage of the violence on television. The FBI would come to regularly invoke the concept of "terror" to characterize Weatherman. Meanwhile, legitimizing the FBI's efforts to destroy Weatherman, the *Tribune* called on police to stamp out the "New Barbarians."[49] Chicago FBI agents, in turn, seized on the fact that the Days of Rage had "resulted in wide spread publicity unfavorable to the Weatherman faction of SDS." They proposed new counterintelligence actions designed to eliminate the group's remaining popular support.[50]

The FBI accurately foresaw the Days of Rage as a prelude to Weatherman's involvement in a new form of violence: clandestine urban guerrilla warfare. In a memo sent to thirteen major field offices on October 23, 1969, Director Hoover reported receiving intelligence, likely gleaned from informants, "that the New York City area 'Weatherman' faction of SDS is going underground and forming commando-type units which will engage in terroristic acts, including bombings, arsons and assassinations."[51]

Hoover still had no clear strategy for combatting clandestine leftist guerrillas, however. Instead, the director and his agents drew on time-tested "preventative" surveillance techniques. Noting that members of the Ohio SDS Regional Office organized weekly karate and firearms training courses during the summer of 1969, Hoover directed his agents to "thoroughly review pertinent files" and consult "logical knowledgeable sources." The goal, Hoover explained, was to "determine whether any indications of such activity exists in those territories" and if "the 'Weatherman' faction intends to follow this pattern on a national basis."[52] In late November, under Hoover's direction, FBI offices throughout the country began compiling biographies of all known Weathermen. Special agents gathered approximately 270 bios in under a month and added most names to the bureau's Security Index. Hoover also ordered over a dozen field offices to develop informants capable of infiltrating local Weatherman collectives.[53]

FBI investigators nonetheless remained frustrated with their limited knowledge of Weatherman's plans and activities. Charles Brennan and William Sullivan also continued to resent Hoover's ban on illegal surveillance techniques. Brennan conveyed such feelings in a memo to Sullivan on December 19, 1969. Because of Weatherman's secrecy, Brennan lamented, the bureau remained "unable to obtain the penetrative coverage we desire."[54]

In spite of their growing tensions, Sullivan, Brennan, Hoover, and Nixon shared a common understanding of law and order. Their political outlook put less emphasis on law, and more on restoring a political order rooted in racial, gender, and economic inequality at home and U.S. imperialism abroad. In keeping with this selective, politicized interpretation of the law, they accepted the idea that there would be a different legal standard for radicals and dissidents than the one applied to police and intelligence personnel. Naturally, they perceived their actions as necessary to defend national security from law-breaking revolutionaries and criminals.

Where Hoover and Nixon diverged was over how much illegal police activity they were willing to support toward this end. This difference was not because they had serious moral qualms with illegal police actions, but because they recognized the need to maintain legitimacy in the public eye—too much police violence and criminality would undermine their law-and-order agenda. But ongoing police violence only fueled the leftist violence that officials sought to prevent. Police violence against the BPP in particular helped steel Weatherman's resolve to prepare for guerrilla warfare.

Chicago Murders and the Flint War Council

During the icy, predawn hours of December 4, 1969, in an alleged effort to seize illegal weapons on behalf of the Illinois State's Attorney, fourteen Chicago police raided the Monroe Street apartment of the city's Black Panther leader, twenty-year-old Fred Hampton. They came armed with five shotguns, a submachine gun, and twenty-one other firearms.

When the occupants of the apartment refused to let them in, the police opened fire through the door. They continued shooting as they barged their way inside, unloading over ninety rounds in a matter of minutes. When the shooting stopped, Fred Hampton lay dead on his blood-soaked mattress. The police killed him in his sleep.

The police also killed Mark Clark, leader of the Peoria BPP chapter, who had spent the night in the apartment. Fellow Panther Deborah Johnson, Hampton's pregnant fiancé, miraculously survived the attack from the other side of the bed. She was immediately arrested along with six surviving Panthers, most of them teenagers, four with serious wounds.

The police initially asserted that they had opened fire in response to shots coming from inside the apartment, a claim reprinted without question in the next day's newspaper. A few months later, however, an FBI investigation carried out on behalf of the Justice Department's Civil Rights Division determined that all of the bullets fired in the raid had come from police guns with the exception of one: Mark Clark fired a single shot into the floor after a police round penetrated his heart.[55]

Like other police killings of Black Panthers, the deaths of Fred Hampton and Mark Clark occurred amid mounting violence between local police and Panthers. Tensions in Chicago had been building since the previous summer, when Hampton was serving a jail sentence for "appropriating" seventy-one dollars' worth of ice cream bars from an ice cream truck and distributing them to neighborhood children. FBI agents and Chicago police carried out several raids on the local Panther office during the summer and fall of 1969, resulting in arrests and shots fired. On September 4, Chicago Panther Larry Robinson died of police gun wounds inflicted during an incident several months earlier. The violence the Panthers experienced was, in turn, only part of what the city's African American community endured as tensions rose in Chicago. Fifty-nine Blacks died at the hands of Chicago police in 1969 and 1970.[56]

This epidemic of police violence pushed a nineteen-year-old Panther named Spurgeon Jake Winters over the edge. On November 13, 1969, Winters was holed up in the abandoned Washington Park Hotel with a pair of rifles when police arrived in response to a call. When the first officer approached the building, Winters opened fire, shooting the cop dead. For the next twenty minutes, amid screeching sirens and an onslaught of police gunfire, Winters scurried between the hotel's rooms, returning fire through the windows. In the process, he wounded nine officers and destroyed five cop cars. After fleeing the building, Winters managed to ambush and kill one more police officer before perishing in a final flurry of police gunfire.[57]

Many in the law enforcement community blamed this outburst of antipolice violence on Hampton, even though he had been out of town during the November 13 attack. Hampton had been one of the most successful Panther organizers in the country, overseeing a successful free breakfast program and free health clinic, and forging alliances with Weatherman, the radical Puerto Rican Young Lords organization, the Blackstone Rangers street gang, and a gang of white men from the South called the Young Patriots Organization. Hampton was the main figure responsible for forging Chicago's original "rainbow coalition," a term used for the multiracial alliance that supported 1980 and 1984 presidential bids by the city's prominent civil rights activist, Jesse Jackson.[58]

Hampton's rainbow coalition was not always harmonious, however. On more than one occasion, egged on by the FBI's counterintelligence operations, Hampton and other Chicago Panthers physically attacked local Weathermen. The worst incident occurred on Thanksgiving Day 1969, when Panther leaders erupted in rage over Weatherman members' claims that they could not afford printing costs for a memorial poster for the slain Spurgeon Jake Winters. Hampton showed up at Weatherman's office with five other Panthers and robbed the place at gunpoint. Accompanied by FBI informant William O'Neal, who would play a role in the chairman's assassination a week later, Hampton and his crew pistol-whipped Ron Fliegelman, knocked Russel Neufeld over the head with a two-by-four, and then took off with cash and a typewriter.[59]

Neufeld later attributed the attack to the stress the Panthers were under because of escalating police repression: "They were getting killed. They were literally under siege and they weren't prepared to deal with it."[60] Weatherman Jonathan Lerner, who had Panther guns pointed at him during the assault, saw things differently. He attributed the violence to "the toxic ecosystem of sycophancy, bullying, degraded principle, and madness that was our relationship with the Black Panther Party."[61]

With police violence against the Panthers intensifying in Chicago and beyond, Hampton, like Bobby Seale, opposed immediate offensive armed attacks on police officers. Instead, he saw Panther "survival programs" as a means to unite oppressed communities into a social movement that would violently overthrow U.S. capitalism and imperialism in the *future*. "We not gonna fight reactionary pigs . . . with any reaction on our part," he told a large multiracial audience in 1969. "We gonna fight their reaction when all of us get together and have an international proletarian revolution."[62] Seale, then on trial in the Chicago Eight case, spoke at the same gathering. "We're going to stand together," he exclaimed to the crowd. "We're going to have a Black Army, a Mexican American Army, and alliance in solidarity with progressive Whites, All of us. And we're going to march on this pig power structure. And we're going to say: 'Stick 'em up motherfucker. We come for what's ours.'"[63]

Police and other officials, however, were unconcerned with the nuances of violent Panther rhetoric. They simply saw Hampton as a lethal threat. After the bloody November 13 gun battle, rumors began to spread on Chicago's streets that the police wanted Hampton dead. Some activists urged him to leave the city.[64] He didn't, and the cops caught up with him while he was in bed asleep.

The Black Panthers portrayed the Hampton and Clark killings as premeditated murder, part of the state's larger campaign of political repression. Given the facts of the raid, their argument was convincing. For several days after the killings, Chicago Panthers kept Hampton's apartment open to the public. Taking careful precautions to ensure that nobody disturbed the crime scene, Panthers toured neighbors, activists, and journalists through the apartment to view Hampton's bloody mattress and the dozens of bullet holes that riddled the apartment's walls. Media coverage of the apartment generated international outrage and forced the Justice Department to mandate an FBI investigation into the matter.[65]

Rather than clarifying the circumstances surrounding the deadly police raid, the FBI's handling of the case fueled further suspicions of a violent government conspiracy to suppress the Panthers. No police were ever charged for the killings, and for nearly a decade the FBI concealed its own role in the Hampton-Clark slayings through its paid informant William O'Neal. The formerly incarcerated O'Neal agreed to spy for the bureau in exchange for cash payments and the dropping of several criminal charges. Gaining the trust of Panther leadership, O'Neal had earned a position as Hampton's bodyguard. In the fall of 1969 he provided his handler, FBI special agent Roy Mitchell, with a hand-drawn floor plan of Hampton's apartment featuring the location of the Panther leader's bed. Mitchell provided O'Neal's sketch to Chicago police before the raid.[66] Under the initial orders of Director Hoover, the FBI hid this information from the public until 1978, when a lawsuit filed by the Hampton and Clark families forced it into the light, leading to an eventual $1.85 million settlement.[67]

Critical facts surrounding the Hampton-Clark killings remain unknown and hotly debated to this day. In particular, the belief persists that Hoover's FBI ordered the killings as part of its COINTELPRO against the Black Panthers.[68] Special Agent Mitchell had indeed participated in COINTELPRO operations against the Chicago Panthers as part of the local field office's domestic security unit. And it is true that he provided Chicago police with O'Neal's floor plan of the Hampton apartment and encouraged them to carry out the raid. Declassified documents also reveal that Director Hoover and the bureau's top domestic security officials knew of O'Neal's intelligence gathering. Six days after the deadly raid, Hoover sent Special Agent Mitchell a two hundred dollar "incentive award" along with a personal note commending him for his "aggressiveness and skill in handling a valuable source, [who], is able to furnish information of great importance to the Bureau in this vital area of our operations."[69]

Yet while we know that Hoover had no regard for the lives of Black radicals, there remains no documentary evidence to support the notion that he directly ordered Hampton's murder, and innumerable questions persist surrounding the scarce evidence that exists. It is unclear why Mitchell provided the floor plan of the Hampton apartment. Did he do so under orders from FBI Headquarters? Or did he and Chicago's chief Marlin C. Johnson act on their own? And did they know how the Chicago police were going to use the drawing?[70] Furthermore, while it is indisputable that Hoover concealed the FBI's connection to the raid, it remains unclear exactly why. To cover up an FBI plot? To cover up other illegal FBI activity? To preserve the bureau's public image?

Although it is unlikely that we will ever have definitive answers to these questions, one critical fact is clear: the Hampton-Clark killings fueled militant leftists' suspicions that the government would stop at nothing, including murder, to crush America's radical Left. As historian Jeremy Varon explained, "Hampton's murder deeply affected the Weathermen, underscoring a basic premise of theirs and the New Left as a whole: that race constituted a primary basis of oppression and vastly separated the experiences of black and white activists."[71] Weatherman David Gilbert recalled, "It was the murder of Fred Hampton more than any other factor that compelled us to take up armed struggle."[72] Similarly, Cathy Wilkerson remembered, "the murders [of Hampton and Clark] seemed to call for yet a greater escalation, so that at least this kind of police behavior would not silently become the accepted norm. . . . The rules had changed, and whatever Weatherman was planning, I wanted to be part of it."[73]

Three weeks after the Hampton-Clark killings, from December 27 to December 30, 1969, Weatherman engaged in a frenzied, final call for armed revolution during its National Council in Flint, Michigan. The meeting of about 300 people, dubbed the "National War Council" by organizers, was Weatherman's last public gathering, and the group's final effort to openly recruit young radicals into its urban guerrilla army.

At the Flint War Council, Weatherleaders deployed some of the most flamboyantly violent rhetoric to ever come out of the New Left. Organizers of the event couched their exhortations to armed revolution in counterculture imagery and parlance. They decorated their meeting area with images of Ché Guevara, Fred Hampton, and other slain revolutionaries. Prominent posters featured hand-drawn gun sights and the words "P-I-E-C-E N-O-W," a sardonic play on the antiwar slogan "peace now" ("piece" was contemporary slang for "gun").[74] One of the most widely publicized statements to come out of the gathering was one that Bernardine Dohrn and other Weatherpeople later deeply regretted. Romanticizing the Charles Manson cult's murder of actress Sharon Tate and six other individuals the previous summer, Dohrn exclaimed, "Dig it; first they killed those pigs, then they ate dinner in the room with them, then they even shoved a fork into pig Tate's stomach. Wild!"[75]

Weatherleaders made such proclamations as they announced their plans to go underground, and worked to psych each other up for the task of building a clandestine urban guerrilla organization. At the War Council, Weather militants also conducted martial arts classes and discussed plans for securing weapons, choosing targets, and building a secure underground infrastructure.[76]

FBI officials looked to the Flint War Council as an opportunity to widen their surveillance on Weatherman. Special agents compiled an annotated list of over a hundred core activists who attended the War Council, drawing on information provided by their own informants in the crowd, as well as by the Flint Police Department, whose officers pulled over at least twenty cars containing suspected Weatherman militants en route to the gathering.[77] In their reports on the conference, FBI officials underscored some of the Weatherleaders' most inflammatory comments. Charles Brennan, for example, notified William Sullivan of Bill Ayers's remarks on the "necessity to take on arms and off the pigs."[78]

Weatherleaders' violent rhetoric provided evidence for Sullivan and Brennan to use in their efforts to convince Hoover and the Nixon administration that leftist guerrilla violence posed an imminent threat to U.S. national security. Brennan and Sullivan relayed intelligence on the War Council up the FBI hierarchy, and Director Hoover sent reports on Weatherman to President Nixon, Attorney General John Mitchell, National Security Advisor Henry Kissinger, the State Department, the CIA, the Secret Service, and three different military intelligence agencies. The contents of Hoover's declassified messages are heavily redacted, but the letters probably contained warnings of Weatherman's plans to carry out clandestine guerrilla violence.[79] President Nixon later recalled reading Hoover's reports on Weatherman's War Council with grave unease over the organization's plans to "begin a new campaign of underground warfare, police murder, and bombing."[80]

The FBI gained a great deal of information about those who attended the War Council but remained unable to gather specific knowledge about Weatherman's plans for urban guerrilla warfare. This is because Weatherman militants maintained their usual security precautions. Despite their exuberant calls for armed revolution, they kept most details of their plans hidden from the FBI's snoops and informants. Sullivan and Brennan were correct that Weatherman was hatching violent plans, but they still possessed no legal means to stop them.

Immediately after the conference, Weatherman members began secret preparations for going underground. The group's leaders initiated a process of what they called "consolidation." After closing down the SDS National Office in Chicago in January 1970, the organization orchestrated a series of "purges" designed to eliminate police informants and individuals deemed lacking in commitment. One FBI informant managed to survive Weatherman's purges: Larry Grathwohl, a Vietnam veteran who infiltrated the group the previous summer. Conservative in his political views and with few job opportunities upon his return from Vietnam to his economically depressed hometown of Cleveland, Grathwohl had posed as an antiwar vet as Weatherman radicals recruited for Chicago's Days of Rage. To avoid Weatherman's purges, he endured an "acid test" in which he consumed LSD along with other members of the group while their leaders taunted and interrogated them.[81]

Weatherman's membership subsequently shrank to approximately 150. Reinventing itself as a paramilitary organization, Weatherman fortified a rigidly hierarchical command structure, with a Weatherbureau composed of Bernardine Dohrn, Jeff Jones, John Jacobs, and Terry Robbins making most of the group's major decisions.[82] Members of the group financed their activities with inherited family money, stolen checks, and shoplifting. Several Weatherman "couples" even deceived their families by staging phony weddings in order to cash in on monetary gifts.[83] Most of the members who remained with the group commenced a painful process of breaking ties with family members and aboveground acquaintances. They did so in order to establish new, assumed identities based on fake IDs. In the San Francisco Bay Area, Chicago, Detroit, and New York City, Weatherman established discreet collective apartments in counterculture enclaves or urban white working-class neighborhoods. As they built up their underground, members accumulated skills with guns, explosives, document forgery, and disguise.

After a decade of intensifying political violence, the 1960s was about to birth America's first clandestine urban guerrilla organization.

· · · · · ·

As Weatherman formed an underground infrastructure and plotted urban guerrilla warfare, the FBI faced a challenge distinct from any other in its forty-five-year history. Domestic security officials William Sullivan and Charles Brennan were correct that the bureau was not prepared to confront a clandestine guerrilla insurgency. The threat of Weatherman violence likely informed J. Edgar Hoover's proclamation during a February 1970 congressional hearing that "Weatherman is the most violent, persistent and pernicious of revolutionary groups."[84] Nonetheless, Sullivan and Brennan would continue to team up with Tom Huston in efforts to bypass Hoover and expand the FBI's surveillance in the war on leftist insurgency.

A series of additional attacks fueled the bureau's anxiety. The FBI suspected Weatherman involvement in two February 1970 bombings of Bay Area police stations. The first mangled the arm of Berkeley police officer Paul Morgan; the second killed San Francisco police officer Brian McDonnell. Forty-five years later, it would turn out that their hunch was correct. In 2015 an anonymous former Weather militant confessed to a journalist that the group had staged the attacks.[85]

Late one night in February 1970, Weathermen also firebombed the Manhattan family home of Judge John M. Murtagh, who was then presiding over the New York Twenty-One trial. Murtagh's son John Jr., age nine at the time, recalled his mother waking him in a panic as towering flames from Molotov cocktails illuminated the windows outside their darkened kitchen. After firefighters arrived, John Jr.'s parents took him across the street to spend the rest of the night in their neighbor's eighth-floor apartment. When he woke up the next morning, he looked out the window to see his brownstone home swarmed with police. He also noticed something new on the sidewalk in front of the house: "I could see written in red spray paint, 'FREE THE PANTHER 21—VIET CONG HAVE WON.'"[86]

Weatherman did not publicly take credit for these attacks. As far as the FBI and other law enforcement agencies knew at the time, these incidents could have been carried out by any number of anonymous radicals then involved in nighttime bombing and sabotage activities; in February 1970 at least seventeen leftist bombings occurred throughout the United States.[87] As the group moved toward remaking itself into a clandestine urban guerrilla organization, Weatherman's future violent attacks, and the consequences of such actions, remained impossible to foresee.

In late 1969 and early 1970, Weatherman's leadership had no qualms with killing police officers or other living symbols of state power. The FBI was well aware of this thanks to its surveillance of the December 1969 Flint War Council. An influential Weather faction led by John Jacobs and Terry Robbins also advocated deadly attacks on civilians.[88] They believed the only way to make Americans understand the horrors of the bullets, bombs, and napalm their government used in Vietnam was through civilian casualties at home. But this belief was about to be tested. The deaths of three Weatherpeople in an accidental explosion on March 6, 1970, would shift Weatherman's tactics in important ways, with far-reaching consequences for the FBI, the Nixon administration, and the history of counterterrorism.

· ·

The FBI's war with leftist radicals had been under way only a couple of years when twenty-three-year-old Terry Robbins's fatal mistake changed everything. On the morning of March 6, 1970, Robbins was in the basement of an upscale townhouse in New York City's Greenwich Village. Weatherwoman Cathy Wilkerson's father and stepmother owned the house, but they were away on vacation. In their absence, Wilkerson, Robbins, and other former SDS members had temporarily taken over the place as a staging ground for a guerrilla attack. The basement was their bomb-making laboratory.

The New York Weatherman collective was planning a spectacular act of political violence. The goal was to set off homemade antipersonnel nail bombs in a ballroom on New Jersey's Fort Dix army base during a dance for noncommissioned officers. Far from avoiding casualties, Weatherman hoped to blow up as many army men as possible, along with wives, girlfriends, and anyone else in the vicinity. The self-made guerrillas intended to deliver on their promise to "bring the war home." Americans, Weatherman hoped, would finally get a taste of the violence their government inflicted daily on the people of Vietnam.[1]

But Robbins's mistake stopped the deadly plan in its tracks. While preparing the bombs, he crossed live wires. A series of thunderous explosions leveled the townhouse within an instant. The blast killed Robbins and fellow Weatherpeople Diana Oughton and Ted Gold, mangling their bodies beyond recognition.

It could have been much worse. More than eighty sticks of dynamite stored within the house failed to detonate, thereby saving the surrounding city block from destruction and sparing the lives of Cathy Wilkerson and her comrade Kathy Boudin. Escaping the wreckage, the pair briefly sought shelter in the home of a neighbor before disappearing into Weatherman's nascent revolutionary underground.[2]

The townhouse explosion deeply traumatized Weatherman. Within a few months, the organization's leadership would decide to forgo murder as a political tactic and reorient their organization toward symbolic bombings of empty buildings.[3] To White House and FBI officials, completely unaware of this course correction, the blast demonstrated that Weatherman was serious about forming the country's first clandestine revolutionary urban guerrilla organization. The explosion vindicated their worst fears that the group posed a genuine threat to American lives.

Immediately after the blast, Hoover sent the FBI on a nationwide search for the group's members, while television news flashed mugshots of Bernardine Dohrn, Jeff Jones, and other Weather radicals. But the manhunt and media attention forced members of the group to follow through with their plans to go underground. The group hastily constructed a clandestine infrastructure of safe houses and fake IDs, establishing a secret world beyond the reach of the FBI's paid informants and traditional investigative techniques.

This reality, along with Weatherman's potential for further violence, presented the FBI with an urgent dilemma: How could agents preempt and capture violent revolutionaries whose guerrilla organization was nearly impermeable to surveillance and informant infiltration?

One way the FBI responded to this dilemma was by redefining clandestine leftist guerrilla violence as "terrorism." After the townhouse explosion, Director Hoover, Assistant Director William C. Sullivan, and internal security chief Charles Brennan launched a series of new initiatives designed to counter "extremist terroristic activities." Brennan explained the motivation for such measures in a memo to his supervisor, Sullivan, on April 1, 1970. "It has become increasingly clear," he wrote, "that we are attempting to cope with a large-scale shift to terrorism by New Left extremists." According to Brennan, leftist violence had "erupted into a menace of national proportions."[4]

Brennan overstated the threat leftist guerrilla violence posed to U.S. national security. Despite Weatherman's turn to clandestinity and a growing rate of bombings, the number of leftists willing to carry out violent attacks remained marginal. Leftist militants were not capable of disrupting the day-to-day operation of the U.S. government, military, or economy.

Nevertheless, this was more than just a rhetorical shift. For the first time in FBI history, federal intelligence officials strategized around fighting terrorism. Framing leftist guerrilla violence as terrorism helped the FBI reorganize its domestic security operations and develop distinct strategies and investigative techniques to combat a problem it defined as an urgent threat to U.S. national security. Because of this, the townhouse explosion was a watershed moment in the FBI's gradual construction of terrorism as a central national security priority.

Firefighters and investigators sort through the wreckage from Weatherman's Greenwich Village townhouse explosion, March 6, 1970. AP Photo / Jerry Mosey.

After the townhouse explosion, growing concerns over urban guerrilla violence also prompted heightened conflict among FBI and White House officials. Hoover, Nixon, and their aides could not agree on how best to combat America's guerrilla insurgency. The disgruntled William Sullivan and White House aide Tom Huston seized the townhouse explosion as an opportunity to skirt Hoover, whom they viewed as an obstacle to the state's war on leftist guerrillas. On June 5, 1970, at Sullivan and Huston's urging, Nixon met with the directors of the FBI, CIA, National Security Agency (NSA), and Defense Intelligence Agency (DIA). The president ordered the men to devise a plan to suppress what he called domestic "revolutionary terrorism."[5]

Three weeks later, Nixon approved what would become known as the Huston Plan, a proposal for the greatest consolidation of state surveillance power in U.S. history before 9/11. The initiative called for the coordination of all federal intelligence agencies through an "interagency group on domestic intelligence" under the direct command of the White House and for the lifting of Hoover's mid-1960s' restrictions on warrantless electronic surveillance, break-ins, mail opening, and use of informants under the age of twenty-one.[6]

But it was never implemented.

Since the Senate Watergate Committee first revealed the Huston Plan to the public in June 1973, the secret agreement has typically been understood as a side story in the larger drama of Watergate. Most accounts have interpreted the Huston Plan in the context of the Nixon administration's many "dirty tricks" uncovered in the Watergate investigations—as evidence of Nixon's paranoid desire to gain control over U.S. intelligence agencies in order to undermine anyone he perceived as an obstacle to his personal political agenda.[7] While this interpretation holds some truth, it overlooks the core motivation for the Huston Plan.

The Huston Plan was the White House's first response to the Weather Underground and the broader problem of clandestine political violence. Three decades before President George W. Bush signed the USA PATRIOT Act and unleashed a massive expansion of state spying as part of his global war on terrorism, the Huston Plan outlined tactics and policies designed to preempt clandestine violence with expansive preventive surveillance measures. It was a blueprint for America's first federal institution dedicated to combating terrorism.

Hoover refused to go along with it. Instead, the Huston Plan cranked up the heat on tensions between Nixon and Hoover that had been simmering for the past year and a half. Fallout over the plan led to a full-scale bureaucratic conflict between Hoover's FBI and the Nixon White House, one that would indirectly bring Nixon's presidency to an untimely end.

The Clandestine Violence Dilemma

In the eight months since the June 1969 SDS National Convention, the FBI had been watching the Weatherman faction with growing alarm. But it was only after the townhouse explosion that bureau officials began to fully comprehend the new challenge that Weatherman presented to U.S. police agencies.

Several other developments also raised FBI officials' alarm over Weatherman's plans for future violence. On the same day of the blast, Detroit police located two undetonated bombs, one in a women's bathroom in the department's Thirteenth Precinct, and a second outside the offices of the Detroit Police Officers Association. Like those in the townhouse, the Detroit bombs were constructed of dynamite and designed to kill. The bombs most likely would have taken lives, but faulty ignition devices made of cigarettes and firecracker fuses prevented them from detonating successfully. The FBI knew that Weatherman had planted the bombs because Larry Grathwohl— its sole informant in the organization—had warned them of the Detroit collective's plans for the attack.[8]

Bureau investigators also traced dynamite recovered from the Greenwich Village townhouse to the rural college town of Keene, New Hampshire, where a man identifying himself as David Bellar had purchased it from the New England Explosives Company four days earlier. In an urgent teletype, Hoover ordered agents in Boston, Albany, and other field offices to immediately investigate the incident. Hoover also directed agents to check on a second dynamite purchase by suspected Weatherman Ronald Fliegelman in Barre, Vermont, on the day of the explosion.[9] Chasing another lead, agents uncovered stolen student ID cards and checkbooks from the townhouse wreckage, items they believed Weather militants had used "to fraudulently purchase quantities of firearms."[10]

Further distress ensued on March 12, when a group calling itself Revolutionary Force 9 bombed three Manhattan skyscrapers: the Mobile Oil Building, the IBM Building, and the General Telephone and Electronics Building. Security forces avoided casualties by heeding the bombers' evacuation instructions and shepherding thousands of workers from the towers. Over the following three days, anonymous callers made more than 600 additional bomb threats in New York City. The phony threats wrought havoc in the city as police scrambled to investigate false leads and evacuate thousands of additional people.[11]

After the townhouse explosion and the March 12 bombings, Nixon's Justice Department called on the FBI to put down the leftist bombing surge. Attorney General John N. Mitchell's three assistant attorneys general recommended to Director Hoover that the FBI, rather than local police, lead investigations of all future political bombings in the United States.[12]

Hoover, however, did not appreciate the Justice Department's suggestions. The number of bombings and bomb threats was nearly too great to count, and the FBI lacked the manpower to investigate each incident. For Hoover, this was merely the latest example of Nixon's Justice Department needlessly meddling in the FBI's affairs. The director conveyed his bitterness in a memo to his top administrators. Referring to the recent wave of New

York City bomb threats, Hoover wrote, "Apparently this trio of Asst. AGs would have us go into each."[13]

Hoover brushed off the Justice Department's request, but he remained particularly concerned about Weatherman. More than any other domestic radicals, Hoover believed Weatherman posed the greatest threat to American lives and national security. But the group's members were nowhere to be found, and the FBI had no idea when or where the guerrillas would strike next.

By forming a revolutionary guerrilla underground, Weatherman posed a challenge unlike any the FBI had faced in the past. The organization's clandestinity confounded Hoover because it put the Weatherman militants beyond the reach of the FBI's informants. The FBI's vast network of spies and snitches inside SDS and other organizations was helpful for keeping tabs on the aboveground left, but now that Weatherman had gone underground, the FBI's informants were of little use for tracking down the group's fugitives. Larry Grathwohl was the only paid FBI informant to remain in Weatherman's ranks after the townhouse explosion, and the bureau would soon blow his cover in a frantic attempt to score a Weatherman arrest. The practice known in FBI parlance as "physical surveillance" was also difficult to use because of Weatherman members' "continually changing residences." Moreover, Hoover was unwilling to forgo the bureau's traditional dress code. This was despite the fact that special agents in suits and fedoras with cameras and notepads stood out like a sore thumb in the working-class "poor housing areas" where Weatherman collectives lived.[14]

For the first time in his forty-six-year career as FBI director, Hoover confronted a revolutionary organization that the bureau was unable to infiltrate.

Hoover addressed the FBI's informant problem in a memorandum he sent to field offices in ten major cities on March 12, 1970, six days after the townhouse blast. Because of Weatherman's clandestine status and "use of drugs and extremely immoral conduct," he noted, "it will be extremely difficult to obtain security informants of the type used in the past." "The type of informant now needed," Hoover explained, "may, of necessity, be the street-type, ghetto informant."[15] In other words, because Weatherman guerrillas took shelter within the counterculture, spurned the student Left, and romanticized illegal behavior, Hoover deduced that petty criminals were the FBI's best source for informants capable of infiltrating the organization.

Hoover specifically called on his agents to develop new informants in what he called "communes." Collective living was widespread within the

New Left and the counterculture, in large cities as well as in a growing number of rural areas where thousands of young idealists were going "back to the land" to establish organic farms and intentional communities. Hoover saw such places as potential sanctuaries for Weather Underground fugitives. The director ordered his agents to recruit informants with criminal backgrounds and counterculture credibility who could serve as spies "for possible infiltration into the ranks of the collectives, communes, units, or whatever name they might go by."[16]

Hunting Weatherman was now a top FBI priority. According to Hoover, Weatherman's plans for clandestine guerrilla violence necessitated an urgent "change in investigative procedures." In the weeks that followed the townhouse explosion, Hoover ordered agents to "intensify" their Weatherman investigations—to identify, locate, and apprehend the organization's fugitives and preempt their "plans to direct 'strategic sabotage' against the 'establishment.'" Hoover directed SACs of sixteen major field offices to form "special squads" dedicated to investigating Weatherman and other violent leftist groups. The agents in these squads were to be experienced in apprehending fugitives.[17]

Developing a strategy to counter Weatherman and the unprecedented problem of clandestine guerrilla violence was not a task that Hoover could accomplish alone. This required collective brainpower. Immediately after the townhouse explosion, Hoover conducted a bureau-wide survey of field agents' ideas for combatting leftist guerrillas. The survey helped Hoover develop new tactics, which he outlined in a memo to the field on March 12, 1970.

To help track down Weatherman fugitives, Hoover instructed the FBI's Weatherman squads to develop photo albums with detailed descriptions of the organization's members to aid local police in collaborating with the bureau's investigation.[18] Beginning in 1973, similar "terrorist photo albums" would become standard elements of FBI domestic counterterrorism investigations.[19] Hoover also called on special agents to investigate sales histories of all the nation's commercial explosives dealers, and to track down individuals who may have violated state laws banning the possession of explosives. In addition, he authorized agents to submit requests to FBI headquarters as needed to access the National Crime Information Center (NCIC) for the purpose of tracking potential Weatherman automobiles.[20] The NCIC was the nation's first computer crime database, established in 1967 as part of President Lyndon B. Johnson's War on Crime; the FBI would soon utilize this technology in its war with leftist guerrillas.[21]

Now that Weatherman had gone underground, the FBI determined that its existing COINTELPROs were no longer effective means for fighting the organization. Because it had only one informant within the group, the FBI was unable to sow internal conflict. And because the townhouse blast had already diminished the organization's little remaining public support, it was hardly necessary for the bureau to expend energy discrediting Weatherman. Instead, the bureau hoped to destroy Weatherman by capturing its members and putting them behind bars. Marlin Johnson, the SAC of the Chicago field office, explained this in a memo to Hoover on March 30, 1970: "As the previously applied tactics of embarrassment, degradations, and creation of factional splits do not seem pertinent to the lifestyle of and organization of [Weatherman], the primary tactic being applied is the development of prosecutable federal or local cases against this group."[22]

Hoover also pushed back against the Justice Department. Attorney General Mitchell expected the FBI to expand its bombing investigations, but he had yet to press charges against Weatherman fugitives, despite the fact that Hoover had been asking him to do so since after the Flint War Council in December 1969. Throughout March 1970, Hoover urged Mitchell to promptly indict Weatherpeople on federal charges.[23] FBI agents in Chicago and other cities worked tirelessly to provide the Justice Department with evidence to support indictments, believing that capturing fugitives was "the most effective method to disrupt the activities of this dangerous group."[24]

The Weatherman investigation took on further urgency on March 30, when a pest exterminator tipped off police to a large stockpile of dynamite and guns in a Chicago apartment that the FBI believed belonged to members of the group.[25] A few days later in a memo to Assistant Director William Sullivan, Internal Security Chief Charles Brennan cited the Chicago weapons cache as evidence of Weatherman's plans to carry out "violent, terroristic" acts.[26] Seeking charges with which to indict Weatherman militants, he recommended the bureau determine whether the group's leaders could be prosecuted under the Smith Act of 1940, a controversial law prohibiting "advocating the overthrow of government" that the Justice Department had used to prosecute fascists and Communists during the 1940s and early 1950s.[27]

Attorney General Mitchell finally came through on April 2. In a press conference in Washington, D.C., he announced a fifteen-count indictment charging twelve Weatherman leaders with conspiracy and interstate travel to incite a riot during Chicago's October 1969 Days of Rage. The indictment also named twenty-eight other Weather militants as coconspirators. Now that a large number of the Weatherman's members were federal fugitives, the FBI had jurisdiction to apprehend them.[28]

The Weatherpeople, however, were nowhere to be found. By attracting unexpected police attention, the townhouse explosion had forced Weather militants to either leave the organization or go underground immediately.[29] Bill Ayers recalled the days following the deadly blast in his memoir. "We took new names and fashioned clumsy disguises and kept our living spaces hidden even from each other," he wrote. "We met up mostly at night in elaborately guarded ways, and then usually only briefly."[30] Similarly, David Gilbert remembered rapidly altering his personal appearance. "I'd gone from clean-shaven to a bushy beard," Gilbert recollected, "from short dark hair to long and light, from horn rimmed to rimless glasses, from an informal version of collegiate dress to tie-dyed shirts and bell-bottoms. One day I walked right past an old college friend, who didn't recognize me."[31]

Hoover was right about communes. As they strengthened their underground infrastructure in several cities after the townhouse blast, Weatherman fugitives frequently took shelter in the youth counterculture. Weatherman Brian Flanagan recalled that during his underground years in California, he would "often wind up staying in hippie communes." The problem for the FBI, however, was that a deep antipolice ethos permeated the counterculture. Even if they questioned Weatherman's tactics, members of the counterculture were reticent to cooperate with police, who regularly beat up protesters and arrested marijuana users. At one point, someone on a commune even recognized Flanagan as a Weatherman fugitive but did not turn him in to authorities.[32] A romanticized view of outlaw culture often worked in Weatherman's favor. Bill Ayers remembered, "When we were in trouble, we could just hitchhike and say, 'I'm a fugitive; can you help me out?'" According to Ayers, "If the FBI visited someone . . . and said 'We're looking for Bill Ayers,' or 'We're looking for Bernardine Dohrn,' within a day or two we'd hear about it. So information would not flow their way; it would flow our way."[33]

The loss of three comrades in the townhouse blast had also dealt a severe emotional blow to Weatherman's membership. Unbeknownst to the FBI, at a secret May meeting in northern California, Weatherleaders Bernardine Dohrn, Jeff Jones, and Bill Ayers formulated a new policy of consciously avoiding casualties in future actions. The trio also purged John Jacobs, the organization's remaining advocate of lethal attacks.[34] The group still flirted with lethal violence in subsequent months—in one case an East Coast cell traveled to Maine to kidnap a member of the Rockefeller family but bailed when they could not find him, and in another case Weather militants robbed an upstate New York steakhouse for cash at gunpoint and then felt horrible about themselves afterward. But through a combination of planning and luck, they managed to avoid lethal casualties in future bombings (though at least one resulted in minor injuries).[35]

As far as federal authorities were concerned, however, the group remained an imminent threat to American lives and national security. Hoover was determined to show Nixon that the FBI was leaving no stone unturned in its investigation of the group. In late March 1970, Hoover wrote to Nixon's assistant John D. Ehrlichman and other officials, citing information from an unnamed source who claimed that his daughter, a supposed Weatherperson, had disclosed the group's plans to bomb U.S. passenger airliners.[36] Hoover offered no evidence to corroborate this threat, and the attack never came to pass. But the memo demonstrated Hoover's determination to convince Nixon that the FBI was following all possible leads in its Weather Underground investigation.

White House pressure also prompted Hoover to expose the FBI's lone informant in Weatherman. In mid-April, agents blew Larry Grathwohl's cover by arresting Weather militants Linda Evans and Dianne Donghi in New York City. In his 1976 memoir, Grathwohl claimed that he had urged his FBI handlers to hold off on the arrest until they could also nab Weatherleaders Bill Ayers, Mark Rudd, Bernardine Dohrn, or Jeff Jones. At the time, Grathwohl had been unable to locate the Weatherleaders because of Weatherman's elaborate security measures, which kept each cell's whereabouts secret from other cells in order to prevent the very sort of infiltration Grathwohl sought to accomplish. According to Grathwohl, New York special agent Terry Roberts hinted that his orders came from Hoover. "You may be right, Larry," Roberts replied, "but . . . this decision came from the man in Washington. We need an arrest"[37]

Special agents like Terry Roberts also felt heavy pressure to locate Weatherman guerrillas. In some cases, they resorted to lies and emotional manipulation. In the days after the townhouse explosion, FBI agents visited the parents of several Weatherpeople. In order to get them to provide information on Weather militants' possible whereabouts, agents dishonestly informed some parents that their child had died in the explosion. In one instance, FBI agents visited Anne Stein on Manhattan's Upper West Side and falsely informed her of the death of her daughter, Weather militant Eleanor Raskin. Stein was a former Communist Party radical with previous experience resisting the FBI, and she refused to speak with the agents.[38] It is unknown what information agents may have gleaned using the same trick with parents of other Weatherman fugitives, but there is no evidence that intelligence gathered from such encounters led the FBI to the guerrillas.

While the townhouse explosion spurred FBI panic over Weatherman violence, an incident involving the deaths of two African American leftists aroused fears of attacks by Black militants. On March 15, less than two weeks after the townhouse blast, a car carrying SNCC activists Ralph Featherstone and William "Ché" Payne exploded in the middle of a road in rural Maryland. Both men died on the scene. Police alleged that Featherstone and Payne were on their way to carry out a bombing when a homemade explosive in their vehicle prematurely detonated. Investigators later claimed that the men had constructed the device using a bomb-making manual identical to one that St. Louis police discovered folded up in the boot of another SNCC member after arresting him in September 1968.[39] Within the Left, however, rumors circulated that the FBI or another police agency had covertly assassinated Featherstone and Payne.[40]

Two days after the car explosion, a bomb tore through the corner of a courthouse in nearby Cambridge, Maryland. SNCC leader H. Rap Brown was to be tried there days later on charges of inciting a riot during a 1967 disturbance in the city in which an uprising of local Blacks angered over racism and police brutality clashed with white mobs. An original target of the FBI's COINTELPRO-Black Nationalist/Hate Groups program, Brown was notorious for his highly publicized statements in favor of armed revolution, including a threat on the life of Lady Bird Johnson. After the bombings, Brown immediately went underground.[41]

Hoover viewed the Maryland explosions as evidence that Black militants, like their white leftist counterparts, were preparing for urban guerrilla warfare in the United States. On March 24, 1970, the FBI director warned his agents that "terrorist acts" by "black extremists," in addition to those carried out by Weatherman, would "increase in frequency and violence unless aggressive investigation is undertaken to bring about successful prosecution . . . of guilty parties."[42]

"We Are Attempting to Cope with a Large-Scale Shift to Terrorism"

Hoover's response to leftist bombings was largely improvisational. The FBI had never confronted a clandestine urban guerrilla organization before, and it was doing its best to figure out a response on the fly. The FBI's domestic security officials soon recognized the need for a systematic approach to the problem, however. Three weeks after the townhouse explosion, Internal Security Chief Charles D. Brennan convened a meeting to develop a coordinated FBI response to what he termed domestic terrorism. On March 31, Brennan met with leaders of the FBI's Domestic Intelligence, General Investigative, and Special Investigative Divisions to "coordinate guidelines for recommendations concerning bombing matters and extremist terroristic activities." William Sullivan and the FBI's other assistant directors held a separate meeting on the topic the following day.[43]

Eight months earlier, Brennan had accompanied Sullivan in his first meeting with Tom Huston. Brennan agreed with his supervisor that Hoover's restrictions on illegal surveillance techniques impaired the FBI's investigations of leftist bombers. But within the FBI, Brennan and Sullivan maintained a facade of devout loyalty to the director. The pair used their conferences with FBI officials as opportunities to expand the bureau's capacity for fighting "terrorism," but they did not seek to revive illegal surveillance tactics. They would reserve these efforts for their secret meetings with Huston.

After his conference with FBI officials, Brennan compiled a report for Assistant Director Sullivan and Director Hoover in which he identified leftist guerrilla terrorism as a new type of national security threat, one that the FBI was not fully prepared to confront. According to Brennan, leftist guerrilla violence had arisen in the United States rather suddenly, catching the FBI off guard. In reference to Weatherman, he explained, "a group which emerged only as an ideology in June, 1969, which we obtained authority to conduct individual investigations on in late November, 1969, has erupted into a menace of national proportions in March 1970." Admitting to Weatherman's success in concealing its specific plans for guerrilla warfare from the state, he noted, "our current investigations connected with the New York bombings have shown how little we have seen of the iceberg—just the exposed tip at Chicago in October and at Flint in December." "It has become increasingly clear," he warned, "we are attempting to cope with a large-scale shift to terrorism by New Left extremists."[44]

Brennan and his colleagues believed that the growing leftist guerrilla insurgency required a concerted institutional response. "Despite our voluminous instructions to the field to cope with the emerging Weatherman terrorism," Brennan explained, "the scope of the problem clearly exceeds our existing manpower limitations." Brennan sought new, explicit measures to address guerrilla violence. He recommended that FBI headquarters implement a "special school for field personnel handling these matters," and issue a "letter to all Special Agents in Charge defining our investigative responsibilities . . . in these matters." Moreover, he advised headquarters to conduct a survey of all FBI field offices in order to establish the "cost and manpower requirements expected to be incurred in these intensive intelligence investigations." Brennan suggested that by establishing "hard, specific cost factors," such a survey would provide the bureau with leverage to petition the Department of Justice for the resources needed to expand leftist guerrilla investigations.[45]

Hoover followed through with Brennan's recommendations. Two weeks later, the director issued a memo directing SACs in each of the FBI's fifty-two field offices to "prepare a cost estimate survey of known and anticipated costs" associated with Brennan's proposal for expanded investigations of "leftist terrorist activity."[46] The FBI's extensive survey resulted in no immediate new funding from the Justice Department, but it facilitated the bureau's internal reorganization, as officials transferred personnel from other areas into the Domestic Intelligence Division in order to expand their investigation of Weatherman and other leftist guerrilla groups.[47]

Aside from the arrests of Dianne Donghi and Linda Evans, however, the FBI had made little progress investigating Weatherman. Indeed, youth protest and guerrilla resistance were rapidly expanding.

After President Nixon announced that the U.S. Army was launching a ground invasion of Cambodia on April 30, 1970, mass protests erupted on college campuses across the country. Dozens of ROTC buildings went up in flames. In Ohio, after students from Kent State University smashed downtown shop windows during a spontaneous late-night street gathering, Governor Jim Rhodes called in the National Guard. Confrontation with student demonstrators at Kent State turned bloody when Guard troops opened fire on a crowd of protesters on May 4, killing four and sparking more than 500 additional protests, walkouts, and strikes on other American university campuses. The police killing of two student demonstrators at Jackson State College in Mississippi on May 11 stirred up further protest. Many campus demonstrations shut down classes for the remainder of the semester.[48]

Campus unrest was so widespread that it affected Nixon personally. The president canceled plans to attend his daughter Julie's commencement ceremonies at Smith College in Northampton, Massachusetts, owing to Secret Service warnings of planned student protests and "the possibility of an ugly incident that would mar the graduation."[49] The Cambodia invasion and campus uprisings also forced Nixon to postpone his secret meeting on "revolutionary terrorism" with Tom Huston and U.S. intelligence officials, which he had originally scheduled for April.[50]

Amid the campus unrest, Hoover took additional steps to locate guerrilla fugitives. In early May, he added two more radicals to the FBI's list of Ten Most Wanted Fugitives. The first was Lawrence "Pun" Plamondon, a member of the Michigan-based White Panther Party, wanted for the September 1968 bombing of an Ann Arbor CIA office. Second was H. Rap Brown, sought on interstate flight and riot conspiracy charges.[51]

The FBI's inability to locate leftist guerrilla fugitives was not, as Charles Brennan suggested in his terrorism report, solely a result of limited manpower and inadequate support from the Justice Department. The FBI was also hampered by its own inefficiency. An audit of FBI domestic security investigations published by the U.S. General Accounting Office (GAO) in 1976 determined that the FBI had wasted valuable time and resources with its 1960s' and early 1970s' investigations of hundreds of groups and individuals deemed, under unclear criteria, to be "subversive" or "extremist."[52] While the FBI added personnel to its Weatherman investigation following its April 1970 staff survey, it also maintained extensive surveillance on hundreds of leftist groups and individuals unrelated to the urban guerrillas, including rival SDS factions PLP and RYMII, both of which had officially denounced Weatherman. The GAO report concluded that "rather than concentrating on the most violence-prone groups the FBI has diffused its domestic intelligence investigative coverage to the point where many investigations do not lead to positive results." The study affirmed that "violent groups, such as the present-day Weatherman . . . warrant the FBI's full attention."[53]

Internal bureaucratic conflicts also hindered the FBI's Weatherman investigation. Special Agent M. Wesley Swearingen investigated the group in Los Angeles during the early 1970s following a transfer from New York two months after the townhouse explosion. In his 1995 memoir *FBI Secrets*, Swearingen recalled that an administrative power struggle in the LA field office severely undermined his work. According to Swearingen, Bill Nolan, coordinator of LA's Security Section, rejected Hoover's March 1970 instructions to establish a special Weatherman squad, assuring the director that the guerrilla organization was not active in Los Angeles. This became a problem a few months later when Swearingen identified Weatherman John Fuerst as his top suspect in a case involving the purchase of fifty pounds of dynamite and blasting caps from a store in Tucson, Arizona. When Swearingen informed his boss that Fuerst was living with other Weatherman fugitives in a communal house in LA's Venice neighborhood, Nolan refused to support the investigation, and Fuerst managed to slip out of Los Angeles with the explosives. Swearingen asserted that Nolan did not want to believe him because Nolan "had put his career on the line when he told Hoover there were no Weathermen in Los Angeles."[54]

In May 1970, a bureau spokesperson announced that the Weatherman investigation amounted to "one of the most intense manhunts in FBI history."[55] But Weatherman continued to flaunt its evasion of the FBI in front of the world. In a tape-recorded communiqué issued on May 21, the third anniversary of Ché Guevara's death, Weatherleader Bernardine Dohrn announced a "declaration of a state of war" against "Amerikan imperialism." Within fourteen days, she warned, Weatherman would "attack a symbol or institution of Amerikan injustice."[56]

The guerrillas lacked punctuality, but they made good on their promise. Twenty days later, on June 10 at 6:57 P.M., Weatherman set off a dynamite bomb in a second-story men's room in New York City Police Headquarters. The guerrillas called in a warning fifteen minutes ahead of time, but the explosion still injured seven people in addition to destroying several rooms adjacent to the lavatory. In a communiqué sent to the *New York Times*, Weatherman made clear that its attack was a response to police violence, and it named several victims, including Fred Hampton, New York Twenty-One defendant Joan Bird, and the four students at Kent State. "The pigs in this country are our enemies," it proclaimed.[57]

The authorities responded swiftly. New York City mayor John Lindsay promised a "relentless" police investigation. The New York Patrolmen's Benevolent Society offered a $20,000 reward for information leading to an arrest.[58] J. Edgar Hoover did not leave a record of his response to the latest Weatherman attack, but Los Angeles special agent Cril Payne recalled the director's reaction. "From the reports that circulated in the field," Payne recalled, "Mr. Hoover was outraged. The situation was rapidly progressing to the point where [Weatherman] was becoming an embarrassment to the Bureau."[59]

A Plan to Combat Terrorism

President Nixon was deeply alarmed by the wave of leftist guerrilla violence. The townhouse explosion finally convinced the president of what Tom Huston had been telling him for eight months: that leftist guerrilla violence posed more of a threat to U.S. national security than foreign Communist

President Richard Nixon and aide Tom Huston on the White House lawn, 1971. Photograph by Robert Knudsen. Courtesy of the Richard Nixon Presidential Library and Museum (National Archives and Records Administration).

subversion of American politics. Nixon's change of perspective presented Huston, William Sullivan, and Charles Brennan with an opportunity. The trio could now move forward with a plan to loosen Hoover's grip on domestic federal surveillance and bypass his restrictions on illegal spy tactics.

Nixon convened his "revolutionary terrorism" meeting on June 5, 1970, in the Oval Office. Huston was in attendance along with FBI director Hoover, CIA director Richard Helms, Admiral Noel Gayler of the NSA, Lieutenant General Donald Bennett of the DIA, directors of the Army, Navy, and Air Force intelligence agencies, and cabinet members H. R. Haldeman, John Ehrlichman, and Bob Finch.[60] Nixon did most of the speaking, but he read from a "talking paper" Huston had drafted for him. Huston had developed the ideas outlined in the paper through his meetings over the past year with Sullivan and Brennan. The analysis Huston outlined in Nixon's talking paper bore close resemblance to Brennan's FBI assessment of the domestic terrorism threat.

Nixon commenced the meeting by identifying urban guerrilla warfare as a new type of threat to U.S. national security. America's "internal security problem," the president declared, had moved from the "student activism" and "protest movements" of the 1960s to "revolutionary terrorism being perpetrated today by determined professionals." "We are now confronted with a grave crisis in our country, one which we know too little about," Nixon warned. "Certainly hundreds, perhaps thousands, of Americans—mostly under 30—are determined to destroy our society. . . . They are reaching out for the support—ideological or otherwise—of foreign powers, and they are developing their own brand of indigenous revolutionary activism which is as dangerous as anything which they could import from Cuba, China, or the Soviet Union."[61]

The president acknowledged that clandestine guerrilla organizations posed unique surveillance challenges that set them apart from the FBI's earlier arch-nemesis, the Communist Party. "The new revolutionary groups," Nixon asserted, were "less susceptible to penetration and surveillance." Urban guerrilla cells were also geographically dispersed, requiring "far broader coverage" than previous targets. These organizations, Nixon emphasized, "place a high premium on violence."[62]

The president ordered the country's top intelligence officials to "develop a plan" to thwart revolutionary guerrilla warfare. "Terrorism has replaced subversion as the immediate threat," Nixon stated. "This must be halted before innocent people are killed."[63]

Just as President Johnson sought preventive intelligence to preempt urban riots in 1967, Nixon sought advance warning of leftist guerrilla violence. But instead of leaving this task up to the FBI, Nixon, for the first time in U.S. history, sought direct White House control over America's intelligence agencies.

On several occasions over the following two weeks, representatives of the FBI, CIA, NSA, DIA, and the Army, Navy, and Air Force intelligence divisions met to fulfill Nixon's orders to "review the collection efforts of the intelligence community in the area of internal security and to recommend . . . additional steps which can be taken to strengthen our capabilities in this regard."[64] Under Nixon's orders, Huston oversaw the project, working closely with Sullivan and Brennan. Together, this trio led the Interagency Committee on Intelligence (Ad Hoc) and drafted its "Special Report" to the president outlining what would become known as the Huston Plan.

The Interagency Committee's report sketched an overview of state surveillance on the student New Left, the Black Power movement, Marxist-Leninist parties, and the Puerto Rican independence movement. Though the authors worried that foreign Communist governments could infiltrate these movements for espionage purposes, they viewed homegrown "terrorism" as a far greater threat to "the internal security of the United States." Weatherman and other "New Left terrorist groups" were the committee's most immediate concern. The report also noted an increase in political bombings by Puerto Rican "extremist groups," however, and warned of the "probability" of future "terrorist activities" carried out by "black extremists" associated with the BPP.[65]

The Interagency Committee's "Special Report" concluded with recommendations for overhauling U.S. federal intelligence agencies and domestic surveillance practices. The FBI, CIA, NSA, and DIA would lose much of their autonomy and would coordinate their activities through an "interagency group on domestic intelligence" chaired by a cabinet official appointed by the president.[66] The plan would also expand intelligence agencies' preventive surveillance capabilities by removing Hoover's restrictions on break-ins, mail opening, warrantless electronic surveillance, and use of teenaged informants.

Huston, Sullivan, and Brennan knew that Hoover would never approve the Huston Plan. The director was sure to see the plan for what it was: an effort to exert White House control over the FBI's jurisdiction and autonomous policing powers.

To get around this, Sullivan concocted an elaborate scheme to trick the director into casting his approval. First, Sullivan concealed his role in drafting the report, knowing that Hoover would fire him if he found out. Instead, he gave the impression that Huston was the primary author. Second, instead of making direct policy recommendations, Sullivan crafted the report in a format that offered a series of options outlined next to boxes for the president to check off. The options ranged from making no changes to existing intelligence procedures to implementing the various measures that Sullivan, Huston, and others on the committee hoped to enact. With this arrangement, Hoover could sign the document without having to explicitly endorse any particular policies.[67] Sullivan and Huston also gathered the CIA, NSA, and DIA directors' willing signatures on the report before soliciting Hoover's, hoping that doing so would compel the director to add his signature.[68]

But Sullivan's scheme did not go as planned.

After reading the report's first draft, Hoover was livid. He called Sullivan into his office. "That hippie is behind this," the director exclaimed, disdainfully referring to Huston's two-inch sideburns. According to Sullivan, Hoover said "I'll only accept the recommendations outlined in this draft if the president orders me to. And I'll only carry them out if someone else—the president, the attorney general, anyone else—takes the responsibility."[69]

Hoover knew from his dealings with Nixon over the Kissinger wiretaps that the president would be reluctant to formally sign off on the plan. Both men were concerned that evidence of the plan could be leaked to the media, and neither was willing to risk bearing the brunt of public outrage over illegal state surveillance.

In responding to the report, Hoover engineered a bureaucratic power play of his own. He ordered Sullivan to draft footnotes into the report that formally indicated the FBI director's opposition to a permanent interagency intelligence committee and all efforts to relax the bureau's restrictions on illegal domestic surveillance practices. Sullivan complied, and Hoover signed the final, revised version of the report.[70]

Huston did not give up, however. In early July, after the Interagency Committee finalized the "Secret Report" with Hoover's footnotes, he penned a memorandum urging Nixon to approve its policy recommendations. Though he acknowledged that tactics such as break-ins and mail opening were "clearly illegal," Huston emphasized that Hoover was the only U.S. intelligence official who opposed the measures. Huston explained that Hoover did not object on ethical grounds but because he selfishly worried that "the civil liberties people may become upset." Furthermore, Huston pointed out that "surreptitious entries" and "mail covers" (FBI parlance for break-ins and surveillance of mail correspondence) were not new tactics but ones that "the FBI, in Hoover's younger years, used . . . with great success and with no exposure." Most importantly, Huston urged Nixon to approve the measures in order to combat "the Weathermen and the Black Panthers" and "forestall widespread violence" on American university campuses during the upcoming fall semester.[71]

Nixon approved Huston's plan, but as Hoover predicted, he refused to do so in writing. In an effort to avoid personal liability, the president indirectly approved the Huston Plan through his chief of staff H. R. Haldeman, who sent Huston a memo blandly stating, "The recommendations you have proposed as a result of the review have been approved by the President."[72] Huston then issued his own memo informing federal intelligence officials of the White House's new surveillance initiative.[73]

The Huston Plan was authorized, but it would remain so for only a mere five days.

Immediately after Huston issued his memo instituting the plan, Hoover approached Attorney General Mitchell, who had no prior knowledge of the secret interagency committee. Hoover informed Mitchell that he intended to seek written presidential approval before directing his agents to engage in any of the illegal tactics authorized in the Huston Plan.[74] Mitchell conveyed Hoover's intentions to the president and, according to Nixon, convinced him that "risk of disclosure of the possible illegal actions . . . was greater than the possible benefit to be derived."[75]

The president backed out of the Huston Plan on July 28, 1970. Hoover retained firm control over the FBI. For now, bureaucratic conflict and fears of public disclosure trumped the Nixon administration's efforts to combat domestic terrorism through interagency coordination and the reinstatement of illegal surveillance measures.

· · · · · ·

The Huston Plan was the U.S. federal government's first attempt to confront a problem it defined as terrorism. Nixon, Huston, Sullivan, and Brennan sought to revive illegal surveillance tactics widely utilized in the FBI's war on Communist "subversives" during the 1950s and early 1960s, but in response to a new, distinct threat. The Nixon administration proposed the Huston Plan in an effort to prevent political acts of arson and bombings on America's university campuses and city streets. Nixon made this clear in his 1978 memoir. Reflecting on the Huston Plan, the former president wrote, "In view of the crisis of terrorism and violence visited upon countless innocent people, the recommendations made to me by the interagency intelligence group in its 1970 report were justified and responsible."[76]

According to Nixon, extralegal state action was sometimes necessary to defend America's citizens and national security from terrorist violence. He compared the Huston Plan to President Abraham Lincoln's suspension of habeas corpus during the Civil War and President Franklin D. Roosevelt's internment of Japanese Americans during World War II, other wartime executive decisions he contended "will always be debated."[77] Nixon asked his readers: "Did the threatened and actual bombings of the Weathermen, and the brutal assaults of the Black Panthers, justify an intrusion of their liberties?" "When the issue juxtaposes the lives of innocent citizens against the possible curtailment of personal liberties we all cherish," he continued, "the answers are never easy." Ultimately, however, Nixon believed that American presidents were required to implement "emergency measures to meet emergency situations" when needed "to defend the nation and to protect innocent people."[78]

Nixon's reflections on the Huston Plan were, of course, part of the former president's efforts at redemption following Watergate. Nixon's memoir downplayed his use of domestic surveillance for personal political gain and offered a one-sided perspective on domestic revolutionary violence, one that ignored the reality of police violence against the Black Panthers and other U.S. radicals as well as the military violence he was personally responsible for inflicting on the people of Southeast Asia. Nonetheless, his account sheds light on the origins of a debate on terrorism that would rise to the forefront of American politics in the post-Watergate era, as intelligence and White House officials grappled with both ongoing guerrilla violence and public controversy over intelligence agencies' violations of Americans' civil liberties.

In the meantime, conflict over the Huston Plan brought Hoover's relationship with Nixon to a new low. The fact that the FBI remained unable to prevent leftist violence certainly did not help matters. Over the next two years, Weatherman and other insurgents would continue to bring Nixon's war in Vietnam home to the United States. With each attack, America's guerrillas would widen the rift between Nixon's White House and Hoover's FBI.

· ·

Jonathan Jackson was only seventeen years old when he smuggled a small arsenal into a courtroom in California's Marin County Civic Center. The young African American militant sat quietly in the gallery for several minutes on the morning of August 7, 1970, while the Black revolutionary and prisoner James McClain stood trial for assaulting a white guard in San Quentin Prison. Then Jackson rose to his feet brandishing an assault rifle. "All right, gentlemen," he shouted, "I'm taking over now."

Events unfolded in dizzying succession. Jackson distributed firearms to McClain and defense witnesses Ruchell Magee and William A. Christmas, also radical Black prisoners. The four men seized Judge Harold Haley, District Attorney Gary Thomas, and three female jurors as hostages and then fled to a nearby getaway van. District Attorney Thomas later stated that the men hoped to trade their captives for the release of the "Soledad Brothers"—Fleeta Drumgo, John Clutchette, and Jonathan's older brother George Jackson—three radical Black prisoners indicted on capital charges for killing a white prison guard amid escalating violence between guards and Black revolutionary convicts inside California's prisons. Jonathan Jackson's true aims remain a mystery, since he never had an opportunity to explain them. He died alongside McClain, Christmas, and Judge Haley minutes later. Police and prison guards surrounded the van, shooting broke out inside the vehicle, and hostages and militants alike perished in the firefight.[1]

A high school student from Pasadena, Jonathan Jackson was tormented by the incarceration of his beloved older brother. Through regular written correspondence from prison, George had tutored his younger sibling in *foco* theory and political economy. Like many other young radicals of his time, Jonathan came to believe that revolutionary violence offered humanity's best hope for overcoming the racist state violence of police brutality, prison, and U.S. foreign military intervention.[2] Jonathan Jackson died in an effort to advance socialist revolution. He knew nothing about the Huston Plan, but his bloody attack prompted a chain of unintended consequences.

The timing of Jackson's rebellion was critical. The raid came two weeks after FBI director J. Edgar Hoover pressured President Richard Nixon to abandon the Huston Plan's secret consolidation of America's intelligence agencies. And the attack occurred only days after guerrilla violence abroad claimed the life of a former FBI operative. At the time of the Marin County courthouse incident, President Nixon and his aides remained frustrated by Hoover's sabotage of the Huston Plan and the FBI's failure to stem the tide of leftist bombings. Fueled by the attack to redouble their efforts, they ratcheted up their insistence that the FBI expand its efforts to thwart leftist guerrilla violence.

The White House found the prospect of kidnappings especially concerning. Jackson's raid marked the first time American radicals had taken political hostages. It was already a common tactic among leftist guerrillas in Latin America, West Germany, and Italy, and with the Popular Front for the Liberation of Palestine, which had gained global attention over the past two years by hijacking international passenger jets.[3] Jackson's attack elicited shock and alarm among American political leaders, who viewed the prospect of further political kidnappings on U.S. soil as a red line. Nixon and his men wanted to ensure that America's first leftist hostage-taking incident would also be its last.

Dozens of bombings and other guerrilla attacks over the remainder of 1970 helped amplify the urgency of the Nixon administration's demands. These included the August bombing at the University of Wisconsin that killed a physicist, the September shooting death of a police officer during a bank robbery outside of Boston, and a string of bombings carried out throughout the Northeast as part of the Weather Underground's "Fall Offensive." The Weather Underground bombings took place under the backdrop of the October Crisis in neighboring Canada, where military troops deployed throughout Quebec after the province's separatist guerrillas kidnapped a British diplomat and provincial deputy premier Pierre Laporte, eventually killing the latter.[4]

The pressure on Hoover was enormous.

Jackson's raid was the first of several leftist guerrilla actions that prompted the director—under pressure from Nixon—to reevaluate the FBI's domestic security operations in the wake of the aborted Huston Plan. Within weeks of undermining the Huston Plan, Hoover began to reinstate most of the surveillance practices outlined in the secret proposal. The FBI fought what it increasingly referred to as terrorism by seeking advanced, preventive knowledge of guerrilla attacks. Hoover dramatically expanded the FBI's surveillance of Black Power and New Left activists. He also reauthorized the FBI's use of informants under the age of twenty-one and expanded warrantless wiretaps targeting the BPP and suspected Weather Underground associates.

Yet Hoover's caution endured. The director still worried that leaks of information detailing FBI involvement in illegal tactics could undermine the bureau and personally expose him to criminal charges. Since neither he nor the president was willing to officially authorize mail tracking, mail opening, or break-ins, Hoover passed the liability for such actions down the FBI's chain of command. Through euphemistic threats and suggestions, the director *informally* pressured local field offices to utilize these tactics in conjunction with the bureau's Weather Underground investigation. In August 1970, Hoover's wink-and-nod authorization prompted the FBI's local Weather Underground squads to commence widespread illegal mail surveillance and break-ins. It didn't go as far as Nixon had wanted, but extralegal spy tactics were now back on the table.

August 1970

After the Marin County courthouse attack, Hoover spoke on the phone with Nixon. The details of their conversation are unknown, but a pair of letters Hoover wrote on August 17, 1970, shed light on the topics discussed. The letters—one issued to the FBI's fifty-nine field offices and twenty overseas legal attaches, and the second to Nixon—indicate that the president instructed Hoover to intensify bureau investigations of leftist guerrillas. Nixon was already furious with Hoover over the collapse of the Huston Plan. Jonathan Jackson's raid only increased the president's frustration with Hoover and the FBI's inability to thwart leftist guerrilla attacks.

Recent events in South America amplified Nixon's concerns. In an incident reported throughout the world, Uruguay's Tupamaros guerrillas kidnapped U.S. Agency for International Development advisor and former FBI agent Dan Mitrione on July 31 and executed him on August 6 after the Uruguayan government refused the revolutionaries' demands for the release of 150 leftist political prisoners.[5] Nixon feared that revolutionary guerrillas inspired by the Tupamaros would attempt additional political kidnappings in the United States. Not only did the president want domestic leftist guerrillas apprehended and prosecuted, he also wanted Hoover to obtain advance warning of revolutionaries' violent plans.

The urgency of Nixon's demands came across in Hoover's letter to his SACs and legal attaches: "Recent activities in Latin America as well as in California on the part of revolutionary extremists in the kidnapping of public officials and diplomats for hostage purposes dictate the need for intensification of investigation of such extremist organizations as the Black Panther Party and the Students for a Democratic Society including the Weatherman faction, and similar violence-prone groups."[6]

Hoover transmitted the pressure from Nixon down the FBI hierarchy. Leftist guerrilla investigations, he emphasized, were a "matter of greatest importance." The director warned the supervisors of regional FBI offices that he would hold them "personally responsible for the development of informant coverage in these organizations whereby the bureau is in a position to ascertain the plans of extremist elements." This directive put the heat on local SACs, whose careers relied on positive annual reviews of field office investigations carried out by the FBI's chief inspector. In his letter to the SACs, Hoover stressed, "Your efforts in this regard will be the subject of close scrutiny during future inspections."[7]

In his second letter, Hoover informed President Nixon of the initiatives he had taken within the FBI. "In line with our conversation the other evening," the director wrote, "I have had instructions issued to every one of our field offices and to our Legal Attaches abroad to intensify investigation of such extremist organizations . . . whose members may make an effort to kidnap high-ranking government officials, members of the diplomatic corps and members of their families."[8]

Hoover's latest order for the "intensification" of FBI leftist guerrilla investigations was different from others he had issued since late 1969. Not only did Hoover seek advance knowledge of violent leftist attacks—a nearly impossible task given the guerrillas' deliberate use of clandestinity—he also shifted the onus of responsibility for this effort from himself to the SACs of local field offices. Though providing no specific instructions on how to obtain preventive intelligence, Hoover strongly implied that a field office's success or failure in preempting revolutionary violence would prove pivotal in determining its supervising agent's career prospects.

SACs receiving this order faced a very real quandary. Was the director expecting field offices to reinstitute break-ins and other illegal surveillance tactics he had discontinued in the mid-1960s? Should their involvement in such activities become known, would local supervisors and field agents face government sanctions? In such a scenario, would Hoover support local FBI personnel, or would he disavow responsibility for illegal techniques?

Questions like these severely troubled field agents. Chicago special agent William Dyson later recalled his frustration: "Obviously if there's a bombing, I can do a crime scene. But what else can I do? Can I infiltrate a college classroom? Can I go and listen to a professor? Can I talk to a professor in a college classroom? Can I go to his office? Can I put an informant in the college classroom? Or even on the campus. Can I penetrate any college organization? What can I do?"[9]

The answers to these questions were uncertain, and clarification from headquarters was not forthcoming.

Meanwhile, the FBI investigated the Marin County courthouse attack, hunting for collaborators. Investigators quickly traced Jonathan Jackson's guns to their owner, Angela Davis, a prominent African American Communist and doctoral student who worked as a lecturer in philosophy at the University of California Los Angeles (UCLA). During the previous year, Davis had been the target of an anticommunist smear campaign led by Governor Ronald Reagan, who tried to force UCLA to fire her.[10]

Davis had purchased the guns after receiving multiple death threats. She stored them at the San Francisco Soledad House commune, where she lived for several months while working on a campaign to exonerate the Soledad Brothers. Jackson worked as Davis's bodyguard. He had access to the guns, but Davis has always sworn she had no prior knowledge of his plans for the courthouse attack. Davis feared a federal indictment nonetheless. She went into hiding two days after Jackson's raid. Hoover put Davis on the FBI's Ten Most Wanted Fugitives list on August 18 as agents searched for her throughout the country.[11]

Six days later, on August 24, a fatal guerrilla attack in Madison, Wisconsin, drew additional FBI attention to leftist violence. At 3:42 in the morning, antiwar militants detonated an enormous car bomb next to the University of Wisconsin's Sterling Hall, home to the Army Math Research Center (AMRC), a facility involved in military weapons research. The bomb was made from 2,000 pounds of ammonium nitrate fertilizer and fuel oil packed into a stolen van. Its blast sent a mushroom cloud of burning debris hundreds of feet into the air and startled people awake throughout the sleeping city. The bombers carried out their attack before dawn in an attempt to avoid casualties, but their precautions were inadequate. The explosion killed Robert Fassnacht, a postdoctoral physicist who was conducting research unrelated to the AMRC in Sterling Hall's basement.[12]

Like other guerrilla attacks, the Madison bombing was inspired by state violence. Twenty-two-year-old University of Wisconsin student Karl Armstrong hatched the bombing plan after watching a television broadcast about the Kent State shootings. "My overwhelming feeling," he recalled, "was now they're killing us. It had come to killing us to stop the protests."[13]

Karl teamed up with his brother Dwight Armstrong (aged eighteen) and two other young white radicals involved in Madison's antiwar movement, Leo Burt (twenty-two) and David Fine (eighteen). They chose the AMRC as their target because the facility's researchers helped the army develop counterinsurgency tactics and chemical and biological weapons for the U.S. war in Vietnam and Cambodia.[14] The AMRC had also been an ongoing target of local antiwar protest. In Armstrong's view, "the fact that there were demonstrations, and that the university was well aware of what this institution was all about, gave them moral responsibility."[15]

Hoover launched another nationwide manhunt for the culprits. The bureau sent Chicago-based Weatherman investigator William Dyson to Madison to assist the local field office in its investigation. "At first, the idea was that it was the Weather Underground," he remembered. "But it soon became apparent that it wasn't, and these people were would-be Weathermen."[16]

A University of Wisconsin student activist named Margery Tabankin was home in New Jersey at the time of the bombing. FBI agents knocked on her parents' door at 7:30 the next morning with a list of suspects. "I couldn't believe they found me so quickly," she remembered. Tabankin recognized the names of Leo Burt and David Fine on the list, having worked with them on the university's newspaper, the *Daily Cardinal*, which had printed stories on the AMRC. "These are the quietist, mousiest, and really the shyest people," she told the agent. "There's just no way. Take them off this list."[17]

Meanwhile, the Armstrong brothers, Burt, and Fine showed up a few hours after the bombing in Sauk County, forty miles north of Madison. Local police pulled them over in a car that matched the description of the vehicle seen departing the university. But the police did not have the evidence required under state law to keep the suspects in jail. After a couple hours of detainment, they were free. The four men seized the opportunity to flee the area.[18]

The FBI identified the bombers three days after their escape from Sauk County, and Hoover hoped to score a public relations victory through quick arrests. In an August 24 memo to his field offices, the director wrote, "In view of the seriousness of this case, and possibility this bombing could trigger similar tragic consequences elsewhere, it is imperative that early solution be made in this case." A follow-up memo the next day conveyed Hoover's hopes that the bureau could deter additional attacks through the apprehension "of guilty parties before they flee the country."[19]

But the bombers managed to slip away. Karl Armstrong later revealed that he and Dwight made their way to New York City and then drove a stolen car to Montreal, where they found support from a network of Canadian activists who assisted American draft dodgers.[20]

Leftist insurgents had carried out another deadly attack, Hoover and his men had no idea of the bombers' whereabouts, and the FBI appeared helpless to do anything more. Hoover added all four suspects to the FBI's Most Wanted list on September 4, 1970.[21] But this wasn't enough. Hoover's top deputies insisted that the fight against guerrilla terrorism required more aggressive surveillance.

Bureaucrats and Teenagers

The Marin County courthouse attack and the University of Wisconsin bombing prompted the FBI to reinstitute banned surveillance practices outlined in the Huston Plan. One of these practices was the use of informants under the age of twenty-one. Hoover had restricted the FBI's use of teenaged informants in 1967 in response to new limitations on the bureau's surveillance capabilities imposed by Attorney General Ramsey Clark.[22] But the fact that Jonathan Jackson and two of the suspected Sterling Hall bombers were younger than twenty-one led FBI officials to reconsider.

One of the FBI officials responsible for lowering the FBI's minimum age for informants was W. Mark Felt. Later in the 1970s Felt would gain notoriety for authorizing illegal break-ins as part of the FBI's Weather Underground investigation. While facing a federal indictment for this activity, he appeared frequently on television news programs. With blue eyes, silver coiffed hair, and a maintained physique visible beneath a well-pressed suit, Felt would speak coolly and unapologetically in defense of his actions, claiming them as necessary measures to combat revolutionary terrorism. In 2005, faced with the onset of dementia, he dropped a news bombshell by coming out as Watergate's "Deep Throat," the notorious secret informant who leaked information on Nixon's dirty tricks to *Washington Post* journalist Bob Woodward.

But in August 1970, Felt was the FBI's chief inspector. Raised by stern Presbyterian parents in the small city of Twin Falls, Idaho, Felt had joined the FBI in 1940 shortly after earning his degree at George Washington University Law School. As a field agent in Washington, D.C., during World War II, Felt cut his teeth carrying out counterintelligence operations against Nazi spies. He later took assignments in New Orleans, Los Angeles, Salt Lake City, and Kansas before returning to Washington for a position as an instructor at the FBI's special agent training facility in Quantico, Virginia. In late 1964, Hoover handpicked Felt to lead the bureau's inspection division.[23]

As chief inspector, Felt was responsible for inspecting field offices throughout the country and reporting his findings to FBI headquarters. In other words, when Hoover warned his SACs in August 1970 that they would be "held personally responsible" for their office's preventive measures against leftist guerrillas, it was Felt who would be holding them to "close scrutiny during future inspections."[24]

Felt was not well liked within the bureau. Many agents saw him as cocky and pompous. But he was respected as an honest administrator loyal to the FBI, its mission, and Director Hoover. And when he traveled throughout the country visiting FBI field offices, he listened to agents' concerns. Felt's discussions with domestic security agents influenced his decision to recommend that Hoover lower the minimum informant age. In a memo to Hoover's deputy Clyde Tolson on September 2, 1970, Felt wrote that local FBI officials throughout the country "informally indicated . . . that their productivity would be greatly enhanced by a lowering of the age requirements" for informants.[25]

Felt urged headquarters to lower its minimum age limit for informants on university campuses from twenty-one to the bureau's pre-1967 standard of eighteen. "Never in our history," he warned, "have we been confronted with as critical a need for informant coverage." Felt made little effort to conceal his contempt for leftist guerrillas. Teenaged informants were necessary to prevent "terrorist violence," he argued, including "bombings, assassination of police officers, kidnapping and torture murder" by "Weatherman fanatics" and other "violence-oriented black and white savages . . . at war with the Government and American people."[26]

Felt's recommendation received a key endorsement. In a brief addendum typed onto the bottom of the memo appeared a note of support from Assistant to the Director William C. Sullivan, the third most powerful man in the FBI and an architect of the Huston Plan. "No one can predict with accuracy the outcome of the revolutionary struggle going on in this country at this time," Sullivan cautioned; "Those under 20 years of age are playing a predominant role in campus violence. . . . Two of the subjects in the University of Wisconsin case are under 20."[27]

In their joint plea to Hoover, Felt and Sullivan forged an unlikely alliance. Felt had detested Sullivan since the mid-1960s. After his promotion to chief inspector, Felt clashed repeatedly with Sullivan over Hoover's new restrictions on warrantless wiretaps, break-ins, and teenaged informants. Like many others in the FBI, Felt shared Sullivan's disagreement with Hoover's new policies, viewing the restricted techniques as essential tools in the bureau's fight against Communist subversion. But Felt was an ardent Hoover loyalist who believed that backing the director's orders took precedent over such disagreement.

This is where he differed from Sullivan, who had spent much of 1969 and 1970 secretly plotting to undermine Hoover and reinstate the bureau's old investigative tactics. In his 1979 memoir, Felt asserted that Sullivan tried many times to persuade him to collaborate in disregarding Hoover's orders. In one instance Felt claimed to have replied, "Bill, we've talked about this before. I understand your problems but we are going to get the job done in spite of the restrictions—not in spite of the Boss. I am not against you—I am for you but I am also for the Director."[28]

Felt's willingness to ally with Sullivan in an attempt to reverse Hoover's restrictions on teenaged informants points to the tremendous frustration felt throughout the FBI's ranks as special agents worked, under enormous pressure but with little success, to prevent revolutionary violence and apprehend leftist guerrilla fugitives. Felt and Sullivan sought to lower the minimum age for campus informants in part because they believed that doing so would improve their chances of preventing guerrilla attacks. However, this was not the only driving force behind the memo. Internal bureaucratic struggle likely influenced Felt and Sullivan as well. Both men were probably partially driven by their longtime rivalry and their separate, individual desires to manipulate the FBI bureaucracy according to their personal ambitions and ideals.

For Sullivan, Felt's memo was yet another opportunity to press Hoover for the reinstatement of FBI surveillance tactics he had unsuccessfully sought to implement through the Huston Plan. Sullivan had managed to shield his involvement in the Huston Plan from Hoover by projecting the appearance that Huston was the driving force behind the initiative. Sullivan was so successful in maintaining the facade of loyalty to his boss that Hoover promoted him to assistant to the director on June 10, 1970, and promoted Charles Brennan to Sullivan's former post as assistant director for domestic security.[29] But Sullivan remained convinced of the need to expand the FBI's surveillance capacities. He seized Felt's memo as an opportunity to advance this agenda.

Around the same time, Sullivan's collaborator Tom Huston was trying to get Nixon to reinstate his eponymous plan, but his efforts were less fruitful. In August Huston made an angry plea to his boss, H. R. Haldeman, hoping the chief of staff would convince Nixon and Attorney General Mitchell to change their minds. "At some point," he wrote, "Hoover needs to be told who is President."[30]

Haldeman was not impressed. He kept Huston on the White House payroll but placed Nixon's newly appointed counsel John Dean in charge of intelligence matters. Huston hung around for another year before leaving his post in June 1971 to build his law practice in Indianapolis. Later he admitted that during his last year working for Haldeman, "I was, for all intents and purposes, writing memos to myself."[31]

It is uncertain whether Felt knew about the Huston Plan. But if he did, it is highly unlikely that he would have worked to reinstate the program behind Hoover's back. Felt wrote his memo in an effort to obtain Hoover's written approval for lifting restrictions on student informants. The director's August 17 memo instructing all field offices to "intensify" leftist guerrilla investigations was ambiguous, and Felt sought clarification on domestic security guidelines in order to relieve field agents' uncertainty. In partnering with Sullivan, Felt forged a convenient temporary alliance.

These efforts ultimately panned out, as Hoover approved the measure. In a September 15 letter, Hoover informed SACs that they were "authorized to develop student security and racial informants who are 18 years or older" in order to obtain "reliable information about the activities of violence-oriented youthful groups on campus." "Terrorist violence surrounds us and more has been threatened," Hoover emphasized. "Bombings, assassination of police officers, kidnapping and murder are all part of the picture."[32]

Fall Offensive

Meanwhile, leftist guerrillas continued to vex White House and FBI officials.

The Weather Underground's next action involved counterculture icon and LSD advocate Timothy Leary, then serving a ten-year sentence at California's minimum-security San Luis Obispo Prison on marijuana possession charges. On September 15, 1970, guerrillas broke him out of captivity. The escape required the nearly fifty-year-old Leary to scale a barbed wire fence and hide in a patch of weeds until Weather guerrillas picked him up in a car, transferred him to another vehicle, and spirited him north to Washington state, Canada, and eventually Algeria.[33]

In a communiqué released to the media, the Weather Underground referred to Leary as a "prisoner of war" and pledged to continue its efforts to destroy U.S. imperialism.[34] Leary thanked the Weather Underground for helping him escape. In a letter attached to the communiqué, he vowed to "stay high and wage the revolutionary war." Leary also warned authorities that he was armed. "I should be considered dangerous to anyone who threatens my life or freedom."[35]

Leary's statement was duly noted by longtime FBI domestic security operative Robert L. Shackelford, who had taken over Charles Brennan's position as head of the Domestic Security Division's internal security operations. Shackelford recorded the comment in a September 22, 1970, report to Brennan.[36]

A week after Leary's escape, guerrillas in Massachusetts killed a police officer. The group of white radicals consisted of Stanley Bond, William Gilday, and Robert Valeri, former convicts at Walpole State Prison, and Katherine Power and Susan Saxe, both Brandeis University students. On September 23, Gilday unloaded a submachine gun at Walter Schroeder, the first cop to arrive on the scene as the group held up a bank in the Boston suburb of Brighton. He died on site. The group then escaped with $26,000 they hoped to give to the Black Panthers. Three days earlier the group had raided a National Guard armory in nearby Newburyport, where they stole a truck, military files, and 400 rounds of ammunition before firebombing the facility, causing over $120,000 in damage.[37]

Police caught up with Bond, Gilday, and Valeri shortly after the bank robbery. The police located the men using intelligence from an acquaintance who tipped off the FBI after overhearing them discuss plans to kill police in a New Hampshire bar.[38]

Saxe and Power eluded authorities, however. Like Cameron Bishop, the Weathermen, Angela Davis, and the Madison bombers, they vanished into the revolutionary underground.

On October 6, the Weather Underground carried out another bombing and released an ominous communiqué. Early in the morning, the group blew up Chicago's Haymarket police statue for the second time (the city had rebuilt it after the group's first bombing a year earlier). Later that day in New York City, Chicago Eight defendant and Yippie leader Jerry Rubin held a press conference along with Jennifer Dohrn, fellow Yippie! and younger sister of the notorious Weather Underground fugitive Bernardine Dohrn. The pair played a tape recording of Bernardine announcing a new round of guerrilla assaults.

With a voice steady, confident, and foreboding, Dohrn proclaimed the start of "a fall offensive of youth resistance that will spread from Santa Barbara to Boston, back to Kent and Kansas." She flaunted the Weather

Underground's evasion of the FBI: "J. Edgar himself admitted that 'underground radicals' were the hardest group to infiltrate." *"Next week,"* Dohrn warned, *"families and tribes will attack the enemy around the country."*[39]

Two days later, the Weather Underground followed up with a bomb that destroyed a courtroom and restroom in the Marin County Civic Center, where Jonathan Jackson and three others had died two months earlier. A pair of bombings by unnamed groups took place the same day, one inside the University of Washington's ROTC building, and another outside a National Guard armory in Santa Barbara.[40] The Weather Underground carried out another bombing the next day, blasting a hole in a Long Island City courthouse in solidarity with a prisoner revolt in the Queens House of Detention recently quashed by New York police.[41] On October 12, five unclaimed bombings took place in Rochester, along with two in New York City and one in Orlando.[42]

In the midst of the bombings, the FBI scored a brief public relations victory. On October 13 agents captured Angela Davis in a New York motel room. Agents tracked her down by locating a car belonging to Communist Party member David Rudolph Poindexter Jr., who was staying with Davis at the Midtown Manhattan Howard Johnson Motor Lodge. Both Davis and Poindexter were unarmed at the time of their arrest. Two days later, President Nixon congratulated the FBI for capturing "the dangerous terrorist, Angela Davis."[43]

Nixon made this statement during a public ceremony to mark his signing of the Omnibus Crime Bill of 1970, a critical piece of law-and-order legislation that expanded power and funding for the Johnson administration's Law Enforcement Assistance Administration. In a direct response to America's domestic insurgency, the bill also expanded the FBI's jurisdiction over bombings on college campuses.[44]

But the bombs kept exploding.

On October 14, the Weather Underground's all-female Proud Eagle Tribe bombed the Harvard Center for International Affairs to protest the institution's complicity in the Vietnam War. They claimed their attack in solidarity with Davis, whom leftists throughout the world justifiably viewed as the target of a government frame-up.[45]

Two days later, fake bomb threats, some of them attributed to the Weather Underground, forced "the evacuation of hospitals in Boston, of airports in New York and St. Louis, and of a subway station in Harvard Square in Cambridge, Mass."[46]

"Free Angela Davis" poster. The image on the bottom right shows FBI agents arresting Davis in New York City on October 3, 1970. Courtesy of the Lisbet Tellefsen Collection.

Bombs were exploding on a weekly basis. Hoover may have relaxed FBI rules in a nod to the Huston plan, but the FBI's investigations were still going nowhere.

Informal Counterterrorism

American guerrillas' Fall Offensive heightened a sense of crisis inside the FBI. In September 1970, the bureau had convened a two-day conference with agents from seventeen field offices on responses to "New Left violence and terrorism." The gathering was dedicated to developing new tactics for infiltrating the guerrilla underground and recruiting informants in the youth counterculture.[47] But in the months that followed, guerrilla violence increased dramatically.

Despite his reluctance to expand FBI involvement in illegal activities, J. Edgar Hoover felt compelled to improvise more drastic responses to clandestine guerrilla violence. This included renewing mass surveillance of the aboveground left and reviving illegal spy techniques outlined in the Huston Plan. Hoover brought the illegal practices back on a strictly informal basis, however, in order to shield himself and FBI headquarters from liability for his agents' activity.

According to Los Angeles special agent Cril Payne, Director Hoover "was in a rage" after the Weather Underground's Fall Offensive communiqué and subsequent bombings. Payne recalled that FBI agents around the country "were aware of [Hoover's] displeasure," as field office phones rang "off the wall with calls from Washington demanding a thorough and aggressive investigation with plenty of manpower."[48]

"It was bad enough for these 'revolutionary-guerrillas,' as the Director called them, to set off a few bombs," Payne reflected, "but to announce their intentions to the American people in advance, and then fulfill them, was unthinkable to Mr. Hoover." The director worried deeply that "the public might decide the FBI had lost control of the situation."[49]

Hoover's actions seem to corroborate Payne's statements. Immediately following Dohrn's Fall Offensive communiqué, Hoover sent urgent teletypes warning the president, the vice president, the secretary of state, the attorney general, the army, the air force, the Secret Service, the directors of the CIA, DIA, and the Naval Intelligence Agency, and all FBI field offices of impending revolutionary terrorism.[50] On October 14, the day of the Proud Eagle Tribe's Harvard bombing, Hoover placed Bernardine Dohrn on the FBI's Ten Most Wanted list. He added Boston-area fugitives Katherine Power and Susan Saxe a few days later.[51]

The total new additions to the Most Wanted list for 1970 now numbered twelve, ten of them leftist revolutionaries, seven of whom remained on the lam. There were so many revolutionaries evading U.S. law enforcement that Hoover expanded the total number of fugitives on the FBI's Ten Most Wanted list to sixteen.[52]

With leftist violence on the rise, Hoover felt obliged to warn federal officials of threats to their personal safety. The impetus for this again came,

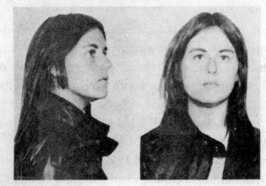

FBI wanted poster for Weather Underground leader Bernardine Dohrn. Director J. Edgar Hoover placed Dohrn on the FBI's list of Ten Most Wanted Fugitives on October 14, 1970. FBI.gov.

in part, from the Nixon administration. On October 22, White House counsel John Dean convened a meeting with cabinet officials and FBI official Rex Schroder about contingency plans for "politically inspired kidnappings." The meeting took place at the height of Canada's October Crisis, just days after Front de liberation du Quebec (FLQ) guerrillas executed one of their hostages, Quebec's deputy premier Pierre Laporte, and as Canadian military troops patrolled the streets of Montreal. During the meeting, Dean and Nixon aide Egil Krogh grilled Schroder on the FBI's efforts to combat leftist guerrilla violence.[53]

The next day, Hoover circulated a bulletin warning government officials to take precautions against political kidnapping and assassination. The director specifically named the Weather Underground, "black extremists," and other leftist radicals as potential assailants. Among other things, Hoover's notice cautioned officials to travel only on main thoroughfares during daylight hours, to speak only before friendly audiences, to keep their home office notified of their whereabouts at all times, and to "vary the pattern of living" in respect to business and social activities to make it difficult for potential assailants to predict their daily routine.[54]

It had come to this. The FBI director was now advising U.S. officials on how to avoid kidnapping and assassination.

Hoover also secretly authorized a revival of mass surveillance. Since his agents were unable to infiltrate the guerrilla underground, Hoover decided to cast a wide surveillance net, hoping such efforts could reap valuable preventive intelligence. His main targets were the aboveground student New Left and Black Power movement. On November 5, Hoover ordered his field offices to open files on "all members of Students for a Democratic Society (SDS) and members of procommunist, militant New Left-type campus organizations who follow SDS advocacy of revolution and violence."[55] As with his lowering the age limit for informants, Hoover made this order at the request of Mark Felt and William Sullivan, who recommended the initiative as members of the FBI's Executive Council.

Hoover's order for New Left surveillance was not limited to the Weatherman faction, whose members had mostly gone underground, beyond the reach of the FBI's gaze. The order also covered unaffiliated campus activist groups as well as SDS factions opposed to the Weather Underground, including Revolutionary Youth Movement II and the Boston-based Progressive Labor Party–affiliated Worker-Student Alliance (WSA) faction, which claimed the mantle of SDS after Weatherman disbanded the organization in early 1970. Despite the fact that both the WSA and RYMII opposed urban guerrilla warfare, Hoover warned that these groups collectively constituted "a breeding ground for revolutionaries, extremists, and terrorists."[56]

Similarly, Hoover's surveillance of the Black Power movement was not confined to the Black Panthers. Hoover also mandated surveillance of every member of "Black Student Unions" and other African American campus groups in the United States. He called for the monitoring of pro-independence Puerto Rican student groups as well. Viewing right-wing nationalist bombers as an additional threat to internal security, Hoover also ordered surveillance of the anticommunist Jewish Defense League, whom the FBI suspected of involvement in a series of attacks on Soviet embassies and consulates.[57]

Expanding domestic surveillance was no easy task. Hoover's measures required field agents to reopen over 10,000 files on student activists that had been frozen since a February 1969 moratorium. Agents were to do so incrementally, completing the task by June 1971. This was Hoover's latest effort to obtain advanced, preventive knowledge of revolutionary violence.

The goal, he explained, was to "identify potential and actual extremists, revolutionaries and terrorists and to assess their threat to the internal security of the Government."[58]

Hoover also expanded the FBI's warrantless electronic surveillance of the aboveground Left. He did so with Attorney General John Mitchell's approval. In late October, the FBI began to wiretap the telephone in Boston's WSA-controlled SDS headquarters, and the phones of suspected aboveground Weather Underground contacts Nancy Kurshan in Cleveland and Nancy Frappier in San Francisco.[59]

The FBI directed the greatest share of its electronic surveillance toward the BPP. From the information it received from informants, as well as the *Black Panther* newspaper's frequent glorification of killing police officers, the FBI suspected that members of the party planned to carry out guerrilla violence.[60] Because the BPP remained an aboveground organization, it was an easier surveillance target than the clandestine Weather Underground. By March 29, 1971, the FBI had telephone surveillance on BPP offices in Chicago, Los Angeles, San Francisco, Oakland, New Haven, and the Bronx, and microphone surveillance inside the San Francisco penthouse suite of the organization's leader, Huey Newton.[61] The FBI now maintained the most extensive electronic surveillance of American leftists since Hoover limited the practice in 1965.[62]

The escalating war with leftist guerrillas also drove Hoover to revive mail covers—illegal and previously restricted surveillance of addresses and return addresses on individuals' mail. Like the use of teenaged informants, mail covers had been a critical tactic outlined in the Huston Plan.

In October 1970, Hoover approved a recommendation from Internal Security Division chief Robert L. Shackelford to his supervisor Charles Brennan, granting permission to initiate mail covers in the FBI's Weather Underground investigation. The FBI targeted Yippie! leaders Jerry Rubin and Jennifer Dohrn, who had exposed themselves as potential aboveground contacts for the Weather Underground with their October 6 press release publicizing Bernardine Dohrn's Fall Offensive statement. In an October 16 memo, Shackelford expressed his view that the FBI "should undertake *every investigative technique possible* to locate . . . Weatherman fugitives." Shackelford's colleagues would have clearly understood this statement as a reference to mail covers and other restricted tactics. Shackelford was specifically concerned with Rubin and Dohrn's public acknowledgment of having received the Weather Underground's tape-recorded communiqué in the mail at the New York Yippie! headquarters. He suggested the FBI "make confidential arrangements through the Old Chelsea Station Post Office to get the lists of postmarks and return addresses on mail sent to individuals at YIP headquarters as well as to the organization itself." Hoover approved the recommendation with his characteristic handwritten initials and a scribbled "OK."[63]

The FBI's illegal surveillance practices went beyond mail covers. Following Hoover's August 1970 call for "intensified" guerrilla investigations, the FBI's Weather Underground squads also engaged in illegal mail opening, warrantless wiretapping, and break-ins. Sources documenting the FBI's use of illegal surveillance techniques are scarce. Since the practices were illegal and unauthorized, agents intentionally kept written records minimal so as to avoid self-incrimination. FBI agents also destroyed many sources documenting illegal surveillance tactics in 1976 as rumors gathered that the Justice Department planned to indict bureau personnel involved in illegal surveillance operations. However, documents from the legal proceedings of John Kearney, L. Patrick Gray, Edward Miller, and W. Mark Felt—FBI officials who faced criminal charges in the late 1970s for their involvement in such activities—offer a glimpse into the FBI's use of illegal surveillance measures in its Weather Underground investigation.

Most of the FBI's illegal surveillance targeted aboveground activists and family members of Weather Underground guerrillas, whom agents hoped would lead them to the revolutionary underground. The Weather Underground squad best known for this activity was New York's Squad 47.

New York City's SAC Joseph H. Gamble initially formed Squad 47 in April 1970, shortly after Weatherman's Greenwich Village townhouse explosion. Special Agent Eugene W. O'Neill was the unit's first supervisor. A pair of memos buried deep in the National Archives suggest that under O'Neill's direction, Squad 47 carried out at least two black-bag jobs targeting Weatherman in the aftermath of the townhouse blast. Both memos are from the New York field office to FBI headquarters. The first memo, from April 17, 1970, reports on the contents of a notebook belonging to townhouse survivor Cathy Wilkerson featuring contact information for several of her associates. The second memo, from May 4, reports on a personal telephone directory belonging to Weatherman leader Jeff Jones. Both memos claim that the items were "furnished . . . by a confidential source," which was the typical euphemism FBI agents used to refer to evidence obtained through illegal break-ins.[64]

Squad 47's involvement in break-ins and other illegal surveillance tactics increased dramatically, however, beginning in August 1970. This was the month of Jonathan Jackson's California courthouse raid and the University of Wisconsin bombing, of Hoover's calls for "intensified" guerrilla investigations, and when the New York field office put John Kearney in charge of Squad 47.

Like many of his colleagues, Kearney was a World War II veteran who signed up to join the FBI after returning home from the war. He served briefly in Butte, Montana, Seattle, and Los Angeles before being transferred to New York City, where he investigated the Communist Party USA (CPUSA) on behalf of the Internal Security Division. Within five years, Kearney earned a promotion to supervisor of the New York FBI office's unit dedicated to the Communist Party, eventually also taking on investigations of the Ku Klux Klan and the BPP.[65]

While investigating the Communist Party throughout the 1950s and 1960s, Kearney became an expert in illegal surveillance tactics and took part in dozens of break-ins. This likely includes a handful of black-bag jobs targeting CPUSA members in 1968 after Hoover officially forbade the practice, and one the same year targeting SNCC's New York office under the auspices of investigating its members' connections with officials in an African country, the name of which is redacted in the FBI memo documenting the break-in.[66] A brief FBI memo on the origins of Squad 47 indicates that "Kearney was recognized by his peers as an aggressive, effective supervisor who was utilized in the most sensitive and challenging assignments," including "'black bag' jobs." "Kearney's assignment to this position," the memo notes, "would serve to impress on the members of the Squad the priority being placed on these investigative matters."[67]

From August 1970 until his retirement from the FBI in June 1972, Kearney led Squad 47's use of illegal surveillance techniques to pursue the Weather Underground. These tactics included illegal mail surveillance. Squad 47 agents acquired keys to New York mailboxes belonging to suspected aboveground Weather Underground supporters, and in a practice they informally referred to as "mail runs," agents would remove mail from their targets' boxes, take it to the FBI office at 201 East 69th Street, and open the envelopes using a special steamer device to avoid noticeable evidence of tampering. After photocopying all of their targets' mail, agents would reseal the envelopes and return them to the mailboxes.[68]

Squad 47 agents also carried out illegal, warrantless electronic wiretaps of suspected Weather Underground supporters as well as individuals suspected of sheltering the FBI's Most Wanted fugitive Cameron Bishop. Kearney held regular meetings with Squad 47 about wiretapping and kept a schedule of agents' shifts monitoring suspects' phone conversations with the bureau's eavesdropping equipment. Kearney also kept files of notes his agents compiled on monitored phone calls. Squad 47 maintained at least eleven illegal wiretaps in New York City between August 1970 and June 1972, though there may have been more.[69]

Weather Underground squads in other cities also used unauthorized wiretaps. Special Agent Wesley Swearingen claimed to have installed over 200 as part of the investigation carried out by the Los Angeles Weather Underground squad, which was known within the bureau as Squad 19.[70]

The FBI's Weather Underground squads carried out an unknown number of unauthorized, illegal break-ins. In some cases, FBI agents may have conducted "surreptitious entries" with the verbal permission of Justice Department officials. SAC Robert Kunkel of the Washington field office recalled that his agents broke in to the residence of a "member of the so-called New Left element" in order to investigate allegations that the individual possessed dynamite that he planned to use in a bombing. According to Kunkel, his agents carried out their black-bag job with permission from Assistant Attorney General William Rehnquist, who verbally authorized a request from the FBI's then assistant director William Sullivan. Kunkel recalled that his office kept no written record of the operation.[71]

For the most part, however, local FBI field offices approved break-ins without authorization from the Justice Department or FBI headquarters. In early 1972, for example, agents from the FBI's Phoenix Weather Underground squad carried out two black-bag jobs in Tucson, Arizona. On March 28, 1972, a Phoenix agent took approximately twenty photographs of documents inside the Tucson apartment of a suspected Weather Underground supporter. Two weeks later, an FBI agent stole from a Tucson apartment a small piece of yellow paper that appeared to contain a handwritten key to a secret communications code.[72] After forging a duplicate version of the paper and returning it to a "small box containing several old letters and other items" located in the apartment, Phoenix agents forwarded the original paper to FBI headquarters in Washington for fingerprint identification and cryptanalysis.[73] Using the typical FBI euphemism, Phoenix agents referred to the break-in as an "anonymous source."[74]

Former special agent M. Wesley Swearingen also recalled conducting break-ins without approval from FBI headquarters. In his memoir, Swearingen wrote that he and other members of Los Angeles's Squad 19 carried out at least seven black-bag jobs. Among the targets were two leftist attorneys who had defended SDS activists.[75] Presumably, like their Phoenix counterparts, Squad 19 agents disguised their sources in their memorandums as "anonymous." However, none of these documents survived the bureau's purging of such sources in 1976.[76]

Hoover took care to avoid any associations with the illegal tactics his agents carried out at his bequest, but he almost certainly knew of their existence. Assistant Director William Sullivan later claimed to have received verbal orders from Hoover to authorize break-ins and other illegal tactics. According to Sullivan, in August or September 1970, Hoover "told me, with some anger, that any means must be used in order to apprehend the fugitives. I gave this information to Mr. Kearney."[77]

Similar claims came from J. Wallace LaPrade, who oversaw the New York FBI regional office's internal security operations from 1971 to 1977, working as a supervisor to Squad 47's John Kearney. In 1977, while facing a Justice Department indictment for his authorization of black-bag jobs, he explained to a reporter that "many instructions from the top were not in writing."[78]

The likelihood that Hoover knew is also supported by the fact that many of the surviving memos documenting illegal FBI activities were sent from field offices to FBI headquarters.[79]

Hoover's informal revival of illegal surveillance consumed tremendous resources and caused great unease among special agents in the field. The director's move also set the stage for the federal indictments of top officials and public outrage that would tarnish the bureau in the years after his death.

But such tactics did little to improve the FBI's success fighting leftist guerrillas. According to Squad 19's special agent Wesley Swearingen, illegal break-ins did not lead to any intelligence that helped the FBI prevent violence or capture Weather Underground fugitives.[80]

Squad 47's John Kearney concurred. "Throughout the entire Bureau we had limited success. . . . Embarrassing, but true."[81]

• • • • • •

Ironically, leftist violence and FBI surveillance increased just as mass radical protest peaked and began to decline. Antiwar demonstrations continued on university campuses during the fall 1970 semester, but not on the scale of the previous spring, when students shut down campuses across the country following Nixon's invasion of Cambodia and the Kent State killings. The disintegration of SDS after June 1969 had left the movement without a national organization capable of keeping up such momentum, while violent tactics alienated America's guerrillas from most of the increasingly fractured aboveground Left. The FBI's annual report for fiscal year 1971 nonetheless emphasized that "New Left extremism posed a serious danger to the Nation's internal security." According to the report, "One of the key extremist groups was the Weatherman, the violence-prone wing of the pre-June 1969 Students for a Democratic Society."[82]

The BPP was also in disarray. In January and February 1971, Huey Newton expelled Geronimo Pratt and most members of New York's Panther Twenty-One after members aligned with exiled Minister of Communication Eldridge Cleaver publicly criticized their leader for moving away from guerrilla warfare as a revolutionary strategy.[83] The FBI noted in its annual report that the BPP's membership had "dwindled" during the first half of 1971 amid the Newton-Cleaver split, which the bureau had actively encouraged through its counterintelligence programs. Nonetheless, the bureau warned that "black extremist groups," particularly the BPP's Cleaver faction, "continue as dangers to national security."[84]

The FBI expanded its surveillance of the U.S. Left in the fall of 1970 in a determined attempt to preempt leftist guerrilla violence. The bureau's improvised tactics would soon become staples of a policing repertoire known as counterterrorism. Much of the FBI's new mass surveillance efforts drew from previous attempts to obtain preventive intelligence of Communist subversion and civil disorder. As in the past, however, mass surveillance did little to help the FBI reach its intended objectives.

Instead, the FBI's incipient counterterrorism backfired. Hoover's zealous efforts to combat guerrilla radicals would lead him to overstate the threat leftist violence posed to U.S. national security. This would set off a series of unexpected events with lasting consequences for the bureau's public image.

The War at Home and the FBI's Public Image

· ·

At the height of America's guerrilla insurgency, on November 27, 1970, FBI director J. Edgar Hoover issued a dire warning. "Extremist elements," he announced, planned an imminent attack in the nation's capital. He described "terrorist tactics" that would encompass the bombing of Washington's power grid and even the kidnapping of a top Nixon administration official.[1]

Hoover outlined this alleged plot to members of the Senate Appropriations Committee as part of his request for increased FBI funding to combat leftist guerrillas. Hoover described the plotters as being associated with the Catholic pacifist organization East Coast Conspiracy to Save Lives. According to Hoover, members of this group planned "to blow up electrical conduits and steam pipes serving the Washington, D.C. area in order to disrupt Federal Government operations." Hoover also accused the group of "concocting a scheme to kidnap a highly placed Government official" as ransom for "an end to United States bombing operations in Southeast Asia and the release of all political prisoners."[2]

Leaks to the press following the testimony—most likely originating from the FBI—named National Security Advisor Henry Kissinger as the official slated for kidnapping.[3] The leaders of this plot, Hoover claimed, were Philip and Daniel Berrigan, a pair of brothers and pacifist Roman Catholic priests then serving federal prison sentences in Danbury, Connecticut, for helping destroy Selective Services records in Maryland in 1968 in a nonviolent act of resistance to the Vietnam War.[4]

It was not normal for the FBI director to reveal details of an active bureau investigation, but these were not normal times. As Hoover outlined in his testimony, leftist violence was on the rise. A growing wave of attacks had convinced the director that the FBI needed increased federal funding to counter this violence.

The problem with Hoover's announcement, however, was that it was not true. In his zeal to combat leftist violence, Hoover stretched the truth beyond credibility, overstating the threat such violence posed to U.S. national security. His overreach would backfire, turning his targets into causes célèbres, and bringing heavy criticism of the FBI. Worse, one of his targets would be inspired to lead a group of pacifist radicals in a burglary of a local FBI office, stealing thousands of classified FBI documents that would reveal the bureau's widespread domestic surveillance and COINTELPROs against dissident social movements.

So it was that Hoover's efforts to bolster congressional support for his strategies brought about a public outcry focused on FBI mass surveillance of the Black Power movement and New Left, including the bureau's efforts to establish informants in all of the country's campus antiwar and Black student organizations. The very measures Hoover had authorized with great reluctance as part of the FBI and Nixon administration's frantic response to leftist violence were exposed.

The dilemma of clandestine political violence had pushed the FBI into a corner. Americans of all stripes were deeply shocked by the unprecedented revelations about FBI operations against fellow citizens' constitutionally protected political activity. For Americans already disillusioned by the war in Vietnam, the new revelations seemed to be the latest proof that their country's political institutions could not be trusted. At the same time, these tactics proved ineffectual at heading off ongoing insurgent plots, leaving others frustrated by the FBI's inability to stop the ongoing domestic guerrilla insurgency.

Hoover's long-standing fears had been realized. Faced with journalists' shocking revelations of domestic spying, on the one hand, and an intractable guerrilla insurgency, on the other, the FBI suffered lasting blows to its popular legitimacy.

Hoover's Overreach

The FBI's war with leftist guerrillas was expensive. When Hoover met with Senators Robert Byrd (D-WV) and Roman Hruska (R-NE) of the Senate Appropriations Committee in November 1970, he requested over $14 million in supplemental funding for FBI operations against organized crime, airplane hijackers, and "black militants and New Left extremists" involved in "violent and terroristic tactics, including bombings."[5] According to Hoover, such activities had led to a 25 percent increase in the FBI's workload over the previous year. With extra funding from American taxpayers, Hoover sought to hire 1,000 new agents and 702 new clerks to expand the FBI's existing staff of 7,869 agents and 10,668 clerks. Hoover also sought to purchase 500 new automobiles in addition to 501 new cars already covered in the FBI's budget for the 1971 fiscal year.[6] For some, the FBI's war on terrorism was creating lucrative career and business opportunities.

Hoover made his funding request as a follow-up to Nixon's recent signing of the Organized Crime Bill of 1970, which expanded the FBI's jurisdiction on political bombings, many of which had previously remained in the purview of local police departments. Hoover was sure to emphasize damage from leftist violence in his statement to the Appropriations Subcommittee. In his "forecast of what might be expected" in the coming year, the director detailed a litany of recent violent incidents, including Weather Underground assaults, the Marin County courthouse raid, and the University of Wisconsin bombing.[7]

Most of the attacks Hoover outlined were real, but the director also exaggerated the threat leftist militants posed to U.S. national security. For example, he cited a Senate Judiciary Committee study that documented more than 5,000 bombings and 1,500 attempted bombings during the fifteen-month period from January 1, 1969, to April 15, 1970 (of the actual bombings, approximately 1,200 were alleged to be of the "high explosive type" while the rest were incendiary). However, he did not mention the fact that these figures contrasted dramatically with those of other government studies, including one by the Senate Investigations Subcommittee that documented 1,188 bombings, acts of arson, and attempted bombings during the same period. He also left out the fact that a large percentage of recent bombings were likely not politically motivated.[8] Hoover's penchant for overstatement was nothing new. For decades he had overstated the threat posed by the Communist Party in order to secure FBI funding.[9]

However, Hoover didn't stop at exaggeration. His accusation that members of the East Coast Conspiracy to Save Lives were plotting to kidnap Henry Kissinger was an outright lie that would incur enormous consequences for both himself and the bureau.

The Kissinger kidnapping conspiracy was not invented from whole cloth. Pakistani American scholar Eqbal Ahmad had floated the idea of a "citizens' arrest" of Kissinger over dinner with some of his Catholic pacifist comrades in Connecticut in late 1970. Whatever "conspiracy" that existed ended that same night, however, after the activists determined that the action posed too much risk of bloodshed. The FBI only learned of this "plot" after Danbury prison officials intercepted a letter—from Sister Elizabeth McAlister to her husband Philip Berrigan—that described the dinner conversation.[10] Hoover's decision to report this detail to Congress would prove to be a fateful one.

While the news media did not regularly scrutinize Hoover's public statements for misrepresentations and exaggerations, this story stood out. The FBI director had announced the existence of a Catholic pacifist terrorist conspiracy. The ensuing firestorm brought on the negative media attention and charges of FBI wrongdoing that Hoover feared most.

Major newspapers such as the *New York Times* and *Washington Post* dug into Hoover's accusations against Catholic pacifists with gusto. Journalists reported that the Berrigan brothers and members of the East Coast Conspiracy to Save Lives publicly denied the charges. At a press conference in Washington, group member Rev. Peter Fordi of Woodstock, Maryland, said that Hoover's testimony was an effort to "create an atmosphere of distrust and terror" within the antiwar movement and to convince the American public that political dissidents were "subversives and careless of human life."[11]

Others took advantage of Hoover's overreach to cast doubt on his many other accusations. At Yale University, leftist students were then hosting thousands of activists from around the country who had come to New Haven to protest the trial of Black Panthers Bobby Seale and Ericka Huggins. Leftist attorney William Kunstler delivered a speech to these supporters that condemned Hoover as "America's Torquemada," the grand inquisitor of late fifteenth-century Spain. Kunstler warned his audience that the FBI director was trying to scare the public into accepting increased FBI repression of the Black Power and antiwar movements. State repression would not stop with militants such as the Chicago Eight, the New York Twenty-One, Huey Newton, Angela Davis, and the New Haven Nine. "If Catholic priests and nuns, sensitive religious people, can be indicted for crimes punishable by the death penalty," Kunstler asked, "who is safe?"[12]

Hoover's accusations also turned members of Congress against him, particularly those in the liberal wing of the Democratic Party. Representative William R. Anderson (D-TN) was a former FBI agent and an esteemed World War II navy veteran who described himself as a "lifelong admirer of Mr. Hoover."[13] After the Berrigan brothers' conviction for sabotaging draft records, however, Anderson decided to visit the priests in prison. Citing the brothers' "philosophy of total nonviolence," Anderson said he "simply could not believe Hoover's allegations."[14] Speaking on the floor of the House of Representatives, Anderson responded to Hoover with what one reporter referred to as "the sharpest criticism of FBI Director J. Edgar Hoover ever heard" in the chamber. Criticizing Hoover for being "involved in a process destructive of the institution he has loved and served with such dedication," Anderson accused the director of utilizing "tactics reminiscent of McCarthyism."[15]

This controversy erupted only days after former attorney general Ramsey Clark publicly criticized the FBI for wiretapping senators and lobbyists during the mid-1960s. Hoover responded by calling his former superior a "jellyfish" who was "soft" on criminals.[16] In a television appearance, Senator Birch Bayh (D-IN) described Hoover's comments as "very unbecoming." "This type of response," Bayh remarked, "would lead me to believe he's forgotten what his job is and perhaps we should find someone who has a better memory."[17]

There are indications that the Berrigan conspiracy blowout may have been another product of the ongoing bureaucratic struggle at the top of the FBI hierarchy. In his 1979 memoir, Mark Felt insinuated that William C. Sullivan fed information about the Berrigan conspiracy to Hoover in an attempt to undermine him, knowing that the director would provoke damaging public backlash if the media picked up his testimony. Sullivan, however, insisted that he had explicitly warned Hoover not to discuss the case.[18]

Whichever the case, the result was increased strain on the FBI's public image—which Hoover's subsequent efforts only worsened. Under pressure to justify his public statement, Hoover persuaded the Department of Justice to convene a grand jury, which indicted Philip Berrigan and seven others on conspiracy charges in early January 1971. On January 12, FBI agents arrested the seven activists, putting all eight members of the group behind bars.

The FBI's actions backfired. Hundreds of protesters demonstrated at the defendants' court hearings as the Harrisburg Eight gained supporters throughout the world. In a direct affront to Attorney General John Mitchell, his predecessor Ramsey Clark served as the defendants' head attorney.[19]

Outcry over the Harrisburg Eight indictment erupted at the same time that other controversies tarnished the FBI's image. On January 31, 1971, Senator George McGovern charged Hoover with "vindictiveness" for firing Jack Shaw, an FBI special agent who had privately critiqued the director in a paper written for a college criminal justice course. Days after Shaw filed a lawsuit against the FBI, McGovern called for a Senate investigation of the matter.[20] Citing Hoover's age of seventy-six, his career spanning over half a century, and growing controversy surrounding his leadership and allegations of illegal surveillance, prominent newspaper editors now called on the director to resign.[21]

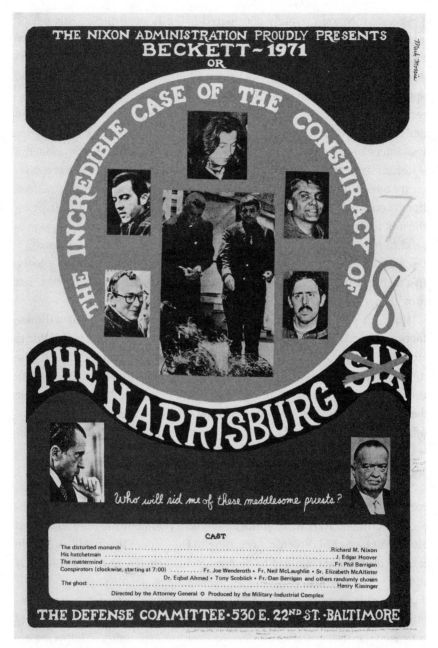

Poster supporting the Harrisburg Eight. After J. Edgar Hoover falsely accused Catholic pacifists of launching a terrorist conspiracy, federal charges generated widespread support for the defendants and undermined the FBI's popular legitimacy. Poster by Markley Morris.

President Nixon privately considered firing Hoover during this period as well, but not because of the director's alleged civil rights violations. On February 3, 1971, Hoover once again blocked the Nixon administration's attempt to revive a version of the Huston Plan. Six weeks earlier, Nixon had approved the formation of an interagency Intelligence Evaluation Committee (IEC) on internal security headed by White House counsel John Dean and Assistant Attorney General Robert Mardian. Recognizing that Hoover was intent on sabotaging the Huston Plan, the IEC's leaders developed a different strategy for establishing executive control over FBI domestic security operations. Instead of reversing all of the FBI's surveillance restrictions at once in a "blanket removal of restrictions," Dean proposed entrusting the unit to determine "the type of intelligence we need . . . and then to proceed to remove the restraints as necessary to obtain such intelligence."[22] Once again, however, Hoover obstructed the Nixon administration's efforts. In a memo to the Justice Department, he indicated that the FBI would "not provide personnel" for the IEC.[23]

Hoover's problem was no longer about using extralegal surveillance tactics—it was that he did not want to put them in the hands of the White House or put in writing that the FBI was engaged in such activities. The director left unmentioned the fact that the FBI had already begun to institute many of the Huston Plan's provisions on its own, albeit with credible deniability allowing Hoover to wink, nod, and look the other way as local offices acted as they saw fit. Hoover's snub compelled the IEC to move forward without the FBI's involvement, a move that prefigured Nixon's formation of the "Plumbers" several months later.[24]

Hoover's problems continued to mount. The day after Hoover issued his memo to the Justice Department, President Nixon, Attorney General Mitchell, and Chief of Staff H. R. Haldeman held a two-hour meeting to discuss Hoover's fate as FBI director. According to Haldeman, the president "made it clear that Hoover has got to be replaced before the end of Nixon's first term."[25]

Hoover's efforts to keep the FBI above partisan reproach were crumbling before his eyes as Americans' views on the bureau grew increasingly polarized. Leftists and liberals decried Hoover's repression of left-wing activists, while growing numbers of other Americans demanded stepped-up efforts to capture leftist guerrillas. At the same time that prominent Democratic lawmakers such as Edward Kennedy and Hale Boggs called for Hoover's dismissal, the FBI endured criticism from the International Association of Chiefs of Police and others who questioned why leftist bomber fugitives continued to elude the FBI despite the bureau receiving "bigger and bigger" appropriations every year.[26]

Still, ongoing leftist violence lent credence to Hoover's warnings that revolutionary guerrillas endangered public safety and national security—and helped him hang on to his job in spite of Nixon's disapproval.

The Capitol Bombing

Catholic pacifists never really planned to bomb anything in Washington, D.C., but the Weather Underground did. Early in the morning on March 1, 1971, in its most brazen attack to date, the Weather Underground bombed the U.S. Capitol Building.

The group carried out the action to protest the U.S. aerial bombardment of Laos, which American jets had littered with millions of cluster bombs and other munitions as part of the government's expansion of the war in neighboring Vietnam. Though far more modest than the deadly ordnance dropped on Laos, the Weather Underground's homemade explosive grabbed the attention of U.S. political leaders. Planted in a seldom-used men's lavatory on the Capitol's ground floor with a timing device set for 1:30 A.M., the dynamite succeeded in demolishing the restroom and damaging some nearby offices. The explosion inflicted a total of around $300,000 in damage.[27]

President Nixon was aboard Air Force One on a trip to Iowa when he heard the news. He issued an immediate statement, calling the blast an "act of shocking violence which will outrage most Americans."[28]

Both parties followed suit. Senate majority leader Mike Mansfield (D-MT) called the action an "outrageous and sacrilegious" attack on "a public shrine." Senate minority leader Hugh Scott (R-PA) called it an act of "terrorism" by those "who believe that if they cannot persuade by reason or by logic, perhaps they can terrify the American people."[29]

Outspoken antiwar senator George McGovern (D-SD) stood alone in connecting the bombing to the carnage in Southeast Asia. While calling the Capitol bombing "barbaric," McGovern blamed "our Vietnam madness." "The massive bombardment we are continuing year after year against the people of Indochina has its counterpart in the mounting destruction of humane values in our homeland," he said. "It is not possible to teach an entire generation to bomb and destroy others in an undeclared, unjustified, unending war without paying a terrible price in the derangement of our society."[30]

The Capitol bombing followed the Weather Underground's December 1970 "New Morning, Changing Weather" communiqué. Bernardine Dohrn used the statement to officially tone down her previously violent rhetoric, renounce the organization's former rejection of grassroots movement building, and pledge that the Weather Underground would consciously avoid casualties in future bombings.[31] The FBI took note of the Weather Underground's newly articulated policy, albeit with a grain of salt. "Whether all Weatherman individuals will follow Dohrn's example," FBI internal security chief Robert Shackelford wrote in a memo to Assistant Director Charles Brennan, "remains to be seen."[32] The organization's status as a dangerous threat remained unchanged.

The Capitol bombing generated further scrutiny of the FBI in Congress. A few weeks after the attack, as hundreds of FBI agents searched for Weather Underground fugitives throughout the country, Hoover told members of the House Appropriations Subcommittee that the bureau was close to making arrests. But the *Washington Post* reported that members of Congress were wary of Hoover's claim.[33] A year later, the Appropriation Subcommittee's Rep. Robert L. F. Sikes grilled Hoover: "What is the status of the Capitol bombing? . . . Almost a year ago, you thought it was ready to break."[34] In the meantime, congressional leaders took matters into their own hands, offering a $100,000 award for information leading to the Capitol bombers. And for the first time, federal authorities installed metal detectors staffed by armed guards in all of Washington's government buildings.[35]

This time, Hoover wasn't lying.

FBI agents had actually just made their first serious break in their Weather Underground investigation while spying on attorney Dennis Cunningham of Chicago's People's Law Office. When agents realized Cunningham had wired $700 to California under an assumed name, they alerted agents in San Francisco, who came close to nabbing Weatherman Jeff Jones when he went to retrieve the funds at a local Western Union office. But the FBI agents did not recognize Jones at first because of his heavy disguise, and when Jones noticed suspicious men hanging around, he jumped into a getaway truck driven by Bernardine Dohrn, who zigzagged through the city to throw off the agents who sped behind them in a black sedan. Though they survived the car chase, Jones and Dohrn soon realized that the license plates of the truck they were driving had been registered with the same fake ID used to rent the apartment the guerrillas were using as their main San Francisco safe house. The group abandoned the apartment first thing the next morning, and FBI agents arrived within a few hours, discovering the place empty of guerrillas but full of bombs and leftist literature.[36]

It was a very close call, and Hoover had real cause for optimism. However, instead of scoring a needed public relations victory, Hoover's FBI took another hit and the Weather Underground continued to elude the world's most celebrated intelligence agency.

The Media Burglary

While the Capitol bombing caused great frustration for the FBI, a nonviolent burglary a week later caused far more damage.

On March 8, 1971, much of the country was transfixed by Joe Frazier's televised championship boxing bout with Muhammad Ali. Calculating that this media phenomenon would serve as a distraction, a team of men and women dressed in suits and female business attire timed their raid to coincide with the highly anticipated bout. They picked the locks of the FBI's Resident Agency in Media, Pennsylvania, and ransacked its filing cabinets. Participants later recalled hearing sportscasters' coverage of the match blaring from a television in the apartment above the office while they hastily stuffed surveillance documents into suitcases.[37]

The operation went off without a hitch. It was all the more impressive considering that the participants were not professionals but eight local peace activists calling themselves the Citizens' Commission to Investigate the FBI. Their leader was William C. Davidon, a physics professor now out on bail after being arrested as a member of the Harrisburg Eight for conspiring to kidnap Henry Kissinger. Infuriated by the government's ongoing attacks on the antiwar movement, and particularly incensed by the recent Harrisburg indictments, the Citizens' Commission had raided the FBI's filing cabinets in search of documentary evidence that the bureau was engaged in covert disruption of the U.S. Left. They were successful beyond their greatest expectations.

Documents uncovered by the Media burglars revealed extensive surveillance of student and Black activist organizations, including Hoover's effort to develop informants in all campus New Left and Black Student Union groups. The documents also exposed the FBI's use of local police, postal workers, telephone operators, and campus security officers in surveillance operations. One document that would be quoted widely in the press conveyed the FBI's attempts to instill in activists the paranoid sense that they were being constantly watched by "an FBI agent behind every mailbox."[38]

Realizing the extraordinary implications of their discovery, members of the Citizens' Commission got to work. They secretly sent the documents to journalists and members of Congress. Despite FBI and Justice Department orders not to publish, the *Washington Post* began running articles on the revelations just over two weeks later.[39] In March 1972, the pacifist *WIN* magazine published the documents in a special issue titled "The Complete Collection of Political Documents Ripped-Off from the F.B.I. Office in Media, PA."[40]

According to the FBI's chief inspector Mark Felt, Hoover was "enraged" when he learned of the document heist.[41] Another source described the director as "apoplectic."[42] Hoover immediately launched an enormous investigation, code-named MEDBURG, which rivaled the Weather Underground investigation in size and scope. MEDBURG consumed vast bureau resources, as investigators followed leads throughout the country, from Los Angeles to North Carolina to Boston. Still more agents drew massive overtime pay for security duty after Hoover, fearful of additional burglaries, closed 103 of the FBI's remote resident agencies and required agents to maintain twenty-four-hour guard at the bureau's more than 400 other small offices. Hoover dispatched over 200 agents to work on the case in the Philadelphia area, where they set up around-the-clock physical surveillance of peace activists in the city's countercultural Powelton Village neighborhood. Using cameras and notebooks, agents stationed themselves in cars and on street corners to monitor activists' comings and goings. Agents also pored over mountains of evidence, including over a decade's worth of surveillance photos of antiwar activists.

On more than one occasion, FBI agents broke into the homes of Philadelphia peace activists whom they suspected of involvement in the Media burglary. The FBI left no documentary record of such "surreptitious entries," but the culprits also made no effort to hide their break-ins, which seemed designed to intimidate as much as to acquire intelligence. Philadelphia peace activists had little doubt that the bureau was behind the break-ins.[43]

The Media burglars managed to escape the FBI's clutches. After mailing off the documents, members of the Citizens' Commission to Investigate the FBI parted ways, agreeing never to speak to one another again. One member of the group, Judi Feingold, moved to the West Coast and went underground, keeping her secret and living under an assumed identity for forty-three years. The rest remained in the Philadelphia area, hiding in plain sight.⁴⁴

The Media burglary prompted an important change in FBI practices. On April 28, 1971, Hoover quietly discontinued all FBI COINTELPROs. He reserved the FBI's prerogative to carry out similar programs in the future on an ad hoc basis, however. In his memo canceling the programs, Hoover notified his agents that "in exceptional instances where it is considered counterintelligence action is warranted, recommendations should be submitted to the bureau under the individual case caption to which it pertains. These recommendations will be considered on an individual basis."⁴⁵ The public had not yet learned of the FBI's COINTELPROs, but Hoover knew it was only a matter of time before activists and journalists began to inquire about the "COINTELPRO" code word typed in the heading of a document stolen from Media. Over the next four years, a series of lawsuits and congressional investigations would bring the FBI's COINTELPROs to light.⁴⁶

By this point the FBI's COINTELPROs against the New Left and Black Power movement were of little use anyway. COINTELPRO-New Left had never been very effective and was of even lesser value to the FBI now that SDS had disintegrated and mass antiwar protest had significantly declined. COINTELPRO-Black Nationalist-Hate Groups had successfully exploited the BPP's internal divisions and violent tendencies, but by April 1971 the party was essentially defunct outside of Oakland.⁴⁷ Furthermore, as FBI officials had acknowledged for the past year, counterintelligence was not an effective tactic for fighting clandestine revolutionary guerrillas. Since clandestine organizations were nearly impossible to infiltrate, the FBI could not sow internal conflict in such groups anyway. Given that leftist violence had failed to win converts or spark revolutionary action, primarily generating highly damaging press coverage and little else, there was little need for COINTELPRO tactics to further discredit the guerrilla underground.

The Media burglary inflicted lasting damage to the FBI's public image. Immediately following the news stories on the stolen documents, public criticism of the FBI surged, particularly among American liberals. Editors of the *Washington Post, New York Times, Philadelphia Inquirer*, and other major papers blasted the FBI's tactics and notion of internal security.⁴⁸ The *Post* called the FBI's tactics "appropriate, perhaps for the secret police of the Soviet Union but wholly inconsonant with the idea of a Federal Bureau of Investigation."⁴⁹ Democratic senators Edmund Muskie of Maine, Gaylord Nelson of Wisconsin, Mike Mansfield of Montana, and John V. Tunney of California joined newspaper editors in calls for congressional investigations of FBI practices.[50] A poll conducted in May 1971 determined that 43 percent of Americans believed Hoover should resign as FBI director.[51]

William Sullivan and J. Edgar Hoover discussed public criticism of the FBI after the Media burglary in an exchange of letters. Always the sycophant, Sullivan initiated the exchange by reaching out to his boss with words of consolation: "It would be misleading to say that the attacks made on you, the FBI, and the rest of us are not damaging," but, he assured Hoover, "you not only have the support and backing of FBI employees but of far greater significance the backing of people throughout the country on a grass-roots level." Sullivan went even further, insisting that "even the critics admit this and point out that your strength is too great for anyone to replace you."[52]

In his reply, Hoover acknowledged that the public criticism was immense, and that he could not help taking it personally. "It was indeed most thoughtful for you to write your most encouraging letter of April 5 commenting on the series of attacks on me and the Bureau," Hoover wrote. "I do not think it is possible to always completely ignore or be able to not let such things get under one's skin, but when one stops to analyze it, the true character of the sources, which is nothing but a pack of jackals, surfaces."[53]

Despite these attempts at optimism, the damage inflicted on the FBI was irreparable. After the Media burglary revelations, the FBI's image, along with Hoover's, entered a long downward spiral. Growing numbers of Americans expressed their distrust of the bureau and its leaders. FBI agents now pursued leftist guerrillas amid intense public scrutiny of bureau tactics.

Reckoning with Mass Surveillance

In terms of political impact, the Media burglary ranks among the most important acts of nonviolent resistance in American history. Since the onset of the Cold War, Americans had been told by political leaders, educators, and Hollywood films that their nation was a virtuous beacon of democracy, defending the free world from the totalitarian Soviet Union, whose secret police agency, the KGB, was supposed to be the antithesis of the FBI. Just as revelations of American atrocities in Vietnam gave lie to the myth of U.S. military exceptionalism, the Media burglary dragged the FBI's top-secret surveillance and counterintelligence activities into the light of day, exposing troubling realities beneath the FBI's mythical G-man image. It turned out that the FBI engaged in covert activities that diametrically contradicted America's democratic values. This did not make Americans happy.

The Media break-in kicked off a heated debate over mass surveillance that rippled throughout American society, from kitchen tables and college dorm rooms to the halls of Congress. This culminated in a series of major government investigations of the FBI and other federal intelligence agencies, most notably, those conducted in 1975 by the Senate's "Church Committee," led by Senator Frank Church (D-ID), which for the first time provided the American public with a full picture of the FBI's covert operations and surveillance of American dissidents. The Media burglary also helped build popular support for the 1974 Privacy Act amendments to the Freedom of Information Act, which expanded Americans' ability to petition government agencies for classified materials—a major check on state power that has led to the declassification of millions of pages of once-secret documents, including most of the FBI documents used to write this book.[54] Impassioned arguments over state power and mass surveillance continue to reverberate through American politics today.

Though he would not live to witness the full consequences, when the Media burglary happened, J. Edgar Hoover immediately grasped the implications. Despite the fact that the FBI itself was engaged in illegal break-ins, Hoover and his men were outraged that leftists had targeted the bureau with a black-bag job of their own. Officials in both the FBI and Nixon's Justice Department were also sour that most news coverage of the documents stolen from the Media office overlooked the main impetus behind the FBI's mass surveillance: preventing leftist violence. Men in power had a point that the news media did not focus on the FBI's motives, but this is understandable given Americans' shock at discovering the bureau's actions.

After the Media burglary, journalists penned exposés on the FBI's invasion of Americans' civil liberties while FBI and Nixon officials bemoaned the news media's downplaying of their antiterrorist motives. In the decades since, most retrospective accounts of Nixon-era FBI mass surveillance have taken one side or the other—this should be understood as one of the Media burglary's legacies. Yet there are other insights to be gained from the declassified documents that have cascaded into the public domain since Media, including on how the FBI's war on leftist guerrillas portrayed entire movements as suspects, and how leftists sometimes overestimated the state's power.

When journalists and newspaper editors wrote about documents uncovered in the Media burglary, they emphasized the negative ramifications of the FBI's intrusion into the lives of law-abiding activists. The *New York*

Times, for instance, charged the bureau with engaging in "political surveillance which far exceed[ed] legitimate efforts to protect the national
interest." The *Washington Post* condemned "the poisonous effect which
[FBI] surveillance . . . has upon the democratic process and upon the practice of free speech.[55] The revelations were particularly shocking given U.S.
officials' repeated denials of such mass surveillance. The day after the Media burglary, for example, Assistant Attorney General William H. Rehnquist
swore to the Senate Subcommittee on Constitutional Rights that U.S. intelligence agencies engaged in virtually no surveillance of Americans. A
couple weeks later, when the new FBI revelations made headlines, reporters made a point of highlighting the falsehood of Rehnquist's testimony.[56]

The FBI's defenders scoffed at the media storm. Attorney General John
Mitchell accused the burglars of taking the documents out of context and
selectively mailing to congressmen and journalists only those that "seem
to discredit the FBI."[57] As an example, Mitchell argued that a memo revealing the FBI's use of local police, a neighbor, a postmaster, campus security,
and a campus switchboard operator to keep tabs on a Philadelphia professor whom agents described as a "hippie" and a "radical" gave the impression that the FBI was watching the man solely because of his political views.
In reality, Mitchell claimed, the document was part of a packet on the September 1970 killing of Massachusetts police officer Walter Schroeder, and
the FBI suspected that Ten Most Wanted guerrilla fugitives Katherine
Power and Susan Saxe might attempt to contact the professor.[58]

Mitchell was probably telling the truth here—in fact, the majority of the
documents uncovered in the Media burglary pertained to surveillance the
FBI had initiated as part of its war against leftist guerrillas. Mitchell would
not comment on journalists' questions about the release of the FBI's September 1970 memo authorizing employment of campus informants aged
eighteen to twenty-one, for instance, but this order, as well as Hoover's
directives massively expanding campus surveillance in November 1970
after the Weather Underground's Fall Offensive, was undertaken as part of
the FBI's desperate hunt for leftist guerrillas.[59]

It is true that journalists like Betty Medsger and Ken Clawson of the
Washington Post downplayed the historic reasons for the FBI's mass surveillance, but that's because what shocked them and many other Americans was the fact that regardless of motives, the bureau's spy tactics trampled
the privacy and civil liberties of people engaged in legal, constitutionally
protected political activities. Most of the FBI's surveillance targeted indi-

viduals who had no involvement in political violence—they were simply protesting war and racism.

In efforts to locate and preempt a small number of leftist guerrillas, the FBI cast an expansive surveillance net, one that stretched from coast to coast, enlisting hundreds of informants, and fixing its gaze on nearly every movement on the American Left. One scholar who documented such surveillance is Ruth Rosen. Rosen was active in the women's liberation movement while a graduate student in history at the University of California Berkeley. Decades later, she used FBI documents obtained through a Freedom of Information Act request to write *The World Split Open*, her classic history of the modern American women's movement, which includes an essential, and frequently overlooked, chapter detailing the bureau's surveillance of feminists.[60]

Rosen's research gives a sense of how far the FBI went in targeting entire activist communities to search for a small number of insurgents. Rosen revealed that although the FBI had been monitoring radical women since the McCarthy era, the FBI maintained an official surveillance program directed at the women's movement from 1969, when Hoover expanded domestic surveillance, to 1973, when L. Patrick Gray began to reduce it in response to public outrage that had grown in the wake of the Media burglary. FBI officials behind the Women's Liberation Movement (WLM) spy program worried about some feminist activists' potential for "subversion," but the bureau conducted much of its surveillance in an effort to detect potential violence and locate female leftist guerrilla fugitives. As Rosen explained, male FBI agents cultivated countless female informants to report on the activities of women's liberation groups and communes across the country, not only in radical hotspots like Chicago, New York, and Berkeley but in dozens of cities from Gainesville, Florida, to Columbus, Ohio, to Lawrence, Kansas. Informants sat in on feminist reading groups and gathered flyers, meeting minutes, and other materials for their handlers, supplying agents with the intelligence they typed in their reports to FBI headquarters.[61]

In cases where it was looking for guerrilla fugitives, the FBI actively disrupted elements of the women's movement. In 1972, the FBI intensified its surveillance of women's activist communities in Boston, Philadelphia, Lexington, Hartford, and New Haven, carrying out hundreds of interrogations while supplying prosecutors with evidence used as the basis for grand jury subpoenas designed to obtain information on the whereabouts of

Katherine Power and Susan Saxe. The pair had become lovers after their 1970 spree of guerrilla actions in the Boston area, and they went into hiding in the lesbian feminist community. One way FBI men tried to extract information on the fugitives' whereabouts was by threatening to tell lesbian feminists' employers and family members about their sexual orientation if they refused to cooperate.[62]

Yet for the most part, the FBI's surveillance of the women's movement was passive. Agents monitored for the possibility of violence or civil disorder, but when groups did not seem violent or disruptive to civic order, the FBI's activities did not go beyond maintaining detailed notes of feminists' political activities. For instance, a 1969 report on the women's movement from the FBI's New York office noted that according to one of its informants, "the WLM is only interested in changing abortion laws and birth control. . . . Women at the meeting on [REDACTED date in 1969] state they are not revolutionaries and would not help anyone in a revolution until the oppression of women was solved first and completely." In 1969 and 1970, the head of FBI's San Francisco field office repeatedly told headquarters that he did not think surveillance of the women's movement was warranted, but he was admonished by Hoover, who insisted that "interwoven with its goals for equal rights for women is the advocation of violence to achieve these goals. . . . It is absolutely essential that we conduct sufficient investigation to clearly establish the subversive ramifications of the WLM and to determine the potential for violence presented by the various groups connected with this movement."[63]

This did not stop members of the women's movement from believing that the FBI and other intelligence agencies were actively disrupting their organizing efforts. Paranoia about state infiltration was by no means confined to radical paramilitary groups like the BPP. Even Betty Friedan—the best-selling author of the *Feminine Mystique* and leader of the National Organization for Women (NOW), well known for promoting the politics of middle-class respectability—believed that the FBI had infiltrated the women's movement. Friedan contended the FBI had manufactured protest by dissident lesbians who resented their exclusion from NOW's leadership and policy decisions, efforts she credited for the women's movement's failure to pass the Equal Rights Amendment to the U.S. Constitution. In one of the most devastating examples of paranoia-driven factionalism, members of New York's radical feminist Redstockings collective accused *Ms.* magazine editor Gloria Steinem of being a CIA informant, a baseless charge that continues to circulate on the fringes of the American Left today.[64]

One of Rosen's crucial findings was that despite its tremendous scope, FBI surveillance did not alter the women's movement's trajectory. Without FBI infiltration, she explained, "women's liberationists still would have trashed their leaders, censored groups members for having the wrong appearance, the wrong partner, or the wrong job," and "Betty Friedan still would have blamed lesbians for causing the gay/straight split." Most of the FBI's surveillance of the women's movement remained passive because most participants were not engaged in violence. This finding cuts against the grain of leftist lore on the FBI and groups like the Black Panthers, which depicts repressive counterintelligence operations as a reflection of such organizations' political effectiveness. Despite its limitations, the women's movement was tremendously successful in transforming relations between the genders, upending cultural norms of women's roles in the family, the workplace, education, and politics. However, as Rosen explained, this was "not what the FBI considered subversive."[65]

This brings us back to one of the great, underappreciated ironies of the Media burglary. The Media burglars discovered that one of the FBI's goals was to make leftists fear that an FBI agent lurked "behind every mailbox," yet this revelation only heightened leftist paranoia about state surveillance. In many cases, oversize fear of the state led activists to deepen suspicions of one another, undermining the solidarity needed to build broad, diverse coalitions capable of achieving systemic change. Even more damaging, some radicals interpreted revelations of FBI operations as confirmation that guerrilla warfare was the only way leftists could ever hope to take on a near invincible U.S. state. In this sense, one could argue that despite the fact that the Media burglary sullied the FBI's image, and despite the fact that the bureau's efforts preempted little if any guerrilla violence, Hoover continued to make headway in his larger goal of undermining the American Left.

The revelations from Media must also be understood in full context. The bureau's late-1970 expansion of domestic surveillance was a product of two dynamics: the FBI's war with domestic leftist guerrillas, and Hoover's battle with the Nixon administration over the conduct of that war. Under intense pressure from the Nixon administration after the collapse of the Huston Plan, the FBI lifted previous restraints on domestic surveillance in late 1970 in an unsuccessful effort to preempt leftist guerrilla violence. As the previous chapter explained, Hoover's expansion of surveillance on the student antiwar and Black Power movements, reauthorization of teenaged informants, and pressuring of field offices to informally partake in mail covers, mail opening, warrantless wiretaps, and break-ins were a direct response to Jonathan Jackson's bloody Marin County courthouse attack, the New Year's Gang's deadly University of Wisconsin bombing, the killing of Officer Walter Schroeder, and the Weather Underground's October 1970 Fall Offensive.

Hoover's long-standing loathing of leftists undoubtedly influenced the measures, and he did himself no favors by overreaching in his remarks to Congress—but a simmering racism and hatred of leftists are insufficient as an explanation for the director's actions. Hoover would not have lifted his restrictions on domestic surveillance and risked the possibility of public exposure tainting the FBI's image if it were not for ongoing leftist guerrilla attacks and the bureau's inability to prevent them.

Still, none of this diminishes the significance of the FBI's operations against American dissidents. The critics who raised alarms after the Media burglary were correct to assert that mass surveillance and domestic counterintelligence violated civil liberties and undermined American democracy. The American Left sought to build a world without racism, sexism, economic inequality, and imperialist war. In contrast, the FBI stood firmly with American political leaders, particularly those on the right, who sought to preserve the prevailing social order. Instead of addressing the violent inequities that fueled political protest, Hoover's FBI cast an entire generation of activists as terrorism suspects.

· · · · · ·

Ultimately, Hoover's worst nightmare materialized. The American public *did* end up learning about FBI domestic surveillance, and the bureau's image suffered as a result. This too was partially an outcome of guerrilla violence. In his zealous attempt to secure funding and support for the FBI's war on guerrilla revolutionaries, Hoover made a calamitous miscalculation when he accused the Berrigan brothers and the East Coast Conspiracy to Save Lives of conspiring to kidnap Kissinger and bomb Washington, D.C.'s municipal infrastructure. In the wake of government efforts to convict several other prominent radicals, and amid continuous police infiltration and attacks on activists, American leftists—including those who went on to carry out the Media burglary—understandably interpreted the Harrisburg Eight indictment as part of an FBI-led assault on the U.S. Left. When he lodged his false allegations against the Harrisburg Eight, Hoover inadvertently provoked the Media burglary.

Hoover's expansion of domestic surveillance did not improve the FBI's success in preventing leftist guerrilla violence. Instead, his announcement of the far-fetched Kissinger kidnap conspiracy backfired. In his frenzy to combat what he called revolutionary terrorism, Hoover badly undermined the public's trust. A growing number of Americans now saw the FBI's politically motivated policing as a far greater threat to their freedom than a handful of guerrilla radicals. As a result of Hoover's actions, the FBI's pursuit of clandestine revolutionaries would only become more difficult, and Hoover's conflict with Nixon even more contentious.

On the evening of May 21, 1971, New York City police officers Waverly Jones and Joseph Piagentini were walking their beat outside a Harlem public housing complex when they became casualties in America's simmering domestic guerrilla war. Two gunmen ambushed the pair from behind, riddling the unsuspecting patrolmen with bullets. Jones, a thirty-two-year-old African American father of two, died instantly when the first of nine rounds entered his body. The twenty-eight-year-old Italian American Piagentini was still alive, and he was left on the sidewalk to slowly bleed out from twelve bullet wounds as the assassins fled on foot.[1]

Two days later, the Black Liberation Army (BLA) took credit for the attack. In a communiqué issued to the *New York Times*, the BLA declared, "Revolutionary justice has been meted out again by righteous brothers of the Black Liberation Army with the death of two Gestapo pigs gunned down as so many of our brothers have been gunned down in the past. But this time no racist class jury will acquite [*sic*] them."[2]

President Nixon convened a private meeting on the killings on May 26, 1971, the same day that thousands of uniformed police and supporters gathered in New York for the slain officers' funerals. The president met in Washington's Executive Office Building with J. Edgar Hoover, Attorney General John N. Mitchell, Chief Domestic Advisor John D. Ehrlichman, and Ehrlichman's deputy, Egil "Bud" Krogh Jr. (Aside from Hoover, all of these men would later serve prison sentences for participating in the crimes of Watergate.) Nixon commenced the meeting by emphasizing his desire for a strong federal response to the police murders.

"Goddamn it," the president declared, "we've got to do something . . . other than just talk about these police killings."[3]

Just as Weatherman's Greenwich Village townhouse explosion had raised alarms over deadly leftist bombings, and just as Jonathan Jackson's California courthouse raid had introduced America to the specter of revolutionary kidnapping, the BLA's assassination of officers Jones and Piagentini spiked U.S. officials' concerns over police killings.

The slayings led to a fresh round of White House pressure on Hoover's FBI over preventive surveillance and revolutionary terrorism. In response, the bureau continued to improvise tactics to combat urban guerrillas. Working with the Nixon administration, Hoover helped organize a meeting of law enforcement officials from around the country to confront the problem of violence against police officers. At the same time, Hoover secretly provided his agents with more ambiguous orders to utilize break-ins, unauthorized wiretaps, and other illegal surveillance tactics, this time directed at the BLA.

The FBI also launched a major investigation into the Jones-Piagentini killings. Code-named NEWKILL (short for New York killings), and led by the New York field office's new Squad-43A, the investigation would eventually link the BLA to the BPP's East Coast "Cleaver faction" and former members of the Panther Twenty-One who had gone underground to wage guerrilla war against U.S. imperialism.

NEWKILL was not simply a criminal investigation. Like other FBI campaigns against leftist guerrillas, NEWKILL was political. The FBI devised NEWKILL's nascent counterterrorism operations in the context of Nixon's law-and-order political agenda. The operation was a direct outgrowth of the FBI's war with the BPP and built on existing surveillance records targeting the group. In its efforts to neutralize the clandestine BLA, the FBI even resorted to counterintelligence operations, targeting remnants of the New York Black Panthers with some of the only documented examples of such operations following J. Edgar Hoover's April 1971 cancellation of COINTELPROs against domestic dissidents.

The political nature of NEWKILL is obvious when one considers the fact that while Nixon and Hoover pursued new measures to prevent the killing of police officers, they did little to prevent police officers' killing of African Americans. As its communiqué stated, the BLA conceived the assassination of Waverly and Jones as retaliation for American police officers' slaying of Black people with impunity. This was a long-standing problem in America, one that went back to the days of slavery. Despite the destructive wave of urban rebellions against police killing and mistreatment of African Americans that washed over U.S. cities during the 1960s, the problem went on unaddressed.

The president and the FBI director remained uninterested in tackling the root causes of BLA violence. When the BLA emerged on the scene in May 1971, the Nixon administration was already immersed in a racially biased War on Crime in which congressional Democrats colluded with the Republican president to defund Lyndon Johnson's Great Society programs while dramatically expanding federal support for urban policing, particularly in African American communities.[4] Four months later, when New York authorities crushed a prisoner rebellion at Attica State Penitentiary with a police massacre of thirty-nine people, Nixon telephoned Governor Nelson Rockefeller to express support.[5] The president was not interested in reducing all violence, only violence he and his administration perceived as criminal, revolutionary, terrorist, or otherwise beyond the norms of a status quo upheld through state violence.

For BLA members, incidents of state violence like the Attica massacre reinforced the belief that America's racist authorities would stop at nothing to crush movements for Black liberation. Each Black person killed by a cop only steeled their resolve to retaliate with more violence of their own. But guerrilla violence did not compel the Nixon administration to change course. On the contrary, the BLA's police assassinations only increased Nixon and Hoover's hostility toward leftists and liberals who promoted government-funded social programming as a solution to poverty and racism. The killings also provided the men with incidents they could use to advance their policy goals. In keeping with their law-and-order political agenda, Nixon and Hoover responded to the Jones-Piagentini killings and other BLA attacks by doubling down on their expansion of policing and state surveillance.

The Jones-Piagentini killings initially rekindled tensions between Nixon and Hoover. But fortunately for Hoover, the FBI made gains in its pursuit of the BLA. This was a matter of both perseverance and luck. The FBI was unable to infiltrate the BLA underground, but steady surveillance and harassment of New York's remaining Black Panthers dried up the guerrillas' limited aboveground support. Meanwhile, a series of high-risk BLA actions during the summer and autumn of 1971 exposed its members to police gunfire and capture. The killing and arrests of several BLA militants opened leads in the FBI's NEWKILL investigation, forcing the BLA's remaining members to flee New York, lay low, and try to regroup. By the spring of 1972, the FBI, New York Police Department (NYPD), and other police agencies had won the first bloody round of their war with the BLA.

Yet the root causes of antipolice violence remained. With the Nixon administration's active refusal to address root causes, and with the FBI's efforts to combat insurgent political violence with policing and preventive surveillance, the state's conflict with the BLA took on a characteristic that would continue to haunt American counterterrorism—its functioning as a "self-fulfilling prophecy"—as disproportionate police tactics that yielded occasional victories in battle ultimately perpetuated a permanent state of war.[6]

"Go In with Everything You've Got"

Though their deaths prompted dramatic responses from Nixon and the FBI, Jones and Piagentini were not the first police victims of a guerrilla ambush. The BLA carried out its first publicized attack two days earlier, when members of the group unloaded a .45 caliber machine gun into a squad car occupied by New York police officers Thomas Curry and Nicholas Binetti. The ambush occurred as the officers stood guard outside the home of District Attorney Frank S. Hogan, head prosecutor of the New York Twenty-One, whose house Weatherman had firebombed a year earlier.[7]

A BLA communiqué took credit: "The armed goons of this racist government will again meet the guns of oppressed Third World peoples as long as they occupy our community and murder our brothers and sisters in the name of American law and order. Just as the fascist marines and army [who] occupy Vietnam in the name of democracy and murder Vietnamese people in the name of American imperialism are confronted with the guns of the Vietnamese Liberation Army, the domestic armed forces of racism and oppression will be confronted with the guns of the Black Liberation Army."[8]

The BLA's two police ambushes occurred amid a growing number of assaults on New York police officers. Twenty-eight other New York police officers had been wounded in the line of duty since the start of 1971, a significant increase in the rate of forty-five wounded the entire previous year. Five officers had died. Edward J. Kiernan, president of the Patrolmen's Benevolent Society, declared, "We're in a war. . . . It's open season on cops in this city."[9]

The BLA's assaults did not come out of nowhere. The group carried out its attacks in the context of ongoing police killings of African Americans. Since the Justice Department does not maintain statistics on people killed by police, the precise body count is unknown. By one estimate, however, between 1971 and 1973 U.S. police killed as many as 1,000 Black people.[10]

But who exactly the BLA *was* remained a mystery. Before the New York police ambushes, neither the FBI nor anyone else outside of the militant Left had heard of the group. This was despite the fact that the bureau had been tracking the BPP's violent rhetoric and advocacy of guerrilla warfare for nearly three years.

President Nixon also demanded answers. The BLA's deadly attack was the topic of Nixon's Executive Office Building meeting on May 26, 1971. The president made it clear that he wanted the New York police murder cases solved quickly. After the Jones-Piagentini killings, Nixon once again pressured Hoover to implement illegal surveillance tactics from the abandoned Huston Plan for the purpose of preventing guerrilla attacks, particularly police ambushes. Little did he know that Hoover had already given his agents unofficial orders to revive such tactics. Hoover kept this information secret from the president, however, in order to shield himself from liability for such unlawful behavior.

At the Executive Office Building meeting, Hoover tried to offer Nixon reassurance. The director informed the president and his aides that he had already ordered the FBI's New York field office to "maintain close liaison" with the NYPD as well as "determine complete intelligence data and . . . identify black extremist influence or participation" in the assaults by reviewing "appropriate files of black extremist organizations, including those of so-called Third World groups."[11] In other words, FBI agents were already busy combing surveillance records on the BPP, the militant Puerto Rican Young Lords organization, and other radical Black, Latino, and Asian American organizations. Nixon and Hoover also made plans for a Washington gathering of chiefs of police from around the country organized in conjunction with the International Association of Chiefs of Police. Set to take place in less than two weeks, the meeting would seek new law enforcement strategies for preventing police assassination. At the conclusion of their ninety-minute meeting, Nixon held a press conference to explain the steps the White House and FBI were taking to address the New York killings.[12]

But Hoover felt the pressure to go further. Immediately after the meeting, he returned to his office in FBI headquarters and telephoned New York's SAC Joseph K. Ponder. The director sought assurance that his men in New York were working overtime. Ponder confirmed that his office had contacted the NYPD immediately after the killings and offered access to the "facilities and services of the FBI, including fingerprints, laboratory, NCIC [the National Crime Information Center] and the handling of out-of-town leads."[13] The New York FBI field office had continued to be in touch with the NYPD every day since, and earlier that morning, Ponder had spoken in person with NYPD commissioner Patrick V. Murphy and several top detectives while attending the funerals for both fallen officers. Ponder also notified his boss that New York City FBI agents had alerted their informants with knowledge of "black extremist activities" that relevant information would be passed to city police, who held legal jurisdiction over the case.[14] Appreciative, Hoover instructed Ponder to have a report on the matter "on his desk" the following morning so that he could share this information with the president.

Nixon was deeply troubled by the latest police officer deaths. At 10:58 P.M., five and a half hours after his Executive Office Building meeting, he called Director Hoover at home. Once again, Nixon conveyed his wish to have the FBI engage in illegal surveillance practices.

When Hoover picked up the phone, the president got right to the point. "Edgar?"

"Yes, Mr. President."

"You're probably way ahead of me, but may I tell you that in terms of the New York situation, at this particular time, since these people have not been apprehended, *the national security information we seek is unlimited*, okay?"

"Okay."

"And you tell the Attorney General that's what I suggested—well *ordered*—and you do it, okay?"

Hoover agreed. "We'll go all out on the intelligence on this thing."[15]

Nixon and Hoover had always more or less agreed about how the state should respond to leftist guerrillas, at least in general terms. They shared the belief that the best way to combat revolutionary violence was not by addressing the sources of radicalism through policies aimed at reducing socioeconomic inequality and state violence, but through punitive policing. During their phone conversation, the pair mocked liberals whom they speculated would attribute the BLA's police ambushes to environmental conditions.

Nixon made no efforts to conceal his resentment: "The *New York Times* will probably write an article saying the man who shot [New York police officer Waverly Jones] was raised in a bad neighborhood."

"It'll be poverty, yes," Hoover agreed, his reply bitter with sarcasm. "The slums of New York, and housing, and all that sort of thing."

"But that's not the reason," Nixon said. "These people are bad people."

Hoover concurred.[16]

Voicing a visceral disgust, Nixon added, "It just sickens me to see people shoot policemen in the back."

To take Nixon's words at face value, he may indeed have been truly shaken by the killings. However, by framing BLA militants as "bad people" rather than as violent radicals who explicitly laid out the political grievances about state violence that had motivated their acts, the president and FBI director avoided reckoning with the assailants' motives. Such active denial of their own complicity in promoting police violence enabled the men to reassure one another of their moral righteousness as they dehumanized the guerrillas, seeking their capture and punishment. As Nixon put it, "By God let's get these bastards!"[17]

Despite sharing Nixon's politics, Hoover remained cautious about tactics. He continued to guard himself and FBI headquarters from connections to illegal surveillance. In his repeated assurances to the president throughout their phone call, he did not specify the surveillance techniques the bureau was using in its investigation of the New York killings.

Hoover was also sure to cover his back. The next morning, he called Attorney General John Mitchell and then fired off a memo to his top deputies: "I called the Attorney General and told him I wanted him to know that the President called me last night after I had reached home and said he wanted to make certain we didn't pull any punches in going all out in gathering information, particularly intelligence information, in this situation in New York (the slaying of the two police officers), and the President wanted me to let him, the Attorney General know. I said the President meant, I assumed, such wiretapping as we feel necessary."[18] In all likelihood, Hoover sought to use this memo to remind his men of his informal orders for illegal surveillance tactics while at the same time creating a documentary record of the president's demands and the attorney general's verbal approval in order to protect himself should news ever leak to the public.

Nixon likely sensed Hoover's reluctance to authorize illegal spy techniques. He was well aware that the director did not want to utilize such tactics without written authorization from the White House or attorney general. He called Hoover again two days later and broached the subject more directly. The president wanted to know—on a "case-by-case basis," if authorized by the attorney general, in cases involving "attacks on law enforcement officials," when "there is evidence or suspicion" that the perpetrators were "Panthers" or other ideologically motivated assailants—would the FBI "go in with everything you've got, in other words surveillance, electronic and everything"?[19]

Again, Hoover was evasive. Instead of answering Nixon directly, he launched into a detailed overview of what the FBI was already doing to investigate the Jones-Piagentini killings and prevent similar attacks in the future. Hoover explained that the FBI's New York field office had assigned an eighty-man special squad to the case and ordered New York–based Assistant

Director John Malone to "take it as an FBI case and break it as an FBI case" (New York FBI agents were to take care, however, to avoid a jurisdictional dispute with the NYPD). The director also discussed his plans to inform members of the International Association of Chiefs of Police about the bureau's new training programs to help local police departments investigate police killings. Hoover assured Nixon that the FBI had the investigation under control, and that he would inform the president if he needed further assistance from the White House. He also promised to prepare a memo that Attorney John Mitchell could use to explain the FBI's handling of the case to the press.[20]

Hoover continued to conceal the fact that the FBI was already utilizing break-ins, unauthorized wiretaps, and other illegal surveillance tactics in its Weather Underground investigation. The director also avoided informing Nixon that he had given the FBI's New York field office a new informal, wink-and-nod authorization to carry out break-ins for the NEWKILL investigation.

Though the White House was kept in the dark, FBI agents on the ground certainly grasped what was expected of them. In a May 27 memo, New York SAC Joseph Ponder indicated that FBI headquarters wanted agents to make an "all out effort to solve this case" using "every resource available." Among field agents—particularly in New York—such phrases were widely understood as euphemisms for illegal surveillance tactics. "We were to understand," Ponder wrote, "that money was no object and that any technical devices we might need should be made the subject of requests to the bureau and the Director was certain that they would be approved." "Technical devices" here referred to electronic listening devices—bugs—that usually required a break-in for installation. Ponder emphasized that Hoover was hoping to have "some positive developments" in the case before the president's meeting with police chiefs in less than two weeks.[21]

The pressure was mounting. In the name of saving police lives, responding to public outrage over police ambushes, and maintaining professional credibility, FBI personnel made hunting down the BLA its top priority.

The Black Liberation Army

The BLA's campaign of police assassinations won the group scarce new support, if any, at the time, and few would embrace similar tactics today. But to say, as Nixon and Hoover did, that those who killed Officers Jones and Piagentini did so simply because they were "bad people" is to warp the historical record beyond meaning. For one, such a characterization overlooks the fact that people can change over time. BLA guerrilla Herman Bell wound up serving a forty-five-year prison sentence for killing Officer Waverly Jones. While incarcerated, Bell expressed remorse for the killings, earned forgiveness from Jones's family members, and devoted much of his time behind bars to volunteer work, mentoring younger prisoners as a football coach and writing tutor. In the face of decades of this kind of self-lessness, empathy, and generosity, the efforts of police, prosecutors, and the press to portray Bell as a one-dimensional, evil "cop-killer" rang hollow.[22]

More crucially, the "bad people" characterization conveniently dodges the BLA's political motives. Above all else, BLA members were united in a visceral determination to retaliate for police violence against Black activists and communities. Former BLA member Assata Shakur remembered, "I understood some of my more impatient sisters and brothers. I knew that it was tempting to substitute military for political struggle, especially since all of our aboveground organizations were under vicious attack by the FBI, the CIA, and the local police agencies. All of us who saw our leaders murdered, our people shot down in cold blood, felt a need, a desire to fight back."[23] As Shakur's statement implied, BLA militants were also informed by Ché Guevara's *foco* theory and the BPP's East Coast–West Coast split, which the FBI covertly encouraged through COINTELPRO-Black Nationalist-Hate Groups. Together these developments pushed BLA members to commit themselves as revolutionaries at war with the police. However, the BLA's tactics never came close to igniting a mass revolutionary uprising as intended.

The BLA began to consolidate in early 1971 after heightened debates over the strategic merits of guerrilla warfare turned a growing cleavage within the BPP into a full-blown rupture. The BPP's partition occurred after the New York Panther Twenty-One issued a statement applauding the Weather Underground—"We wish you revolutionary victory in all you do"—while criticizing Huey Newton and the Panthers' Oakland-based leadership for moving the party away from guerrilla warfare. "Racism, colonialism, sexism, and other pig 'isms,'" they argued, "can only be ended by revolution . . . ARMED STRUGGLE."[24] Newton responded by expelling dissidents from the BPP: the Panther Twenty-One, LA Panther Geronimo Pratt (then incarcerated in Dallas), and the exiled Eldridge Cleaver.[25]

The FBI encouraged the Panther split. Continuing the pattern they had been pursuing since targeting the Panthers with COINTELPRO-BNHG in late 1968, domestic security agents used counterintelligence operations to exacerbate the organization's existing factional disputes and violent tendencies. In April 1970, COINTELPRO agents began sending fake letters to Eldridge Cleaver in Algeria and to Huey Newton and David Hilliard of Oakland's Central Committee to sow distrust and encourage factionalism. For example, a January 1971 letter purported to be from Huey Newton's personal secretary Connie Matthews warned Cleaver, "Things around headquarters are dreadfully disorganized with the comrade commander [Newton] not making proper decisions. . . . We must either get rid of the Supreme Commander or get rid of disloyal members." Another letter warned Huey Newton's brother Melvin that Panthers loyal to Cleaver planned to murder him, while another advised Eldridge Cleaver that other Panthers wished to harm his wife, Kathleen.[26]

FBI headquarters continued authorizing COINTELPROs to encourage the Panthers' East Coast–West Coast split until March 1971, when during a dispute over the *Black Panther* newspaper, Newton-allied Panthers in New York shot dead Cleaver faction member Robert Webb. After this incident, the bureau determined that "the differences between Newton and Cleaver . . . [were now] irreconcilable."[27] The Panthers' fratricide continued. On April 17, 1971, in the headquarters of the Oakland-aligned Corona Queens chapter, Cleaver faction militants gunned down the *Black Panther*'s national distributor Samuel Napier. After shooting Napier three times in the back, the assailants tied him to a bed, shot him in the skull, and burned the building to the ground.[28]

The Panthers expelled by Newton formed the core of the BLA. In February, New York Twenty-One members Dhoruba bin Wahad and Cetawayo Michael Tabor skipped their $150,000 bail and headed for the revolutionary underground along with Tabor's wife (and Newton's secretary) Connie Matthews. Tabor and Matthews resurfaced a few months later in Algeria with Eldridge Cleaver at the Panther embassy, while Wahad remained stateside to organize the BLA. Approximately fifty Panthers loyal to Cleaver soon joined Wahad in building clandestine BLA cells, with the two main cells based in New York City. Included in the ranks of the BLA were many members of the Panther Twenty-One, who were released from jail after receiving acquittals in May.[29] A handful of New York Panthers also remained aboveground to staff their Harlem office and distribute the Cleaver faction's newspaper *Right On!*, a publication printed with the financial support of white radicals that primarily consisted of exhortations to guerrilla warfare and the killing of police officers.[30]

As Wahad and others built the BLA underground, the Cleavers became the main spokespeople for Black urban guerrilla warfare in the United

States. Speaking to a leftist reporter in Algeria in April 1971, Kathleen Cleaver proclaimed, "What is necessary now is a party to advance and expedite the armed struggle. . . . There's a revolutionary war going on. The people are ready for a real vanguard, for military action. . . . We need a people's army and the Black Panther party vanguard will bring that about."[31] Eldridge Cleaver made similar statements in the pages of *Right On!*: "Our guns are turned on them. Let us fire at will. When they scream for law and order, they are asking us to stop. Our answer must be the bark of guns, bigger, better, and louder bombs, better placed and no phone calls warning them. The only open forum now is the barrel of a gun. Let the pigs debate with our bullets and talk back to our razor blades."[32]

Given the degree to which police violence shaped its members' lives and outlooks, it should be no surprise that the BLA moved to adopt Cleaver's concept of "revolutionary executions" of police officers as its central tactic.[33] However, violence begat violence, and escalation led to further escalation. Just as leftist guerrilla violence was succeeded by heavy-handed responses from the FBI and other law enforcement agencies, increasingly violent police tactics further radicalized the Black revolutionary underground.

A cycle of violence and escalation was spinning out of control. Hoover and Nixon used insurgent violence to rationalize punitive policing. Aggressive tactics, they believed, were necessary to fight a ruthlessly violent enemy. Such reasoning built on the violent antipolice rhetoric that Cleaver and other Panthers—including Huey Newton and Bobby Seale—had been promoting for the past three years, and seized upon bombings and assassinations as both vindication and a prompt for even more aggressive tactics.

While Nixon and Hoover misconstrued the insurgents by explaining their actions as simplistic acts of evil, the BLA's analysis of its adversaries suffered from distortions of its own. The turn to guerrilla violence ultimately rested on Cleaver-faction Panthers' analysis of the state. The Nixon administration and police were "fascist" and "Gestapo," and their violence had to be confronted with violence. Strategies that involved building power through labor organizing, nonviolent direct action, or electoral politics were indelibly tainted by the state's illegitimacy—these approaches were therefore ruled out. In a time of escalating repression against a fascist state, the only remaining way to maintain revolutionary resistance was through armed struggle. This hyperaggressive stance sapped the BLA of the ability to build coalitions with less revolutionary forces, forcing the small group into an all-or-nothing standoff against the massive resources of the state.

The BLA's autonomous cells differed from the rigidly hierarchical Weather Underground, as they had the ability to decide on their own what actions to carry out. This structure was a result of Eldridge Cleaver's belief that independent cells of six to twelve guerrillas could evade police surveillance more successfully than a centralized organization that could be neutralized through the arrest of its leader. Cleaver's decision also sprung from his desire to publicly distance himself from guerrilla activity, as Algerian government officials had forbidden him from using their country as a base to organize violence abroad. As Algeria sought to improve its relations with the United States in hopes of increasing oil exports, Cleaver had good reason to worry that his hosts would close the Panther embassy.[34]

The BLA's turn toward high-risk guerrilla actions also reflected its members' social positions. Unlike the white and largely middle-class Weather Underground (with some members from very wealthy families), BLA members were largely working-class African Americans without access to inherited money to subsidize life underground. Their white Weather Underground counterparts could fairly easily get away with shoplifting and check fraud, but in a society that tended to view all Blacks as potential criminals, BLA members did not have this luxury. The Weather Underground's preferred tactic of planting homemade bombs equipped with timing devices in government buildings and corporate offices was also largely off limits to the BLA, whose Black members had few hopes of entering such establishments without drawing suspicion.

Regardless, building an underground infrastructure required funding. To meet this need, New York City BLA members carried out a series of armed robberies (or as they called them, "expropriations") of banks and alleged drug dealers.[35]

These attacks had a second purpose as well. The BLA sought to fight back against a recent flood of heroin into Black communities, which it viewed as part of a government conspiracy to undermine African Americans' collective resistance to racism and oppressive living conditions.[36] Racially biased police neglect seemed to confirm the BLA's theory. Former BLA member Jamal Joseph recalled observing a Harlem drug den "where fifty, maybe a hundred, junkies flitted about buying drugs and running into the shooting galleries in full view of the community, with cops avoiding the area or ignoring it as they rode by in squad cars."[37] As far as Joseph and other Panthers who joined the BLA were concerned, the drug epidemic had been "brought on" with the "assistance and encouragement" of the same government forces that had indicted the Chicago Eight, the New York

Twenty-One, and various other leftists, waged imperialist wars abroad, and killed Fred Hampton and countless Black activists and community members.[38]

Joseph and his comrades had a point. The CIA had indeed covertly facilitated opium cultivation and heroin production in Southeast Asia as part of the U.S. war effort, and a large portion of these narcotics made its way into urban African American communities.[39] This process was part of a secretive multiagency web of state violence and corruption that operated with impunity on an international scale. But heroin trafficking was a vast and complex multilevel problem—not a centralized state conspiracy with the streamlined simplicity that BLA members alleged.

Regardless of the accuracy of their underlying analysis, the BLA also suffered from the reality that every armed action was liable to expose its members to discovery and arrest. A BLA robbery gone awry led to the bureau's first lead in its investigation. Before dawn on June 5, 1971, police officers in the Bronx responded to the sound of gunfire inside the Triple-O, an illegal after-hours establishment dedicated to drinking, gambling, and narcotics. When officers entered a room on the second floor, they found a strange scene. A group of about three dozen men and women stood awkwardly in rumpled clothes, many with their shirts untucked or missing a shoe.

It turned out that four heavily armed men had ordered a group of Triple-O patrons to strip naked. Another assailant combed their garments for money and valuables. The crew's leader had fired a .45-caliber M3A submachine gun into the ceiling, spattering the crowd with dust and plaster. When the cops pulled up outside, the robbers stashed their firearms under a table and tried to blend in with the group. The man with the machine gun ordered everyone to get dressed: "We're going to act like nothing happened, you dig?"

But not everyone complied. Once the police entered, one of the patrons franticly pointed out the gunmen. "That's him, and him and him and him." The police arrested the four men without resistance.[40]

Later that morning at New York's Forty-Eighth Precinct, the police figured out that the man with the machine gun was Dhoruba bin Wahad (a.k.a. Richard Moore), one of the New York Twenty-One. Another of the men was his codefendant, Jamal Jacobs. The police ballistics lab soon identified the seized machine gun as the same one used to ambush officers Curry and Binetti. The FBI laboratory traced fingerprints on the rifle to the BLA communiqués issued after the Curry-Binetti and Jones-Piagentini police ambushes. It turned out that Wahad had authored both statements.

The FBI and NYPD had a major break in their case less than two weeks after launching NEWKILL. In July, New York officials indicted Wahad and Joseph on a slew of charges related to skipping bond in the New York Twenty-One case, the Triple-O holdup, the Curry-Binetti ambush, and the March murder of Oakland-faction Panther Sam Napier.[41]

The BLA's political commitments notwithstanding, its hopes about the formation of a mass revolutionary "people's army" remained unrealized, and its tactics seemed only to push its goals further out of reach. No matter how deeply reasoned its political analysis, or heartfelt its motivations, the more police ambushes and armed robberies it undertook, the more the police mobilized to take it out. State violence only seemed to be getting worse.

Serendipity

The BLA and Weather Underground continued to stage attacks during the fall of 1971, but for many on the left, what was most memorable was the violence the state doled out. Two epochal traumas came in quick succession: the killing of Black revolutionary prisoner George Jackson by guards in California's San Quentin Prison on August 21, 1971, and the Attica prison massacre three weeks later. No criminal investigations followed these punitive spectacles of violence. Instead, Nixon applauded the police violence at Attica. The president called Governor Nelson Rockefeller shortly after New York State Police quashed the prisoner rebellion at Attica State Prison by raiding the facility with an indiscriminate barrage of tear gas and bullets, slaughtering twenty-nine prisoners and ten correctional officers who had been taken as hostages. "You did the right thing," Nixon assured the governor. "It's a tragedy those poor [hostages] were shot, but I just want you to know that's my view, and I've told the troops around here they're to back that to the hilt."[42]

Nixon's support for such brutal, unlawful state violence may seem hypocritical, but it was consistent with long-standing patterns. Nixon and Hoover's calls for law and order were never about the law, but about maintaining a particular political order through the selective use of the law. However, like the Nixon administration's conspiracy indictments and the FBI's COINTELPROs, ongoing police violence produced further ironic, unintended consequences. By defending a status quo built on racist state violence, Nixon and Hoover indirectly encouraged the very guerrilla violence against police officers that had thrown America's law enforcement institutions into crisis.

During the second half of 1971 the FBI was making important gains in its pursuit of the BLA, though it remained stymied in its hunt for Weather Underground fugitives. This divergence largely reflected differences in BLA's and Weather Underground's structures and tactical repertoires. While the BLA's deadly shooting attacks, robberies, and other hazardous actions exposed its members to police capture, the Weather Underground's more elaborate clandestine infrastructure and limited engagement in periodic nighttime bombings enabled its members to maintain evasion of the FBI's surveillance network for longer.

The relative success of the BLA investigation had little to do with the FBI's preventive intelligence efforts. The FBI remained unable to infiltrate the BLA's revolutionary underground or obtain advance warning of guerrilla attacks. But with millions of dollars in resources and man-hours poured into antiguerrilla investigations, FBI agents did manage to identify BLA suspects and distribute photographs and other information to police throughout the country. As with the Triple-O holdup, the FBI, NYPD, and other police agencies were well prepared to capture or kill BLA members when the guerrillas made fateful tactical mistakes—including botched robberies and assassination attempts—that attracted the attention of local police.[43]

The BLA investigation unfolded through a dynamic that Special Agent Ronald Butkiewicz later described as "serendipity." According to Butkiewicz, terrorism investigations "had to have some luck in addition to good work. . . . If you did the work once that luck came through it was like breaking through the barrier and you could really make some great progress."[44] A second round of breakthroughs in the FBI's BLA investigation picked up after a pair of muddled guerrilla actions in the summer of 1971.

On August 4, police surrounded a taxi that BLA guerrillas had commandeered after holding up an illicit Black social club in Harlem called Thelma's Lounge. Teenaged BLA member Twymon Myers temporarily held off the police with a spray of machine gun fire and escaped to a BLA safe house. But others were less fortunate. The clash resulted in the arrests of his three accomplices and the taxi driver's death.[45]

In the second incident, on August 27, San Francisco police officer George Kowalski arrested nineteen-year-old Jalil Muntaqim (a.k.a. Anthony Bottom) and thirty-year-old Albert Nuh Washington after the pair had attempted to assassinate Kowalski with a machine gun but missed their target. With his adrenaline surging and the nighttime city air rushing in through his squad car's blown-out windows, Kowalski managed to chase down his assailants and corner them in an alley.

Muntaqim's adolescent ego led to another FBI break in the NEWKILL case. In the police station's holding cell, while passing the hours in conversation, the young man mentioned to a cellmate that he and other Bay Area Panthers were responsible for a string of unclaimed local bombings and other attacks over the previous year. These included an ambush on a police station in San Francisco's Ingleside neighborhood that resulted in the death of Sergeant John Young two days after Muntaqim's and Washington's arrests—Muntaqim had cased the station five days earlier while filing a phony stolen bicycle report. Muntaqim also indicated that he had participated in the killing of New York police officers Jones and Piagentini.

Muntaqim's cellmate was an informant in the pay of the police, however, and gladly passed the information on to his handlers. San Francisco police officers' discovery of Waverly Jones's service revolver in Muntaqim and Washington's car corroborated Muntaqim's confession to the New York killings.[46] Muntaqim's loose talk also provided police with information used to identify other suspects in the Jones-Pagentini case. Principal among them was Herman Bell, who had gone into hiding in New Orleans.[47]

Hoover was sure to share the good news with Nixon and his staff. After the arrests of Muntaqim and Washington, the director sent John Ehrlichman several memos outlining the bureau's progress in its BLA investigation.[48]

All the while, the drumbeat of state violence was unrelenting. Police arrested Muntaqim and Washington just six days after guards in San Quentin Prison shot and killed Black revolutionary icon George Jackson, theorist of urban guerrilla warfare and older brother of the deceased Jonathan Jackson. Guards shot Jackson in the middle of the prison yard after he and other convicts staged a rebellion in which they took five correctional officers hostage—the latest episode in a two-year cycle of deadly violence between guards and revolutionary prisoners in California's prison system. San Quentin officials later claimed that Jackson's attorney Steven Bingham had smuggled a handgun into the prison during a visit, and that Jackson had hid it under a wig covering his Afro, though there are ample reasons to doubt this narrative.[49]

Even at the time, many on the left rejected the official story. With the assassinations of Malcolm X, Martin Luther King Jr., Fred Hampton, and many others fresh in their memories, Jackson's death was the latest example of a state conspiracy to violently repress dissent in America. Literary icon James Baldwin expressed such sentiment when he quipped, "No black person will ever believe George Jackson died the way they say he did."[50]

Over 2,000 supporters gathered for Jackson's funeral on August 28, 1971, spilling onto the sidewalk outside the overcrowded St. Augustine's Episcopal Church in Oakland. Huey Newton and other Black Power leaders gave eulogies.[51]

Leftist guerrillas swiftly struck back. A few hours before Jackson's funeral, a pair of Weather Underground bombs exploded in Sacramento and San Francisco, each damaging buildings that housed offices of the California Department of Corrections. In a communiqué issued to the *San Francisco Examiner*, the Weather Underground explained its attack as retaliation for Jackson's "assassination."[52]

Once again, the Weather Underground articulated a conspiratorial analysis of American state violence, one that generalized state actors and their motives, conceiving every act of violence inflicted upon a leftist as part of a conscious, coordinated plan to crush dissent. According to the Weather Underground, Jackson's death was part of a broader "pattern" in America's "attempts to control colonial peoples" through the "periodic assassination of major leaders" such as Patrice Lumumba—the socialist Congolese president killed by domestic rivals in 1961 with CIA backing—and Malcolm X, whom Nation of Islam gunmen murdered in 1965. The Weather Underground downplayed Jackson's violent role in the conflict at San Quentin, asserting that his "execution represents a major attempt at mass propaganda—to convince the youth who are now entering the Folsoms and the Quentins that rebellion is hopeless, that those who inspire and lead will pay the price of death."[53]

The BLA promoted a similar view. In a communiqué taking credit for the August 29 Ingleside police station attack, the BLA's "George L. Jackson Assault Squad" announced that it had killed Sergeant Young to avenge the "intolerable political assassination of Comrade George Jackson, in particular, and the inhumane torture of P.O.W. (Prisoner of War) Camps in general."[54]

George Jackson's killing unleashed another round of bloodshed: more political rebellion, another major incident of state violence against incarcerated people, and further leftist guerrilla retaliation.

On September 9, in New York's Attica State Prison, a silent protest mourning Jackson's death escalated into an all-out four-day uprising as prisoners—Black, Puerto Rican, and white—overtook the institution's D yard. Holding forty-two guards hostage, Attica's prisoners ignited a twenty-four-hour television news drama viewed throughout the world as they issued a list of demands for basic reforms in the institution's policies. "We are men, we are not beasts, and we do not intend to be beaten or driven as such," the prisoners declared. Their rebellion, they explained, was a response to the "unmitigated oppression wrought by the racist administration network of this prison."[55] Governor Nelson Rockefeller refused to negotiate, however, and the uprising ended in a police-inflicted bloodbath.[56]

The Weather Underground hit back once again. Four days later, the guerrillas' bomb exploded in a ninth-floor women's bathroom next to the offices of the New York State Commissioner of Corrections in Albany. "We must continue to make the Rockefellers, Oswalds, Reagans, and Nixons pay for their crimes," the group stated in its subsequent communiqué. "We only wish we could do more to show the courageous prisoners at Attica, San Quentin, and the other 20th century slave ships that they are not alone in the fight for the right to live."[57]

Yet a coordinated state conspiracy at the level the Weather Underground, BLA, and other militant leftists insinuated was not necessary to explain the George Jackson killing and Attica massacre. Both incidents were far more easily explained by long-standing patterns of federal officials looking the other way, or even offering encouragement, while local police and prison guards inflicted violence on political dissidents and racialized minorities.

This political analysis mattered because it framed the operating capacity of activists to make change. If, as Weathermen and the BLA believed, the United States was a fascist society bent on systematically stomping out resistance through coordinated Gestapo tactics, clandestine insurgent violence was the only recourse. But there were counterexamples that suggested that such claims may be overly simplistic. In some instances in the American past, organized leftist social movements had managed to pressure the federal government to take action against local repressive police violence. This was the case in 1964, when an international outcry over the murders of Mississippi civil rights workers James Chaney, Andrew Goodman, and Michael Schwerner compelled President Johnson to demand that Hoover's FBI crack down on the Klan and its collusion with southern police forces. Movements had the power to make demands and force change—but context mattered. Such federal intervention was not forthcoming, however, amid the disintegration of the U.S. Left and the Nixon administration's law-and-order crackdown on political rebellion.

Nixon and Hoover continued to condemn leftist violence while condoning police violence. Instead of mandating an FBI investigation of laws broken by New York State officials at Attica, the president praised the mass killing of prisoners and hostages, reiterating to Governor Rockefeller his belief that if he had granted the prisoners' request for immunity from prosecution, "it would have meant that you would have prisoners in an uproar all over the country." "The courage you showed . . . it was right," Nixon told Rockefeller, "and I don't care what the hell the papers or anybody else says."[58] Meanwhile, in response to a request from the Justice Department's Civil Rights Division, which faced pressure from liberals in Congress to oversee San Quentin guards' handling of the incidents that led to George Jackson's death, Hoover revealed his clear sympathies with the prison authorities. The director explicitly instructed his agents to inform San Quentin officials and staff that the FBI was conducting the investigation at the "specific request" of David L. Norman, assistant attorney general in charge of the Justice Department's Civil Rights Division.[59] By relaying such information to San Quentin officials, FBI agents signaled that their investigation was a formality undertaken begrudgingly on behalf of the Justice Department. In October 1971, after conducting a "limited" three-day investigation of George Jackson's death, FBI agents determined that prison staff had committed no wrongdoing.[60]

Nixon and Hoover were not alone in supporting the state violence in San Quentin and Attica. Many Americans were understandably horrified by the television news media's initial false reports that the Attica prisoners had castrated and slit the throats of their correctional officer hostages as police stormed the facility. After a steady media diet of violent prison uprisings and urban guerrillas, some were inclined to see the epidemic of violence as symptomatic of a breakdown in traditional respect for political authority. Historian Heather Ann Thompson has explained that among white Americans in particular, there was a widespread feeling that "it was now time to rein in 'those' black and brown people who had been so vocally challenging authority and pushing the civil rights envelope."[61]

California governor Ronald Reagan spoke to these feelings when he praised San Quentin and Attica officials' use of deadly force against prisoner rebellions. The *New York Times* published an op-ed by Reagan that discussed George Jackson in terms reminiscent of Hoover and Nixon. All Americans, Reagan insisted, would "become prisoners" of deadly chaos if they accepted "the falsehood that violence, terror and contempt for the moral values of our society are acceptable methods of seeking redress of grievances."[62] No one could have predicted at the time that California's right-wing governor would go on to win the 1980 presidential election, and once in office, make fighting terrorism a cornerstone of his efforts to both undo post-Watergate restrictions on FBI domestic surveillance and launch U.S. military interventions in Latin America and the Middle East.

In the meantime, while police continued to kill people and get away with it, Hoover worried that the BLA had more violence in store. "During the past several months," the director alerted his men in late September 1971, "the Cleaver faction of the Black Panther Party has moved on a course of increased violence, lawlessness, and terror. . . . Although many of these criminals have been arrested for extremist-related activity, a substantial hardcore of fanatics remains highly active and I consider their potential for violence and disruption greater today than ever before." Relaying information gleaned from paid informants, Hoover warned that Cleaver-faction Panthers were considering kidnapping businessmen or police officers in efforts to bargain for the release of "jailed extremists."[63]

In hopes of preventing such violence, Hoover provided FBI field offices with a new round of ambiguous orders, directives that some agents likely interpreted as euphemistic encouragement to utilize illegal surveillance practices.

Hoover instructed his men to pursue the BLA "with renewed vigor and imagination." "I consider no extremist investigation to be routine," he emphasized. "Investigations must be of the highest degree of thoroughness and informant coverage must never be considered adequate." The aim of FBI operations, the director stressed, was to prevent leftist guerrilla attacks. Surveillance, he explained, "must have preventative capabilities, that is, we must know in advance, wherever possible, of plans and propensities for violence."[64]

Hoover also gave his agents a green light to utilize counterintelligence operations against aboveground supporters of guerrilla violence, a tactic he had banned for domestic use six months earlier. Such operations were to include "disruptive efforts to be aimed at the Cleaver Faction and similar groups" and "use of news and publicity media to counter frequent proextremist programs."[65] The extent of the FBI's use of illegal counterintelligence and surveillance tactics into its BLA investigation is unknown. A document buried in the National Archives verifies that the FBI's New York office carried out illegal break-ins and wiretaps targeting New York Panthers in late 1972, after Hoover's death in May. Such activities likely started earlier, however, following Hoover's September 1971 orders to the field.[66]

FBI and police harassment contributed to the disintegration of New York's remaining aboveground Black Panther chapter. From their headquarters on Harlem's Seventh Avenue, New York Panthers with secret connections to the BLA underground used stolen credit cards to make international calls to the Panther embassy in Algiers to speak with Don Cox, Sekou Odinga, Cetawayo Tabor, and occasionally Eldridge Cleaver. FBI agents listened in from their wiretap. During a call in the summer of 1971, former Panther Twenty-One defendant and secret BLA member Lumumba Shakur lamented on the dwindling of the New York Panthers' membership after the Jones-Piagentini killings. "Everyone is just too scared," he groaned. "They all running and hiding in fear."[67]

The New York Panthers' disintegration occurred amid the organization's decline on a national level. In August 1971, the FBI's Domestic Security Division boasted a drastic decrease in the organization's membership from a high of over 1,000 in January 1968 to approximately 710. According to the bureau, 156 of these members—21.7 percent of the party—were FBI informants.[68]

There is no evidence, however, to suggest that counterintelligence, mass surveillance, or illegal spy tactics helped the FBI capture BLA guerrillas or prevent their violence. Those speaking with exiled comrades in Algeria had enough sense to avoid discussing sensitive information on the phone. Instead, authorities made gains on the BLA when the guerrillas made mistakes. The police managed to capture or kill many BLA members between October 1971 and February 1972 as the guerrillas unleashed a haphazard crescendo of holdups and police assassinations stretching from New York to Atlanta to St. Louis. When it was over, the body count included three more cops and two more BLA soldiers, and thirteen more guerrillas were in police custody, including Most Wanted fugitive H. Rap Brown.[69]

The FBI, NYPD, and other police agencies continued their investigations of the BLA after the last round of arrests in St. Louis. And in March, a group of BLA members who remained at large managed to release a wordy, twenty-eight-page "message to the Third World" in which they evaluated their guerrilla activities and promised further violence. The authors dedicated their manifesto to several Black radicals who had died at the hands of police officers as well as "the brothers who were murdered at Attica." The BLA, the document proclaimed, consisted of "small urban guerrilla units . . . the embryonic form of the People's Army . . . waging armed struggle against the agents of death—the United States government."[70]

But the group was severely damaged. The BLA would not launch another attack on police until nearly a year later.

· · · · · ·

At the height of the FBI's war with the BLA, on November 22, 1971, President Nixon phoned J. Edgar Hoover to express his approval of the bureau's performance hunting down the men who killed New York officers Waverly Jones and Joseph Piagentini. Hoover had just announced that the FBI had ascertained the identities of the "five black terrorists who participated in the planning and assassination of these two officers": Jalil Muntaqim and Albert Washington, still held in California for the attempted murder of a San Francisco police officer, and Herman Bell, Gabriel Torres, and Francisco Torres, who remained at large.[71]

"That's a fantastic story," Nixon gushed. "I'm just delighted. . . . Be sure you let the boys over there [in the FBI] know I think it's just great."[72]

Without knowledge of the wider context, someone today listening to Nixon's secret tape recording of this conversation might presume the president and the FBI director were getting along swimmingly. In their brief phone call, each man lavished praise on the other and poured scorn on New York's liberal police chief Patrick V. Murphy, whom they both despised. (Nixon called him a "jackass"; Hoover replied, "I have no use for him.")[73]

Beneath the macho veneer of collegiality, however, Nixon and Hoover's relationship was at an all-time low. The institutional conflict between Hoover and Nixon that began with the Huston Plan had taken a new turn in June 1971 following the leak of a massive classified military intelligence report known as the *Pentagon Papers*. In its battle with the BLA, the FBI had informally expanded its illegal surveillance operations and improvised new counterterrorism methods. Though such efforts were limited in effectiveness, the capture of key BLA assailants like Muntaqim and Washington were welcome victories for Nixon's racially biased law and order, and temporarily eased strains between the president and the FBI director. But the good feelings did not last long.

As the FBI's war with the Weather Underground and the BLA continued to rage, a surprise career breakthrough set the bureau's chief inspector on a new and fateful trajectory. On July 1, 1971, J. Edgar Hoover called W. Mark Felt into his office. The director immediately rose to his feet and cut to the chase. "Felt, I am creating a new position in the chain of command. I am calling it Deputy Associate Director, and it will be the number three position in the Bureau. You are the one I have selected for this assignment."[1]

Felt was astonished. "While I was sure I had been handling my job in a way that would please the Director," he later recalled, "it had never occurred to me that such high responsibility was so close." But Felt contained his awe and responded to his boss as professionally as he could. "Mr. Hoover, I am extremely gratified—more than I can say. I will try to do a good job for you."[2]

Hoover made it clear that something other than merit was behind Felt's promotion. In truth, he was still waging bureaucratic war against President Nixon and the FBI's assistant director William Sullivan after coming to a head a year earlier over Hoover's refusal to go along with the Huston Plan. Now it was reaching a breaking point, and the new position set Felt up to offer Hoover cover that he desperately needed.

The latest flare-up came in response to the actions of a CIA-trained policy analyst named Daniel Ellsberg. After experiencing a crisis of conscience over the U.S. war in Vietnam, Ellsberg leaked to journalists a massive classified Defense Department report known as the *Pentagon Papers*. The meticulously researched monograph offered an astonishing revelation: every president from Harry Truman to Lyndon Johnson had lied to the American people about the efficacy of the United States' escalating military operations in Southeast Asia. Though the *Pentagon Papers* did not implicate him, Nixon worried that further leaks could undermine both his presidency and his efforts to win the war he had inherited against South Vietnam's guerrilla insurgents.[3]

In order to suppress the *Pentagon Papers*, Nixon flexed his executive powers. The White House filed an injunction in the name of national security to bar the *New York Times* and *Washington Post* from printing Ellsberg's leaked government documents. Nixon officials also sought to influence the FBI's investigation of the matter. The president had learned from William Sullivan that Hoover did not want his agents to interview Ellsberg's father-in-law Louis Marx, a wealthy toy manufacturer who contributed annually to a Christmas charity run by the FBI director.[4] Hoover had explicitly denied a request to interview Marx from Sullivan's right-hand man, Charles Brennan, but the domestic security chief had already gone ahead with the interview without his boss's permission. Hoover was furious. As soon as he heard the news, he demoted Brennan to the position of SAC of the FBI's Cleveland field office, but Attorney General John Mitchell quickly intervened on behalf of the president. Mitchell successfully persuaded the director to reinstate Brennan.[5]

More than two years after Sullivan and Brennan first went behind his back to collaborate with Tom Huston on a White House plan for combatting guerrilla terrorism, Hoover finally realized that his top domestic security officials were disloyal. Hoover now promoted Felt in order to isolate Sullivan and Brennan and to maintain the FBI's autonomy from the White House. The director made his intentions crystal clear. "Felt, I need someone who can control Sullivan," he said. "Watch everything that comes out of the Domestic Intelligence Division very closely. I want to slow them down. They are going too far."[6]

Felt's activities at the top of the FBI hierarchy would have far-reaching consequences. It is widely understood that in his role as the Watergate leaker known as Deep Throat, Felt would help bring down the Nixon presidency. Until now, however, scholars have yet to explain why Felt decided to expose Nixon's use of illegal break-ins while at the same time secretly working with Edward Miller, his handpicked replacement for Charles Brennan as head of domestic intelligence, to achieve official FBI reauthorization of the very same sort of break-ins for investigations of the Weather Underground and other leftist guerrillas.

W. Mark Felt was not the Deep Throat figure mythologized in Woodward and Bernstein's 1973 best seller *All the President's Men* or in Felt's 2006 autobiography cowritten with John O'Connor, which served as the basis for the 2013 film *Mark Felt: The Man Who Brought Down the White House*, starring Liam Neeson as the virtuous protagonist. Though guided by a certain set of principles, Felt was no selfless hero acting purely to defend the U.S. Constitution and the American presidency from Nixon's unlawful abuses of executive power.[7] The real Felt had no problem using break-ins to go after leftist guerrillas and others the FBI deemed a threat to U.S. national

W. Mark Felt speaking on the television show *Face the Nation* in 1976, as he prepared to face a federal indictment for his authorization of FBI break-ins targeting suspected supporters of the Weather Underground. In 2005, at age ninety-one, Felt would admit to his role as "Deep Throat," the secret source whose leaks to the press helped fuel the Watergate scandal. AP Photo/File.

security. Like Hoover, he was not opposed to illegal surveillance techniques per se, but to Nixon's use of such tactics for partisan political objectives.

As both a Hoover loyalist working to defend the bureau from the Nixon White House and a leader of the FBI's war on leftist guerrillas, Felt shaped the FBI and American politics in two important ways. The first was by taking the mantle from Hoover in his bureaucratic war with the Nixon administration. The *Pentagon Papers* leak precipitated a final rift between Hoover and Nixon. A day after the Supreme Court ruled that the newspapers could continue publishing excerpts of the *Pentagon Papers*—and the very same day of Felt's promotion—Nixon telephoned Hoover to pressure the FBI director to pursue an aggressive investigation of Daniel Ellsberg, one that would include the use of break-ins and other illegal surveillance practices. Using such tactics to hunt down leftist guerrillas was one thing, but deploying them against Ellsberg was a line Hoover would not cross. When Hoover refused Nixon, the president set off on the road to Watergate.

Nixon's men quickly formed their own secret intelligence unit. Dubbed "the Plumbers," the shadowy band of former federal intelligence agents and Cuban counterrevolutionaries got paid in cash to stop leaks of classified information damaging to the president. Nixon's covert operatives did what Hoover would not. They carried out their first illegal break-in in September 1971, burglarizing the Los Angeles office of Daniel Ellsberg's psychiatrist. The following June, five of Nixon's Plumbers got caught red-handed breaking into the headquarters of the Democratic National Committee in Washington's Watergate office complex.

At FBI headquarters, bureaucratic conflicts unfolded at breakneck speed. In the fall of 1971, Hoover fired Sullivan and Brennan and promoted Edward Miller. Sullivan tried to blackmail Hoover in retaliation, and Nixon attempted to fire the FBI director, yet neither could unseat Washington's most powerful bureaucrat.

But like other mortals, Hoover could not live forever. Felt noticed something different about Hoover during their brief meeting about his promotion. "The Director looked tired," he recalled.[8] Ten months later, Hoover was dead. On May 2, 1972, after leading the FBI for nearly forty-eight years, the director, age seventy-seven, died in his home of a heart attack.

Felt fully expected an appointment as Hoover's successor. After all, the FBI's number two man, Hoover's best friend Clyde Tolson, was aging and in poor health. However, the president instead chose L. Patrick Gray, an assistant attorney general and bureau outsider whom Nixon hoped would serve as a dutiful White House ally.[9] With Nixon's appointment of Gray as acting director of the FBI, Felt took on a role as heir to Hoover's bureaucratic war with the White House. After the Watergate break-in, Felt escalated his bureaucratic conflict with Nixon into a secret counterintelligence war, anonymously leaking critical information from the FBI's Watergate investigation to journalists such as the *Washington Post*'s Bob Woodward.

But Felt influenced history in a less widely known way through his contributions to the development of American counterterrorism. Much of this happened in collaboration with Assistant Director for Domestic Security Edward Miller. Felt supervised Miller as he listened to the concerns of FBI field agents involved in leftist guerrilla investigations, who worried over whether headquarters would support them if they got caught carrying out illegal break-ins. Like Sullivan and Brennan, Felt and Miller wanted the FBI to reinstitute illegal surveillance tactics on an official basis, hoping to boost field agents' morale as they hunted for clandestine guerrilla revolutionaries. But unlike their predecessors, Felt and Miller remained loyal to Hoover, even after his death. Felt and Miller's efforts to compel both J. Edgar Hoover and L. Patrick Gray to reauthorize FBI break-ins were part of their broader endeavor to modernize the bureau. Over the course of shifting domestic security priorities from fighting Communist subversion to combating revolutionary terrorism, the men laid the groundwork for the FBI's emerging counterterrorism doctrine.

Bureaucratic War and Nixon's Break-Ins

President Nixon began discussing break-ins as a response to the *Pentagon Papers* leak on the morning of July 1, before his phone call to J. Edgar Hoover that evening. Nixon's secret White House tape recording system captured him speaking with his chief of staff H. R. Haldeman about his belief that the Brookings Institution, a liberal Washington think tank, might have files linking Ellsberg to a wider conspiracy to leak classified state secrets.[10] "We're up against an enemy, a conspiracy. . . . We're going to use any means!" he exclaimed. The president knocked on his desk with each word for emphasis. "I want the Brookings Institute safe cleaned out!"[11]

Nixon's idea to use break-ins probably came from the FBI. Edward Miller later recalled that William Sullivan and Tom Huston had convinced the president that "surreptitious entries" were a "gangbuster investigative technique."[12] At any rate, Nixon telephoned Hoover at six in the evening.[13]

Just as he did after Jonathan Jackson's Marin County courthouse raid and after the BLA's assassination of New York police officers Waverly Jones and Joseph Piagentini, Nixon contacted Hoover to let him know that he wanted the FBI to pursue an aggressive investigation of Ellsberg.

The president fell short of making a direct request, though. Instead, he eased into the matter diplomatically by first asking Hoover for advice on public relations. The director cautioned against making any public statements about the matter. "We oughta be awful careful about what we do in the case of this man Ellsberg," Hoover said. The press would "make a martyr" out of Ellsberg, he warned, if it seemed that the government was persecuting the whistleblower. Always sensitive to public perceptions, Hoover knew that such a scenario would undermine the credibility of both the FBI and the Nixon administration. "I doubt whether we're going to be able to get a conviction of him," Hoover asserted, referring to the Justice Department's indictment of Ellsberg under the Espionage Act of 1917. "I hope so, but I doubt it."[14]

Nixon was not satisfied. "Well I'd like to check some of the other people around him," he said. "I think there's a conspiracy involved."

Hoover dodged Nixon's comment. The director launched into a rant complaining about journalists at the *Times* and *Post* before returning the conversation to the president's press strategy.[15] As he had done a month earlier in response to Nixon's suggestion that the FBI utilize illegal surveillance techniques in its BLA investigation, Hoover resisted Nixon's efforts to influence the FBI's investigation of the *Pentagon Papers*.

The call ended and Nixon flew into a rage. The president interpreted Hoover's evasiveness as a refusal to investigate the *Pentagon Papers* leak beyond Ellsberg. Nixon complained to Haldeman the next day: "I talked to Hoover last night and Hoover is not going after this case as strong as I would like. There's something dragging him." Again, Nixon brought up his suspicion of a conspiracy. "I want to go after everyone. I'm not so interested in Ellsberg," Nixon said, "but we have to go after everybody who's a member of this conspiracy."[16]

When Hoover refused to go along with Nixon's plans, the president's men formed the Plumbers. As Nixon recalled in his memoir, "If the FBI was not going to pursue the case, then we would have to do it ourselves."[17]

The president put Ehrlichman in charge of establishing the unit. On July 17, 1971, Ehrlichman assigned Egil Krogh and Kissinger's former National Security Council staffer David Young to take direct charge. Lacking intelligence training, Krogh and Young hired former CIA investigator E. Howard Hunt and FBI veteran G. Gordon Liddy to assist them.[18] There is no evidence that the operatives ever carried out the proposed Brookings Institution break-in, but in late August, Ehrlichman approved the unit's plans to break into the Los Angeles office of Ellsberg's psychiatrist, Dr. Lewis Fielding. Ehrlichman authorized the raid on one stipulation: "that it is not traceable."[19]

Hunt and Liddy traveled to Los Angeles and carried out the break-in on September 3, 1971, with the assistance of anti-Castro Cuban operatives Bernard Barker, Eugenio Martinez, and Felipe de Diego. Inside Dr. Fielding's office, the Plumbers used a crowbar to open a locked metal filing cabinet, leaving it visibly dented. In their search for information that could damage or discredit Ellsberg, however, the operatives came up empty-handed.[20]

While Nixon's staff formed the Plumbers, Hoover and Mark Felt dealt with William Sullivan and Charles Brennan. Hoover had begun to question Sullivan's loyalty in October 1970 after the FBI's arrest of Angela Davis in a Manhattan hotel, where she had been hiding from charges related to Jonathan Jackson's Marin County courthouse raid. At a press conference, Sullivan had publicly cited guerrilla violence as a greater threat to America's domestic security than Communist subversion. The United States would be confronting violence from radical students and Black militants "to a greater or lesser extent if the Communist Party in this country didn't exist at all," he said.[21] Though it was an off-the-cuff statement, the press circulated it widely. Sullivan's remarks infuriated the director, who viewed the comment as an act of insubordination that undermined the bloated FBI Domestic Security Division's raison d'être. Hoover sternly rebuked Sullivan in a handwritten note: "We must be *most careful not to downgrade the activities of the C.P.*," inaccurately describing the ailing Communist Party as "*a real continuing factor to our unrest.*"[22]

Felt believed that the Angela Davis incident, along with a desire to replace Hoover as FBI director, prompted Sullivan to "come out in the open in his bid for power."[23] That is certainly how it seemed after the *Pentagon Papers* leak—when Charles Brennan interviewed Daniel Ellsberg's father-in-law against the director's wishes, and Sullivan went to Nixon to get Hoover to reverse Brennan's demotion. To make matters worse, shortly after Felt's promotion, the *Washington Post* published a series of articles by journalists Robert Novak and Roland Evans asserting that in his old age, the director was no longer fit to run the FBI. Hoover and Felt believed that the articles had been written using information leaked from Sullivan.[24]

After Felt's promotion, however, it did not take long for Sullivan to figure out that his days working for Hoover were numbered. In early September, at Felt's suggestion, Hoover promoted Edward Miller to Charles Brennan's post at the head of the Domestic Intelligence Division and isolated Brennan by putting him in charge of a new special unit dedicated to the *Pentagon Papers* case (Nixon would not object to this, Felt speculated, since it would be "giving the White House exactly what it asked for").[25] At this time Hoover also formally instructed Sullivan to submit his application for retirement. Before he complied, however, Sullivan engaged in another showdown with Mark Felt.

It turned out that in an effort to blackmail Hoover, Sullivan had instructed Brennan to relocate secret files pertaining to the "Kissinger wiretaps," the illegal bugs of Justice Department officials and journalists that Nixon and Henry Kissinger had persuaded Hoover to establish in early 1969 to uncover the source of leaks about the president's war in Cambodia. Hoover had been reluctant to authorize the wiretaps, and at the time he ordered Sullivan to keep the files in a special location outside the bureau's top-secret Official and Confidential filing system. In case the public ever found out, Hoover wanted evidence that orders for the wiretaps had come from the White House. But before his ouster, Sullivan removed the files in a last-ditch effort to topple Hoover. Unbeknownst to the director, Sullivan ordered Brennan to transfer the files to the office of their ally in the Justice Department, Assistant Attorney General Robert Mardian, who passed them along to Nixon's advisor John Ehrlichman.[26] Under Hoover's orders, Felt and Miller spent over a week scouring FBI headquarters for the files, to no avail.

Felt learned of the files' location on October 6, after Sullivan returned to his office from his last paid annual leave in order to pack his belongings. When Felt confronted Sullivan about the matter, he responded with bitterness. "If you want to know more, you'll have to talk to the Attorney General." When Felt called him a "Judas," Sullivan challenged Felt to a fistfight. "He was like a little banty rooster," Felt recalled, "and I think he really would have fought me had I accepted the challenge, although I am half again his size."[27]

Sullivan's machinations nearly succeeded in ousting Hoover. Nixon attempted to fire the FBI director, in part, because of Sullivan telling him that Hoover "was trapped in outdated notions of the communist threat and was not moving with flexibility against the new violence-prone radicals."[28] Nixon tried to ask the director for his resignation on September 20, 1971, during a private breakfast that he had arranged precisely for this purpose. "As gently and subtly" as he could, the president urged Hoover to resign on his own accord. Nixon later remembered telling Hoover "it would be a tragedy if he ended his career while under a sustained attack from his long-time critics instead of in the glow of national respect that he so rightly deserved."[29]

But the president backed down after Hoover pulled yet another classic bureaucratic power maneuver. The director informed his superior that he would resign only under direct orders. "More than anything else, I want to see *you* re-elected in 1972," Hoover replied. "If you feel that my staying on as head of the Bureau hurts your chances for re-election, just let me know." Afraid of alienating the director's large base of conservative supporters ahead of the 1972 election, Nixon ultimately decided that firing Hoover "would raise more political problems than it would solve."[30] Just as he had maintained control over the FBI in the aftermath of the Huston Plan, the New York police shootings, and the *Pentagon Papers* leak, Hoover once again blocked Nixon's effort to control the FBI.

It was only a matter of time until the next showdown between the FBI and the White House. It came in March 1972, this time with Mark Felt at the forefront. Muckraking journalist Jack Anderson had just published a story based on a leaked memo from a woman named Dita Beard, who worked as a lobbyist for the ITT Corporation. In the memo, Beard had boasted to her employer that Attorney General Mitchell agreed to quash an antitrust case against the company in exchange for a $400,000 contribution to the Republican Party for the 1972 National Convention. When the story broke, Beard insisted the memo was forged, and Nixon's staff sent the document to the FBI laboratory to corroborate the lobbyist's claim.[31]

The Nixon administration's request arrived on Mark Felt's desk on March 10. It came from L. Patrick Gray, a former World War II navy submarine captain and longtime Nixon supporter who had assumed the position of assistant attorney general a little more than a week earlier (he had taken the place of Richard Kleindienst, who had become attorney general-designate after Mitchell stepped down on March 1 to direct Nixon's reelection campaign).[32] Felt attested that Assistant Attorney General Gray, Assistant Attorney General Robert Mardian, and White House counsel John Dean repeatedly interfered with the FBI lab's analysis over the course of the following week in an attempt to pressure the bureau to conclude that the Beard document was a forgery. To the chagrin of the White House, however, the FBI lab determined that Beard's memo was authentic.[33]

Nixon was furious when he heard that Hoover and Felt stood behind the analysis.[34] But as far as Felt was concerned, the Dita Beard incident was just the latest example of Nixon's many attempts to wield control over the FBI in order to advance a partisan political agenda. "Looking back," Felt later wrote, "I am glad that the FBI was able to resist White House pressure to take part in a cover-up which in some ways was a prelude to Watergate."[35]

It would be the last of Hoover's duels with Nixon. The war between the bureau and the White House was far from over, but less than six weeks after the ITT–Dita Beard showdown, Hoover died in his sleep.

L. Patrick Gray was as surprised as anyone when Nixon appointed him to serve as the FBI's acting director—when he received notice that the president wanted to speak with him, he assumed that Nixon wanted to discuss a development in the ITT controversy. To Felt, the president's choice for Hoover's successor sent a clear signal: Nixon wanted "his man" to control the FBI.[36]

You would not have known that Hoover and the president had been butting heads for the past three and a half years if you were one of the thousands of Americans watching the late FBI director's funeral during its live television broadcast. Nixon praised Hoover and his forty-eight-year career as "the invincible and incorruptible defender of every American's precious right to be free from fear."[37] Instead of letting on that Hoover had blocked his administration's efforts to manipulate America's political institutions, Nixon responded to criticism of FBI domestic surveillance by promising to uphold Hoover's policing practices. "There is a belief that the changing of the guard will also mean a changing of the rules," Nixon declared. "With J. Edgar Hoover this will not happen. The FBI will carry on in the future, true to its finest traditions in the past."[38]

Despite his frustrations with Hoover, Nixon fully supported the FBI's mass surveillance of America's antiwar and Black Power movements, especially when carried out in an effort to prevent leftist guerrilla attacks. Now, with Hoover out of his way at last, the president sought to exert direct White House influence over the bureau.

The FBI's Break-Ins and Domestic Counterterrorism

Throughout these bureaucratic battles and Hoover's shuffling of his top administrators, the FBI continued its war with domestic leftist guerrillas. By the time of Mark Felt's promotion, the FBI and local police agencies had scored key arrests and leads in their investigations of the BLA. The Weather Underground remained at large, however, having pulled off four bombings during the fall of 1971, including a blast at the Massachusetts Institute of Technology on October 15. Yet the Weather Underground's pace was slowing as internal differences threatened to tear the group apart from the inside. Members continued to grapple with an existential crisis amid their failure to revive a declining U.S. Left. Unaware of these dynamics, bureau officials worried about the possibility of another high-profile guerrilla attack. Their fears were realized on May 19, 1972, two weeks after L. Patrick Gray took on the position of acting director of the FBI, when the Weather Underground bombed the Pentagon. In response to these developments, and with Felt in a critical position of leadership, the FBI took important new measures to overhaul its domestic security operations.

The main person responsible for revamping the FBI's urban guerrilla investigations was Assistant Director for Domestic Security Edward Miller, who led the bureau's Domestic Security Division as Felt's handpicked successor to William Sullivan's retainer, Charles Brennan. Like many of Hoover's FBI men, Miller was a World War II veteran and a devout Catholic. He was also a firm believer in break-ins as a necessary tactic for defending U.S. national security from revolutionary dissidents. "Revolutions always start in a small way," he argued, and the FBI "must be able to find out what stage the revolution is in."[39] During the 1950s, Miller participated in dozens of top-secret black-bag jobs against alleged Communists. In 1969, after a promotion to the position of assistant SAC of the bureau's Chicago field office, he oversaw surveillance of Weatherman's Days of Rage and helped persuade Chicago Eight trial judge Julius Hoffman to place the disruptive defendant Bobby Seale in shackles.[40] More recently, Miller had been working under Felt in the FBI's Inspection Division.[41]

Both Felt and Miller shared core beliefs with their predecessors, Sullivan and Brennan. They believed that the FBI needed to update its approach to domestic security to address the threat of urban guerrilla insurgency and felt strongly that the FBI should reauthorize break-ins, mail opening, and warrantless wiretapping for leftist guerrilla investigations. The critical difference, of course, was that the newly promoted officials were loyal to Hoover and the FBI, remaining so even after the director's death.

With Miller leading the initiative and Felt acting in a supervisory role, both men worked during the year after their promotions to improve the bureau's effectiveness in suppressing America's urban guerrilla insurgency. Beginning under Hoover and continuing under L. Patrick Gray, Miller developed knowledge on investigating clandestine urban guerrilla organizations through discussions with FBI field agents and members of other police agencies. He refined his findings into a theoretical doctrine and tactical repertoire—a nascent counterterrorism. Feedback from FBI field agents and members of urban police forces informed Miller's appeals to Hoover, and then to Gray, for changes in FBI policies and practices that would eventually come to form the FBI's domestic counterterrorism operations. Critically, this included calls for FBI headquarters to officially authorize break-ins and other illegal surveillance tactics that units like New York's Squad 47 had been carrying out on an informal basis since August 1970.

Miller's strategy for revamping the FBI's domestic security operations involved crowd-sourcing knowledge at a series of special conferences for bureau field agents and other law enforcement personnel. The first conference came in response to the FBI's BLA investigation. On November 29–30, 1971, Miller hosted the "Urban Guerrilla Seminar" at FBI headquarters, which was attended by approximately fifty-two state and local law enforcement officers from around the country. The purpose of the gathering was to conduct collective research on combatting "urban guerrilla warfare."[42]

In his opening remarks at the conference, Miller made an important modification to previous FBI officials' framing of guerrilla insurgency: he explicitly defined the problem and its perpetrators as "terrorism" and "terrorists." "It would give me great pleasure to welcome each of you experts in urban guerrilla activity to this seminar if it were not for the fact that all of us are here because our country has become a battleground," he said, "a battleground in our cities and towns involving those who espouse a destructive, violent, revolutionary philosophy of terrorism."[43]

Miller's framing outlined terrorists' tactics but obscured their motives. "We all know that the twisted logic of the terrorist, his murder and mayhem, have now thrust their way into the fabric of urban life," he told the police personnel gathered at Quantico. For Miller, it was a given that BLA guerrillas were not rational actors responding to rampant police violence but crazed madmen who posed an existential threat not only to police officers but also to American society itself. And there was only one thing standing between American democracy and violent Hobbesian disorder: the nation's police agencies. "The challenge to law enforcement, to each of you and to us, is going to be an awesome one," Miller told the police in the crowd. "The theorists of urban terror boast that police officers are their main target. The logic of the urban guerrilla is simple—and sobering: if law enforcement officers cannot protect themselves from ambushes, snipers, and bombings, then what chance has the private citizen against the revolutionary's rifles, explosives, and Molotov cocktails?"[44]

Inquiry into the root causes of guerrilla violence was not up for discussion. Instead, America's political leaders expected police and intelligence agencies to suppress such violence, whatever the cost.

So that is what they sought to do. In the case of police ambushes, this job fell mostly to local police agencies, which typically held jurisdiction over such crimes. Since the BLA's May 1971 assassination of New York police officers Waverly Jones and Joseph Piagentini, however, Nixon had demanded greater FBI involvement in such cases. The FBI was also concerned about an October 18 robbery of a church outside St. Louis, Missouri, by four individuals whom local police arrested after a shootout. Among the assailants was a forty-year-old Catholic priest from Milwaukee named Nicholas J. Riddell, whom the FBI had been seeking for his involvement in a 1969 raid of a Chicago draft board. Searches of the suspects' homes uncovered six rifles, bomb-making guides, and birth certificates used for forging fake IDs. Police had unwittingly broken up an urban guerrilla cell.[45]

Miller's "Urban Guerrilla Seminar" was the FBI's latest effort to research and develop interagency coordination and tactical knowledge for combatting "terrorism." Each attendee received a copy of a thirty-five-page report prepared by Miller's office titled "Profile of Urban Guerrilla Activity: Groups, Leaders, Incidents," which provided detailed overviews of several organizations identified as "terrorist," including the Weather Underground, the BLA, two New York–based Puerto Rican independence guerrilla groups, and Southern California's Chicano Liberation Front.[46] As the gathering commenced, Miller called for collaborative research. "We want your suggestions and ideas as to how we can help you in combatting the urban terrorist."[47]

Miller also hinted at legal challenges involved in combatting clandestine political violence. He noted "judicial restrictions on release of information that might prejudice the defendants' rights in a pending case," a likely reference to illegal surveillance techniques. Miller sought to create a space for police to openly discuss such tactics, but he did not want word of this to reach the public. "We want a frank discussion of all cases relating to urban guerrilla activity," Miller announced, "but we will confine these discussions . . . to the seminar itself."[48]

There is no surviving record of the conversations had at the "Urban Guerrilla Seminar," but they almost certainly involved illegal surveillance tactics. Shortly after the conference, Miller made his first formal request for the FBI's reauthorization of break-ins. The document Miller wrote to make this request was so sensitive that he marked it "DO NOT FILE," instructing the recipients to return the memo to his office after reading. Miller also kept Hoover's name off the document, addressing it instead to Assistant Director Alex Rosen, who served with Felt on Hoover's elite executive council.[49] The only reason Miller's memo ever saw the light of day is because federal prosecutors obtained it through a subpoena during his 1979 trial. In the memo Miller discussed the FBI's failure to obtain adequate information on the Weather Underground's membership through wiretaps, physical surveillance, and informants and noted the bureau's "excellent use of the technique of surreptitious entry" against the Communist Party in the 1950s. Miller called on Hoover to reauthorize break-ins for the FBI's Weather Underground investigation, citing their use as an "absolute necessity." Miller also proposed personally coordinating such efforts as head of the Domestic Security Division.[50]

Hoover never fully reauthorized black-bag jobs. However, on March 27, 1972, five weeks before his death, the director authorized a break-in to the New York City apartment of Jennifer Dohrn, sister of Bernardine Dohrn, the Weather Underground leader and FBI Most Wanted fugitive. In his memo authorizing Squad 47's break-in, Hoover used the FBI's typical euphemism for agents engaged in black-bag jobs, referencing "two highly sensitive sources" involved in surveillance of Dohrn's residence. *"Every logical effort must be immediately expended to capitalize on the above-enumerated assets,"* Hoover stressed, *"as it is unknown for how long this opportunity will exist or if it can be repeated."*[51]

Squad 47 went through with the break-in. However, with the issue of surreptitious entries unresolved, the question of reauthorizing the technique would fall to L. Patrick Gray.

Gray faced multiple challenges upon stepping into his role as the FBI's acting director. For one, Nixon demanded that Gray ensure the FBI's fidelity to the White House. According to a memo penned by his aide, Nixon instructed Gray during their first meeting, immediately after Hoover's funeral on May 4, 1972, "to consolidate control of the FBI, making such changes as are necessary to assure its complete loyalty to the Administration."[52] In Gray's recollection of the Oval Office encounter, Nixon called for a "house-cleaning" of the FBI after the bureau's top officials had time to mourn Hoover's death.[53] At the same time, Gray felt tremendous pressure from members of Congress, the press, and the American public to reform the FBI's outdated administrative practices and intrusive domestic surveillance operations, which had come under increasing scrutiny during Hoover's final year in office. On top of all this, Gray also inherited Hoover's war on domestic leftist guerrillas.

Upon assuming his position as the FBI's acting director, Gray was "appalled to learn" that despite one of the most intense manhunts in its history, the bureau had captured only three Weather Underground fugitives.[54] In the approximately two years since the Greenwich Village townhouse explosion, the FBI's nationwide Weather Underground investigation (WEATHFUG) had generated more than 90,000 pages of documents, focusing on 280 individuals throughout the country. This included twenty-six fugitives and forty other individuals, whereabouts unknown, whom the FBI suspected of Weather Underground membership. In a report on WEATHFUG issued five days after Gray's appointment, Miller's domestic security deputy R. L. Shackelford noted, "only a few fugitives have been apprehended" while "the key Weatherman leaders remain at large."[55] More than two years after Hoover initiated the FBI's Weather Underground investigation, the massive WEATHFUG operation remained largely fruitless.

In order to make progress in their hunt for the Weather Underground, Miller urged Gray to reauthorize break-ins and other illegal surveillance. Gray later recalled that during his first two weeks as acting director, Miller informed him that the FBI maintained eight warrantless wiretaps on individuals suspected of involvement in revolutionary violence, all of them targeting either the BPP or alleged Weather Underground associates. According to Gray, Miller wanted to drastically expand the FBI's usage of restricted surveillance techniques. "I could use sixty-five taps, thirty-three microphones, and seventy mail covers," Miller supposedly said.[56] Miller later recalled that field office directors around the country whom Gray visited during his first months in office also implored the acting director to reauthorize surreptitious entries.[57] Felt claimed that Gray ordered a survey to determine "the feasibility of reinstituting FBI participation in this activity."[58] It remains unclear, however, whether Miller or Felt made Gray aware of the full extent of the informal, unauthorized break-ins that agents in New York, Los Angeles, Seattle, San Francisco, Portland, and Phoenix had already been conducting in search of leads in the WEATHFUG investigation.[59]

As if to taunt the FBI's new acting director, the Weather Underground detonated a bomb in the Pentagon just two weeks after Gray took office. The guerrillas outlined the reasons for the bombing in an erudite, six-page communiqué, explaining their attack as a means to protest President Nixon's recent orders for the mining of North Vietnamese harbors and intensified aerial bombardment of both North and South Vietnam. "It has become clear to everyone that the [South Vietnamese] Thieu regime and the Army of the Republic of Viet Nam would collapse within a matter of days without U.S. air and naval power," the Weather Underground wrote. "The risk taken by the Vietnamese at this time is to face that U.S. military might in a fight to regain their homeland."[60] Viewing Nixon's military escalation as cruel and pointless, the Weather Underground urged Nixon to accept the Provisional Revolutionary Government of South Vietnam's recent peace proposal.[61]

The Weather Underground's bomb, detonated at 12:53 A.M. in a fourth-floor women's restroom, caused minor damage.[62] However, the organization's ability to strike the symbolic center of American military power underscored its members' continued evasion of FBI surveillance. The headline of a *Washington Post* article on the bombing emphasized this point: "Who Are Weather People—Ask FBI."[63]

While the Weather Underground and other domestic guerrillas remained at large, attacks by Palestinian militants and their allies in Western Europe and Israel prompted growing concern throughout the world, including within the FBI, over the problem of international terrorism. On February 22, 1971, Palestinian nationalist guerrillas gained $5 million in ransom after hijacking a Lufthansa airliner departed from Delhi with the aim of freeing Palestinian captives held in West Germany.[64] On May 8, militants from the Black September Organization—a faction within the larger Palestinian Liberation Organization (PLO)—hijacked a Belgian Sabena passenger jet en route from Vienna to Tel Aviv. The guerrillas wanted to swap the plane's passengers for the release of a hundred Palestinians held in Israeli prisons, but after a twenty-three-hour standoff, Israeli commandos stormed the jet. Two hijackers and a passenger perished in the ensuing gun battle.[65] An even bloodier incident occurred at Tel Aviv's Lod Airport on May 30, when three Japanese Red Army guerrillas working under the command of the Popular Front for the Liberation of Palestine (PFLP), a Marxist-Leninist PLO faction, fired machine guns and hurled hand grenades into a crowd, killing twenty-six and injuring seventy-eight.[66]

This series of attacks brought global attention to the Palestinian struggle while also rousing fears of what governments and media outlets increasingly called international terrorism. Acting Director Gray later recalled the period after the Lod Airport massacre as "a time of great unease among all the responsible agencies in the federal government," when "international terrorism was a new and fast-growing phenomenon."[67]

Amid growing concerns over terrorism at home and abroad, Miller sought ramped-up FBI surveillance ahead of the Democratic and Republican National Conventions, respectively scheduled for June and August 1972, in Miami. After violence marred the 1968 Democratic National Convention in Chicago, FBI officials were eager to prevent a repeat scenario at either party's 1972 convention, particularly the Republicans', which Miller predicted would draw more "power and fire" owing to popular opposition to Nixon's prolonging of the war in Vietnam.[68] FBI officials also hoped they could locate Weather Underground fugitives among the crowds of radical protesters gathered outside the conventions. Miller informed Gray that 8 percent of the FBI's 2,100 "domestic security" informants would be attending the Republican Convention. In keeping with long-standing practices, the FBI focused on preventing violence by protesters while implicitly condoning police violence through their silence on the matter.[69]

Gray declined to approve Miller's request for expanded warrantless wiretapping and mail surveillance after determining that such actions would not hold up in court, but he did approve a request from Miller to order LA undercover agents who had infiltrated VVAW to participate in a cross-country caravan of activists heading to the summer 1972 Democratic and Republican Conventions.[70] None of the longhaired, bearded agents whom the Los Angeles field office had unofficially sent undercover approximately two years earlier had yet infiltrated an underground guerrilla cell or prevented revolutionary violence. Nor had they uncovered evidence of VVAW members plotting violent attacks. Nonetheless, Gray saw promise in the use of undercover agents. This was a departure from Hoover, who had felt that the tactic violated the FBI's traditional dress code and put agents in harm's way. The FBI sent to the conventions a total of ten undercover agents "with appearance to readily be accepted by New Left street people" in hopes of locating Weather Underground fugitives. However, their search came up empty.[71]

Gray officially authorized use of undercover agents for the first time in FBI history on July 24, 1972, making an important contribution to the development of U.S. counterterrorism. Gray's coded teletype sent to seventeen field offices stressed the extra secrecy and "extreme importance" of undercover operations aimed at leftist guerrilla groups: "I expect Weatherman and similar groups to be hunted to exhaustion. This can only be done by utilization of sufficient manpower and penetration into the underground by informants and agents where warranted. You are reminded of the two objectives to be achieved in these cases: one, short-range, the immediate apprehension of the fugitives and two, long-range, penetration and neutralization of the underground apparatus."[72] Gray's orders formalized a practice that had been going on since August 1970 in Los Angeles, where "deep cover" agents had infiltrated VVAW, and in San Francisco, where bearded undercover agents had been searching the hippie counterculture for Weather Underground fugitives. In his memoir, Gray recalled that he authorized "carefully selected young special agents" to go undercover on a full-time basis, "to live with these people [leftist guerrillas], to sleep with these people, to make love to women if necessary, to smoke marijuana if necessary."[73]

In August, the FBI formalized a program for developing undercover agents and new informants capable of infiltrating the clandestine Weather Underground. It was called the Special Target Informant Development Program, or SPECTAR.[74] None of the FBI's deep-cover agents ever successfully infiltrated a leftist guerrilla cell, though some developed leftist sympathies. While undercover in British Columbia, Canada, Special Agent Cril Payne encountered the family of an American draft resister but declined to turn them in out of compassion for their situation. He also recalled that a couple other "deep cover" agents ended up going rogue, fully adopting the counterculture lifestyle and an affinity for marijuana and LSD.[75]

In addition to enduring FBI surveillance, VVAW was a target of the Committee to Reelect the President (CREEP), a group whose members John Mitchell, Jeb Stuart Magruder, G. Gordon Liddy, and E. Howard Hunt later served prison sentences for their involvement in the Watergate scandal, the latter two for their activities with the Plumbers. Before the 1972 Republican Convention, Liddy and Magruder discussed ideas for covertly disrupting VVAW or using the group to publicly embarrass the McGovern campaign. Pablo Manuel Fernandez, a paid informant with links to Watergate burglary mastermind Howard Hunt, attempted to sell hand grenades, machine guns, and other weapons to VVAW members ahead of the Miami convention, though the antiwar veterans had the sense to turn him down.[76]

The motives and nature of the bureau's investigation of VVAW still have not been adequately explained, but it is clear that Gray's reasons for investigating VVAW went beyond supposed violence prevention.[77] On May 31, 1972, less than a month into his term, Gray provided President Nixon with intelligence on links between VVAW and the McGovern campaign. Gray wrote confidential memos to the president's assistant H. R. Haldeman and Attorney General Mitchell stating that an unnamed representative of the McGovern campaign had attended a VVAW meeting in Los Angeles and agreed to lend a station wagon leased by McGovern's campaign committee to VVAW members for the purpose of "barnstorming" California college campuses to "voice opposition to the Vietnam War."[78] Though the document did not explicitly say, this information likely came from the bureau's undercover agents in VVAW.[79]

By providing the president with information that could be used to smear an election opponent, Gray demonstrated his willingness to use FBI surveillance in the service of Nixon's stealth reelection efforts. After the Watergate break-in, Gray's partisanship would make him a target of Felt's Deep Throat covert counterintelligence operations. In the meantime, Miller continued to pressure Gray to reauthorize FBI break-ins.

In his 2008 memoir—written largely as a final attempt to exonerate himself from both the FBI's break-ins and Nixon's attempted Watergate cover-up—Gray insisted that he never approved FBI black-bag jobs for domestic investigations. This was a continuation of the argument that won him an acquittal in his 1979 trial: that all break-ins for the Weather Underground investigation had been taken on by Felt and Miller without his knowledge. Felt and Miller claimed otherwise, however, and declassified FBI documents seem to back them up.

Gray may not have provided written authorization for all FBI break-ins, but the records show that on May 22, 1972, three days after the Pentagon bombing, he approved additional break-ins at Jennifer Dohrn's residence. Using the same terminology Hoover used a mere six weeks earlier, Gray ordered Squad 47 agents to "continue to insure [*sic*] that every logical effort is made to capitalize" on both their round-the-clock physical surveillance of Dohrn and their "sensitive sources."[80] Gray noted that Dohrn was a "known Weatherman courier" who had "travelled around the U.S. setting up an underground Weatherman communication system." The goal of the break-ins and intense physical surveillance was to obtain "foreknowledge of Weatherman revolutionary terrorist activities" and locate "her fugitive sister [Bernardine] and other Weatherman fugitives."[81]

Mark Felt later recounted other instances in which Gray provided authorization for FBI break-ins verbally or through written euphemisms. "It was crystal clear to me that Gray intended to reinstate the use of surreptitious entries, particularly in cases involving terrorists," he recalled.[82]

Gray sent Felt a memo on July 18, 1972, conveying his intentions. The acting director wanted "the full resources of the FBI to be placed behind" FBI agents involved in leftist guerrilla investigations, "in the most innovative manner." "I want no holds barred," he stressed, "and I want to hunt Weatherman and similar groups to exhaustion."[83]

Like Hoover, Gray avoided explicitly reauthorizing break-ins and other illegal tactics in writing. Instead, he used heavily euphemistic language to express his wishes while leaving room for plausible deniability should his orders ever get leaked to the public. In his 1979 memoir, published while he and Gray were on trial, Felt cited this memo as indicative of the acting director's "extreme interest" in break-ins.[84] Miller also recalled that many field officers and their agents interpreted Gray's repeated orders to hunt leftist guerrillas "to exhaustion" as signals to continue use of such tactics.[85]

Much of the pressure on Gray to reauthorize break-ins came from Miller as he worked to streamline the FBI's Weather Underground investigation. Gray penned his memo to Felt shortly after Miller hosted a one-day conference on the Weather Underground at FBI headquarters on June 22 attended by high-ranking agents from the twelve offices around the country. Miller and other domestic security officials set the agenda beforehand. Like the "Urban Guerrilla Seminar" the previous November, the "Weatherman Conference" and a longer, ten-day "Weatherman Matters School" scheduled for the coming August were designed to collaboratively research and develop tactics for combating leftist guerrilla "terrorism." Miller also hoped the June conference would build support for Gray's authorization of break-ins and undercover agents. Additionally, he sought to loosen FBI requirements for developing informants so agents could recruit "narcotics addicts, ex-convicts, individuals awaiting prosecution and [those] who may be 'unstable.'"[86]

These objectives were part of Miller's larger efforts to reconfigure FBI domestic security operations in response to the problem of clandestine guerrilla violence. Miller and his associates also sought to centralize the Weather Underground investigation under one nationally coordinated special squad that would give agents involved in the case greater opportunities for inter-office travel and coordination.[87] While awaiting Gray's approval of these measures, Miller instituted other incipient counterterrorism practices. He oversaw an expansion of the Domestic Security Division's computerized Telephone Number File tracking use of phone numbers "by Weatherman support individuals and possible Weatherman Underground personnel." Agents also compiled an "auto hot sheet" to "identify important Weatherman vehicles used by both underground and support individuals."[88]

When it came to break-ins, Miller's desire to obtain official FBI reauthorization of the tactic was not motivated solely by ideology or by his belief that it was an effective investigative technique. He also sought to restore FBI field agents' sagging morale. FBI agents were on the front lines of the war on leftist guerrillas, and they took on the difficult task of investigating guerrilla violence under extreme pressure while trying to follow their supervisors' ambiguous orders and guidelines. To complicate matters, on June 19, 1972, the Supreme Court ruled in the *Keith* case (named after Eastern Michigan federal district judge Damon Keith) that Attorney General John Mitchell could not withhold evidence of FBI warrantless wiretaps in the federal government's case against Lawrence "Pun" Plamondon, the former White Panther leader and Ten Most Wanted fugitive charged with dynamiting an Ann Arbor CIA office in 1968. In its first-ever decision on warrantless wiretapping, the Supreme Court ruled that authority for conducting warrantless surveillance, which attorneys general had authorized without congressional or judicial oversight since the Roosevelt administration, was illegal under the Fourth Amendment.[89] According to Gray, three days after the court's decision Attorney General Richard Kleindienst ordered the FBI to drop four warrantless wiretaps and two microphones targeting the Black Panthers and suspected Weather Underground associates.[90] To

FBI field agents, the *Keith* decision and Gray's "hunt to exhaustion" order sent mixed messages. Rank-and-file special agents wanted to know that their supervisors would support them if they ever got caught illegally breaking and entering, opening mail, or setting up wiretaps in efforts to preempt guerrilla violence.

Special agents made their feelings known at the FBI's August Weatherman In-Service. They were encouraged to do so by Miller, who asked them to be "frank and objective" in their discussions.[91] The content of the in-service was top secret, but Detroit special agent Robert Knapp later attested to the climate of pressure and uncertainty that pervaded the FBI's Weather Underground investigation. He recalled how investigators at the conference discussed the fact that agents from several field offices were engaging in break-ins but disagreed over whether the tactic should be used and sought approval for its use from FBI headquarters. He also recounted that some agents on leftist guerrilla assignments resorted to using "suicide bugs"—warrantless electronic wiretaps or hidden microphones applied without authorization, for which "if you got caught you were on your own."[92] Under relentless pressure from FBI headquarters to apprehend guerrilla fugitives, but lacking clear guidelines on how to do so, local supervisors and their field agents weighed utilizing illegal surveillance practices in regard to efficacy, ethics, legality, and their future careers.

By pressuring Gray to reauthorize break-ins and other illegal surveillance techniques, Miller sought to soothe his agents' anxieties. Although the term had not yet been invented, Miller's efforts and the conversations surrounding them were an important part of the development of counterterrorism.

The Watergate Break-In and Deep Throat's COINTELPRO

While Mark Felt supported Edward Miller's efforts to get Acting Director L. Patrick Gray to reauthorize the FBI's use of illegal surveillance tactics, he widened Hoover's posthumous war against Nixon and Gray. Immediately after the June 17, 1972, Watergate break-in, Felt opened a new front by secretly going to the press. Journalist Max Holland has aptly described Felt's Watergate leaks, attributed at the time to Deep Throat, as "Felt's private COINTELPRO."[93] Felt's leaks exposing Nixon followed the template of the very covert counterintelligence operations the FBI had waged against the BPP and New Left.

Felt's resentment toward Gray had begun before the Watergate break-in. He had first clashed with Gray during the ITT–Dita Beard controversy and had bristled at Nixon's appointment of Gray to the position of acting director of the FBI after Hoover's death. And he was not alone in resenting Gray's appointment. Many senior FBI officials shared the view that Gray was an interloper, a Nixon lackey who was wholly unqualified for his position. A journalist close to the FBI reported, "So tenuous were the links between some of the FBI's key personnel and the Justice Department that in the 24 hours following the death of Hoover . . . several assistant directors of the bureau seriously considered resigning."[94] Gray narrowly averted a mutiny by convening a meeting of Hoover's top fifteen assistants less than two hours after his appointment. The new acting director assured the men that both he and Nixon intended to "maintain the FBI as an institution."[95] During this meeting, Gray made a critical alliance with Felt, whom he promoted to associate director, the number two position in the FBI hierarchy.[96] Felt's loyalty was less certain than he realized, however.

Gray assumed power at a time of growing public concern over the FBI's role in American society. The FBI's public image had taken a serious beating since journalists' disclosure of declassified surveillance documents from the March 1971 burglary in Media, Pennsylvania. In the wake of J. Edgar Hoover's death, Americans from across the political spectrum publicly questioned the FBI's integrity and competency and called for major reforms, particularly in the area of domestic surveillance. Determined to restore the FBI's popular legitimacy, Gray instituted historic changes immediately after taking office. He signed an order allowing women to become FBI agents for the first time, formed an Equal Opportunity board to explore avenues for recruiting more minority special agents, and enacted a new dress-code policy permitting male agents to grow longer hair and mustaches in keeping with early 1970s' fashion trends.[97]

A *Washington Post* editorial on May 15, 1972, conveyed the pressure Gray faced as Hoover's successor, as critics demanded the acting director move quickly and decisively to demonstrate the FBI's commitment to safeguarding Americans' civil liberties. While the editorial applauded Gray's hiring and dress-code reforms, calling them "pleasantly surprising and remarkably daring," it also called on Nixon to appoint a "Presidential Commission to Study the FBI." The goal of such a commission would be to determine whether the FBI required oversight from Congress or another arm of the executive branch.[98]

Gray responded to the FBI's flagging image with a public relations campaign. The acting director spent much of his one-year term on the road, visiting field offices and giving public addresses throughout the country. With Gray away from FBI headquarters, responsibility for most of the bureau's "day-to-day" operations fell to Felt.[99] Felt treated his boss with courtesy and professionalism in person. In private, though, he resented taking orders from someone widely perceived as "a neophyte not only to the FBI, but to the profession of law enforcement."[100] Private resentment would transform into covert attacks once the FBI launched an investigation into the Watergate burglary.

Nixon's Plumbers actually conducted two Watergate break-ins—the first one was the one they got away with. Howard Hunt and Gordon Liddy broke into the Democratic National Committee headquarters on May 28, 1972, and successfully installed a hidden microphone. Their aim was to find out whether DNC chairman Larry O'Brien possessed information that could damage Nixon's reelection campaign.[101]

But there was some sort of problem with the microphone, and it did not work. So on June 17, James McCord, Frank Sturgis, Bernard Barker, Eugenio Martinez, and Vergilio Gonzalez made a second break-in. This time the operation went sour. Washington police arrested the men inside the DNC headquarters and confiscated the operatives' cameras, eavesdropping equipment, and large sum of cash, which included thirteen new one-hundred-dollar bills with their serial numbers in sequence.[102]

The Plumbers' bungled Watergate break-in did not initially make major news headlines, but the FBI immediately opened an investigation. Hearing about the news while in California, Gray promptly called Felt, who provided a summary of what the FBI then knew about the arrests. Unaware of the Nixon administration's role in the operation, Gray ordered his associate director to investigate the Watergate break-in "to the hilt."[103]

And then Deep Throat started his counterintelligence operations.

Felt began leaking classified information to the press two days after the Watergate arrests. In mid-June, *Washington Post* reporter Bob Woodward phoned Felt looking for information on Howard Hunt, whose name appeared in two address books found on the Watergate burglars. Woodward figured out that Hunt was a former CIA agent and worked at the White House with Special Counsel Charles W. Colson, but he sought further confirmation before publishing a story connecting the Nixon staffer to the break-in. Felt gave Woodward the confirmation he was looking for. The FBI had found a check bearing Hunt's name in the Watergate burglars' hotel room; Felt informed Woodward that the FBI considered the former CIA operative a "prime suspect" in its investigation. The tip enabled Woodward to publish his first major story on the Watergate break-in on June 20, 1972.[104]

Felt had begun a delicate balancing act. He simultaneously oversaw the FBI's Watergate investigation and covertly leaked information to the press. Circumstantial evidence also ties Felt to two more June 1972 leaks pertaining to the Watergate investigation: one to *Time* journalist Sandy Smith and the second to *Washington Daily Post* reporter Patrick Collins.[105]

Nixon officials hastily moved to stall the bureau's investigation. On June 18, the day after the Watergate break-in arrests, Nixon's chief domestic advisor John Ehrlichman put White House counsel John Dean in charge of handling the cover-up. President Nixon became directly involved on June 23, having learned that FBI investigators were close to tracing the one-hundred-dollar bills discovered on the Watergate burglars to funds from a reelection campaign donation laundered through a Mexican bank. That same day, in a recorded conversation subsequently known as the "smoking gun" tape, Nixon instructed his chief of staff H. R. Haldeman to have CIA director Richard Helms ask Acting Director Gray to limit the FBI's Watergate investigation. The president invoked national security, claiming that if the FBI followed the Mexican lead it would uncover information on the CIA's top-secret role in the failed 1961 invasion of Cuba's Bay of Pigs. Haldeman and Ehrlichman subsequently met with Helms and CIA deputy director Vernon Walters. Afterward, Walters telephoned Gray to request a meeting, which took place at 2:30 that afternoon.[106]

From his meeting with Walters onward, Gray wavered, torn between his loyalties to Nixon and the FBI. During his meeting with the deputy CIA director, Gray agreed to limit the FBI's Watergate investigation to the seven arrested men. Gray then reversed his decision at the request of Felt and Assistant Director Charles Bates, and then once again flopped back to limiting the investigation under orders from John Dean. However, on July 5, Gray decided to move forward with a full investigation after the FBI's Watergate case agent Angelo Lano wrote a teletype complaining that headquarters was delaying his efforts.[107]

Even after committing to investigating, Gray agreed to provide Dean with documents pertaining to the FBI's Watergate investigation. This was consistent with his previous complicity in the Nixon White House's corrupt practices, which included his meddling in the FBI's ITT investigation and his decision to tell Nixon about VVAW members' support of George McGovern. Gray committed his most serious act of collusion in June when Dean requested that he destroy two manila envelopes containing classified documents removed from the safe of Watergate burglar and CREEP member Howard Hunt. Continuing to vacillate, Gray held on to the envelopes until late December and then burned the secret documents in an incinerator behind his house in New London, Connecticut.[108]

Felt never described his personal motives for waging his secret war, and we can only infer what drove his actions. By the time he came forward as Deep Throat in 2005, dementia had already set in, preventing the former expert in deception from unburdening his conscience. It is clear, however, that Felt did not leak information from the FBI's Watergate investigation because he morally objected to illegal break-ins. It is also evident that Felt carried out his actions in the context of the FBI's ongoing institutional conflict with the Nixon White House. As Woodward recalled in 2005, Felt "never really voiced pure, raw outrage to me about Watergate." "The crimes and abuses were background music," he wrote. "Nixon was trying to subvert not only the law but the Bureau. Watergate became Felt's instrument to reassert the Bureau's independence and thus its supremacy."[109]

Felt's 1976 remarks on the television news program *Face the Nation* support Woodward's assertion. Amid rumors of an impending federal indictment for his authorization of the Weather Underground break-ins, Felt directly denied that he was Deep Throat. But he stated that he "wouldn't be ashamed to be." "I think that whoever helped Woodward helped the country," Felt explained. Felt professed a belief similar to that held by Hoover, that the FBI functioned best when autonomous from the influence of partisan politics. "I think that the Justice Department should be a completely independent department, completely removed from politics," he argued. "The positions should all be career positions, then the FBI and the other Bureaus in the Department of Justice would be under a career type individual and not under a politician."[110]

Whatever Felt's personal motives, his leaks demonstrated that the acting director had little control over the FBI. Throughout the summer John Dean complained to both Gray and Felt about information reported in the press that he believed came from the FBI. Meanwhile in the White House, Nixon and his top aides were confident that a series of bribes paid out to Hunt and his accomplices would limit their testimonies, and that their trial would not take place until after the November election. But thanks to Felt's counterintelligence operations, Nixon still questioned Gray's ability to control the FBI. The president expressed his doubts on August 1 in a conversation with Haldeman. He offered his chief of staff a blunt assessment: "I don't believe that we oughta have Gray in that job."[111]

. . . . . .

In August 1972, Mark Felt's leaks enabled *Time* magazine reporter Sandy Smith to uncover the existence of the Plumbers unit. Smith's August 7 article reviewed the Watergate burglars' connections to CREEP and recently dismissed White House consultants Gordon Liddy and Howard Hunt. "Liddy and Hunt," the story revealed, "were part of a White House team known as 'the plumbers,' because they were assigned to investigate the source of leaks to the press like that of the Pentagon papers."[112] Two weeks later, Smith published another article in which he asserted that the Watergate burglary "grew out of a team of so-called 'plumbers,' originally recruited by the Administration to investigate leaks to the media." "The Watergate affair," *Time*'s top reporter predicted, "promises to be the scandal of the year."[113]

As more information about the Watergate break-in went public, Felt's colleague Edward Miller continued to pressure Gray to reauthorize FBI break-ins. From August 21 to August 31, Miller hosted the bureau's intensive "Weatherman Matters School" at Quantico. Once again, special agents from around the country gathered to coordinate the Weather Underground investigation, as Miller provided in-depth training on the bureau's new SPECTAR undercover agent program and crowdsourced information on illegal surveillance tactics that he could use to make his case to Gray that break-ins needed to be reauthorized.

Felt's secret war on Gray and Nixon cannot be understood apart from his efforts to reauthorize break-ins as part of the FBI's war on the Weather Underground. After the arrests of the five burglars at the DNC headquarters, Felt managed aspects of both the FBI's Watergate investigation and Weather Underground investigation on a daily basis. In both cases, Felt's secret wars built on the bureaucratic conflicts over political dissent and state surveillance that he stepped into when Hoover promoted him to associate director.

Yet as the summer of 1972 approached autumn, Felt's leaks were not yet provoking the political scandal that *Time* magazine predicted. Despite Felt's continued assistance with investigative reporting in both *Time* and the *Washington Post*, the Nixon administration's cover-up would keep a lid on the scandal until after the November election.

For American voters, distractions abounded, with the Olympics looming large. On August 26, the 1972 Summer Olympic Games opened in Munich, West Germany, and Americans were among the millions who tuned in to watch live television coverage of the ceremony, as crowds in Munich's sleek new Olympic Stadium cheered the dozens of teams who marched in procession beneath their countries' flags.

No one could have predicted that this year's games would be marred by a gruesome guerrilla assault. Four months after J. Edgar Hoover's death, the Munich attack would prompt an urgent new round of FBI and White House efforts to combat terrorism.

9 Arab Scare

In the predawn hours of September 5, 1972, eight commandos from the Palestinian nationalist Black September Organization stormed an apartment unit on the site of the Twentieth Summer Olympic Games in Munich, West Germany. Inside slept the Israeli men's Olympic team. After killing two team members who resisted the siege, the heavily armed guerrillas held nine athletes and coaches hostage. The militants sought to exchange their captives for the freedom of 234 Palestinians held in Israeli prisons as well as two Red Army Faction guerrillas imprisoned in West Germany.

As television crews covering the Olympics shifted their focus to the hostage crisis, the Munich siege became an international media sensation. For eighteen hours, an estimated 900 million viewers throughout the world watched the unfolding drama: as West German officials negotiated with the hostage takers; as Israeli prime minister Golda Meir announced her government's refusal to meet the guerrillas' demands; and as West German police bungled a rescue mission that resulted in the deaths of a police officer, five Black September guerrillas, and all of the Israeli hostages.[1]

The Munich siege forever changed how the world thought about political violence. The bloody incident brought world attention to the Palestinian nationalist struggle while media coverage and contentious United Nations debates on the matter conveyed global panic over a new and seemingly urgent problem: international terrorism.[2] Fearing a similar attack in the United States, the FBI and Nixon administration responded to Munich with several new initiatives designed to preempt domestic and international terrorism.

Historians have previously understood the Munich attacks as the starting point for American counterterrorism. However, the FBI and Nixon administration's efforts to combat terrorism after Munich were informed by their previous four years of conflict with domestic leftist guerrillas. Since Director J. Edgar Hoover's death in May 1972, the FBI's associate director W. Mark Felt, assistant director for domestic security Edward M. Miller, and acting director L. Patrick Gray had been leading the bureau's efforts to counter clandestine political violence. The Munich attacks gave these efforts greater urgency.

After Munich, Felt and Miller acted on their goal of reauthorizing FBI break-ins. They took aim not only at the Weather Underground but also at organizations and individuals supportive of Palestinian rights. The FBI cast a broad net in its search for Palestinian nationalist guerrillas in the United States, spearheading an Arab scare that targeted many Arabs and Arab Americans with no direct connections to guerrilla violence. Arab American political activists who survived this state harassment recalled these operations as a "dry run" for U.S. intelligence agencies' targeting of Muslims and people of Middle Eastern descent in the post-9/11 era.[3]

The FBI carried out its post-Munich operations under a great deal of pressure from Nixon. The president and his aides had tried to craft a federal response to terrorism in 1970 with the short-lived Huston Plan. After the Munich attacks, the Nixon White House established the Cabinet Committee to Combat Terrorism (CCCT), composed of Secretary of State Henry Kissinger, FBI acting director L. Patrick Gray, and several other executive branch officials. This was America's first federal institution explicitly dedicated to fighting terrorism.[4] But the Cabinet Committee's authority was extremely limited. While the Huston Plan attempted to consolidate and expand the surveillance powers of all federal intelligence agencies under the direct command of the White House, the main purpose of the CCCT was to provide policy analysis, most of which would be undertaken by the committee's separate working group.[5] In the midst of the simmering Watergate scandal, Nixon did not risk another attempt to seize control of the nation's intelligence agencies. Instead, with his founding of the CCCT, the president made the FBI the sole federal agency responsible for "combatting foreign terrorists inside the United States."[6]

The pressure on L. Patrick Gray alone was surely intense. The FBI was now expected to head off a Munich-style attack in the United States. If the bureau failed, the acting director knew that Nixon and the American people would hold him accountable. By the same token, if he got caught authorizing illegal surveillance techniques, he could face prosecution. Either scenario could cost him his job. Gray later remembered that when Nixon's advisor John Ehrlichman announced the FBI's antiterrorism responsibilities at the first meeting of the CCCT, the other intelligence and military officials in the room "washed their hands like Pontius Pilate."[7]

Drawing from the preemptive surveillance tactics the bureau had deployed while waging war on the Weather Underground and the BLA, the

FBI set about launching an Arab scare. On September 7, two days after the Munich bloodbath, Mark Felt and Edward Miller authorized a request from the FBI's Dallas field office for a break-in to the office of the Arab Information Center, a public relations outfit affiliated with the Arab League.[8] FBI agents stole a briefcase from the office containing a list of ninety-four Arabs and Arab Americans living in the United States. Alleging that the individuals on the list were involved in a conspiracy linked to Black September, FBI agents visited, interrogated, and harassed Arabs and Arab Americans across the country. Meanwhile, the State Department launched its own program called Operation Boulder, which enlisted the FBI and other federal intelligence agencies for intensified screenings of visa applications from Arab countries.[9]

The exact nature of the threat that Palestinian nationalist violence posed to the United States after Munich is unclear. Most FBI documents on the matter were either destroyed in the 1970s or remain classified today. As with the Weather Underground and the BLA, however, Palestinian clandestine political violence indisputably existed, developing from larger political conflicts with deep historical roots. Palestinian nationalist violence was an outgrowth of the creation of the State of Israel in 1948, the displacement of approximately 1 million indigenous Palestinian Arabs from Israel, and a series of wars between Israel and neighboring Arab states— most recently, the Six Day War of June 1967, which resulted in Israel's occupation of Palestinian lands in the West Bank and Gaza.

The FBI was charged with keeping Americans safe, but as had been the case when Hoover expanded mass surveillance of campus New Left and Black Student Union groups in the fall of 1970, the FBI's post-Munich tactics did not seek to address root causes of political violence. Instead, the FBI engaged once again in broad preemptive action against groups and individuals based on their racialized status or political affiliations. Arabs and Arab Americans suddenly became suspect communities.

The Dallas Break-In

The sense of dire urgency that pervaded federal agencies after the Munich attack gave Mark Felt and Edward Miller an opportunity to enact their goal of officially reauthorizing FBI break-ins. The Dallas Arab Information Center break-in was the first one they approved. On September 7, 1972, Miller documented Felt's verbal authorization of the break-in in a short memo. Keeping with previous bureau policies for black-bag jobs, Miller referred to the break-in as "contact with an anonymous source" and marked the memo with a "Do Not File" caption that reminded Felt to store the documents in a secret location outside the FBI's official filing system.[10]

Miller captioned the memo "Al Fatah; Internal Security—Middle East." This indicated that the operation was part of an FBI internal security investigation of Fatah, the largest faction of the PLO, led by Yasser Arafat.[11] Black September, the organization responsible for the Munich attack, was a subfaction that had recently split from Fatah.[12] Miller's memo indicated that the request to conduct the break-in had originated from the domestic security supervisor at the Dallas field office, who sought approval from FBI headquarters: "On 9/7/72 Security Supervisor [name redacted] Dallas Office, telephonically contacted Bureau Supervisor [name redacted] and requested authorization to contact an anonymous source in connection with captioned matter [Al Fatah] at the Arab Information Center, Suite 1302, Hartford Building, 400 North St. Paul, Dallas, Texas. He assured that such contact could be accomplished with full security. I was advised of the Dallas request during the course of this telephone call by Supervisor McDonnell and authorized the contact of an anonymous source provided full security was assured."[13]

Mark Felt and L. Patrick Gray each later asserted that the Dallas break-in was crucial to thwarting deadly attacks by Palestinian nationalists in the United States. Their two accounts were contradictory, however, and little evidence exists to support their claims.

Felt, Miller, and Gray gave divergent accounts of who authorized the break-ins targeting Palestinian nationalists, when they did so, and under what conditions. This is not surprising since all three men faced legal consequences for their actions. In 1978 the Justice Department indicted the trio for authorizing the illegal Weather Underground break-ins. A federal jury convicted Felt and Miller in 1980, but a judge dropped the charges against Gray, who maintained that he had authorized the black-bag jobs targeting foreign "Arab terrorists" but not the operations targeting the domestic Weather Underground. Felt and Miller nonetheless insisted that Gray had verbally authorized break-ins against both targets.[14] The Justice Department never charged FBI officials for break-ins related to the Palestinian investigation, however.[15]

Self-interest was a central motivation behind Felt and Gray's later outspoken defense of the FBI's post-Munich operations against alleged Palestinian nationalist terrorists—after the Justice Department indictments, both men defended their personal freedom and professional reputations by insisting that break-ins were necessary responses to terrorism. They argued that although the FBI's tactics were illegal, they were justified because they protected American citizens and national security from foreign terrorist violence.

In his 1976 interview on *Face the Nation*, Felt defended the Weather Underground break-ins by pointing to the supposed success of the Dallas operation. "The Palestinian Liberation Organization," Felt claimed, was "planning on all sorts of terrorism in the United States, and I think we stopped them because we took that action."[16] Felt made such claims again in his 1979 memoir, contending that the FBI's Dallas black-bag job and subsequent campaign of interviewing, fingerprinting, and photographing the men on the list uncovered in the break-in convinced "foreign terrorists" that "the FBI was all-knowing and ever-present" and "ended the Palestinian terrorist threat of hijacking, massacres, and bombings in the United States."[17]

Similarly, Gray claimed in his 2005 memoir that the FBI "harassed . . . dozens of Al Fatah assassins . . . out of the country by knocking on their doors and saying we wanted to fingerprint them." "Though it was clearly illegal," he wrote, "the niceties of due process weren't applied; nobody in the intelligence community, the Justice Department, or the White House was willing to risk the time that might allow one of them to slip free and commit the atrocity he was here for."[18]

Neither Felt's nor Gray's assertions should be taken at face value, however. Felt was never specific about what terrorist threats the FBI supposedly preempted. Gray provided more specific details, but his account is full of misstatements.[19] Declassified FBI documents provide some information, but it is limited.

Fundamental questions about the Dallas break-in remain unanswered. Were Palestinian nationalist militants really preparing a Munich-style attack in the United States? If so, who were these people, and what sort of operation were they planning? Did the FBI really prevent an attack? Or did it carry out its preemptive actions merely as precautionary measures amid fear generated by the Munich siege and pressure to avert similar violence in the United States?

There is evidence that some Palestinian nationalists and their allies sought to carry out political violence in the United States after the Munich siege, but it is unclear which organizations they were affiliated with. We do not have evidence that the FBI preempted any specific attack, though it is possible that one or more of the individuals whom authorities chased or barred from the country were planning acts of violence. We do know, however, that the Munich siege put the FBI and the Nixon administration under tremendous pressure to keep Americans safe. In the name of fighting terrorism, the Nixon administration formed the CCCT while the FBI streamlined its break-in operations, chased false leads, and harassed Arabs and Arab Americans throughout the United States. The FBI also developed contingency plans for hostage crises as Gray, Felt, and Miller continued their process of reorganizing the bureau's domestic security operations to confront clandestine guerrilla violence. These efforts laid the foundation of American counterterrorism.

The FBI had begun surveilling Arab American political activists back in 1967, following the Six Day War. It ramped up its efforts a year later after June 6, 1968, when Sirhan Bishara Sirhan, a lone Palestinian gunman suffering from trauma and mental illness, assassinated Democratic presidential hopeful Robert F. Kennedy. At the center of the FBI's surveillance was Abdeen Jabara, a Lebanese American attorney and political activist based in Detroit. After Robert Kennedy's assassination, Jabara took on a controversial role as Sirhan Sirhan's legal counsel. Agents also spied on other members of the Association of Arab American University Graduates, an organization Jabara helped found after the 1967 war that promoted Arab American civil rights, a one-state solution in Palestine, and the establishment of socialism in the United States and throughout the Arab world.[20]

Conservative American political leaders, as well as Zionist organizations like the American Israeli Public Affairs Commission (AIPAC) and the Anti-Defamation League seized on growing violence in the Middle East and the Kennedy assassination to call for increased surveillance of Arab and Arab American university students sympathetic to the Palestinian struggle. Congressman Gerald Ford made such a suggestion in a speech at a 1969 AIPAC conference, as he denounced Palestinian "terrorism" and attributed Kennedy's assassination to "Peking-trained agitators from the Middle East" who had infiltrated American college campuses.[21] CIA reports conducted in 1968 and 1969 found that embassies of Middle Eastern countries had funneled some money to Arab student organizations in the United States but that members of such groups had "no significant connection" to Palestinian guerrilla organizations, nor had they engaged in any violence or illegal activities.[22]

Two classified FBI reports issued in 1970 came to similar conclusions but documented ties between the U.S.-based Organization of Arab Students and Fatah, asserting that the latter sought to build support among students at American universities. Domestic security officials expressed concern about the possibility of Arab students collaborating with Fatah to carry out attacks on Israeli targets in the United States. One of the FBI's reports warned that if Palestinian guerrilla organizations "do carry out terrorist acts in the United States, they will probably rely on the large segment of Arab students residing here for at least the planning stages of the operation."[23]

Felt's approval of the Dallas Arab Information Center break-in gave the FBI license to act on these concerns. The break-in was an act of preventive surveillance intended to preempt potential Palestinian nationalist terrorism in the United States. As Felt wrote in his 1979 memoir, he and Miller authorized the Dallas supervisor's request for "permission to make a surreptitious entry into the offices of a suspected Palestinian terrorist group to learn of any terrorist plans for the United States and to identify any possible terrorists who were residing here."[24] Agents also used the break-in as an opportunity to ascertain whether it was possible to install a listening device in the office. After the agents in Dallas affirmed that this was possible, Felt and Miller approved a second break-in on September 20, during which agents bugged the office. The FBI maintained both microphone and telephone surveillance of the Arab Information Center office until June 1973.[25]

Dallas FBI agents determined they could break in to the Arab Information Center without getting caught because the organization's director, Seif El-Wadi Ramahi, had been out of the country since mid-August.[26] Dallas agents knew this because they maintained a tap on his phone. Because local FBI offices rarely initiated unusual actions independently, it is likely that the Dallas field office requested permission to conduct the break-in in response to a request from FBI headquarters, whether a direct request for specific information on the Arab Information Center or a general request to multiple field offices for intelligence on possible terrorist attacks. There is no documentary evidence to determine this, though a journalist with sources on the Church Committee reported in 1975 that the FBI had acted at the request of the CIA, which was "following up on intelligence received from foreign governments," likely Israel.[27]

Though we may never know exactly who initiated the FBI's post-Munich pursuit of preventive intelligence on Arabs in the United States, it is clear the Dallas field office issued its request in the context of the FBI's ongoing war with domestic leftist guerrillas and surveillance of Arab American political activists. FBI headquarters had been pressuring field offices to preempt guerrilla attacks for over two years. With the global panic over

Palestinian terrorism that followed Munich, the Dallas field office's domestic security supervisor must have felt morally and professionally compelled to seek a preemptive break-in into the Arab Information Center office. The Dallas supervisor made his decision knowing that if a group like Black September carried out a deadly attack in the United States and it was later determined that the FBI had forgone an opportunity to prevent it, he would be held personally responsible by FBI headquarters, the White House, and the American people. By officially authorizing the break-in, however, Felt and Miller departed from FBI headquarters' practice of *informally* encouraging black-bag jobs and provided the Dallas supervisor and his agents assurance that bureau officials supported the action and would take responsibility for its criminal nature if necessary.

Institutionalizing Domestic Counterterrorism

Just as he had fretted about leftist insurgent violence earlier in his presidency, President Nixon spent the months after the Munich siege worrying about a Palestinian nationalist attack in the United States. Shortly after the Munich attack, Jean Dixon, a purported psychic with a popular syndicated column, predicted that Black September would carry out a terrorist attack targeting Yitzhak Rabin, Israeli's ambassador to the United States. On September 21, after his secretary Rose Mary Woods told him about Dixon's prediction, Nixon shared his concerns with his national security advisor, Henry Kissinger. "Suppose [Black September] kidnap[s] Rabin, Henry, and demand[s] that we release all blacks who are prisoners around the United States, and we didn't and they shoot him? . . . We have got to have a plan." He was adamant. "We have got to have contingency plans for hijacking, for kidnapping, for all sorts of things that [could] happen around here."[28] Nixon made his comment a few days after Palestinian militants based in Amsterdam sent letter bombs to Israeli targets in multiple countries, stoking further post-Munich hysteria over the threat of international terrorism. One of the explosives killed an Israeli diplomat in London, though officials intercepted the remaining bombs in Brussels, Geneva, Paris, Jerusalem, Montreal, Ottawa, and New York.[29]

At Kissinger's suggestion, Nixon formed the CCCT less than three weeks after the Munich attack. Kissinger conceived the CCCT as a way to placate Israel, whose air force had just killed more than 200 Arab civilians in raids on PLO bases in Lebanon and Syria in retaliation for the Munich attack.

Kissinger hoped to prevent further Israeli escalation by demonstrating that the United States was taking the problem of international terrorism seriously. Nixon's feelings about the CCCT were far more earnest.[30] In the aftermath of the Huston Plan that Nixon aborted two years earlier, the CCCT at last provided the president with a federal agency dedicated to combating terrorism. After more than three years of conflict with domestic leftist guerrillas, the CCCT's formation marked the federal government's formal institutionalization of counterterrorism.

L. Patrick Gray attended the CCCT's first meeting on September 25, 1972. Presiding over the meeting was the committee's appointed chair, David Young, who codirected the Plumbers on behalf of his boss, Nixon's assistant for domestic affairs and fellow Watergate conspirator, John Ehrlichman. Ehrlichman also attended the meeting, where he announced that the FBI, rather than the CIA or State Department, would be the sole agency responsible for fighting terrorism inside the United States.[31]

By coincidence, the CCCT meeting took place in Washington on the very same day that Mark Felt convened a conference of FBI SACs from around the country. According to Edward Miller, Felt had organized the conference at the request of Gray, who had decided to reauthorize surreptitious entries for both the Al Fatah and Weather Underground investigations. The point of the conference was to inform FBI field officers of the bureau's new policy of permitting break-ins for terrorism investigations. Miller recalled that Gray made an appearance during Felt's conference to announce: "I want you to make damn sure that you don't do any of these [break-ins] without the Bureau's authority!"[32] Felt also recollected Gray's statement, adding in his 1979 memoir that the acting director "ordered an all-out effort to prevent terrorism in the United States."[33] In all likelihood, Gray addressed the FBI field supervisors' conference after having just left the CCCT meeting. Because the minutes to the first CCCT meeting are classified, it is unknown whether Ehrlichman and Gray discussed reinstituting break-ins. What is known is that immediately after the CCCT meeting, Gray verbally instructed FBI officials to reauthorize break-ins, submitting at last to the White House's long-standing demand since shortly after Nixon came into office.

After Munich, the FBI shifted from a focus on urban guerrilla warfare toward terrorism. The new language was all over a memo Gray wrote to Edward Miller about the FBI's new efforts to develop contingency plans for high-profile terrorist attacks:

We are in an age of terrorism. A potential attack of the sort which occurred at Lod Airport or which occurred at the time of the Munich massacre could happen in the U.S. The tactic of the urban guerrilla, often used in Latin America Algeria, the Middle East and elsewhere in the world, was introduced into the U.S. about five years ago and we have seen ample evidence of it in the form of ambushed police officers and terrorist bombings which have included the U.S. Capitol and the Pentagon. We now accept the existence of urban guerrilla terrorism and the fact that the urban guerrilla's philosophy of terrorism has made it necessary for law enforcement to adopt new standards and adapt to the constant threat of terrorist attack. We recognize that FBI personnel have been targeted for assault or assassination.[34]

Gray also argued that the terrorist threat required major FBI field offices to acquire caches of weapons and other equipment left over from the army's use in Vietnam. This included body armor, shotguns, gas masks, and bullhorns. Ironically, U.S. counterinsurgency tactics in Vietnam that had helped inspire leftist guerrilla resistance inside the United States were now coming home in the form of domestic counterterrorism.[35]

While the Munich attacks compelled Gray to focus bureau resources on combating guerrilla violence, he also had to navigate economic, legal, and political restraints on the bureau's surveillance powers. Public scrutiny over FBI surveillance practices unleashed by the April 1971 burglary in Media, Pennsylvania, intensified over time, particularly in early 1973. On January 31, NBC television journalist Carl Stern sued the Justice Department and FBI under the Freedom of Information Act for access to files related to the mysterious COINTELPRO-New Left program that had been referenced in a document uncovered through the Media burglary. Over the next three years, Stern's lawsuit led to the declassification of the FBI's COINTELPRO documents and, eventually, the 1975 Senate Church Committee reports on mass surveillance and covert operations carried out by the FBI and other federal intelligence agencies.[36]

Meanwhile, the FBI's Watergate, Weather Underground, BLA, and MEDBURG investigations used a massive amount of FBI resources. Each involved special investigative units that consumed manpower throughout the FBI's fifty-nine field offices. Nixon's mandate through the CCCT, that the FBI take responsibility for all terrorist attacks in the United States, demanded still more bureau resources. After Munich, FBI officials rapidly worked to develop training and operational protocols for hostage negotiation and armed standoff situations, both of which required coordination with outside police and military agencies.[37]

In response to the changing political climate, Gray significantly reorganized the bureau's domestic surveillance practices. During the 1973 fiscal year (FY), which roughly covered the period of Gray's tenure, the FBI reduced its use of informants in "extremist" investigations by approximately 20 percent.[38] Much of this reduction was due to Gray's elimination of the FBI's Ghetto Informant Program, which Hoover established in 1967 in an attempt to gain advance warning of popular rebellions in African American inner-city communities.[39] Gray also "drastically reduced" the number of Americans on the FBI's Administrative Index (ADEX), which listed individuals deemed a threat to national security. Though the precise number of individuals on the ADEX under Gray's tenure is unavailable, his efforts contributed to a reduction of names on the list from over 12,000 in November 1971 to 1,250 in November 1975.[40]

Gray's reduction of domestic surveillance did not reflect changes in FBI officials' attitudes toward mass surveillance. Rather, this was part of a calculated effort to placate the FBI's critics while more efficiently redirecting domestic security operations toward communities he and other state officials deemed prone to terrorism. After Munich, Palestinians and others of Arab descent quickly became the number one community targeted for suspicion of supporting terrorism, and the FBI's activities demonstrated little regard for civil liberties.

Harassing Arabs

L. Patrick Gray and Mark Felt asserted that the Arabs and Arab Americans they targeted after Munich were foreign "assassins" and "terrorists," and that the bureau successfully "harassed" them "out of the country."[41] Though the threat of Palestinian nationalist violence was real, these were gross exaggerations that served to whitewash the FBI's harassment of innocent people.

Among those targeted by the Arab scare, the FBI's post-Munich harassment of Arab Americans and Arab students in the United States is typically remembered as "Operation Boulder": the obscure name for the State Department's program of intensified screening of visa applications from people of Arab descent. Operation Boulder lasted from September 1972 until officials called it off in April 1975, claiming the program was not cost-effective, though the cancellation coincided with lawsuits launched by Abdeen Jabara and the opening of the Church Committee and Pike Committee investigations of federal intelligence agencies.

In just over two years of existence, Operation Boulder screened more than 150,000 Arab visas through the CIA, FBI, Immigration and Naturalization Service (INS), and Secret Service, but only twenty-three applicants were denied entry on security grounds. INS agents also investigated all of the approximately 80,000 Arabs present in the United States on student or visitor visas, many of whom they interrogated about their views on Palestine and Israel. By January 1973, just over three months after initiating the program, INS agents had coerced more than one hundred Arabs to leave the country. A majority of these cases involved formal deportation proceedings, with the most common violation being employment without permission. However, with one or two possible exceptions discussed below, federal officials did not find any Arabs in the United States who were involved in guerrilla activity.[42]

FBI and State Department officials claimed Operation Boulder was effective in keeping dangerous terrorists out of the country. Arab Americans and their allies, on the other hand, considered the program an example of biased ethnic profiling. The critics had a point. Federal authorities' broad preemptive policing actions cast all members of an ethnically diverse cultural-linguistic group as terror suspects.[43] In the name of fighting terrorism, the state sent waves of terror through America's Arab diasporic communities.

The FBI's harassment campaign, operating in parallel with Operation Boulder and the INS's own campaign of harassment, was at the center of the Arab scare. Numerous Arab Americans recalled their frightening encounters with FBI agents after the Munich attacks. Contrary to claims by Mark Felt and L. Patrick Gray, the vast majority of these individuals were not terrorists.

Jamil Azzah was a senior engineer for the Missouri Highway Department. In the fall of 1972, an FBI agent visited his Kansas City apartment and demanded his fingerprints for an alleged terrorist investigation. Azzah denied the accusation, however, and the FBI did not follow through in pressing charges. After he complained to the bureau about his treatment, the supervisor of the agent who harassed him apologized. "Such accusations," the local FBI official admitted, "are a tactic sometimes used by agents to obtain information."[44] In Chicago, Arabs reported being detained by FBI agents who took them on "night rides" to interrogate them about their political beliefs and affiliations.[45]

The FBI's questioning of Arab Americans demonstrated that agents perceived any opposition to Israel or sympathy for the Palestinian freedom struggle as potential support for terrorism. Consider the interrogation of Ishan Diab, a professor of pharmacology at the University of Chicago who had come to the United States from Palestine at age twelve. When an FBI agent asked him about his views on Fatah, Diab was astounded by his interrogator's political bias and ignorance of Arab views on Middle Eastern affairs. "Ninety percent of the 15,000 Arabs in the Chicago area sympathize with Fatah!" he replied.[46] FBI agents' questioning confirmed that in their effort to prevent clandestine political violence, the bureau was taking preemptive police action against a broad, stigmatized ethnic community. Pierre Alwan, a naturalized immigrant from Lebanon residing in Southern California, remembered FBI agents questioning him about his connections with Palestinian political groups as well as the political activities of other Arab Americans. "We are checking on you Arabs because we don't want a repeat of Munich," the agents told him.[47]

Arab American political activists bore the brunt of FBI harassment. Attorney Abdeen Jabara kept records of such activity, documenting examples of at least thirty-one Detroit-area activists visited by the FBI. This included most of the prominent political figures in the Arab American enclave of Dearborn, Michigan. Among them was Don Unis, a third-generation Lebanese American activist with the Arab Community Center for Economic and Social Services (ACCESS) in Dearborn's Southend neighborhood. Agents showed Unis photographs of local Arab Americans and asked if they had connections to Palestinian militant groups. Unis recalled the FBI's questions: "What is ACCESS, AACC, Arab Center? Do Red Crescent and UHLF send money to fedayeen? Do you donate? . . . What kind of meetings do you go to and where? Will you cooperate and give information if you know of some terror activities? Do you think the above names are capable of doing terror?"[48]

In addition to prompting preemptive police action, panic over a Munich-style terrorist attack in the United States sent FBI agents chasing false leads as they sought to defend Americans from phantom terrorists. Declassified FBI documents indicate that on September 12, 1972, a week after the Munich attack, special agents mobilized throughout the eastern United States in response to intelligence from an undetermined source warning that Black September militants sought to blow up airliners at an East Coast airport. The attack was supposedly scheduled to happen before the close of the Munich Games, which Olympic officials had resumed after a brief suspension to mourn the murdered Israeli athletes.[49] FBI agents from Boston to San Juan spent approximately forty-eight hours alerting local airport security agencies of possible violence and searching for the origins of the intelligence before the New York FBI office determined that the investigation was "the outgrowth of a rumor running rampant the last several days and has no validity whatsoever."[50] The FBI dropped the investigation and the attack never materialized.

A couple months later, the FBI scrambled in response to another false alarm in Chicago. On November 24, 160 armed FBI agents converged on O'Hare International Airport in response to information that terrorists were planning a "Lod-style" massacre.[51] The threat proved to be a nonstarter. Nevertheless, Gray considered the FBI's response to be "an excellent field test for evaluating our emergency procedures for dealing with threatened terrorist attacks."[52]

Felt and Gray's claims that the Arab scare prevented planned guerrilla attacks were exaggerations, if not outright lies. Gray, for instance, falsely claimed that Black September's plot to blow up an airliner at an East Coast U.S. airport was authentic, and that the FBI thwarted it using information obtained from the Dallas break-in.[53] But investigators' many misrepresentations shouldn't be taken as proof that there was nothing to investigate. A few scraps of evidence found in the National Archives suggest that the FBI may have foiled at least one potential plotter.

The Dallas Arab Information Center's director, Seife Wadi, was a Palestinian with a degree from Southern Illinois University. He did not initially flee the United States when the FBI singled him out. On the contrary, the State Department denied him a return visa when he sought to come back to Texas after traveling in the Middle East. Wadi's successor at the Arab Information Center, Palestinian American Munir Bayoud, later asserted that his predecessor had been out of the country on his honeymoon.[54] However, in their secret documents, FBI officials referred to Wadi as the "leader of Fatah in the United States" and alleged that he was using his travels to gain approval and funding for attacks inside the country. Even though officials denied his multiple visa renewal requests, Wadi managed to sneak back in to the United States in late November using a Qatari diplomatic passport issued to him in Kuwait. The FBI learned of Wadi's presence in the United States through its tap on the Dallas Arab Information Center's office phone. At the FBI's request, officers from the INS arrested Wadi in New York City's Drake Hotel on December 5. At the urging of federal authorities, he "voluntarily" left the country the next day.[55]

In reports to the CCCT, the FBI hailed Wadi's deportation as a successful move to preempt Palestinian nationalist terrorism in the United States. As of December 7, 1972, the FBI also reportedly had under surveillance "another fedayeen [PLO guerrilla] member, who may have participated in previous skyjackings." At the time, agents were preparing to arrest and deport the individual.[56] Though further documentation of Wadi's alleged plans remains unavailable, the fact that he had the resolve and resources to surreptitiously enter the United States after multiple visa rejections gives some credence to the FBI's assertions. Wadi's actions also raise doubts about claims that he was merely trying to return from his honeymoon. On the other hand, the fact that federal agents deported Wadi rather than indicting him suggests they may not have possessed solid evidence linking him to a violent plot. It is also entirely possible that the FBI targeted Wadi to impress the CCCT and made inaccurate claims about him to justify its illegal break-ins to the Senate Watergate Committee.

It is unclear whether Munir Bayoud really meant it a few years later when he claimed that Wadi had no ties to terrorism. Did Bayoud sincerely believe this? Was he just covering for a friend? Or was this in fact true? Whatever the case, Bayoud's statement was certainly informed by his own experience of harassment by FBI agents after the Munich attacks, which made him feel so threatened that he sought an attorney.[57] Bayoud was an American, however, and the FBI was not successful in driving him from his country. Bayoud also insisted that the document FBI agents stole from Wadi's briefcase in the Arab Information Center safe was not a list of terrorists but a mailing list containing names of students and other people of Arab descent living in the United States.[58]

Though the Wadi case remains a mystery, it is clear that a few supporters of the Palestinian cause did attempt attacks in the United States. These individuals managed to bypass Operation Boulder and other preemptive counterterrorism measures.

In January 1973, a small group of Middle Eastern guerrillas made their way to New York City during Israeli prime minister Golda Meir's visit to the United Nations. PLO-affiliated Iraqi militant Khalid Duhhan Al-Jawary and two accomplices set up three car bombs outside Israeli banks in Manhattan and the El Al terminal at Kennedy Airport. If the bombs had exploded, it would have been a realization of Gray's worst fears. However, the guerrillas were thwarted not by the FBI's post-Munich security efforts but by their own mistakes—faulty design prevented the homemade bombs from detonating.[59] Much like Weatherman's botched efforts to bomb a Detroit police station in March 1970, the Al-Jawary group's technical error averted bloodshed, and spared the FBI, Nixon, and other authorities a major crisis.

Later in 1973, assailants with likely connections to the Palestinian struggle carried out a successful attack inside the United States. Though far less dramatic than the Munich bloodbath, the incident vindicated CCCT and FBI fears that militants would seek to attack Israeli diplomatic personnel. The target was Colonel Yosef Alon, a handsome forty-three-year-old Israeli Air Force veteran who served as military attaché for the Israeli embassy in Washington, D.C., where he worked to secure F-4 Phantom jets and other U.S. weapons for his country's wars with its Arab neighbors. Early in the morning of July 1, Alon and his wife Dvora pulled into the driveway of their home in Chevy Chase, Maryland, after returning from a dinner party. As Alon stepped out of his car, a gunman opened up on him with five rounds from a foreign-made .38-caliber revolver. He died on site.[60]

Later that day, a PLO radio broadcast in Cairo took credit for the action. Voice of Palestine broadcasters claimed Alon's assassination was retaliation for the death of Algerian PFLP commander Mohamed Boudia, whom Mossad agents had slain with a car bomb in Paris a few days earlier as part of Operation Wrath of God, a covert Israeli military campaign dedicated to killing suspected perpetrators of the Munich attack.[61]

The CIA initially believed that Alon's assassination had been carried out by a two-man Black September hit team that managed to slip in and out of the United States. The FBI investigated the case but closed it in 1978 after failing to turn up sufficient evidence. In 2011, however, the bureau reopened the case in response to an unexpected turn of events. In a letter to an American journalist penned in a French prison, Ilich Ramírez Sánchez—the notorious incarcerated Venezuelan militant popularly known as "Carlos the Jackal," who succeeded Mohamed Boudia as European commander of the PFLP in 1973—claimed to have information on the identities of Alon's assassins. When an FBI agent interrogated Ramírez Sánchez, the veteran Marxist-Leninist guerrilla claimed that the attackers were a trio of American Vietnam War veterans (at least one of them African American). According to Ramírez Sánchez, in the early 1970s the veterans resided in Paris, where they frequented a bookstore owned by Mahmoud Saleh, a Mauritanian man with links to the PLO. When the vets expressed interest in supporting the Palestinian liberation struggle, Saleh introduced the men to Black September operative Kamel Kheir Beik, who suggested they kill Alon.[62]

The Alon assassination remains unsolved, but whether the assailants were foreign Black September commandos or American military veterans, the case underscores the limits of counterterrorism. Despite the CCCT, the State Department's Operation Boulder, INS and FBI investigations, mass surveillance of American dissidents, FBI break-ins, and the harassment of hundreds of Arabs and Arab Americans, determined clandestine operatives still managed to assassinate a prominent Israeli diplomat outside his suburban Washington home. Counterterrorism could certainly *counter* terrorism, but such policing efforts could neither prevent all insurgent violence nor eliminate its root causes.

· · · · · ·

Four months after the Munich attacks and Nixon's founding of the CCCT, L. Patrick Gray addressed an audience of police and intelligence agents in a speech at the National Symposium on Terrorism held at the FBI Academy in Quantico, Virginia. His remarks were part of a new global conversation about fears of international terrorism.

"The terrorist," Gray proclaimed, "is an outlaw, a wild animal, a jungle killer!" "How the terrorist got that way is not important," he continued. "We're not interested in the psychological, philosophical, sociological factors on the terrorist scene." The priority of law enforcement, Gray asserted, was not to understand "terrorists" and their motives but to forcibly prevent them from killing "innocents."[63]

Gray's remarks attacked not only terrorism but also intellectualism. He actively refused to examine terrorists' motives and seemed to imply that those who employed scholarly research to understand insurgent violence were themselves suspect. To some this may seem counterintuitive. After all, wouldn't it make sense for the head of the FBI to understand why terrorists engaged in violence? Couldn't understanding this help the FBI and other agencies take steps to prevent such violence from taking place?

Gray's anti-intellectualism highlights an important dynamic in the early development of American counterterrorism. From the outset, as they built institutions like the CCCT, overhauled the FBI's Domestic Security Division, and improvised new policing tactics and investigative practices, key officials involved in the invention of counterterrorism engaged in what sociologist Lisa Stampnitzky has called a "politics of anti-knowledge."[64] As the FBI's Domestic Security Division hosted its latest terrorism conference, Gray made it clear that terrorism should be combatted through policing and militarism: "I have just ordered within the last two days further action to be taken on the creation of hypothetical [terrorism] situations and that those situations be war gamed and practiced out under the most realistic of conditions."[65]

Other political discussion on how to address insurgent violence was off the table, much as Communist politics was not up for discussion among American political leaders during the early years of the Cold War. Implicitly—based on Gray's dismissing the fields of psychology, philosophy, and sociology—topics to avoid included consideration of police oversight, conflict resolution, transformative justice, social democracy, and foreign policy rooted in a commitment to peace and human rights. Decades before President George W. Bush answered the question *Why do they hate us?* by calling the 9/11 attackers "evil doers," America's founding counterterrorism officials engaged in an "active refusal of explanation itself."[66] By framing the FBI's work as an urgent crusade against maniacal "jungle killers," Gray dehumanized those he considered terrorists, creating an environment in which his agents could feel morally justified in preemptively harassing people based on their Arab ethnicity or other characteristics that marked them as potential terrorism supporters.

American leaders avoided addressing the causes of insurgent violence, but they continued to beef up security. Just days before Gray's speech at the FBI's National Symposium on Terrorism, the Department of Transportation began implementing a new federal policy of screening all luggage and passengers boarding planes at U.S. airports. The new policy was a response to more than four dozen plane hijackings that had taken place in the United States over the past decade. Though most of these attacks had been carried out by apolitical criminal extortionists, a few had involved leftist militants seeking passage to Cuba or Algeria. The federal government's new screening policy led to a dramatic decrease in skyjackings and laid the foundation for the militarized airport security that Americans in the post-9/11 era have come to take for granted. Around the same time, the Department of Justice also quietly signed an agreement with the Department of Defense to make military assistance available to the FBI in the case of a terrorist crisis.[67]

Terrorism was not the only thing on L. Patrick Gray's mind at the beginning of 1973, however. The Watergate scandal was now erupting into public view. At the same time that he sought to balance pressure to prevent terrorism with the need to comply with legal restrictions on preventive surveillance tactics, Gray sought to navigate Mark Felt's secret "Deep Throat" counterintelligence operations, on the one hand, and Nixon's efforts to enlist him in his Watergate cover-up, on the other. Over the next several months, such feats would prove to be beyond Gray's capacity.

10 Implosion

· ·

Not long after starting his second term, President Richard Nixon decided to give the FBI's acting director L. Patrick Gray a promotion. Nixon would change Gray's title to director, making him a permanent successor to the legendary J. Edgar Hoover. On February 16, 1973, the president received Gray in the Oval Office to share his news. It was only their second meeting since nine months earlier, when on the day after Hoover's death, Nixon instructed his new appointee to clean house in the FBI and ensure that the loyalties of bureau officials aligned with the White House rather than with the deceased director.[1]

Gray's promotion came with conditions, of course. The president again demanded loyalty from his prospective FBI director, a demand that held particular importance as the Watergate scandal spiraled quickly out of control.

Just a few months earlier, in November, Nixon had won his reelection in a landslide. The cover-up directed by John Ehrlichman and John Dean had successfully convinced a majority of voters that the summer's break-in at the Democratic National Committee office was, in the words of White House press secretary Ron Ziegler, nothing more than a "third-rate burglary attempt" with no connection to the president.[2] But new evidence increasingly pointed to ties between the Watergate burglars and the White House, and the public was beginning to take notice. In January, Plumber ringleaders Howard Hunt and Gordon Liddy took guilty pleas along with all five of the Watergate burglars. In exchange for hundreds of thousands of dollars withdrawn from the coffers of the Committee to Reelect the President (CREEP), the men concealed their connections to Nixon cabinet members Egil Krogh and David Young, chair of the Cabinet Committee to Combat Terrorism (CCCT). On February 2, however, Judge John Sirica announced his belief that the full Watergate story had yet to be revealed. Five days later, the Senate voted unanimously to establish a bipartisan committee to investigate the scandal.[3]

Nixon understood that Gray's confirmation hearings before the Senate Judiciary Committee would present hostile Democratic congressmen their first opportunity to grill an official with ties to Watergate. The president demanded assurance that Gray would stand up to hard-hitting questions about the FBI's Watergate investigation and recent revelations of FBI spying on American citizens. Moreover, Nixon wanted his presumptive FBI director to defend the federal government's prerogative to engage in warrantless wiretapping and other illegal surveillance. Gray was to justify his position by citing the threat of terrorism. "There's this violent Jewish committee that wants to kill the Arabs, and the Arabs want to kill the Jews. . . . Hijacking is another thing," the president exclaimed. "Some of that requires wiretapping. It's your responsibility to do this, and your authority. I just don't think that we should be defensive. . . . We must not be denied the use of the weapon. The idea that we're wiretapping a lot of political groups is bullshit."[4]

Nixon also demanded that Gray eliminate the leaks he believed were coming from within the FBI, specifically from Associate Director Mark Felt. "You haven't been able to do anything—or have you?—about the leaking coming out of the Bureau," the president stated. "The lines lead very directly to [Felt]."[5]

Gray insisted that he had the FBI under control and that the leaks were coming from outside the bureau. The acting director still believed Felt's repeated personal avowals that he was not involved in the leaks. Gray could hardly get a word in, however. This was not a true meeting—it was more of an unhinged monologue, as Nixon vented his frustrations over the unfolding Watergate scandal.

Ironically, amid the deepening political crisis, the president longed for the leadership of his erstwhile friend J. Edgar Hoover. As much as the deceased FBI director had frustrated Nixon in private, Hoover always maintained discipline within the FBI, and in public he never hesitated to support the president's calls for law-and-order policing to suppress civil disorder, insurgent violence, and leaks of classified information. "This stuff didn't leak when Hoover was there," Nixon declared. FBI personnel, the president insisted, need "to fear the man at the top, and you've got to get that again." "You remember in World War II," he continued, "the Germans, if they went through a town and one of their soldiers was hit by a sniper, they'd line up the whole goddamned town and say, 'Until you talk every one of you is going to be shot.' I really think that's what has to be done. I mean, I don't think you can be Mr. Nice Guy over there."[6]

With nods of assurance and the few sentences he managed to insert into the gaps in the president's tirade, Gray managed to convince Nixon that he could handle the position of FBI director. A "Nixon loyalist. You're goddamn right I am," Gray assured his boss.[7] He left the Oval Office with the nomination.

Within two months Gray would be out of a job. The confirmation hearings turned out to be a disaster for the Nixon administration, especially after Gray spilled information uncovering more White House links to the Watergate cover-up. As the scandal widened, Nixon withdrew Gray's nomination, and Gray decided to resign from his post as the FBI's acting director.

Gray's political downfall was yet another unexpected consequence of the bureaucratic conflict between J. Edgar Hoover's FBI and the White House that began shortly after Nixon took office four years earlier. Though concerns over leftist guerrilla violence and state surveillance had been at the center of this conflict from the outset, in the hands of Hoover loyalist W. Mark Felt it had transformed into a covert information war to defend from Nixon the FBI that Hoover had built as an autonomous federal intelligence agency. Gray was at once a pawn of Nixon's efforts to control the FBI and a helpless victim of Felt's covert campaign to make Watergate Nixon's epitaph.

Gray was caught in the middle, torn between his responsibilities to lead an independent federal intelligence agency and his sense of obligation toward a president who expected him to do his political bidding. Balancing these conflicting priorities became untenable after the Watergate break-in, as Felt's secret leaks severely undermined Gray, giving Washington the impression that he had no control over the FBI.

Felt's leaks continued throughout the fall of 1972 and into early 1973, as Gray prepared for his confirmation hearings before the Senate Judiciary Committee. However, in addition to bringing down Gray, Felt's private COINTELPRO had another unintended consequence: it brought down his career as well. Though Gray had believed Felt when he denied accusations that he was the anonymous source known as Deep Throat, Gray's replacement, Acting Director William D. Ruckelshaus, did not. In one of the most significant actions of his five-week term at the top of the FBI, Ruckelshaus forced Felt into retirement on May 15, 1973.[8]

The Hoover-Nixon conflict culminated with the downfall of the two men who became the most powerful figures in the FBI after Hoover's death. Above all, Hoover's foremost concern had been protecting the FBI's public image, which he knew was necessary to uphold the bureau's power and autonomy. But leftist guerrilla violence and other resistance to violent U.S. government activities locked the FBI and White House in an ongoing battle. As officials sought to both prevent violent attacks and minimize public outcry over intrusive surveillance practices, Hoover and Nixon, and officials inside the FBI, staunchly disagreed over what kinds of surveillance practices to implement and who should authorize and control such activities. After Hoover's death, Felt and Gray had led efforts to update the FBI's domestic security operations to confront the problem of terrorism, but it turned out that neither man would get to follow through with this task. Instead, this responsibility would fall to former Kansas City police chief Clarence M. Kelley, who gained an appointment as the second permanent FBI director on July 9, 1973.

And of course, Nixon would end his career in disgrace as well. Nixon's authoritarian insistence on using break-ins to defeat his critics had led to the Watergate debacle, and Felt's leaks had played a critical role in exposing the White House cover-up. On August 9, 1974, facing the likelihood of impeachment and removal from office, Nixon resigned the presidency.

But the fall of Nixon, Gray, and Felt was not the only irony of the FBI's war with leftist guerrillas. All of the manpower and tremendous resources the FBI had dedicated to fighting guerrilla violence—and that leadership had spent dueling over tactics and control—proved largely ineffectual in preempting clandestine revolutionaries.

The Weather Underground and the BLA both effectively imploded on their own in 1973 and 1974. The Weather Underground withered quietly, while the BLA sputtered out in a wave of violent clashes with police that opened up investigative leads for the FBI and the New York Police Department, whose investigators collaborated in an interagency task force.

The FBI's war with domestic leftist guerrillas was far from over, however. In early 1974, the FBI took on a new leftist guerrilla organization, the cult-like Symbionese Liberation Army out of the San Francisco Bay Area. On February 4, the group kidnapped nineteen-year-old newspaper heiress Patty Hearst from her Berkeley apartment, unleashing an enormous, nationwide FBI investigation. Under the leadership of Director Kelley, the FBI continued to improvise its approach to counterterrorism, with limited success, as the bureau's public reputation continued its downslide.

The Fall of Gray and Felt

President Nixon did not really want Pat Gray to be his FBI director. On January 8, 1972, just five weeks before nominating Gray to the position, the president repeated to H. R. Haldeman an opinion he had shared with his chief of staff back in August: "Gray can't cut it."[9]

Gray's credibility had been undermined by Mark Felt's leaks. Felt had continued to feed information to journalists at the *Washington Post* and *Time* throughout the fall of 1972. Most of his leaking amounted to corroborating information that journalists Bob Woodward and Sandy Smith had gathered from other sources, but he occasionally offered up new information as well. The most important story to come out that autumn was one published after Bob Woodward spent five and a half predawn hours interviewing Felt in a parking garage beneath the Oakhill Office Building in the Washington suburb of Rosslyn, Virginia. The next day, the *Post* printed Woodward and Bernstein's cover story, with the headline, "FBI Finds Nixon Aides Sabotaged Democrats." "FBI agents," the article revealed, "have established that the Watergate bugging incident stemmed from a massive campaign of political spying and sabotage conducted on behalf of President Nixon's reelection and directed by officials of the White House and Committee for Reelection of the President." Anonymously citing Felt as "federal investigative officials," the story reported that operatives working for the Nixon administration were engaged in an "offensive security" program that involved "trying to disrupt and spy on Democratic campaigns." Most of these activities, the article noted, had been bankrolled by a fund controlled by John Mitchell, both while he was attorney general and while he was Nixon's reelection campaign manager.[10]

The *Post* story was a bombshell, but it did not result in the preelection scandal the authors had predicted. The indicted Plumbers were keeping quiet thanks to CREEP hush money. Nixon's law-and-order campaign message also remained popular among white voters, and the president successfully tarred his opponent, George McGovern, as the candidate of "Acid, Amnesty, and Abortion."[11] The story did, however, lead President Nixon to realize that Mark Felt was Deep Throat.

Nixon found out thanks to the chief manager of his Watergate cover-up, John Dean. Dean had learned about Felt's leaking from Henry E. Petersen, head of the Justice Department's Criminal Justice Division, who had received this information from an undisclosed attorney who worked for either the *Washington Post* or *Time*.[12]

Nixon and his men were livid when they learned the news. "Now why the hell would he do that?" Nixon asked.

But they realized they could not do anything to stop Felt. He had too much power. "If we move on him, he'll go out and unload everything," Bob Haldeman warned. "He knows everything that's to be known in the FBI."[13]

News of Felt's leaking came to Gray via Attorney General Richard Kleindienst and White House special counsel Charles W. Colson. The acting director was unconvinced, however. When Gray asked Felt about the accusations, he firmly denied it. "You can transfer me if you don't believe it," Felt said. "But those allegations are not true."[14]

Gray believed Felt. The assistant director had come to rely on Felt during his frequent absences from FBI headquarters, and as the associate director had helped him manage the Watergate investigation as well as the FBI's war on leftist guerrillas and suspected Palestinian nationalist militants. Felt had never revealed his disloyalty to his supervisor. Instead, working as a skillful manipulator of the FBI bureaucracy, he had ingratiated himself to the acting director, earning Gray's trust while making himself indispensable.

Gray later recalled his trust in Felt, and his skepticism of Kleindienst, who claimed to have learned of Felt's leaking from an attorney who worked for *Time* magazine: "Choosing between the personal word of the number two man in the FBI, a man sworn to uphold the law, and the frequent unreliability of a reporter, I chose the former without a second thought."[15]

With this vote of confidence, Felt's leaks continued straight up to the time of Gray's confirmation hearings.

By February 1973, the president concluded he had no choice but to nominate Gray as permanent FBI director. Gray's credibility may have been undermined by the ongoing leaks, but Nixon knew that whether he appointed him or not, Gray would get called to testify before the new Senate Watergate committee. He sought to avoid the appearance of attempting to cover up the Watergate investigation and calculated that if Gray was going to testify about Watergate, it would be better for him to do so during his confirmation hearings, as a loyal ally to the White House rather than as an adversary in the Senate Watergate investigation. As John Dean later put it, "The only thing worse than nominating Gray would have been not nominating him."[16]

Perhaps Nixon felt cautiously optimistic after congratulating Gray on becoming his nominee at their February 16 Oval Office meeting. If so, such feelings did not last long. Gray's Senate Judiciary Committee hearings, which lasted from February 28 to March 22, could not have gone worse for the president or his nominee.

Felt made sure the hearings got off to a rocky start. In late February, Felt informed Sandy Smith about the "Kissinger Wiretaps" that Hoover had installed at Nixon's insistence back in 1969. Gray had nothing to do with these wiretaps—he didn't even know about their existence. But the story Smith published ensured that Gray would have to answer for Hoover's illegal surveillance during his confirmation hearings. *Time* published the article "Questions about Gray" on February 26, two days before the start of Gray's hearings. Smith characterized Gray as a partisan hack committed to "turning the FBI into an arm of the administration." He also exposed the Kissinger wiretaps to the public for the first time and alleged that Gray had extended approval of the surveillance after Hoover's death.[17]

Smith's article suffered from a number of falsehoods. Gray's partisanship was overstated, and the claim that the acting director had extended the Kissinger wiretaps was patently false—Hoover had discontinued this surveillance in February 1971. Felt had fed Smith a bit of false information, and in printing it, the journalist had become an unwitting accomplice in Deep Throat's private counterintelligence campaign. The result was a hearing that could hardly have gone better, from Felt's perspective. On the second day of the hearings, Senator Ted Kennedy (D-MA) grilled Gray about the wiretaps. Gray's insistence that he knew nothing about them was met with disbelief. He later faced a perjury investigation on the matter, but the Watergate special prosecutor dropped the charges in early 1974.[18]

A new and unexpected domestic insurgency cast a further cloud over Gray's confirmation hearings. On the night of February 27, less than twenty-four hours before the start of the hearings, the American Indian Movement (AIM) led an armed seizure of Wounded Knee, South Dakota, site of the U.S. Army's massacre of more than 200 Lakota Sioux eighty-three years earlier. Like other recent instances of armed insurgency, the Wounded Knee occupation had deep historical roots in unresolved political conflicts. In this case, AIM and traditional Oglala Sioux elders sought to unseat the Pine Ridge Reservation's controversial president Dick Wilson and compel the U.S. government to return lands that had been seized from the tribe in violation of the 1868 Treaty of Fort Laramie.[19] "For the rest of my confirmation hearings," Gray later recalled, "I would have to alternate between defending myself and the FBI against the partisan jabs of the Democratic senators on the Hill and trying to oversee the federal response to an armed insurrection 1,500 miles away."[20]

In reality, Gray's attention wasn't as divided as he claimed. As with most major crises undertaken during Gray's tenure, FBI activities at Wounded Knee would be coordinated primarily by Mark Felt, who took instructions from Attorney General Kleindienst. From FBI headquarters, Felt gave orders by phone to Joseph Trimbach, SAC of the bureau's Minneapolis field office, who led efforts on the ground in South Dakota in collaboration with representatives of the Justice Department and U.S. Marshals Service.[21]

The FBI was compelled to respond to Wounded Knee because Nixon's recently established CCCT designated the bureau as the primary federal agency responsible for incidents of terrorism. Though bureau officials did not consider the siege to be an act of terrorism, AIM militants initially took eleven white townspeople hostage when they raided the hamlet. AIM radicals also fired on the FBI's vehicles as agents set up roadblocks to keep out two caravans of AIM reinforcements who were driving up from Denver and Nebraska. With South Dakota's governor refusing to deploy the National Guard and Nixon denying Mark Felt's request to send in the army, federal authorities deferred to the new CCCT guidelines, and the FBI was left to manage the siege in conjunction with the Justice Department and the U.S. Marshals (though the army secretly sent in a team of "advisors" to test a secret plan for managing civil disturbances hatched in 1968 called Operation Garden Plot).[22]

The standoff quickly escalated into the largest federal military mobilization on U.S. soil since the Indian wars of the late nineteenth century. Lasting seventy-one days and garnering international media coverage, the Wounded Knee siege pit a few hundred American Indian militants fortified behind sandbags and trenches and armed mostly with hunting rifles against more than 200 FBI agents, U.S. Marshals, and Bureau of Indian Affairs officers. The army quietly supplied federal forces with a military arsenal that included "15 armored personnel carriers, 100,000 rounds of M-16 ammunition, 1,100 parachute flares, 20 sniper rifles with scopes, plus gas masks, bulletproof vests, C-rations, ponchos, blankets, canteens and helmets."[23] Federal forces were goaded on and sometimes assisted by Dick Wilson's hundreds of Indian vigilantes, the Guardians of the Oglala Nation, otherwise known as the GOONs. Thousands of bullets were fired during the siege, which resulted in the deaths of an FBI agent, a U.S. Marshal, and two Indian activists.[24]

The Wounded Knee incident further damaged the FBI's reputation, as public opinion largely favored AIM and the Oglala Sioux elders. One poll found that approximately 51 percent of Americans sympathized with AIM while only 21 percent sided with the government.[25] In one of the most visible displays of support for the Native American activists, actor Marlon Brando boycotted the 1973 Oscar Awards. On live television on March 27, Apache actor and activist Sacheen Littlefeather accepted Brando's award for Best Actor in the film *The Godfather* and afterward read to the press a

Acting director of the FBI L. Patrick Gray testifying before the Senate Judiciary Committee, March 1, 1973. Gray's testimony contributed to the unraveling of his career and that of President Nixon. AP Photo.

fifteen-page speech Brando had written in support of the Indians at Wounded Knee.[26]

The Senate Judiciary Committee hearings were over by the time of Littlefeather's Oscar performance, but Gray's testimony had already done its part in making the FBI look bad. The fiasco started on the second day of the hearings when Gray informed his questioners that he would gladly share the FBI's full classified Watergate file with the committee's chairman and ranking member, and that he would make key bureau investigators available for questioning. This was a sharp reversal from Gray's promise to Nixon that he would lodge an unapologetic defense of the FBI's Watergate investigation. Gray's efforts to appease the committee revealed his astonishing naïveté of the Nixon administration's involvement in Watergate. Gray did not yet realize that the president and his top advisors, including Ehrlichman, Haldeman, and Mitchell, had all conspired to obstruct the FBI.[27]

Gray's performance only got worse from there. For the next three weeks, members of the Judiciary Committee and a string of expert witnesses hammered Gray on his role in the ITT–Dita Beard controversy, on Hoover's secret files on American politicians, on warrantless wiretaps, on his sharing FBI surveillance on Vietnam Veterans Against the War and the McGovern campaign with the Nixon administration, on his long periods of time spent away from bureau headquarters, and on his forwarding of Watergate investigation files to John Dean.[28] Gray used his opening statement to highlight recent FBI initiatives to combat terrorism, including the bureau's hosting of multiple symposia and training courses for special agents and members of other law enforcement agencies. But Gray did not adopt Nixon's suggestion that he cite the threat of terrorism to deflect from criticism of the bureau. The onslaught of interrogation was too great.

The most damning portion of Gray's testimony came after members of the Judiciary Committee sifted through the FBI's Watergate investigation documents and concluded that John Dean had lied to special agents in June when he concealed the contents of Howard Hunt's safe. On March 22, when Senator Robert Byrd asked Gray if Dean had lied to the FBI, the acting director replied in the affirmative: "I would have to conclude that that probably is correct."[29]

Gray avoided mentioning the fact that he had destroyed the classified documents from Hunt's safe at Dean's request, but he would be compelled to do so soon. In the meantime, as Gray turned against the White House, and the Judiciary Committee turned against the acting director, Nixon decided to withdraw Gray's nomination. The president told Haldeman that Gray had "been irreparably damaged."[30]

Gray was allowed to keep his position as acting director while the president searched for a new candidate, but it was too late for him to salvage his career. In early April, facing a federal indictment, John Dean began confessing his Watergate crimes to a grand jury and told prosecutors about giving the secret Hunt documents to Gray. On April 27, 1973, Gray resigned from his position. In his resignation letter, he cryptically cited "serious allegations concerning certain acts of my own during the ongoing Watergate investigation."[31]

As the FBI's number two official, Mark Felt was Gray's logical successor, but there was no way Nixon would allow it. Attorney General Kleindienst called Nixon after receiving Gray's resignation letter. As he broached the subject of appointing Felt, the president cut him off. "No! I tell you, I don't want him. I can't have him." Nixon's choice was his former director of the Environmental Protection Agency, William Ruckelshaus, who was neither a Watergate participant nor a Hoover loyalist. "Bill is a Mr. Clean and I want a fellow in there that is not part of the old guard and that has not had a part of the infighting there."[32]

Felt and other FBI officials viewed Ruckelshaus's appointment as yet another attempt by Nixon to extend White House control over the FBI. So, they pushed back. On his first day in the office, Ruckelshaus found on his desk a telegram to Nixon signed by Felt, all fifteen of the FBI's assistant directors, and the SACs of almost every field office in the country. The message called on the president to choose a new permanent FBI director from among the ranks of the bureau's existing officials.[33]

Nixon warned Ruckelshaus that Felt had been leaking to the press when he appointed the FBI's new acting director, but his decision to fire the associate director came after an interaction with Felt's old nemesis, William Sullivan.[34] At the center of the FBI's bureaucratic conflicts since 1970, when he began complaining about J. Edgar Hoover's reluctance to combat leftist guerrilla violence to Nixon's aide Tom Huston, Sullivan was still jockeying for a position as FBI director.

On May 11, 1973, Sullivan called Ruckelshaus pretending to be John Crewdson, a *New York Times* reporter who had just published a story on the Kissinger wiretaps. Sullivan had supplied Crewdson with new information on the taps—the names of several journalists and National Security Council staff members targeted in the surveillance. But in his phone call to Ruckelshaus, Sullivan, posing as Crewdson, told the acting director that Felt had been the source for the article. Ruckelshaus confronted Felt about leaking a few days later.

Facing the likelihood of being fired, Felt submitted his resignation on May 15.[35] Felt's secret counterintelligence operations had backfired. Hoover had promoted him back in 1971 to control Sullivan, but now Sullivan had his revenge.

The Fall of the Weather Underground and BLA

The bureaucratic conflict that brought down L. Patrick Gray and Mark Felt had revolved around surveillance practices. White House and FBI officials argued over which spy tactics were best suited for preempting guerrilla violence and other politically motivated lawbreaking, and over who should be responsible for authorizing such techniques. Remarkably, while conflict over surveillance tactics led to the downfall of Gray and Felt, the tactics themselves did little to prevent guerrilla violence.

After J. Edgar Hoover's death, Gray and Felt had helped build the foundation of FBI counterterrorism. They had overseen Edward Miller's revamping of the FBI's Domestic Intelligence Division, hosted multiple national law enforcement conferences on guerrilla violence, reauthorized break-ins for terrorism investigations, and instituted a new undercover agent surveillance program, all while overseeing massive investigations of the Weather Underground, the BLA, and other leftist guerrilla groups. Yet in the spring of 1973, when their professional careers came crashing down, the Weather Underground remained at large and lingering members of the BLA managed to pull off a second wave of violence in the New York metro area. The bureau's preemptive surveillance activities were limited in effectiveness. It was only when guerrillas' careless actions made them vulnerable that the FBI and other police agencies could make arrests.

FBI agents had been frustrated with the Weather Underground investigation for some time. The Pentagon bombing in May 1972 had certainly been an embarrassment to the bureau and had spurred the newly appointed acting director Gray to amplify the FBI's WEATHFUG investigation. But this had been the first Weather Underground bombing in seven months. The next would not occur until a year later. Amid the long gaps between Weather Underground bombings, as agents expressed their frustrations about FBI headquarters' unclear guidelines for break-ins, mail opening, and warrantless wiretaps, they also questioned the tremendous resources the bureau was pouring into the investigation. Privately, special agents chided the guerrillas as the "terrible toilet bombers," since the group's main activity consisted of periodically planting bombs in restrooms.[36]

The FBI's break-ins targeting the Weather Underground proved ineffectual. Mark Felt and Domestic Security Chief Edward Miller began to authorize break-ins for the Weather Underground investigation after the September 1972 Munich Olympics attacks, at the same time they began authorizing break-ins for their investigation of alleged Al Fatah operatives. The first authorized Weather Underground break-in took place on October 24, 1972, in a leftist print shop in Eugene, Oregon, run by supporters of the guerrillas. Felt and Miller authorized six more Weather Underground break-ins over the next six months, most of them in the New York metro area targeting fugitives' friends and family members.[37] None of these operations uncovered information leading to the capture of the organization's members.

Special agents on the FBI's Weather Underground squads joked about the futility of their break-ins even before Felt began to officially authorize the actions. In June 1972, for example, agents of New York's Squad 47 gathered to celebrate the retirement of their supervisor, John Kearney. "We haven't managed to actually capture any of the Weather leadership," one squad member declared, "but we have come awfully close." The agent then produced an item taken from the apartment of Jennifer Dohrn, the above-ground Weatherman spokesperson who had become the most frequent target of FBI burglaries. On behalf of the squad, the agent handed Kearney a clear plastic envelope containing his gift: a pair of Dohrn's underwear.[38]

The FBI did not fully realize it, but the Weather Underground was gradually disintegrating on its own. This was partly due to the FBI's close encounter with Jeff Jones and Bernardine Dohrn in March 1971. After the pair narrowly escaped their undercover FBI pursuers in a car chase through the streets of San Francisco, the group had to ditch its underground safe houses in the Bay Area and begin anew in other parts of the country. The group was also shrinking as its members concluded that their bombings had done little to reverse the U.S. Left's steady decline. After the San Francisco debacle, the Weather Underground's leadership ordered several of its lesser-known members to surface and rejoin society with the aim of reestablishing leftist contacts and building an aboveground revolutionary socialist organization. Other members drifted away from radical politics altogether, including Mark Rudd, who took refuge in Santa Fe with his girlfriend. By 1972, the Weather Underground had about thirty-five clandestine members, and only a dozen or so actively participated in bombings.[39]

The Weather Underground's contraction mirrored a broader waning of mass antiwar mobilization as Nixon wound down the U.S. war in Vietnam. Though he opportunistically touted his actions as attaining his long-promised "peace with honor," Nixon's signing of the Paris Peace Accords on January 27, 1973, signaled the coming victory of Vietnam's Communist guerrilla resistance. Four bloodstained years of war had gained the United States nothing since Nixon's associates covertly sabotaged Lyndon Johnson's peace efforts in 1968. Nixon's decision came in response to years of disruptive antiwar protest, George McGovern's presidential campaign, and a state of utter dysfunction within the U.S. armed forces, as American troops regularly disobeyed orders and even killed officers to avoid being sent into the jungle on suicide missions.[40] Though he never would have admitted it, by signing the Peace Accords, Nixon also conceded to the central demand behind the Weather Underground's May 1972 bombing of the Pentagon.[41]

The Weather Underground carried out its next bombing on May 18, 1973, to protest a New York police officer's killing of Clifford Glover, an unarmed African American boy, age ten.[42] The explosion destroyed a police car in Queens.

Four months later, by a total fluke, off-duty FBI agents in New York arrested Weather Underground fugitive Howard Machtinger. Squad 47 member Special Agent Michael Kirchenbauer recognized Machtinger as he and an unknown woman strolled through evening rush hour crowds on 86th Street and 2nd Avenue, not far from the apartment of Machtinger's brother Leonard, which had been a target of FBI break-ins. As soon as he spotted the fugitive, Kirchenbauer summoned two fellow FBI men in the area and made the split-second decision to make an arrest. It was the first arrest of a Weather Underground fugitive since FBI agents stumbled upon Judy Clark in a Manhattan movie theater three years earlier. The FBI's informants and undercover agents had not been able to infiltrate the Weather Underground, but extensive investigations and training had prepared Kirchenbauer and his fellow special agents to make an arrest when Machtinger made the mistake of appearing in public in an inadequate disguise. It was a perfect example of investigative serendipity.[43]

But the FBI did not keep its prized captive for long. Machtinger's attorney, the famous William Kunstler, persuaded a federal judge to release his client to his mother on a $2,500 bond. "Going underground is a political move," Kunstler explained, and once a fugitive has surfaced, "they do not become fugitives again."[44] Machtinger showed up for a hearing on September 26 but then jumped bail, disappearing back into the radical underground.

The Weather Underground carried out its next bombing two days later. This one came in response to the CIA's backing of a September 11 coup in Chile at the urging of National Security Advisor Henry Kissinger. Right-wing forces had overthrown the country's democratically elected socialist president, Salvador Allende, and installed a brutal military dictator, Augusto Pinochet. The Weather Underground targeted the International Telephone and Telegraph corporation for its collaboration with the Chilean right. At 2:19 A.M., dynamite exploded on the ninth floor of ITT's Manhattan office, hurling shattered windowpanes to the empty sidewalk below.[45]

By the fall of 1973, however, the nation was far more concerned about Watergate than it was about the Weather Underground's sporadic early-morning bombings. On October 24, the Justice Department dropped federal charges of weapons possession and bombing conspiracy against thirteen Weather Underground leaders to avoid incriminating the FBI and other intelligence agencies for warrantless wiretapping. Two months later, for similar reasons, the government withdrew charges of conspiracy and riot stemming from the 1970 Chicago Days of Rage. Though most still faced minor state charges, many members of the Weather Underground were no longer federal fugitives.[46]

In contrast to the Weather Underground, the FBI had more success investigating the BLA. As was the case after May 1971, when the group burst onto the scene with a string of police assassinations in New York and other cities, the FBI's success fighting the BLA was largely due to the deadly, high-risk nature of the group's actions, which exposed it to police.

By early 1973, police bullets and handcuffs had greatly reduced the membership of the BLA. The Algerian government also kicked Eldridge Cleaver and his companions out of the Black Panther embassy in the fall of 1972, depriving the group of its previous link to international prestige. But fifteen or so BLA guerrillas began to regroup in New York City in late 1972. Around this time, incarcerated member Anthony "Kimu" White and six other prisoners escaped from the fourth floor of the Manhattan House of Detention using hacksaw blades and a ladder fashioned from knotted-up bedsheets.[47]

In September 1972, agents in the New York FBI office formed a special interagency squad that worked with New York City police to investigate a rash of bank robberies attributed to the BLA. The FBI-led squad gave its new investigation the code name CHESROB for Joanne Chesimard (who called herself Assata Shakur), the twenty-five-year-old former City College student suspected of leading the BLA's robberies.[48] The squad's agents in New York coordinated with FBI investigations in Atlanta, New Orleans, and San Francisco. Having evolved out of the NEWKILL investigation of the BLA's May 1971 New York police ambushes, the bank robbery squad was a predecessor to the interagency Joint Terrorism Task Forces the FBI would establish in the early 1980s as the front line of U.S. domestic counterterrorism operations.[49]

The FBI's war with the BLA took on greater urgency after an outbreak of violence in January 1973. On January 7 in New Orleans, snipers armed with multiple firearms and hand grenades wrought havoc during a thirty-six-hour siege in a seventeen-story downtown Howard Johnson's hotel. The attack killed ten people including five police officers and wounded a dozen more. Police eventually used a marine helicopter gunship to kill one sniper, twenty-three-year-old Navy veteran Mark Essex, but they suspected that two other snipers got away. Police traced weapons found at the crime scene to the assassination of a New Orleans police officer on New Year's Eve. Louisiana's attorney general believed a "national terrorist group" was behind the attack.[50] FBI acting director L. Patrick Gray mentioned the incident during his remarks at the FBI's National Symposium on Terrorism on January 16.[51]

A short time later, violence flared in New York. On January 23, New York detectives staked out BLA members Woody Green and Kimu White when they followed Green's wife to the Big T Lounge in Brooklyn on the couple's wedding anniversary. The detectives' efforts to approach the underground BLA guerrillas erupted into a wild gun battle that tore the bar to shreds and ended with the wounding of two officers and the deaths of Green and White. Over the next week, the BLA launched two ambush attacks on police officers in their cruisers: one in Brooklyn on January 25, and another in Queens on January 27. Neither attack was fatal, but each resulted in the wounding of two police officers.[52]

Just over two months later, Assata Shakur turned up on the New Jersey Turnpike. The capture of the woman whom New York police called the "heart and soul" of the BLA followed a traffic stop that turned into another gunfight. This one resulted in the deaths of New Jersey state trooper Werner Foerster and Zayd Malik Shakur, a former leader of the New York Black Panthers. Assata Shakur and trooper James M. Harper both suffered gunshot wounds in the battle. The next morning in nearby woods, police captured the car's driver, Sundiata Acoli (a.k.a. Clarke Squire), a former Panther Twenty-One defendant. The New Jersey Turnpike incident came about after Assata Shakur and her comrades were driving at night in a beat-up Pontiac LeMans on a highway notorious for racially biased police stops of Black motorists. In terms of clandestine guerrilla security, this transportation choice was not ideal, but in all likelihood, the BLA members were desperate to escape a police dragnet in New York City. The police initially pulled the car over for a broken taillight.[53]

As the BLA's membership dwindled, the FBI ramped up its investigation. On May 9, Acting Director William Ruckelshaus placed Herman Bell on the FBI's Ten Most Wanted list, hoping the move would lead to the capture of the last BLA guerrilla sought for the May 1971 killing of New York police officers Jones and Piagentini. Agents caught up with Bell in New Orleans in September after police there arrested a group of men involved in a bank robbery ring they suspected of fund-raising for the BLA. Evidence uncovered in the New Orleans bank robbery investigation enabled the FBI's interagency squad to track down Bell at a safe house where he was living with his wife and two-year-old son. With Bell in custody, the FBI replaced him on the Ten Most Wanted list with Twymon Myers, an elusive twenty-three-year-old BLA gunman involved in various robberies and shooting incidents.[54]

Back in New York, investigators on the FBI's interagency squad developed a BLA informant. Her name has never been revealed to the public, but as the girlfriend of an imprisoned BLA member, she faced charges of her own and agreed to cooperate in exchange for leniency. The informant notified FBI agents of BLA rendezvous points and safe houses, enabling agents to capture Freddie Hilton and Andrew Jackson in June 1973.[55]

In November, a tip from another BLA informant led the FBI to Twymon Myers. This time the information came from a man named Joe Lee Jones, who had robbed banks with Myers and turned himself in to the FBI to face an old army desertion charge. Investigators traced Myers to a Bronx apartment where he was hiding out with his girlfriend. On November 7, nearly 150 police and FBI agents staked out the area around the apartment and watched as he strolled into a local bodega. When an officer tried to arrest Myers upon his exiting the store, he whipped out a 9mm submachine gun and started shooting. The police responded with their own flurry of gunfire that cut Myers down on the sidewalk.[56]

Law-and-order advocates celebrated the killing of Myers by declaring victory over the BLA. The Nixon administration had done nothing to address police violence, and FBI surveillance was unable to prevent the BLA's violent retaliation. But a massive investigation by the FBI's interagency task force prepared law enforcement to respond with guns drawn when the guerrillas' violent miscalculations exposed their underground to the state. Shortly after the killing of Myers, New York police commissioner Donald Cawley proclaimed that the FBI and local police had "broken the back" of the BLA.[57] The FBI's war with leftist guerrillas, however, was far from over.

Clarence M. Kelley and the Symbionese Liberation Army

Clarence M. Kelley was sworn in as the new FBI director on July 9, 1973. Nixon nominated him because of his distance from both the contemporary FBI leadership and the Watergate scandal, hoping the appointment would lend greater legitimacy to the bureau and his administration alike. Kelley had worked for the FBI from 1940 to 1961, climbing his way up the ranks from a firearms instructor to SAC of the bureau's field offices in Birmingham (1957–60) and Memphis (1960–61).[58] For the past decade, he had served as the chief of police in Kansas City, Missouri, where in the eyes of

white political leaders like Senator Thomas F. Eagleton he earned a reputation as "an individual of unquestioned integrity" for his successful efforts
to boost officer morale and build public confidence in law enforcement.
Kelley's reputation was less favorable among Kansas City's African Americans, however. Many felt that Kelley had not gone far enough in replacing
racist whites on the force with Black officers, and disapproved of his handling
of the uprising that swept the city for three days in April 1968 after the assassination of Martin Luther King, when six Black residents died amid violent clashes with police.[59] Kelley was a reformer, but he had no intentions
of using the FBI to fundamentally challenge America's entrenched inequities or the role of police in upholding them. Nevertheless, upon taking his
oath of office, Kelley vowed to "serve only justice and to avoid any other force
or influence which hurts the cause of justice."[60]

It did not take long for Kelley to begin feeling overwhelmed by his job's
responsibilities.[61] Kelley's term, lasting until early 1977, was marked by a
crisis of legitimacy, as the FBI director juggled public controversy over
mass surveillance and counterintelligence, the Watergate scandal, sinking
morale within the bureau's ranks, and a resurgence of violence from new
guerrilla groups like the Symbionese Liberation Army (SLA).

In one way or another, all of these problems were linked to the FBI's war
on leftist guerrillas. Hoover had launched COINTELPROs against the Black
Power movement and the New Left in an effort to preempt these movements' capacities for violent civil disturbance, but such efforts had helped
push some radicals toward clandestine guerrilla warfare. Institutional conflict over state surveillance and how to respond to leftist guerrillas had de-
moralized FBI agents and led to fallout between Hoover and Nixon, whose
secret Plumbers squad committed the Watergate burglary. And despite
consuming massive federal resources, the FBI's mass surveillance of American political dissidents was unable to preempt the emergence of groups
like the SLA.

As a result, the FBI's once-heroic G-man mystique was replaced with an
image of the bureau as authoritarian secret police, on the one hand, and,
on the other, as an organization of bungling Keystone Cops who were unable to keep Americans safe. A Gallup poll published in mid-1973 illus-
trated the bureau's diminished stature. Only 52 percent of respondents
gave the FBI a "highly favorable" rating, compared with 84 percent in 1964
and 71 percent in 1970.[62]

Like L. Patrick Gray before him, Kelley walked into his position with
little understanding of the complex power dynamics that surrounded him.

On his first day in the office, Kelley read a two-page memorandum by the outgoing acting director William Ruckelshaus, titled "Substantive Issues Regarding the Future of the FBI." It outlined the issues Ruckelshaus believed required immediate attention from the new FBI director. Topping the list was moral and legal considerations around mass surveillance and illegal spy tactics.[63] A week later, in response to a lawsuit by NBC journalist Carl Stern, Kelley delivered two FBI COINTELPRO documents to a federal judge. In December, the judge handed them over to Stern, who immediately requested more documents and told the world, for the first time, the story of how Hoover's FBI had launched a covert campaign to "expose, disrupt, and otherwise neutralize" the student New Left.[64] Kelley was now embroiled in public outcry over FBI counterintelligence and mass surveillance. The controversy would snowball over the next two years as the Justice Department, the House's Pike Committee, and the Senate's Church Committee all conducted lengthy investigations of U.S. intelligence agencies.

And then there was Watergate. Two weeks after Kelley started his position, special prosecutor Archibald Cox asked a Watergate grand jury to subpoena the White House for a slew of Nixon's secret tape recordings and other classified materials. As Cox and the Nixon administration battled it out in federal court, Kelley was tasked with managing investigations requested by the special prosecutor's office while also overseeing the bureau's main Watergate investigation. The special prosecutor's struggle with Nixon came to a head on October 20, 1973, in a major crossroads in the Watergate scandal. That evening, Kelley's boss, Attorney General Elliot Richardson, resigned from office to protest Nixon's orders that he fire Cox. William Ruckelshaus, who took a position as deputy attorney general after leaving the FBI, also resigned. Cox's firing was quickly carried out by the Justice Department's number three official, Robert Bork. American television stations interrupted their scheduled programming to report on what newscasters were calling the "Saturday Night Massacre."[65]

Kelley later recalled his reaction when Nixon's chief of staff Alexander Haig called him at home to tell him the news: "My heart sank. I almost fell to the floor."[66]

At Haig's urging, Kelley immediately dispatched FBI agents to guard the offices of Richardson and Ruckelshaus. These orders were carried out by Assistant Director for Domestic Security Edward Miller, who had managed the FBI break-ins under Mark Felt and Pat Gray. The agents, from the FBI's Washington field office, ensured that no sensitive files left the offices.[67]

The demands of Watergate continued to dog Kelley for the remaining nine months of Nixon's truncated term. The director managed requests to the FBI from the new Watergate special prosecutor Leon Jaworski multiple times each week as the nation absorbed around-the-clock news coverage of the widening scandal.[68]

In the middle of all this, a new guerrilla insurgency splashed onto the scene. On the evening of February 4, 1974, members of the SLA carried out a sensational political kidnapping, dragging nineteen-year-old Patty Hearst from her Berkeley apartment at gunpoint after beating up her fiancé, Steven Weed.[69]

Seven months earlier, President Nixon had tried to deflect attention from the Watergate scandal by using FBI director Kelley's swearing-in ceremony as an opportunity to celebrate his administration's success heralding a "new era" of domestic peace. Commenting on the state of America's university campuses, Nixon boasted, "This last academic year was the first one in eight years that did not have destruction and violence."[70]

But the emergence of the SLA revealed that the FBI's war with leftist guerrillas was far from over. Dubbed HEARNAP, for Hearst kidnapping, the FBI's SLA investigation enlisted even more manpower than the Weather Underground and Media burglary investigations. The nationwide investigation lasted nineteen months and cost taxpayers over $5 million in FBI salaries alone, as special agents throughout the country pursued the SLA's elusive guerrillas on a violent wild goose chase.[71]

The SLA was a small, mostly white group of radicals led by Donald De-Freeze, a Black escaped prisoner who assumed the nom de guerre General Field Marshal Cinque. While serving time for armed robbery in Vacaville Medical Facility during the early 1970s, DeFreeze immersed himself in revolutionary literature and gained recognition as a leader of the institution's radical Black prisoners' movement. White Bay Area radicals Angela Atwood, Bill and Emily Harris, Russell Little, Nancy Ling Perry, Patricia Soltysik, Joseph Remiro, and Willie Wolfe all lived in or frequented Berkeley's Peking House commune. They met DeFreeze while visiting the prison as volunteers. When DeFreeze escaped captivity in spring 1973, Peking House gave him shelter.[72]

The SLA carried out its first attack on November 6, 1973, using cyanide-laced bullets to assassinate Marcus Foster, Oakland's popular African American superintendent of schools. In a communiqué released to the media, the group accused Foster of waging "genocide" against the Black community for proposing to institute student identification cards in the city's schools. The Foster murder drew wide condemnation throughout the U.S. Left—even the Weather Underground critiqued the action, questioning the ethics and logic of executing "a black person who is not a recognized enemy of his people." Through his reading of *foco* theory, DeFreeze believed the assassination would prompt massive police retaliation in Oakland's Black communities, which he hoped would spark a widespread popular revolt. Neither anticipated outcome panned out, but the Foster murder did grab California headlines and spur a major Bay Area police investigation.[73]

The SLA's second action gained it even greater notoriety. By kidnapping Patty Hearst, the daughter of powerful white newspaper magnate Randolph Hearst, the guerrillas had seized the national media spotlight. Now, they were the FBI's problem.

Clarence Kelley had never heard of the SLA before the Hearst abduction. But on the morning after the kidnapping, a telex documenting "all activities and available history" on the group arrived on his desk at FBI headquarters. Charles W. Bates, SAC of the FBI's San Francisco office, happened to be visiting the capitol for a meeting with Kelley on the day of the abduction, but he returned to California "almost immediately" to oversee the bureau's investigation.[74] Later that morning, Kelley accepted a telephone call from Randolph Hearst, whose wealth and power ensured him a personal audience with the nation's top police official.

"We are thunderstruck, Mr. Kelley. May I have your assurance that everything possible will be done?" asked Hearst.

"I want you to know, Mr. Hearst, that we will do everything in our power to return your daughter to you as quickly as possible," Kelley vowed.

The FBI director made his promise with sincerity, believing that Patty was "too well-known to be kept hidden." Surely, he and his assistants thought, "our informants would know who she was—and where she was."[75]

Kelley felt sure of the FBI's abilities because of the bureau's sprawling surveillance network. Although L. Patrick Gray reduced the surveillance of American leftists that Hoover had expanded in 1970, when Kelley took the helm of the FBI, the Domestic Security Division still maintained about 22,000 active probes on groups and individuals the bureau deemed prone to violence or vaguely defined "subversion" (a catch-all term usually designated for foreign radicals, members of sectarian Marxist organizations, and individuals suspected of involvement in international espionage). Targets included AIM, the Attica Brigade, the Institute for Policy Studies, the Puerto Rican Socialist Party, the Puerto Rican Independence Party, the

Revolutionary Union, the Socialist Workers Party, Vietnam Veterans Against the War, the Young Workers Liberation League, and New Hampshire's Seacoast Area Workers Committee. The FBI also maintained an extensive network of informants within the Bay Area Left.[76]

The FBI's mass surveillance network proved ineffective in preventing the emergence of the SLA. It was also useless for tracking down the guerrillas.

Immediately after the Hearst abduction, SAC Charles Bates assigned San Francisco special agent Monte A. Hall to lead a team of several agents who worked full time on the case, along with a special clerical staff, which helped organize the investigation's massive catalog of index cards. The FBI sent over one hundred additional agents to San Francisco to assist Hall's team, while hundreds of others followed leads and conducted over 5,000 interviews throughout the mainland United States, as well as in Hawaii, Europe, the Caribbean, and South America. Hall also rented a helicopter to use during the investigation, a first in FBI history, at a cost of approximately $6,000 per week.[77] Additionally, the FBI established a command post in the Hearst family's mansion in the San Francisco suburb of Hillsborough, where two agents worked around the clock "to take hundreds of phone calls, check leads and extortion attempts, monitor police-band radios, and ensure the security of the Hearst home itself." Kelley personally reviewed developments in the Hearst case daily for the first few weeks of the investigation and received updates from Bates over the phone at least once a week for the first several months.[78]

The FBI's HEARNAP investigation underwent numerous strange twists and turns and became a major national news story, rivaling the Watergate scandal for coverage.[79] In February 1974, Randolph Hearst, under an extortion threat from the SLA, spent millions of dollars to fund a series of free food distributions to poor people around the Bay Area. On March 9, in a tape recording released to local radio stations, Patty shocked listeners as she dismissed her father's efforts as an inadequate "disaster" and announced her sympathy for the revolutionaries' efforts to defeat "fascism in America."[80] It would later become known that Hearst spent her first six weeks with the guerrillas locked in a closet, where SLA members subjected her to psychological manipulation, death threats, and rape, in addition to Mao-inspired "political reeducation" involving extensive lectures on U.S. complicity in war, racism, sexism, and economic inequality. The SLA's political reeducation opened Hearst's eyes to a world of social conflict and inequity from which her elite upbringing had previously shielded her, while her captors' coercive tactics instilled in her a constant fear of death,

The SLA's Donald DeFreeze and captive-turned-guerrilla Patty Hearst robbing a Hibernia Bank in San Francisco, April 15, 1974. FBI.gov.

as well as a determination to take any measures necessary in order to survive her daily ordeal.[81]

Patty Hearst then joined her captors as an SLA guerrilla. On April 15, she helped rob the Sunset Branch of the Hibernia Bank in San Francisco. In a subsequent tape recording she announced that her fellow combatants had given her the name "Tania," the nickname of revolutionary icon Tamara Bunke, who had died fighting alongside Ché Guevara in Bolivia.

Yet the FBI could not track down the guerrillas. Much to the chagrin of Kelley and his agents, the SLA evaded the state for as long as it did because the FBI and other police investigators lacked reliable informants inside the group. Kelley later recalled, "The absence of even one solid lead was almost unbelievable in a case like this. But the fact of the matter was that the SLA had gone underground, and none of our many informants could—or would—give us any information concerning their whereabouts."[82] As was the case with the Weather Underground, the FBI was unable to infiltrate the SLA because of security measures the group had taken in its members' decision to become a clandestine urban guerrilla organization.

Aside from Jonathan Jackson's short-lived effort to take captives at the Marin County courthouse, the SLA's abduction of Hearst was also America's first political kidnapping. It differed from ordinary kidnappings in that

Hearst's captors demanded no ransom, which investigators typically used as a key source for clues. As Kelley recollected, "We at the FBI had never faced this type of kidnapping. Thus, no casebooks could be followed; no precedents had been set."[83]

Lacking informants, the FBI was left to improvise investigative techniques in its hunt for the SLA. After learning through interviews with his former prison mates that Donald DeFreeze enjoyed plum wine, the FBI sent information about the fugitive to every plum wine dealer in the United States. The FBI also launched a "Sniff Program," in which agents trained two German shepherds to track the scents of Patty Hearst and Emily Harris by making the dogs sleep on pairs of the fugitives' underwear. In addition, Special Agent Hall's SLA squad attempted to look up every new gas and water hookup in San Francisco and run them against the Department of Motor Vehicles' list of recently issued drivers' licenses, "just to see who had rented a new apartment in that area." For the first time in its history, the FBI issued bulletproof vests to agents, who wore them while checking San Francisco's newly rented apartments for SLA members.[84] In another first, the FBI printed 60,000 SLA "wanted" posters in Spanish for distribution in Latin America.[85] When word got out that the SLA had moved down to Los Angeles, FBI agents began a strategy of profiling Black men in the company of white women. "We were working twelve hour shifts every day, pulling over and jacking up every black pimp and white hooker in LA," Special Agent James Botting recalled.[86] The FBI consulted with experts on kidnapping and political violence as well. At one point in early 1974, agents even resorted to meeting with a psychic, "who on one particular day presided over a prolonged séance." (Director Kelley later recalled that the information produced by the psychic "was not worth the paper it was written on.")[87]

Building on the rhetoric of his recent predecessors, J. Edgar Hoover and L. Patrick Gray, Director Kelley framed SLA violence as terrorism. Kelley launched a public relations campaign after taking office, using more than twenty-three speaking engagements during his first year in office to project a fresh image for the FBI based in the principles of public service, accountability, and compliance with the law. In his speeches, Kelley emphasized fighting terrorism as a core FBI responsibility and upheld the bureau's prerogative to utilize preventive surveillance to preempt terrorist violence. On March 29, 1974, at his alma mater, the University of Kansas, Kelley delivered a speech titled "The FBI's Role in Protecting America." Kelley used the speech to defend the covert, extralegal COINTELPROs the bureau had carried out under Hoover. COINTELPROs had been necessary during the

FBI director Clarence M. Kelley speaking at a press conference, 1975. AP Photo.

"crisis in the 1960's and early 1970's," Kelley insisted, in order to "weaken extremist groups, such as the Students for a Democratic Society (SDS) [and] the Weathermen," and to protect "innocent citizens" and America's "constitutional system of government" from "violent revolution and insurrection."[88] While emphasizing that all FBI COINTELPROs ceased in April 1971, and insisting that he had no plans to reinstitute them, Kelley upheld the bureau's prerogative to engage in "anticipatory" intelligence operations. Such actions were required, he argued, in order to defend society from a "malignant cancer" of "terrorism and extremism" still practiced in the United States by "guerrilla-type groups."[89]

But despite the tough rhetoric, FBI surveillance had not preempted the SLA. Nor had any of the FBI's investigative tactics helped locate SLA guerrillas. As was the case with the BLA, the bureau gained leads only when the guerrillas made fatal errors that compromised their security.

The SLA drama reached its climax on May 17, 1974, when over 600 police officers, including teams of SWAT sharpshooters, backed by two helicopters and over 300 other police vehicles, surrounded a small stucco house in the African American neighborhood of South Central Los Angeles where DeFreeze and five other guerrillas were hiding. SLA members had commandeered the house from its occupants after fleeing another safe house in Los Angeles. The location of the first house became compromised the previous day when Patty Hearst fired a machine gun into the facade of a sporting goods store in Inglewood in order to free SLA members Emily and Bill Harris, whom store security had detained for shoplifting. The shooting incident alerted the FBI that the guerrillas had moved to LA, and a caller from the neighborhood tipped off police to the presence of multiple white people with rifles in the South Central bungalow.[90]

After surrounding the house, police fired teargas canisters through the windows. Then a firefight broke out. Over the next four hours, SLA guerrillas and the Los Angeles Police Department exchanged over 8,000 rounds of ammunition (most of it fired by the police), as television networks carried live broadcasts of the entire ordeal. The siege ended after a massive fire consumed the house. All six of the SLA members inside died, either from smoke inhalation or gunshot wounds.[91]

Hearst was not there, however. She watched the conflagration on a television in a hotel room near Disneyland with Emily and Bill Harris. The three surviving SLA members spent most of the following year hiding from law enforcement.

The Hearst investigation delivered further bruises to the FBI's reputation. To many, the bureau and its director emerged from the episode looking wholly incompetent. Director Kelley later recalled his humiliation upon confessing to the *Los Angeles Times* in April 1974 that the bureau had no idea where Patty Hearst was. "That admission hurt," he remembered, "but we had indeed turned the entire Bay Area upside down, with no luck."[92]

Press inquiries on the Hearst case numbered in the hundreds. They were so intense that on May 9, 1974, Kelley "held the first national news conference ever conducted by an FBI director."[93] Though he promised that the FBI would eventually find Hearst and apprehend the SLA, Kelley used the occasion to admit that the case had him "stumped."[94]

The FBI's inability to find Patty Hearst even cut against Kelley's confidence in his manhood. Men, after all, were supposed to protect women, especially wealthy white "girls" like Hearst, whose supposed youthful feminine vulnerability gained much play in the media.[95] Kelley recalled the tremendous pressure he felt when fielding the "often-asked" question: "What's wrong with the FBI? Why can't you find that girl?"[96]

To make matters worse, Patty Hearst herself emerged as a critic of the FBI. Hearst criticized the FBI in several of the tape recordings the SLA issued to the media. In her recording on February 16, 1974, she opined that "her biggest worry" was that the FBI would "come bursting in" to the SLA's safe house and "kill everyone," including her.[97] In a March 9 tape she went further: "The SLA are not the ones who are harming me. It's the FBI." Hearst went on to purport that "the FBI and other federal agencies" sought to murder her, and that "in the event of an attack by the FBI, I have been told that I will be given an issue of cyanide buckshot in order to protect myself."[98]

Hearst's assertions were at least partly a product of psychological manipulation, but they were not completely unfounded. Two weeks after her abduction, Attorney General William Saxbe shocked the Hearst family and members of the press when he called Patty a "common criminal," implying during a public statement that the FBI would be justified to risk Patty's life in a shootout in order to defeat the SLA. Saxbe quickly retracted his remarks, but the May 17 police siege on the group's Los Angeles hideout, undertaken without authorities knowing whether Hearst was inside, seemed to confirm her fears.[99]

As far as Kelley was concerned, Patty Hearst's claims were "nonsense." Still, the FBI director was deeply disturbed that as a result of both the SLA's propaganda and the FBI's lack of success, "the image of the Bureau was taking a battering."[100]

Though he was no longer employed by the FBI when Kelley came into office, Mark Felt later claimed that morale within the FBI plummeted under the new director because special agents felt that Kelley was diminishing their capacity to combat domestic terrorism.[101] In his first three years as FBI director—responding to widespread criticism of J. Edgar Hoover's mass surveillance and COINTELPROs—Kelley reduced the FBI's domestic security probes by approximately 82 percent.[102] Before the Justice Department's declassification of Hoover-era COINTELPRO documents, Kelley issued a memo to all bureau field offices stating, "FBI employees must not engage in any investigative activity which could abridge in any way the rights guaranteed to a citizen of the United States by the Constitution."[103] The new director's strict ban on break-ins and other illegal surveillance tactics was a sharp reversal of Felt's previous efforts to reauthorize such practices in the name of combating terrorism.

Kelley claimed to have reined in domestic surveillance in order to regain the FBI's popular legitimacy, to establish "a Bureau that would be more efficient, more responsible, and more professional and that would operate well within the law."[104] Felt, however, believed that Kelley phased out "domestic security investigations to placate the media and liberals in Congress." "My conception," wrote Felt, "that it is the function of the FBI to prevent violence and other subversive acts rather than to wait until the bomb has exploded before investigating became an abandoned policy under Director Kelley."[105]

Felt's perspective was biased of course. He wrote these words in his 1979 memoir as he endeavored to exonerate himself from federal charges of authorizing warrantless wiretaps in the FBI's Weather Underground investigation. But his perspective was undoubtedly shared by other FBI personnel, especially senior officials who remained loyal to Hoover. Felt's outlook also speaks to the internal rift over surveillance practices that continued to exist in the bureau during Kelley's tenure and that was exacerbated by the SLA.

The SLA indeed stained the FBI's reputation. Members of the group eluded capture and gained celebrity status through their outrageous, widely publicized guerrilla actions. They taunted the bureau in their tape recordings, which radio and TV outlets broadcasted throughout the world. The SLA did not achieve its goal of rousing America's poor and downtrodden into revolutionary action. But it did make the FBI appear incompetent, just as Kelley sought to improve the bureau's image and contain the COINTELPRO controversy.

Much of this was unintentional. The Foster murder, for instance, spawned conspiracy theories within the Bay Area Left that "the SLA was actually some sort of elaborate government scheme to accomplish the long-anticipated persecution and repression of radical dissent in the area."[106] Such speculation broadened in early May 1974, when newspapers reported that DeFreeze had worked as an informant for the Los Angeles Police Department while incarcerated during the late 1960s. In the context of the COINTELPRO controversy, this news convinced many leftists that DeFreeze was an agent provocateur, and seemed to confirm rumors that the SLA was a creation of the FBI or CIA.[107]

The SLA embarrassed the FBI by carrying out urban guerrilla war from the underground, beyond the reach of the bureau's surveillance network. After the inferno in South Central Los Angeles, the SLA's remaining members—Bill and Emily Harris and Patty Hearst—continued hiding until September 18, 1975, when FBI agents tracked them down in a San Francisco apartment. The FBI's inability to utilize its informants in the service of HEARNAP contradicted Director Kelley's assertions that the bureau needed to maintain preventive intelligence in order to preempt terrorist violence. If such intelligence could not help the FBI preempt the SLA, let alone find its members, what use was it?

· · · · · ·

Facing certain impeachment and removal from office, President Richard Nixon resigned from office on August 9, 1974. His decision was long overdue. Nixon's presidency was effectively over after April 1973, when his closest aides fell like dominoes. Soon after the FBI's acting director L. Patrick Gray incriminated John Dean in front of the Senate Judiciary Committee, Dean confessed to his Watergate crimes and implicated John Ehrlichman and Bob Haldeman, whom Nixon fired on April 30. Without his trusted lieutenants, Nixon was left to battle his enemies alone. The president's frustration with this reality boiled over on May 1, when Attorney General Richardson dispatched FBI agents to guard documents in the former offices of Dean, Ehrlichman, and Haldeman, which were located just outside the Oval Office. Infuriated by this perceived affront to his authority, Nixon shoved one of the agents into a wall.[108] For the next fifteen months, Nixon's base of support gradually eroded, as the Senate Watergate Committee's investigation closed in on the Oval Office.[109]

Nixon's resignation was the culmination of his administration's institutional conflict with J. Edgar Hoover's FBI. Yet the primary organization responsible for prompting the FBI-Nixon feud—the Weather Underground—continued to elude law enforcement. The Weather Underground was decaying from within at this point, but the group managed to plant a few more bombs and publish its 1975 book-length manifesto *Prairie Fire: The Politics of Revolutionary Anti-imperialism* before disbanding in 1976.[110]

The Weather Underground's guerrillas did not realize, however, that they had helped ignite what was then the greatest political scandal in U.S. history. Of course, clandestine urban guerrillas were not the only reason for Watergate, but without them, it is unlikely that institutional conflict between Hoover's FBI and the Nixon administration would have escalated as far as it did. There would have been no Huston Plan; no mass expansion of domestic surveillance in 1970; far fewer controversial surveillance files uncovered in the Media, Pennsylvania, burglary; and no revival of FBI black-bag jobs. Perhaps Hoover would have still refused to go after Daniel Ellsberg, and Nixon's cabinet would have still formed the Plumbers. But without the bitterness engendered by the bureaucratic struggle over "revolutionary terrorism," it is unlikely that Hoover would have fired his domestic security chief William Sullivan or that Mark Felt would have risen to the top of the FBI hierarchy, taken on his Deep Throat operations, and exposed Nixon's Watergate cover-up to the world.

The Weather Underground's bombings had failed to spark a socialist revolution or overthrow the state. But inadvertently and indirectly, it had taken down an American president and irreparably tarnished Hoover's FBI.

The SLA followed with uppercuts to Clarence M. Kelley. Its blows made it impossible for the FBI's second permanent director to repair the damage already done to the bureau's reputation.

Yet the fall of Hoover's FBI and the Nixon White House was not the only outcome of America's war with domestic leftist guerrillas. This conflict bequeathed a more enduring legacy: the formation of American counterterrorism.

The FBI and the Nixon administration improvised what would become counterterrorism in response to clandestine urban guerrillas, who launched hundreds of armed attacks from the revolutionary underground, where they could conceal themselves from police investigators and informants. As they waged war on domestic leftist guerrillas like the Weather Underground, the BLA, and the SLA—and on the Palestinian nationalist Black September Organization—American officials increasingly framed their opponents as terrorists, contributing to a growing international political discourse on guerrilla warfare. To protect police officers, politicians, and other Americans, the FBI sought not only to investigate bombings and other attacks but also to preempt terrorism—to stop terrorists before they carried out their violence. Preemption became the core tenet of counterterrorism.

The concept of counterterrorism was not yet developed at this time. Intellectuals, politicians, and law enforcement officials did not explicitly elucidate the concept of counterterrorism until the late 1970s and early 1980s.

Nevertheless, in the early 1970s, as they popularized the notion of terrorism, the FBI and the Nixon administration built the foundation of American counterterrorism. This foundation included a network of informants in and around dissident political organizations and racialized suspect communities (particularly the Arab diaspora); break-ins; mail opening; warrantless wiretapping; the SPECTAR undercover agent program; data collection through the National Crime Information Center computer database; interagency investigative task forces; police training programs on political bombings, kidnapping, airplane hijacking, sniping, and ambushes; and the CCCT, America's first national institution dedicated to fighting terrorism, which sponsored a new field of terrorism research.

Preventive intelligence was sorely limited in effectiveness, but it became the basis of a lucrative terrorism industry reliant on taxpayer funding.

Counterterrorism did not develop in a political vacuum. Policing has never been politically neutral. Counterterrorism developed as part of the punitive, law-and-order turn in American politics, as the Nixon administration steered the country away from the limited social democracy of the

New Deal and Lyndon Johnson's Great Society and set us on the road to mass incarceration. The badly fractured Left lacked the power to move history in a different direction, and guerrilla violence played into Nixon's law-and-order agenda.

Yet it took several more years for counterterrorism to take hold and become the raison d'être of America's national security state. A big reason for this was Watergate. The CCCT lost its founding chair in May 1973 when David Young, who was also a leader of the Plumbers, resigned from the Nixon administration and began cooperating with the Senate Watergate Committee in exchange for immunity from prosecution.[111] The CCCT's working group continued to meet through 1977 but operated primarily as a sponsor of terrorism research.[112] Clarence Kelley also dramatically reduced the FBI's surveillance operations in 1974—and other federal intelligence agencies and local police departments did as well—in response to a wave of lawsuits and in anticipation of unprecedented Justice Department, Senate, and House investigations of government spying.

Over subsequent decades, the politics of terrorism and counterterrorism would be inseparable from contentious debates over insurgent violence, state violence, national security, mass surveillance, policing, civil liberties, racial justice, and U.S. foreign policy. Federal and state governments, along with private security companies, would build a massive counterterrorism infrastructure during the administrations of Ronald Reagan and George W. Bush. But the contours of such debates and the foundation of counterterrorism were constructed earlier, in the era of Black Power, the New Left, and the U.S. war in Vietnam, during Nixon's war at home.

Epilogue

The Politics of Counterterrorism

· ·

During a March 1974 speaking engagement, FBI director Clarence M. Kelley articulated core tenets of what would become counterterrorism. "The FBI," he proclaimed, "simply cannot wait until the terrorist or extremist—the individual whose allegiance is to violence—strikes before we act."[1] In Kelley's view, terrorism was not something to be understood as a reflection of serious political grievances—it was a "malignant cancer" that posed an existential threat to U.S. national security and the American way of life. In turn, preemptive surveillance was needed to prevent terrorism in advance.[2] It would take more than six years, however, for counterterrorism to gain a footing in American political and policing institutions.

For the rest of the 1970s, public concerns over government abuse of authority and violation of Americans' civil liberties prevailed over fears of terrorism. To a majority of Americans, the crimes of Watergate overshadowed the emergence of new domestic leftist guerrilla groups such as the New York–based Puerto Rican nationalist Fuerzas Armadas de Liberación Nacional (FALN), the Bay Area's New World Liberation Front, Seattle's George Jackson Brigade, and New England's Sam Melville–Jonathan Jackson Unit, as well as Palestinian militants' continued international bombings, kidnappings, and hijackings.

Some U.S. political leaders sought to emphasize the threat terrorism posed to U.S. national security. Former segregationist and longtime anticommunist Senator Strom Thurmond (R-SC) presided over more than a dozen hearings on "terroristic activity" and political violence from 1974 to 1976 as chair of the Senate Judiciary Committee's Internal Security Subcommittee. Gathering testimonies from police, intelligence officials, and academic experts, Thurmond revived the Internal Security Subcommittee, an institution typically dismissed as a relic of the McCarthy era, to investigate groups such as the Weather Underground, the SLA, and the FALN.[3] Thurmond's efforts had little influence on federal policy in the short term, but they revealed the fact that debates over terrorism and counterterrorism, like earlier debates over Communism, were part of much larger political battles.

By contrast, investigations of federal intelligence agencies conducted by the Church Committee and other government bodies led to substantial new limits on the state's surveillance powers. In 1976, Attorney General Edward Levi issued new guidelines for FBI domestic security investigations that required the bureau to base investigations of American citizens on "specific and articulable facts giving reason to believe that an individual or group is or may be engaged in activities which involve or will involve the use of force or violence and which involve or will involve the violation of federal law." The Foreign Intelligence Surveillance Act of 1978 established a special court to oversee new limits on CIA and NSA international surveillance.[4]

America's prevailing views on terrorism changed dramatically, however, after the 1980 election of President Ronald Reagan. During the 1980s, notions of state overreach and repression did not anger Americans nearly as much as concerns that the federal government was failing to protect them from terrorism. Reagan came to power after Jimmy Carter's presidency became bogged down in the 444-day-long Iranian hostage crisis, in which a group of Iranian student revolutionaries stormed the U.S. embassy in Tehran and held ninety people captive; the nightly ABC television news program *America Held Hostage* served as a reminder of the Carter administration's inability to resolve the conflict.[5] In what some have suspected was the result of a secret deal between the incoming Reagan administration and the Iranian revolutionaries, the American hostages in Tehran gained their freedom on January 20, 1981, the day of the new president's inauguration. A week later Reagan proclaimed, "Let the terrorists beware that when the rules of international behavior are violated, our policy will be one of swift and effective retribution. We hear it said that we live in an era of limits to our powers. Well, let it also be understood, there are limits to our patience."[6]

That April, Reagan fulfilled a campaign promise by issuing presidential pardons to Mark Felt and Edward Miller, whom a federal jury had convicted five months earlier for authorizing illegal FBI break-ins to the homes and workplaces of suspected Weather Underground supporters. Richard Nixon privately sent each man a bottle of champagne along with a note that said, "Justice ultimately prevails."[7] Reagan issued a public statement praising the former FBI officials as "two men who acted on high principle to bring an end to the terrorism that was threatening our nation."[8]

The conservative "Reagan revolution" was advantageous for Strom Thurmond and others who sought to revive U.S. intelligence agencies' preventive intelligence capacities in the name of fighting terrorism. Reagan appointed Thurmond to take fellow ex-segregationist Senator James O. Eastland's long-held position as chair of the Senate Judiciary Committee. In this capacity, Thurmond established the new Subcommittee on Terrorism and Security. Freshman southern conservatives, including chairman Senator Jeremiah Denton (R-AL) and John P. East (R-NC), dominated the new subcommittee. The Subcommittee on Terrorism and Security was the first congressional body dedicated to fighting terrorism, and it laid the groundwork for American counterterrorism in the Reagan era.[9]

One person who was particularly influential on the subcommittee was a highly ideological paleoconservative policy analyst named Samuel T. Francis, who worked for Senator East. Francis had published a report on U.S. intelligence agencies in *Mandate for Leadership*, the 1,093-page publication of the conservative Heritage Foundation think tank that became the Reagan administration's policy bible.[10] Seeking to restore federal surveillance capabilities of the early Cold War in order to combat terrorism, Francis called for an overhaul of Attorney General Levi's FBI Domestic Security Guidelines; greater cooperation between intelligence agencies and local police departments; reinstitution of the McCarthy-era Attorney General's List of Subversive Organizations; FBI exemption from the Freedom of Information Act; and a revival of break-ins, mail covers, and warrantless wiretapping. Francis argued that intelligence agencies needed to detect terrorist plots in advance: "Authorities must keep extremist movement under at least moderate surveillance, become familiar with the public positions and members as well as their unstated goals, adherents, and fringe elements, and be prepared to escalate surveillance of whatever groups seem likely to engage in more extreme activities."[11] Francis's suggestions read as though he had copied them straight from the Huston Plan.

From February 1982 to March 1983, Francis was instrumental in drafting policy recommendations for the Subcommittee on Terrorism and Security's hearings on the attorney general's Domestic Security Guidelines and in shaping Attorney General William French Smith's new Guidelines for Domestic Security / Terrorism.[12] The new Smith Guidelines limited Justice Department oversight of FBI operations and removed the requirement that the bureau obtain evidence of illegal activity before opening an investigation. FBI officials were now empowered to "anticipate or prevent crime" by initiating surveillance whenever "facts of circumstances reasonably indicate that two or more persons are engaged in an enterprise [to further] political or social goals wholly or in part through activities that involve force or violence."[13]

A deadly leftist guerrilla attack carried out by remnants of the BLA and Weather Underground helped create the political climate necessary for the Smith Guidelines' expansion of FBI surveillance powers. The Revolutionary Armed Task Force's botched robbery of an armored Brinks truck in Nyack, New York, on October 20, 1981, left a security guard and two police officers dead and led to the arrests of several guerrillas, including BLA members Sekou Odinga, Kuwasi Balagoon, and Mutulu Shakur and former Weather Underground members Kathy Boudin, David Gilbert, and Judy Clark.[14] FBI director William Webster, President Carter's replacement for Clarence Kelley, had opposed the Smith Guidelines, viewing them as unnecessary, but the Nyack fiasco was a horrible embarrassment that led him to change his mind.[15]

The Nyack robbery and a series of other attacks by leftist guerrillas also prompted the formation of the United States' first FBI-led interagency Joint Terrorism Task Forces (JTTFs), formed in New York, Chicago, and Boston from 1980 to 1983.[16]

Ironically, at the very same time that the FBI was establishing counterterrorism institutions to combat America's last domestic leftist guerrillas, the CIA was exporting terrorism throughout the world, ensuring the counterterrorism industry would stay in business for decades to come. The Reagan administration embraced covert operations and proxy wars as a way to fight the Cold War after Vietnam, when Americans no longer had the stomach to support another costly overseas military invasion.[17] In Nicaragua, the CIA supported the Contras, whose brutal paramilitary efforts sought to topple the socialist Sandinista regime that came to power in 1979 after leftist guerrillas overthrew U.S.-backed dictator Anastasio Somoza Debayle. Throughout Latin America, Reagan supported right-wing military regimes whose leaders justified their repressive rule as necessary to protect their nations from leftist insurgents and other dissidents they dismissed as terrorists. The CIA's largest paramilitary operation was in Afghanistan, where from 1979 to 1989, U.S. operatives funneled weapons, intelligence, and hundreds of millions of dollars through Pakistani intermediaries to sustain a vicious insurgency led by Islamic jihadi extremists. With the help of Saudi elites, somewhere in the ballpark of 100,000 fighters were recruited from throughout the world to fight Afghanistan's Communist government and the Soviet military, who invaded the country in an ill-fated effort to keep their allies in power. One of these fighters was Saudi millionaire Osama bin Laden, who in 1989 founded al-Qaeda, the organization that went on to perform the 9/11 attacks a decade later.[18]

After 9/11, American leaders had an opportunity to reckon with the consequences of American imperialism. They could have started with an examination of former CIA analyst Chalmers Johnson's book *Blowback: The Costs and Consequences of American Empire*. Published just before 9/11 and reprinted with a new introduction shortly thereafter, the book introduced readers to the concept of "blowback," a CIA term used to describe retaliation for U.S. covert operations that were hidden from the American public but widely known and reviled in the countries where they had taken place.[19] The 9/11 attacks had been a casebook example.

Instead, many of the same conservatives who supported Reagan's proxy wars blamed the FBI's failure to prevent the September 11 attacks on post–Church Committee intelligence reforms. The day after 9/11, former secretary of state James Baker (who served in the cabinets of Presidents Reagan and George H. W. Bush) claimed in a television news interview that the Church Committee hearings had caused the United States to "unilaterally disarm in terms of our intelligence capabilities."[20] Speaking on Fox News' right-wing talk show *O'Reilly Factor*, spy novelist Tom Clancy charged, "The CIA was gutted by people on the political left who don't like intelligence operations. . . . And as a result of that, as an indirect result of that, we've lost 5,000 citizens this week."[21] A similar view was articulated by the new FBI director Robert Mueller, who had cut his teeth in the early 1980s as an assistant attorney general working with Boston's JTTF to indict members of the United Freedom Front, who carried out bombings in New York to protest U.S. support for the Nicaraguan Contras and South Africa's racist apartheid regime.[22] "We need a different approach that puts prevention above all else," Director Mueller affirmed. FBI headquarters needed the "capability to anticipate attacks."[23]

Like Richard Nixon, J. Edgar Hoover, L. Patrick Gray, and Clarence M. Kelley before them, officials in the 9/11 era were not interested in understanding terrorists' motives. America's new counterterrorism warriors focused on fighting terrorism with surveillance, policing, and military action. The FBI and the White House had their share of bureaucratic conflicts after 9/11, but root causes of violent conflict were not up for serious discussion. Counterterrorism officials' analyses of terrorists' motives rarely went beyond those of President George W. Bush, whose explanation for the 9/11 attacks was completely void of historical context: "They hate our freedoms."[24]

Within seven weeks of 9/11, President Bush signed the USA PATRIOT Act, the greatest expansion of preventive surveillance powers since the Huston Plan. Under the act, U.S. intelligence agencies seeking to preempt terrorism could engage in warrantless wiretaps and computer searches; enter homes without warrants; seize library, internet, and business records; and detain resident aliens without charges for seven days to six weeks. The new rules also empowered FBI agents to recruit informants and conduct other surveillance without approval from bureau headquarters.[25] After 9/11, the FBI also multiplied its number of JTTFs—institutions initially formed to combat domestic leftist guerrillas—from thirty-five to over one hundred, including one in every one of its fifty-six field offices.[26]

Federal agents began to carry out preemptive arrests even before Bush's signing of the PATRIOT Act. In the weeks following 9/11, authorities rounded up and detained over 1,000 immigrants, mostly of Middle Eastern descent, and transferred an unknown number of Arab, Arab American, and Muslim federal prisoners to segregation units, where they were held in solitary confinement. This was like the 1972–73 Arab scare but on a much larger scale, and widened to target not only the ethnically and religiously diverse Arab diaspora but also the broader Muslim community.

Federal prison authorities also transferred several incarcerated former leftist guerrillas into solitary confinement after the 9/11 attacks. Targets included Richard Williams, Tom Manning, and Raymond Luc Levasseur of the United Freedom Front; Antonio Camacho Negrón and Carlos Torres of the FALN; Sundiata Acoli of the BLA; and white BLA supporter Marilyn Buck.[27] The documents that ordered this round-up of incarcerated dissidents remain classified, but they appear to have come from the office of Attorney General John Ashcroft, who on October 26, 2001, signed new federal rules authorizing "special administrative measures with respect to specified inmates." Outlined in a document published in the *Federal Register* titled "National Security: Prevention of Acts of Violence and Terrorism," the rules enable the Department of Justice to hold prisoners deemed a "threat to national security" incommunicado for up to a year and deny them the right to attorney-client privilege.[28]

By the time President Bush's global war on terrorism began raining missiles from the skies over Afghanistan and Iraq, the short-lived surveillance reforms instituted after the Church Committee hearings were all but forgotten (the top-secret Foreign Intelligence Surveillance Court, established in 1978, offered little more than a fig leaf for the new electronic mass surveillance unleashed by the PATRIOT Act). In addition to the lengthy wars in Afghanistan and Iraq, Bush's war on terrorism was characterized by drone wars and other covert operations in Pakistan and Yemen and throughout the Middle East and Africa; indefinite detainment of terrorism suspects in secret CIA "black sites" and at the U.S. prison in Guantanamo Bay, Cuba; water-boarding (a form of simulated forced drowning) and other state-sanctioned torture; the NSA's expansive bulk electronic data collection programs; and numerous FBI arrests of alleged terrorists (most of them Muslim) that seem to be examples of entrapment rather than preemption of authentic terrorist plots.[29]

The state power accumulated under Bush dwarfed that of the early Cold War and was well beyond what Nixon and his supporters could have ever dreamed of in a time before the internet. Yet if the goal of the war on terrorism was to actually end insurgent violence, Bush and his successors have been no more successful than Nixon. Sure, police raids, military operations, and drone strikes may have occasionally resulted in the capture or extrajudicial execution of key terrorists. But just as Nixon and Hoover's crackdowns inspired clandestine insurgents, U.S. military, police, and intelligence agencies' involvement in countless civilian deaths, arrests, detainments, and torture sessions, along with the destabilization of Iraq and the greater Middle East, inspired new terrorist organizations. The clearest example is the so-called Islamic State in Iraq and Syria, which emerged in 2014 and soon spread to Europe, Afghanistan, and Libya.

American political leaders have also yet to resolve the underlying problems of poverty, racism, and police violence. From 2014 to 2020, uprisings under the banners of Black Lives Matter, workers' rights, and indigenous land and water protection, among others, brought issues of social and environmental justice back to the center of public conversation, though economic inequality in America is now worse than it was during the Nixon era.

Today, if we are going to use the word "terrorism" as it came to be understood in the early 1970s, the greatest terrorist threat to the United States comes from the Right. Since 9/11, white racists have carried out far more violent attacks inside the United States than have Islamic extremists and have left more victims dead.[30] Yet President Donald Trump downplayed, and even goaded, white supremacist and rightwing insurgents. "There were very fine people on both sides," Trump announced after a neo-Nazi intentionally slammed his car into counterprotesters at the 2017 Unite the Right rally in Charlottesville, Virginia, killing antiracist activist Heather Heyer. This book goes to press just days after the majority of Senate Republicans concluded Trump's second impeachment trial by refusing to convict him for inciting the deadly rightwing mob that stormed the U.S. Capitol on January 6, 2021 in an effort to overturn the 2020 presidential election. The hypocrisy of the Republican Party's claims to support "law and order" in response to "terrorism" is more glaring than ever, and for now, despite losing both his reelection and efforts to remain in office through extralegal means, Trump maintains a level of corruption, power, and impunity well beyond what Nixon ever achieved.

Where do we go from here? Anthropologist Mahmood Mamdani had this question in mind in 2004 when he reflected on the world wrought by the Cold War and Bush's war on terrorism. "Caught in a situation where both adversaries in the war on terror claim to be fighting terror with weapons of terror," Mamdani wrote, "nothing less than a global movement for peace will save humanity. If we are to go by the lesson of the last global struggle for peace—that to end the war in Vietnam—this struggle, too, will have to be waged as a mass movement."[31]

The American antiwar movement did help bring our nation's war in Vietnam to an end, but the 1960s' Left lacked the power to end the totality of U.S. state violence at home and abroad. Instead, the Left splintered before it was even close to having built such power, and though they composed a small fraction of the activists who fought for social justice and an end to U.S. militarism, the guerrillas played a big part in this splintering. They also played a part in the creation of counterterrorism, which would allow the worst of federal intelligence agencies' preemptive tactics to be deployed both domestically and abroad for decades to come.

Today, as a new generation seeks to figure out how to build a better world, there is much they can learn from the American movements of the 1960s and 1970s, as well as from political struggles of other places and times. I hope this book will help participants in today's movements avoid the trap of viewing paramilitary groups like the Black Panthers and Weatherman with uncritical nostalgia, and of mistakenly viewing the police repression they faced as evidence of their political effectiveness.[32] And as we examine how the FBI and other state institutions are responding to today's movements for social justice, I hope this history can help us do so with greater sophistication, and help us realize that the state is not omnipotent—we can transform our world if we avoid the pitfalls of giving in to cynicism or insisting on easy answers.[33]

Fundamentally, I hope this book can help us rethink counterterrorism.[34] If we truly want a more peaceful world, we must work to minimize all forms of violence, not just violence carried out by those we wish to vilify as terrorists. This is a necessary first step to overcoming endless wars on terrorism, wars fought to preempt insurgent violence carried out in response to state violence.

Acknowledgments

While working on this book for nearly a decade, I've benefited from the support, encouragement, and camaraderie of many friends, family members, and colleagues. While I cannot name them all, there are some I must acknowledge.

Christian G. Appy was my primary academic advisor throughout my time in graduate school, and he supported me and this project through all sorts of intellectual and professional challenges. I cannot thank him enough for the time and energy he has poured into my career, and for all I have learned from him about teaching, writing, and the historian's craft. While studying in the University of Massachusetts Amherst / Five Colleges Graduate Program in History, I worked closely with Jennifer Fronc, who supported my work with great enthusiasm, provided detailed comments on early drafts, and always pushed me to ground my research and writing in a strong theoretical foundation. John Higginson offered pivotal feedback at the early stages of this project as well; I am particularly grateful for his pointing out to me the difference between radicals' revolutionary intentions and an actual revolutionary historical moment. Jennifer Guglielmo is a shining beam of positivity who never stopped believing in me and my work. I am especially appreciative of our conversations on social movements, violence, and historical methodology. I was the beneficiary of several fellowships from the UMass Amherst History Department, Graduate School, and W.E.B. Du Bois Library that provided critical funding for my research.

I am incredibly thankful to Heather Ann Thompson and Rhonda Y. Williams, editors of the Justice, Power, Politics series at University of North Carolina Press. Both are fine historians committed to social justice, and I feel deeply honored to be included among the esteemed authors in this series. Heather has been particularly supportive of my work over the years, and I thank her for encouraging me to submit my book proposal. I am also immensely grateful to my editor Brandon Proia, who has demonstrated a deep investment in this project from the outset. Brandon and I always seemed to be on the same page in our vision for this book, and his thorough, insightful feedback has consistently pushed me to improve my arguments and prose.

I'd like to shine a light on several others who were particularly helpful or influential. Ray Luc Levasseur is a long-standing friend and comrade, and I am thankful for our countless conversations on politics and history. I also appreciate his granting me access to his treasure trove of personal papers, which are now archived at UMass Amherst. Erika Arthur introduced me to the concept of prison abolition in graduate school while we read our way through the foundational literature of what is now known as carceral studies in an independent study with

Amherst College's Martha Saxton. Our many conversations on transformative justice inform this book's core arguments. Trevor Griffey, one of the most generous scholars I know, shared multiple hard-to-access primary sources, offered useful research tips, and commented on early draft material. Daniel Burton-Rose shared an unpublished paper, and Dan Berger mailed me a bunch of photocopied FBI documents—and I appreciate these fellow men named Daniel who write about leftist guerrillas for our many conversations on this topic. Ryan Shapiro helped me navigate my requests for FBI documents through the Freedom of Information Act. My dear friends Peter Pihos and Mohammad Ataie each provided helpful input on portions of my manuscript, as did Atiya Husain. The reviewers for UNC Press— Jeremy Varon, Michael Koncewicz, and Susan Reverby—expended great time and effort on my manuscript, each offering extensive critical commentary. I extend to these distinguished historians my deepest gratitude for their invaluable feedback, which proved essential in helping me craft this into a stronger book.

I could not have completed my research without the assistance of archivists and librarians, particularly those at Amherst College Library Special Collections, Freedom Archives, Marquette University Library Special Collections, the National Archives and Records Administration, the Nixon Presidential Library, and UMass Amherst W.E.B. Du Bois Library Special Collections and University Archives. A special thanks is due to Rob Cox, the former director of the latter institution, who passed away before he had the opportunity to see this book in print.

I must also thank those who supported me from the beginning of my path to becoming a professional historian. At the University of Southern Maine, several wonderful staff and faculty mentors nurtured my writing, love of history, and undergraduate research on Maine's prisoners' rights movement of the 1970s, which later morphed into this project. Thank you to Pat Finn, George Caffentzis, David Carey, the late Diana Long, and especially Adam Tuchinsky.

In addition to those already named, several other mentors and colleagues at UMass Amherst / Five Colleges supported me or helped me work through aspects of my research. Thank you to Diana Carolina Sierra Beccara, Aviva Ben-Ur, Anne F. Broadbridge, Joye Bowman, Julie de Chantel, Amy Fleig, Holly Hanson, Jess Johnson, Barbara Krauthamer, Mary Lashway, Toussaint Losier, Michella Marino, Laura Miller, Marla Miller, Alice Nash, Brian Ogilvie, Sigrid Schmalzer, Matt Spurlock, Ekwueme Michael Thelwell, Chris Tinson, Stellan Vinthagen, Rob Weir, Leah Wing, and Kevin Young.

This project also evolved in conversation with other scholars in my field, including fellow panelists at meetings of the American Historical Association, the American Studies Association, the European Social Science History Conference, and the Organization of American Historians, and during a 2017 seminar I led at the Center for the United States and the Cold War at New York University's Tamiment Library. Thank you to Josh Cerretti, Doug Charles, Robert Chase, Richard English, Beverly Gage, Steve Hewitt, Rebecca Hill, Elizabeth Hinton, Elissa Underwood Marek, Melani McAlister, Timothy Naftali, Jessica Pliley, Vijay Prashad, Ian Rocksborough-Smith, Marie Breen Smyth, Lisa Stampnitzky, and Akinyele Umoja.

Since arriving at Western Washington University, I have been fortunate to join the company of a fantastic group of scholars in the History Department and across campus. I am particularly indebted to the History Department's chair Johann Neem, whose support for my career and research cannot be measured, and whom I am pleased to call a friend. A WWU Manuscript Completion Grant provided essential funding, and my colleagues' supportive feedback in a History Department "work in progress" seminar organized by Sarah Zimmerman and Charles Anderson helped me develop chapter 7. The department's office manager Becky Hutchins helped with crucial last-minute logistical support. In addition to other Western colleagues I've already mentioned, I'd like to acknowledge my appreciation for the supportive friendships of Stefania Heim and Dharitri Bhattacharjee. Furthermore, my students at both UMass Amherst and Western Washington University deserve a word of thanks for helping me develop many of the ideas that made their way into this book.

In addition to all of this, the book is a product of my involvement in various radical social movements since the late 1990s. My ideas on history and politics have developed through my conversations and relationships with political activists of all ages, including veterans of 1970s' leftist guerrilla organizations. I would like to thank the many nonacademic political radicals whom I have known, loved, annoyed, spoken with, struggled with, lived with, argued with, and built with over the years. There are too many to name, lest I accidentally leave someone out, but I would like to express my particular appreciation for those involved with the Victory Gardens Project and the Portland Victory Gardens Project in Athens and Portland, Maine, and the Rosenberg Fund for Children in Western Massachusetts (and beyond). I do not expect you all to agree with my interpretations of the past, but I want you to know that I appreciate your efforts to build a better world. You have enriched my life, inspired me, shaped my thoughts, and helped motivate me to write this book.

Finally, I'd like to thank my family. My mother, father, stepmother, mother-in-law, and father-in-law are pillars of love and encouragement, as are my siblings—biological, step, and in-law. Close friends back in New England are part of our extended, "chosen" family and have cheered me on throughout the process, as have new friends in Bellingham. My two daughters are constant sources of inspiration, love, and joy. And I cannot imagine getting through this project without Julie—my spouse, my closest collaborator, my best friend.

Notes

Abbreviations in the Notes

BLA FBI Gale Cengage Learning, Archives Unbound Digital Database, *The Black Liberation Army and the Program of Armed Struggle, 1970–1983*

Bloom Alternative Press Collection

  Amherst College Archives and Special Collections, Amherst, MA, Bloom (AC 1966) Alternative Press Collection

Church Committee (Books II and III)

  U.S. Congress, Senate Select Committee to Study Governmental Operations with Respect to Intelligence Activities, Final Report, Book II, *Intelligence Activities and the Rights of Americans*, and Final Report, Book III, *Supplementary Detailed Staff Reports on Intelligence Activities and the Rights of Americans*, 94th Cong., 2d Sess. (1976)

CMK FBI Freedom of Information Act acquisition, FBI, Clarence R. Kelley, Director's File

COINTELPRO-Black Extremist

  FBI Vault, https://vault.fbi.gov, COINTELPRO-Black Extremist Files

COINTELPRO-New Left

  FBI Vault, https://vault.fbi.gov, COINTELPRO-New Left Files

DDRS Gale Cengage Learning, Declassified Documents Reference System, http://gdc.gale.com/products/declassified-documents-reference-system/

FBI NEWKILL

  FBI NEWKILL documents. Free Jalil website. http://www.freejalil.com/newkilldocuments.html

FBI WUO Federal Bureau of Investigation, *FBI File on Students for a Democratic Society and the Weather Underground Organization* (Wilmington, DE: Scholarly Resources, 1991), microfilm

Huston Plan

  U.S. Congress, Senate Select Committee to Study Governmental Operations with Respect to Intelligence Activities, *Hearings on Intelligence Activities*, Vol. 2. *The Huston Plan*, 94th Cong., 1st Sess. (1975)

KORM Special Collections and University Archives, Raynor Memorial Libraries, Marquette University, Milwaukee, WI, Kenneth O'Reilly Research Materials, FBI Investigation and Surveillance Records Series 90

LPG FBI   Freedom of Information Act acquisition, FBI, L. Patrick Gray,
             Director's File
Nixon White House Tapes
             President Richard Nixon's White House recordings are available online
             in the following three locations: Nixontapes.org; Miller Center,
             millercenter.org, Richard Nixon White House Recordings; and Richard
             Nixon Presidential Library Online Archive, https://www.nixonlibrary
             .gov/, White House Tapes Collections
US v. Felt   National Archives and Records Administration, College Park, MD,
             Record Group 60, Department of Justice Case 177-16-13 (U.S. v. Gray,
             Felt, Miller)
WCS FBI   Internet Archive, archive.org, Ernie Lazar FOIA Collection, William C.
             Sullivan FBI Personnel File
WUR   U.S. Congress, Senate Subcommittee to Investigate the Administration
             of the Internal Security Act and Other Internal Security Laws,
             *Weather Underground: Report of the Subcommittee to Investigate the
             Administration of the Internal Security Act and Other Internal Security
             Laws*. 94th Cong., 1st Sess. (Washington, DC: U.S. Government Printing
             Office, 1975)

Introduction

1. Stampnitzky, *Disciplining Terror*, 4, 106.

2. Naftali, *Blind Spot*, xv–xvi.

3. Mueller and Stewart, *Chasing Ghosts*; Priest and Arkin, *Top Secret America*, 86. On the Bush Doctrine, see Bacevich, *America's War for the Greater Middle East*, 245.

4. Schrader, *Badges without Borders*, documents how urban police officials responded to 1960s' domestic civil disorder by importing counterinsurgency tactics utilized by U.S. forces in the global South; Stampnitzky, *Disciplining Terror*, explains how intellectuals in the new field of terrorism studies, which emerged in the mid-1970s, drew from scholarship on counterinsurgency. However, my research in declassified internal documents shows that the FBI based its response on the bureau's domestic institutional experience with dissident organizations.

5. The U.S. incarceration rate was second only to the Soviet Union's under Joseph Stalin. This book adds to a burgeoning scholarship on the rise of mass incarceration and the related systems of state punishment, policing, and control that historians have dubbed the "carceral state." The following essays offer interpretive overviews of the historical literature on this topic: Hinton and Cook, "The Mass Criminalization of Black Americans"; Clegg and Usmani, "The Economic Origins of Mass Incarceration"; Hernandez, Muhammad, and Thompson, "Introduction: Constructing the Carceral State"; and Thompson and Murch, "Rethinking Urban America through the Lens of the Carceral State." Foundational works in this field include Hinton, *From the War on Poverty to the War on Crime*; Thompson, "Why Mass Incarceration Matters"; Alexander, *The New Jim Crow*; and Flamm, *Law and Order*.

6. I conducted archival research in declassified FBI documents and other government sources at the Nixon Presidential Library, in the U.S. v. Felt trial document collection at the National Archives and Records Administration in College Park, Maryland, and in Kenneth O'Reilly's research collection at Marquette University in Milwaukee, Wisconsin (where a friendly librarian kindly scanned my requested files). I also researched FBI documents on microfilm and in numerous digital archives. Additionally, I researched FBI Director's Files of L. Patrick Gray and Clarence R. Kelley, both of which I acquired through Freedom of Information Act requests (historian Ivan Greenberg initially gained access to these files through a 2008 lawsuit).

7. This conservative estimate comes from Sale, *SDS*, 632, and draws from several sources outlined below. More research is needed to arrive at a precise number, though most government reports put the numbers much higher. A July 1970 report by the Senate Investigations Subcommittee, for example, documented 1,188 bombings, acts of arson, and attempted bombings during this period. Another report drafted around the same time by the Alcohol, Tobacco, and Firearms Division of the U.S. Treasury documented 40,934 bombings, attempts, and threats during this period, of which Sale extrapolated approximately 2,800 were leftist bombings. In his memoir, Richard Nixon (presumably drawing from the Treasury report) stated that there were over 40,000 bombings during this period. A January 1971 special issue of the leftist magazine *Scanlan's*, titled "Guerrilla War in the U.S.A.," documented over 1,000 examples of "guerrilla acts of sabotage and terrorism in the United States" in 1969 and 1970. All of these studies, however, included many examples of unclaimed bombings at schools, businesses, homes, and other locations that were not necessarily politically motivated. Both radicals from *Scanlan's* and conservative proponents of law and order, including Nixon and politicians who chaired the government investigating committees, had political motivations for overstating these numbers: the former to celebrate a supposed incipient guerrilla revolution in the United States, and the latter to emphasize the need for a stronger federal response to such activity. See Senate Committee on Government Operations, Permanent Subcommittee on Investigations, *Riots, Civil, and Criminal Disorders*; Nixon, *RN*, 470; and *Scanlan's* 1, no. 8 (January 1971), copy in author's possession courtesy of Trevor Griffey. Journalist Bryan Burrough wrote in his 2015 book that there were over 2,500 bombings "during an eighteen-month period in 1971 and 1972," 1,900 of them in 1972. Burrough cited an interview with a retired FBI agent as his source for this information but provided no documentary evidence. The dates attributed to this figure are almost certainly the result of the agent's mistaken memory, since the peak of leftist bombing activity occurred from 1969 to 1971 and dropped precipitously in 1972. See Burrough, *Days of Rage*, 5. For a more conservative quantitative study of political bombings from 1969 to 1975 that is missing data from 1969 but shows 1972 and 1973 as a low point in the period's bombings, when fewer than sixty occurred over a two-year period, see National Advisory Committee on Criminal Justice Standards and Goals, *Report of the Task Force on Disorders and Terrorism*, 509.

8. I define clandestine urban guerrilla organizations as groups whose members developed underground infrastructures of safe houses, fake IDs, and secret communication networks for the purpose of evading state surveillance while conducting sustained campaigns of politically motivated urban guerrilla warfare in the form of bombings, police assassinations, and other attacks. For more on the concept of clandestinity, see della Porta, *Clandestine Political Violence*; and Zwerman, Steinhoff, and della Porta, "Disappearing Social Movements."

9. Groups and individuals motivated by right-wing ideologies also carried out bombings, acts of arson, and other attacks during this period—violent attacks on public school property by people opposed to mandatory busing were particularly destructive in Boston, Pontiac, Michigan, Newark, New Jersey, and other locations during the early 1970s. However, because most of such violence was sporadic, episodic, or isolated to local police jurisdictions, it did not attract widespread media attention or prompt the attention of the FBI. An exception was the far-right Jewish Defense League (JDL), which was centered in New York with aboveground and underground factions, and carried out several attacks; a January 1971 firebombing of the offices of an artist-activist who was working to normalize U.S. relations with the Soviet Union, which the JDL opposed because of its barring Soviet Jews from migrating to Israel, killed one person and injured thirteen others. Anti-Castro Cuban counterrevolutionaries also carried out a wave of more than a dozen acts of arson and bombings in New York, Los Angeles, Chicago, and Miami in 1968. See Eckstein, *Bad Moon Rising*, 94; and Perlstein, *Nixonland*, 339–40, 587. Further examples are listed in the sources outlined in note 7. On the FBI and the Ku Klux Klan in the 1960s, see Cunningham, *Klansville, U.S.A.* and *There's Something Happening Here*; and on the FBI and violent white power organization in the 1980s and 1990s, see Belew, *Bring the War Home*.

10. For more on the international dimensions of clandestine urban guerrilla warfare, see Churchill, *Becoming Tupamaros*; Varon, *Bringing the War Home*; della Porta, *Social Movements, Political Violence, and the State*; and Wickham-Crowley, *Guerrillas and Revolution in Latin America*.

11. As Cedric Johnson put it, the "crucial distinction between movement notoriety and actual popular power is conflated within the scholarship and folklore of Black Power. . . . How many middle-class or working-class Americans fully embraced the [Black Panther Party]'s call for socialist revolution, as they had the civil rights movement? And was this perspective, one inflected with Third Worldism and allusions to armed struggle, at all suited to the affluent, advanced industrial society in which it was propagated? These are questions that latter-day historians and fans of the Black Power movement have, for the most part, failed to answer or even to pose." Johnson, "The Panthers Can't Save Us Now," 70. For more on the concept of a "revolutionary situation," see Aya, *Rethinking Revolutions and Collective Violence*, 71. On the Black Panthers and the media, see Rhodes, *Framing the Black Panthers*.

12. The preeminent scholarly study of the Weather Underground is Varon, *Bringing the War Home*, which compares the organization to West Germany's Red Army Faction. Eckstein, *Bad Moon Rising*, offers more information on the FBI's Weather Underground investigation and argues that the group "beat" the FBI,

largely owing to the bureau's ineptitude. For more on this book, see Chard, review of *Bad Moon Rising*. Also see Berger, *Outlaws of America*; and Jacobs, *The Way the Wind Blew*. For a documentary history of the group, see Dohrn, Ayers, and Jones, *Sing a Battle Song*. Several former Weather Underground members have published memoirs: Lerner, *Swords in the Hands of Children*; Gilbert, *Love and Struggle*; Rudd, *Underground*; Wilkerson, *Flying Close to the Sun*; Ayers: *Fugitive Days*; Stern, *With the Weathermen*. For a documentary film on the group, see *The Weather Underground*. For a historian's family history featuring insights on the lives of his parents, Weatherpeople Eleanor Raskin and Jeff Jones, see Jones, *A Radical Line*. For a true-crime-style journalistic account of the Weather Underground and other armed leftist groups of the era, featuring new revelations on leftist violence culled from other journalists and nonrecorded oral history interviews (some of which have been disputed) by an author who said that FBI files "are almost useless to a historian," see Burrough, *Days of Rage* (xi), along with Varon, "Dumbing Down the Underground." Several oral histories of former Weather Underground members are available in Bingham, *Witness to the Revolution*.

13. Former Weather Underground sources told journalist Bryan Burrough that members of the group were responsible for a pair of bombings of San Francisco Bay Area police stations in February 1970 that killed one police officer and maimed another. Burrough also revealed that the group planned other lethal actions after the townhouse explosion—and robbed an upstate New York steakhouse for cash—before settling into a pattern of bombing buildings while avoiding casualties. Burrough, *Days of Rage*, 94–97, 126–27, 141. As I discuss in chapter 4, on the night of the townhouse explosion, Weatherman guerrillas in Detroit also planted two anti-personnel bombs outside of police stations that failed to detonate.

14. Historians have yet to publish a full history of the BLA. The most balanced scholarly source is Reverby, *Co-conspirator for Justice*, which explains the BLA in relation to the white anti-imperialist May 19th Communist Organization and the life of radical doctor-turned-guerrilla Alan Berkman. Reverby focuses more on the years from the mid-1970s to 1981, after the BLA's most violent period in the Nixon era. For an earlier historical overview of the organization, see Umoja, "The Black Liberation Army and the Radical Legacy of the Black Panther Party." For a more sensational journalistic account of the group, see Burrough, *Days of Rage*, chapters 8–11. For a very sympathetic dissertation on the BLA, see Faraj, "Unearthing the Underground." For a short overview of the BLA's history by one of its former members, see Muntaqim, *On the Black Liberation Army*. For a police perspective drawn from journalistic and other secondary sources, see Rosenau, "Our Backs Are against the Wall." For a memoir by a former BLA member, see Joseph, *Panther Baby*.

15. In addition to the sources listed above, see Burton-Rose, *Guerrilla USA*; and Graebner, *Patty's Got a Gun*.

16. Analysis of leftist violence is almost entirely absent from scholarship on the FBI during the late 1960s. Exceptions include Eckstein, *Bad Moon Rising*, which examines the FBI's Weather Underground investigation but offers little explanation of how this investigation influenced broader changes in the FBI and American politics; O'Reilly, *"Racial Matters,"* which offers a brief explanation of how Black

Panther violence and violent rhetoric influenced FBI operations targeting the group; and Davis, *Spying on America*, which provides a good overview of the FBI's five major domestic counterintelligence programs and explains how fears of civil disturbance prompted the formation of COINTELPROs against the Black Power movement and the New Left.

Most writing on FBI operations against American leftists during the late 1960s and early 1970s reflects the viewpoint of the Senate Select Committee to Study Governmental Operations with respect to Intelligence Activities, popularly known as the "Church Committee" after its chair, Senator Frank Church (D-ID). In January 1975, in the aftermath of Watergate and President Nixon's resignation, the Senate charged the Church Committee with the task of investigating American federal intelligence agencies' involvement in "illegal, improper, or unethical activities" (Book II, page v). Based on unprecedented congressional access to thousands of formerly classified intelligence documents, the Church Committee's nearly 1,400 pages of reports on the FBI revealed for the first time how the bureau used electronic surveillance, informants, mail opening, break-ins, and covert counterintelligence programs against American citizens in order to undermine political dissidents, manipulate the mass media, and influence government policy from 1936 through the early 1970s.

The Church Committee reports offer what remain the most detailed studies of FBI operations against dissident social movements during the late 1960s and early 1970s and include extensive evidence on how insurgent violence influenced the FBI during this period. However, because of their post-Watergate focus on uncovering FBI improprieties as a step toward reforming U.S. intelligence agencies, and because of their thematic rather than chronological framework, the Church Committee reports do not sufficiently analyze how domestic revolutionary violence contributed to changes in FBI practices over time.

Since 1976, the Church Committee reports have offered the central body of primary sources and the key analytical framework for subsequent literature on FBI operations against radical social movements of the late 1960s and early 1970s. Much of the subsequent literature has replicated the Church Committee reports' expository format. See Church Committee, Books II and III.

Other works on FBI operations against the U.S. Left during this period include Greenberg, *The Dangers of Dissent*; Cunningham, *There's Something Happening Here*; Donner, *Age of Surveillance*; and Theoharis, *Spying on Americans*. For a sociological study of FBI reforms and institutional changes during the 1970s and 1980s, see Poveda, *The FBI in Transition*. Scholarly works covering the sweep of FBI history from 1908 to the early twenty-first century include Jeffreys-Jones, *The FBI*; Theoharis, *The FBI and American Democracy*; and Powers, *Broken*. Much of the FBI's history has been written as biographies of J. Edgar Hoover. See Summers, *Official and Confidential*; Gentry, *J. Edgar Hoover*; Theoharis and Cox, *The Boss*; and Powers, *Secrecy and Power*. For a journalistic overview of the history of the FBI that references Nixon-era leftist violence, see Weiner, *Enemies*.

17. The Bureau of Investigation was renamed the Federal Bureau of Investigation in 1935. See the previous note for a list of Hoover's biographies.

18. Cecil, *Hoover's FBI and the Fourth Estate*.

19. Theoharis, *Spying on Americans*, 18.

20. FBI airtel [Airtel is the name for a high-priority internal FBI memorandum that was typed and sent on the same day via mail or teletype. A teletype is a device that transmitted instant typed communication over wire], Director to SAC [special agent in charge] Albany, "Counterintelligence Program, Black Nationalist—Hate Groups, Internal Security," August 25, 1967, 1–2, COINTELPRO-Black Extremist, Section 1; FBI memo, C. D. Brennan to W. C. Sullivan, "Counterintelligence Program, Internal Security, Disruption of the New Left," May 9, 1968, and FBI memo, Director to SAC Albany, "Counterintelligence Program, Internal Security, Disruption of the New Left," May 10, 1968, COINTELPRO-New Left, Headquarters file, Number 1.

21. Davis, *Spying on America*, 33–34.

22. This is particularly true of most scholarship on the Black Panther Party, including Bloom and Martin's influential *Black against Empire*. See my notes in chapter 2 for further discussion and citations. Examples of works on 1960s-era radical social movements that provide more accurate accounts of FBI operations include Carson, *In Struggle*; Rosen, *The World Split Open*; and Schmalzer, Chard, and Botelho, *Science for the People*.

23. Medsger, *The Burglary*, 7.

24. One example is the documentary film *COINTELPRO 101*. For an older but influential work exhibiting such tendencies, see Goldstein, *Political Repression in Modern America*. Also see my notes in chapter 2.

25. Cunningham, *There's Something Happening Here*, 8–9.

26. Churchill and Vander Wall, *Agents of Repression*, 384. Also Churchill and Vander Wall, *The COINTELPRO Papers*.

Churchill and Vander Wall based their work largely on previous scholars' research (much of which they misrepresented) and memoirs by leftist activists and police informants. Among other works, the pair uncritically drew on former Black Panther leader Huey P. Newton's questionable PhD dissertation "War against the Panthers." Churchill and Vander Wall wrote *The COINTELPRO Papers* in response to a review of *Agents of Repression* published in the *Washington Post* by preeminent FBI historian Athan Theoharis, which argued that the authors did not provide evidence to back their claims. See Athan Theoharis, "Building a File: The Case against the FBI: AIM and the FBI," *Washington Post*, October 30, 1988.

Though *The COINTELPRO Papers* includes excerpts of some FBI documents, the authors misrepresented many of these sources, or interpreted them out of historical context, just as they did in their previous book. In 2007, Ward Churchill (who never earned a PhD) was forced from his faculty position in the Ethnic Studies Department at the University of Colorado Boulder after a panel of experts determined that he had misrepresented evidence in several of his books on Native American history (the panel did not review his books on the FBI). Because the university launched the investigation in response to complaints from right-wing activists about a sensational essay he wrote after the 9/11 attacks arguing that some of the victims deserved their fate, some of Churchill's supporters on the militant left continue to believe that his dismissal was entirely politically motivated rather than motivated partly by politics and partly by his inflammatory writing and spurious scholarship.

It is difficult to overstate Churchill's impact in distorting the historical record on the FBI and the U.S. Left. A Google Scholar search at the time of this writing shows 634 citations of *Agents of Repression* in scholarly books and articles. Churchill and Vander Wall's books on the FBI also continue to circulate in radical movement circles.

27. For examples of historical literature that uses 9/11 as a starting point for U.S. counterterrorism operations, see Greenberg, *Rogue Justice*; and Mayer, *The Dark Side*.

28. This book explores the history of terrorism and counterterrorism before 9/11, but it takes a different approach than most scholarship on the history of terrorism. Most work on the topic analyzes the history of terrorism through what I call a *definitional* framework. With this framework, scholars adopt a contemporary state definition of terrorism—typically understood as political violence carried out by nonstate actors for the purpose of instilling fear in an audience beyond the immediate target—and apply it to examples from various times and places throughout world history. This is a useful approach for understanding how states have responded to violent insurgents in a variety of past situations, but it also has its problems.

The definitional framework presumes a commonality between an incredible diversity of insurgents and vigilantes. This has included George Washington and the American Revolution's Sons of Liberty; John Brown and fellow armed abolitionists; anarchist bombers and assassins; the Ku Klux Klan and other white racists; Irish, Zionist, Palestinian, and Puerto Rican nationalists and a range of ethnonationalist separatists; post–World War II anticolonial rebels; leftist guerrillas; and religious extremists of varying faiths, including al-Qaeda. As critics have pointed out, lumping these disparate groups together as "terrorists" can remove them from their specific historical contexts.

These problems are compounded by the fact that terrorism is a contemporary term fraught with political controversy. Since the emergence of counterterrorism in the 1970s, neither terrorism experts, U.S. state agencies, nor the United Nations has been able to agree on a single, shared definition for terrorism. Specialists continue to disagree, for example, over whether the term should encompass property damage, attacks on military targets, or state violence. This is because the act of labeling an individual or group as "terrorist" is inherently political: such categorization works to delegitimize "terrorist" (usually nonstate) violence while implicitly legitimizing "counterterrorist" (typically state) violence. Conventional terrorism scholars rarely discuss state terrorism, and when they do they typically reserve the term for regimes hostile to the United States. The term is unquestionably pejorative and state-centric.

Using "terrorism" to describe historical actors whose contemporaries did not use the term as we understand it today brings harmful present-day bias to our analyses of the past. By vilifying history's violent insurgents, a definitional framework can limit our understanding of what social, economic, and political conditions motivated past incidents of nonstate political violence. It can skew our awareness of how incidents of insurgent violence relate to other forms of violence, including that carried out by states. Even worse, the definitional framework can inadvertently help legitimize harmful—and often racist—forms of contemporary state violence carried out in the name of counterterrorism, including torture, rendition, police brutality, and military intervention.

Instead of a *definitional* framework, this book draws from Stampnitzky, *Disciplining Terror*, and Thorup, *An Intellectual History of Terror*, to analyze terrorism history through what I call a *diachronic* framework. With this approach, I analyze how the FBI and the Nixon administration's war with leftist guerrillas influenced changes in the political meaning of terrorism. My aim is not to impose a present-day definition of terrorism on past historical actors. Nor do I wish to minimize the real pain and lasting trauma that resulted from political violence in the 1970s. Rather, I seek to uncover how and why U.S. state officials in this period began to constitute leftist guerrilla violence as terrorism, and how this development shaped critical changes in American politics, policing, and global power.

The term "terrorism" was originally used to describe state violence. During the French Revolution's "Reign of Terror" (1793–94), Maximilien Robespierre's guillotines decapitated 40,000 aristocrats and other accused counterrevolutionaries in a campaign designed to secure revolutionaries' control over the new republic. Terrorism became more closely associated with nonstate political violence during the late nineteenth and early twentieth centuries, when European revolutionary nationalists and anarchists carried out various attacks with guns and dynamite. State officials and revolutionaries of the time sometimes described insurgent political violence as "terrorism," but they used other words too, like "assassination," "nihilism," "anarchy," "revolutionist," and "fanaticism."

A key antecedent to international antiterrorism agreements forged in the 1970s was the Petersberg Protocol of 1904, an international policing agreement signed by ten European countries and designed to suppress anarchist violence. Importantly, this agreement set out to combat "anarchist" rather than "terrorist" violence, since "terrorism" did not carry today's connotations of a pathological threat to civilization. In 1901, after a young anarchist's assassination of President William McKinley, Theodore Roosevelt expressed this very point, proclaiming that "anarchy is a crime against the whole human race, all mankind should band against the anarchist."

The contemporary meaning of the term "terrorism" did not take hold until the Cold War, particularly during the 1970s, when state officials also invented counterterrorism.

Works that employ a definitional approach to terrorism history include Law, *The Routledge History of Terrorism* and *Terrorism*; Gage, "Terrorism and the American Experience"; and *The Day Wall Street Exploded*; Laqueur, *A History of Terrorism*; Rapoport, "The Four Waves of Modern Terrorism"; Kumamoto, *The Historical Origins of Terrorism in America*; Jensen, *The Battle against Anarchist Terrorism*; and Messer-Kruse, *The Trial of the Haymarket Anarchists*. For histories of terrorism based on alternative, unconventional definitions, see Miller, *The Foundations of Modern Terrorism*; and Fellman, *In the Name of God and Country*. For historians' criticism of this approach, see Larabee, "Why Historians Should Use Caution When Using the Word 'Terrorism'"; Mulloy, "Is There a 'Field'?"; and Varon, "A History of Violence and the Myth of American Exceptionalism." For more on debates over the definition of terrorism, see Stampnitzky, "Can Terrorism Be Defined?" For more on state terrorism and political biases in orthodox terrorism studies, see Blakely, "Constructing State Terrorism"; Rafael, "In the Service of Power"; Jackson, "Knowledge, Power and Politics in the Study of Political Terrorism"; and Jackson, Smyth, and Gunning, "Critical Terrorism Studies." On shifting definitions of terrorism from the French Revolution to anarchist and nationalist insurgencies of the late nineteenth and early twentieth centuries, see Hoffman, *Inside Terrorism*, 3–12; and Thorup, *An Intellectual History of Terror*, 89–94, 103–7. On the Petersberg Protocol and Roosevelt's quote on anarchism, see Jensen, "The United States, International Policing, and the War against Anarchist Terrorism," 15, 19.

29. After Russia's Bolshevik Revolution of 1917, U.S. authorities also decried Bolshevism and Communism. See Schmidt, *Red Scare.*

30. U.S. State Department, "A Report to the National Security Council—NSC 68," 4–6.

31. Bacevich, *The Long War.*

32. Schrecker, *Many Are the Crimes*, 203. Also, Storrs, *The Second Red Scare and the Unmaking of the New Deal Left.*

33. Prashad, *The Darker Nations*, 15, 107.

34. Townshend, "'Methods Which All Civilized Opinion Must Condemn," 35–39.

35. Barak-Erez, "Israeli Anti-terrorism Law," 598.

36. Cohen, "1967 Terrorism Act, 83 of 1967."

37. Naftali, *Blind Spot*, 25–26.

38. Organization of American States, "Convention to Prevent and Punish the Acts of Terrorism Taking the Form of Crimes against Persons and Related Extortion That Are of International Significance."

39. Chamberlin, *The Global Offensive*, 88–92.

40. Chamberlin, 161–72.

41. Arafat quoted in Hoffman, *Inside Terrorism*, 38. Ironically, Arafat's covert sanctioning of deadly international attacks such as those carried out by the Black September Organization had helped give rise to the very accusations of terrorism that he criticized.

42. Hewitt, *The British War on Terror*, 19–20.

43. Hewitt, "Cold War Counter-Terrorism," 4.

44. Varon, *Bringing the War Home*, 256.

45. Interagency Committee on Intelligence (Ad Hoc), "Special Report," June 1970, Huston Plan, Exhibit 1, 141–88.

46. Stampnitzky, *Disciplining Terror*, 27–28.

47. In doing so, this book also provides the most detailed analysis to date of the various and often contradictory roles the FBI and its leaders played in the Watergate saga. For decades, Kutler's 1990 book, *The Wars of Watergate*, has remained the definitive account of the Watergate scandal, though Kutler expanded scholars' access to Watergate research in 1997 with his publication of *Abuse of Power*, an

annotated guide to transcripts of the Nixon tape recordings. Since then, a handful of scholars have shed further light on the FBI's roles in Watergate, which Kutler did not explore in depth. This includes journalist Tim Weiner, who discusses this topic in his book *Enemies*, and historian Beverly Gage, whose 2012 article "Deep Throat, Watergate, and the Bureaucratic Politics of the FBI" outlined the Huston Plan as a critical part of an institutional conflict between the FBI and the White House that led to Watergate, but did not explain how leftist violence influenced this conflict. Journalist Max Holland's book *Leak*, published around the same time as Gage's essay, offers a well-researched account of Mark Felt's activities as Deep Throat, though he also does not analyze leftist violence or Felt's authorization of FBI break-ins, and does not provide sufficient evidence to support his claim that Felt's Deep Throat activities were motivated primarily by a personal ambition to succeed Hoover as FBI director. More recently, Michael Koncewicz's 2018 book *They Said No to Nixon* uses fresh archival research in the Nixon Library and the Nixon Tapes to explain how moderate Republicans such as Attorney General Elliot Richardson and Deputy Attorney General William Ruckelshaus (who previously served a short term as interim FBI director) helped prevent Nixon from fulfilling his deeply authoritarian political aspirations. My work builds on all of this research, explaining how leftist guerrilla violence fueled the FBI-Nixon institutional conflict and Nixon's grab for power.

48. This research expands on recent work on the U.S. State Department's post-Munich Operation Boulder in Pennock, *The Rise of the Arab American Left*; and Yaqub, *Imperfect Strangers*.

Chapter 1

1. UPI, "Grand Jury Indicts Man for Bombing," *Lodi News-Sentinel*, February 15, 1969; AP, "2 Witnesses Admit Joining Bishop in Bombing Towers," *Greeley Daily Tribune*, December 31, 1969; United States v. Bishop, 555 F.2d 771 - Court of Appeals (10th Cir. 1977), 772–73; Cameron Bishop interview, June 5, 1975, audio recording, Freedom Archives, call number PM 197A.

2. Nixon, inaugural address (1969).

3. Ben A. Franklin, "Young Demonstrators at Parade Throw Smoke Bombs and Stones at Nixon's Car," *New York Times*, January 21, 1969. For further accounts of the 1969 counterinaugural protests, see Rudd, *Underground*, 131; Emerson, *Winners & Losers*, 314–17; and Perlstein, *Nixonland*, 357–59.

4. National Advisory Commission on Civil Disorders, *The Kerner Report*; Graham and Gurr, *Violence in America*.

5. Bloom and Martin argued that the BPP grew significantly over the course of 1969, expanding its chapters from approximately twenty cities to sixty-eight. The evidence casts doubt on this assertion, however, since as Bloom and Martin acknowledge, and as I analyze in chapter 2, Bobby Seale froze the party's membership in January 1969, at which time he claimed that the party already had over forty chapters. It appears that the fall of 1968 was actually the party's greatest period of national growth, though it was also a time of heightened factionalism amid

increasing violent confrontations with police. Bloom and Martin, *Black against Empire*, 2, 179–98, 344–45.

6. Scholars have estimated that between twenty-four and twenty-eight members of the Panthers were killed by police over the course of the party's existence. See Murch, *Living for the City*, 162, 262n209. On police raids, see Bloom and Martin, *Black against Empire*, 212–15; and Donner, *Protectors of Privilege*, 180.

7. See chapters 2 and 3 for further discussion of BPP and SDS conflicts with police over the course of 1969.

8. UPI, "Grand Jury Indicts Man for Bombing"; United States v. Bishop, 555 F.2d 771 - Court of Appeals (10th Cir. 1977), 773.

9. Sale, *SDS*, 632. For a discussion on bombing statistics, see note 7 in my introduction.

10. The Justice Department charged the Chicago Eight under provisions of the Civil Rights Act of 1968, which Congress had passed in response to militant Student Nonviolent Coordinating Committee (SNCC) leaders Stokely Carmichael and H. Rap Brown, whom the FBI inaccurately accused of inciting the hundreds of urban riots that disrupted American cities in 1967 and 1968. The Chicago Eight also faced charges of conspiring to cross state lines to teach the making of incendiary devices and committing acts to impede police officers from their lawful duties. Dellinger, Davis, Hayden, Hoffman, Rubin, and Seale also faced charges of crossing state lines to incite a riot, and Froines and Weiner faced charges of instructing other persons how to make incendiary devices. In addition, the indictment named sixteen unindicted conspirators from various segments of the antiwar movement. Farber, *Chicago '68*, 147; Stone, *Perilous Times*, 484; "Indictment in the Chicago Seven Conspiracy Trial," Famous Trials.

11. Eckstein, *Bad Moon Rising*, 249.

12. These indictments should also be understood as part of Nixon's authoritarian efforts to repress his political enemies, which included attempts to use the Internal Revenue Service (IRS) to audit his perceived foes and to use the Office of Management and Budget to cut federal research funds to the Massachusetts Institute of Technology because of its leadership's perceived lax handling of student antiwar protest. Moderate conservatives within the administration blocked these efforts. See Koncewicz, *They Said No to Nixon*.

13. Perlstein, *Nixonland*, 335; Schrecker, *Many Are the Crimes*, xi, 213.

14. Gentry, *J. Edgar Hoover*, 362; Powers, *Secrecy and Power*, 301.

15. National Advisory Commission on Civil Disorders, *The Kerner Report*, 1–2.

16. King, "Why I Am Opposed to the War in Vietnam."

17. The *Kerner Report* also called for increased policing to manage urban unrest, providing an intellectual foundation for Johnson's War on Crime, which Nixon expanded while cutting back on social democratic aspects of the Great Society. See Schrader, *Badges without Borders*, 4.

18. From 1960 to 1970, in American cities with populations of more than 1 million, the homicide rate tripled and robberies increased sixfold. Clegg and Usmani, "The Economic Origins of Mass Incarceration," 19.

19. Ehrlichman, *Witness to Power*, 233; Alexander, *The New Jim Crow*, 44.

20. Nixon, "Failure of Leadership." Also see Bernstein, *America Is the Prison*, 27–38.

21. Flamm, *Law and Order*, 167.

22. Huston oral history, 1–3.

23. Interagency Committee on Intelligence (Ad Hoc), "Special Report," June 1970, Huston Plan, Exhibit 1, 141–88.

24. Crespino, *Strom Thurmond's America*, 3, 7, 219–22, 225–28.

25. Crespino, 210; Schaller, *Right Turn*, 20.

26. Senate Subcommittee to Investigate the Administration of the Internal Security Act and Other Internal Security Laws, Annual Report, 1976, vi.

27. Stampnitzky, *Disciplining Terror*, 122; see my epilogue for further discussion.

28. Thompson, "Why Mass Incarceration Matters"; Gilmore, *Golden Gulag*.

29. Hinton, *From the War on Poverty to the War on Crime*, 2.

30. O'Reilly, *"Racial Matters,"* 254–56.

31. J. Edgar Hoover testimony, Senate Committee on Appropriations, *Hearings on H.R. 19928*, 1079; Medsger, *The Burglary*, 34.

32. Bishop interview, June 5, 1975; Hoecker, "The Black and White behind the Blue and White," 61–62.

33. "CSUPD History," Colorado State University Police Department, https://police.colostate.edu/history/ (accessed May 24, 2020).

34. Levasseur, "Trouble Coming Every Day."

35. *United States v. Bishop*, 555 F.2d 771, 773; Bishop interview, June 5, 1975.

36. *United States v. Bishop*, 555 F.2d 771, 773.

37. UPI, "Grand Jury Indicts Man for Bombing"; U.S. Department of Justice, *United States Attorneys Bulletin*, 210.

38. In 1973, a special Senate committee led by Frank Church (D-ID) and Charles Mathias (R-MD) determined that a series of vaguely defined "states of emergency" declared since the Roosevelt administration remained in effect during the Nixon presidency. A February 1969 Justice Department memo noted that the section of the Federal War Sabotage Act of 1918 used to indict Bishop had been "extended to cover a period of national emergency declared by the President." It is unclear, however, whether this statement refers to Eisenhower, whose administration amended the act, or Nixon. See James N. Naughton, "Wartime Powers Studied by Panel," *New York Times*, January 14, 1973; "National Emergency," *New York Times*, April 19, 1973; and U.S. Department of Justice, *United States Attorneys Bulletin*.

39. *United States v. Bishop*, 555 F.2d 771, 774.

40. U.S. Federal Bureau of Investigation, "FBI's Ten Most Wanted Fugitives"; UPI, "Radical Leftists Dot Most Wanted List," *Hartford Courant*, October 21, 1971. Bishop's three alleged coconspirators were Steven Knowles, Susan Parker, and Linda Goebel. Parker and Goebel testified against Bishop in exchange for immunity. Knowles also went underground. The FBI targeted Bishop on its Most Wanted list because he was considered the group's leader. He was the 300th individual to appear on the list.

41. O'Reilly, *"Racial Matters,"* 185–86.

42. Johnson quoted in Nixon, *RN*, 358.

43. Church Committee, Book III, 403. In 1924, after the Palmer Raids of 1919–20 and the Teapot Dome Scandal of 1921–22—a bribery scandal involving the Department of Justice that ruined the reputation of President Warren Harding and was widely considered the greatest political scandal in U.S. history before Watergate—Attorney General Harlan Fiske Stone banned the Bureau of Investigation from engaging in political surveillance. President Calvin Coolidge appointed the young J. Edgar Hoover to serve as the bureau's acting director (he was promoted to permanent director the following year). See Schmidt, *Red Scare*, 324–26.

44. Church Committee, Book III, 403.

45. Kornweibel, *"Seeing Red"*; Charles, *J. Edgar Hoover and the Anti-interventionists*, 1–6. The FBI also dedicated vast resources to policing sexuality and persecuting gay men. See Charles, *Hoover's War on Gays*; Pliley, *Policing Sexuality*; and Fronc, *New York Undercover*.

46. Church Committee, Book III, 412–13.

47. Church Committee, Book II, 60–65, and Book III, 228–29.

48. FBI personnel officially referred to break-ins as "surreptitious entries" while colloquially using the term "black bag jobs" in reference to the black bags containing lock-picking tools agents would bring with them on such operations. For an overview of the FBI's extralegal surveillance techniques directed at the CPUSA, see Church Committee, Book II, 60–65, and Book III, 228–29.

49. Schrecker, *Many Are the Crimes*, 192, 203.

50. Julius Rosenberg led a spy ring that transferred information about the U.S. military and weapons technology to the Soviet Union, but he was not, as the government claimed, responsible for passing the secrets of America's nuclear bomb to the USSR (Union of Soviet Socialist Republics) or for starting the Korean War. The 2015 declassification of the 1950 grand jury testimony of David Greenglass, Ellen's brother and a member of Julius's spy ring who worked in Los Alamos labs, confirms the long-held suspicion of Rosenberg supporters that Greenglass fabricated a story of Ethel's involvement in the espionage that the government used in an effort to compel Julius to confess. Schrecker, *Many Are the Crimes*, 176–78; Michael Meeropol and Robert Meeropol, "The Meeropol Brothers: Exonerate Our Mother, Ethel Rosenberg," *New York Times*, August 10, 2015.

51. Hoover launched COINTELPRO-CPUSA in response to a Supreme Court ruling on the Smith Act of 1940 that limited the state's power to investigate and prosecute individuals deemed "subversives." While the Smith Act made it a crime to advocate "the overthrow of any government in the United States by force of violence," the court's new interpretation determined that promotion of ideas alone was not punishable. The director continued to emphasize the CPUSA's supposed threat to U.S. internal security to American officials after the ruling, despite the party's greatly diminished stature and his knowledge that the Soviet Union had ceased using the organization for espionage since Nikita Khrushchev replaced Joseph Stalin as the country's leader in 1953. Hoover gained President Dwight Eisenhower's approval for a covert effort to defeat the CPUSA during a National Security Council meeting on March 8, 1956. For more on COINTELPRO-CPUSA, see Davis, *Spying on*

America, 31–32. On the FBI's development of COINTELPRO operations against Axis and Soviet spies, see Batvinis, *Hoover's Secret War against Axis Spies* and *The Origins of FBI Counterintelligence.*

52. Davis, *Spying on America,* 29, 33–34.

53. Davis, *Assault on the Left,* 6.

54. On the FBI's COINTELPRO against the SWP, see Blackstock, *COINTELPRO.* More research is needed on the FBI's 1960s' COINTELPRO against "Groups Seeking Independence for Puerto Rico," which was not covered in the Church Committee reports because the FBI did not make the program's existence known to the public until after the committee's hearings. Declassified documents from this operation available in the FBI's online archive suggest that the program's purported mission shifted over the course of the 1960s from one of countering "subversion" to preventing revolutionary anticolonial violence. See FBI Vault, COINTELPRO-Puerto Rican Groups Files.

55. Agents had secretly taped King's illicit encounters using hidden microphones (bugs) in his hotel rooms. "There is only one way out for you," the letter threatened. "You better take it before your filthy, abnormal fraudulent self is bared to the nation." Assistant Director William Sullivan wrote the letter and ordered an agent in Miami to mail it to King from Atlanta. The FBI carried out this operation before King's acceptance of the prestigious Nobel Peace Prize, amid bureau officials' anger over his association with Communists, secret extramarital affairs, and public criticism of the bureau for not protecting civil workers from violent white racists. The American public first learned of the FBI's "suicide letter" to King during the Church Committee hearings. The Church Committee based its reporting on a heavily redacted version of the letter received from the FBI. In 2014, however, researchers discovered the original letter in Hoover's "Official and Confidential" files at the National Archives. See Gage, "What an Uncensored Letter to M.L.K. Reveals." The online version of the article includes a digital copy of the uncensored letter. In 2019, David Garrow found evidence that this operation was directly approved by Hoover.

56. Church Committee, Book III, 319, 476.

57. Church Committee, Book III, 253–55; O'Reilly, *"Racial Matters,"* 267–68.

58. Jack Ryan, oral history interview.

59. Church Committee, Book III, 490.

60. Church Committee, Book III, 491 (emphasis in original).

61. Cecil, *Hoover's FBI and the Fourth Estate.*

62. Theoharis, *Spying on Americans,* 17.

63. According to one of Hoover's biographers, Johnson did this because Hoover had ingratiated himself to the president after John F. Kennedy's death, and LBJ sought the FBI director's alliance in a power struggle with Attorney General Robert F. Kennedy. See Powers, *Secrecy and Power,* 392.

64. Theoharis, *Spying on Americans,* 18.

65. Church Committee, Book III, 180.

66. O'Reilly, *"Racial Matters,"* 199, 225–26.

67. FBI airtel, Director to SAC Albany, "Counterintelligence Program, Black Nationalist—Hate Groups, Internal Security," August 25, 1967, 1–2, COINTELPRO-Black Extremist, Section 1. The FBI Vault currently refers to this program as

COINTELPRO-Black Extremist, but at the time it was called COINTELPRO-Black Nationalist—Hate Groups.

68. For more on the FBI's COINTELPRO operations against SNCC, see Carson, "White Repression."

69. FBI airtel, Director to SAC Albany, "Counterintelligence Program; Black Nationalist-Hate Groups; Racial Intelligence," March 4, 1968, COINTELPRO-Black Extremists, Part 1. This document is also reprinted in Churchill and Vander Wall, *The COINTELPRO Papers*, 108–9. Also see Bloom and Martin, *Black against Empire*, 202.

70. FBI airtel, Director to SAC Albany, March 4, 1968. At this point COINTELPRO-BNHG named "the radical and violence-prone leaders, members, and followers" of SNCC, SCLC, RAM, and NOI as its primary targets.

71. FBI airtel, Director to SAC Albany, March 4, 1968.

72. FBI memo, C. D. Brennan to W. C. Sullivan, "Counterintelligence Program, Internal Security, Disruption of the New Left," May 9, 1968; FBI memo, Director to SAC Albany, "Counterintelligence Program, Internal Security, Disruption of the New Left," May 10, 1968, FBI COINTELPRO-New Left, Headquarters file, Number 1.

73. National Advisory Commission on Civil Disorders, *Kerner Report*, 107.

74. Davis, *Assault on the Left*, 41.

75. "Text of F.B.I. Report to President on Summer Riots in 9 Cities over Country," *New York Times*, September 27, 1964; Church Committee, Book III, 25.

76. O'Reilly, *Black Americans*, 10–11.

77. Hoover quoted in O'Reilly, 7.

78. Howard Saffold quoted in *Eyes on the Prize, America's Civil Rights Movement 1954–1985*, Season 2, Episode 6, *A Nation of Law? 1968–1971*.

79. FBI memo, Brennan to Sullivan, May 9, 1968.

80. In the words of war correspondent Gloria Emerson, U.S. state violence in Vietnam was "normal—war normal." Emerson, *Winners & Losers*, 314.

81. Theoharis, *Spying on Americans*, 15.

82. Prados, *The Family Jewels*, 39–46.

83. Theoharis, *Spying on Americans*, 121–22.

84. Ehrlichman, *Witness to Power*, 159.

85. Powers, *Secrecy and Power*, 443.

86. Church Committee, Book III, 495–500.

87. Church Committee, Book III, 508.

88. Theoharis, *Spying on Americans*, 16.

89. William Beecher, "Raids in Cambodia by U.S. Unprotested," *New York Times*, May 9, 1969; Gentry, *J. Edgar Hoover*, 632–37.

90. Farrell, "When a Candidate Conspired with a Foreign Power to Win an Election."

91. Nixon claimed in his memoirs that his administration faced twenty-one serious leaks during his first five months in office, and a total of forty-five during his first term. Nixon, *RN*, 386. For more on Nixon's response to leaks, see Gentry, *J. Edgar Hoover*, 632–38; Powers, *Secrecy and Power*, 444–48; and Theoharis, *Spying on Americans*, 191–94.

92. Gentry, *J. Edgar Hoover*, 637.

93. Church Committee, Book III, 508–9.

94. Gentry, *J. Edgar Hoover*, 636.

95. Theoharis, *Spying on Americans*, 16.

96. John Kifner, "Lesbian Groups and Militant Feminists Questioned in Search for Fugitives," *New York Times*, April 9, 1975; Chard, "SCAR'd Times." A pair of police officers approached Bishop and Levasseur's vehicle when they recognized it as matching the description of a car reported to have been parked outside another local bank for several hours a couple days earlier. The pair had hooked up in Portland, Maine, where Levasseur was active in the prisoners' rights movement and helped run a leftist bookstore. Levasseur skipped bail after his Rhode Island arrest and went on to lead a guerrilla cell that carried out bombings throughout the Northeast during the late 1970s and early 1980s to support the struggle for Puerto Rican independence and protest U.S. support for South Africa's apartheid regime and Central American counterrevolutionary death squads. Levasseur earned a spot on the FBI's Most Wanted list in 1976.

97. *United States v. Bishop*, 555 F.2d, 773, 778.

Chapter 2

1. *Black Panther*, Vol. 2, No. 19 (January 4, 1969), 1, Bloom Alternative Press Collection, box 032, folder: Black Panther (Jan.–Mar. 1969).

2. *Black Panther*, Vol. 2, No. 19, 12.

3. Murch, *Living for the City*, 133.

4. Newton quoted in Murch, 135.

5. *Black Panther*, Vol. 2, No. 19.

6. Georgakas, "Armed Struggle—1960s and 1970s," 58; Rhodes, *Framing the Black Panthers*, 106.

7. "Pigs Raid De Moines Panthers," "Indianapolis Panthers Target of Pig Attack," and "Pigs Uptight: Bomb N.J. Panther Office," *Black Panther*, Vol. 2, No. 20, January 15, 1969, 8–9, Bloom Alternative Press Collection, box 032, folder: Black Panther (Jan.–Mar. 1969); Bloom and Martin, *Black against Empire*, 212–13.

8. *Black Panther*, Vol. 2, No. 20, 1, 3.

9. In his 1980 doctoral dissertation, Huey Newton argued that "agencies and officers of the federal government" endeavored to destroy the BPP because of the organization's "political ideology and potential for organizing a sizeable group of the country's population that has been historically denied equal opportunity." Newton, "War against the Panthers," 9.

10. In their influential book on the Black Panthers, for example, Joshua Bloom and Waldo Martin argue that the organization gained the FBI's attention in September 1968 owing to its "growing national scope, and the political challenge it now posed to the status quo." While the authors took the Panthers' claims at face value, they offered no evidence that the party's organizing posed a credible threat to America's political order. Bloom and Martin, *Black against Empire*, 203. For similar arguments, see Murch, *Living for the City*, 148; Alkebulan, *Survival Pending*

Revolution, 83–86; Austin, *Up against the Wall*, 191–93, 246–47; and Spencer, *The Revolution Has Come*, 89–90. For an argument claiming COINTELPRO was a core reason for the decline of the Young Lords Party, presented with scant evidence, see Fernández, *The Young Lords*, 372–77. For a critical review of Bloom and Martin, see Johnson, "Panther Nostalgia as History." Panther memoirs that underscore factionalism and dogmatism as central to the decline of the BPP include Cox, *Just Another*, and Dixon, *My People Are Rising*.

11. FBI memo, G. C. Moore to W. C. Sullivan, "Counterintelligence Program; Black Nationalist-Hate Groups; Racial Intelligence; (Black Panther Party)," September 27, 1968, in Churchill and Vander Wall, *The COINTELPRO Papers*, 124. The FBI's annual report for fiscal year 1968, issued on October 1, 1968, only briefly mentioned the Panthers as an Oakland-based group that advocated "the use of guns and guerrilla tactics to end their alleged oppression." The 1967 report did not mention the FBI at all. See Bloom and Martin, *Black against Empire*, 210, 445n46.

12. FBI memo, Moore to Sullivan, September 27, 1968.

13. Though much has been written about the FBI's COINTELPRO operations against the BPP, the best study remains that published by the Church Committee in 1976. See "The FBI's Covert Program to Destroy the Black Panther Party," Church Committee, Book III, 187–223.

14. Nixon was indeed highly authoritarian and sought to wield the state to crush his political adversaries. Obstacles to his efforts included moderate Republicans within his own administration, Democratic majorities in both houses of Congress, public sentiment spurred by movements of the Left, Hoover, and the decentralized nature of policing under the United States' federal system of government. See Koncewicz, *They Said No to Nixon*.

15. Murch, *Living for the City*, 65–66.

16. Kuwasi Balagoon quoted in "The Collective Autobiography of the Panther 21" (1971), republished in kioni-sadiki and Meyer, *Look for Me in the Whirlwind*, 205.

17. In addition to *Look for Me in the Whirlwind* and various Panther memoirs cited throughout this book, see Shih and Williams, *The Black Panthers*.

18. Others in the African American freedom struggle questioned nonviolence earlier. Many southern Black activists, for example, adopted nonviolence reluctantly, after a great deal of persuasion from movement leaders such as Bayard Rustin and Martin Luther King Jr. Most embraced nonviolence not out of a commitment to pacifism but because of their belief in its strategic value in the struggle to overturn southern states' racist Jim Crow regimes. Moreover, the southern civil rights movement was not as nonviolent as it typically appeared in the media. Throughout the late 1950s and early 1960s, activists including King kept firearms for self-defense and groups of armed African Americans provided security for nonviolent activists in a variety of settings, in some cases exchanging fire with white racist vigilantes. See Cobb, *This Nonviolent Stuff'll Get You Killed*; and Umoja, *We Will Shoot Back*.

19. Malcolm X, "The Ballot or the Bullet," in *Malcolm X Speaks*, 38. Also Marable, *Malcolm X*.

20. Malcolm X, "The Black Revolution," in *Malcolm X Speaks*, 49.

21. Tyson, *Radio Free Dixie*, 88–89.

22. Robert F. Williams, "USA: The Possibility of a Minority Revolution," *Crusader* 5, no. 4 (May–June 1964), Freedom Archives, 6. Williams's essay does not specifically use the term *foco*, but the guerrilla strategy it promotes is essentially *focoist*. It is unclear to what extent Cuban president Fidel Castro's foreign policy, which involved promoting *foco* theory internationally, influenced Williams's writings. Williams continued to publish the *Crusader* until 1968, after moving from Cuba to China. According to his biographer, Williams's isolation likely contributed to the "frustrations, delusions," and "apocalyptic visions" that characterized his writings on guerrilla warfare. See Tyson, *Radio Free Dixie*, 298–99.

23. Williams, "USA: The Possibility of a Minority Revolution," 6.

24. Marable, *Malcolm X*, 303.

25. Williams, "USA: The Possibility of a Minority Revolution," 5–6.

26. Bloom and Martin, *Black against Empire*, 42–50. For a firsthand account, see Seale, *Seize the Time*, 85–99.

27. The program's tenth point called for "a United Nations-supervised plebiscite to be held throughout the black colony [meaning African American communities] in which only black colonial subjects will be allowed to participate, for the purpose of determining the will of the black people as to their national destiny." The Black Panther Party for Self-Defense, "The Ten-Point Program: What We Want / What We Believe," October 1966, in Gosse, *The Movements of the New Left*, 103–6.

28. Bloom and Martin, *Black against Empire*, 61–62; Austin, *Up against the Wall*, xviii.

29. Prashad, *The Darker Nations*, 15, 107 (italics in original).

30. Prashad, 11, 108.

31. Guevara, "Message to the Tricontinental," in *Guerrilla Warfare*, 175–76; Prashad, *The Darker Nations*, 108–9.

32. Debray, *Revolution in the Revolution?* and *Strategy for Revolution: Essays on Latin America*.

33. Loveman and Davies, introduction to Guevara, *Guerrilla Warfare*, 34n22.

34. Varon, *Bringing the War Home*, 57.

35. Mumford, *Newark*, 125, 142–47.

36. Newton, "On the Correct Handling of a Revolution." Also see Umoja, "The Black Liberation Army," 227. Robert F. Williams's influence on Newton's essay is obvious.

37. Newton, "On the Correct Handling of a Revolution."

38. Cox, *Just Another*, 6.

39. Cox, 9.

40. Cox, 25.

41. "Most of the integration I saw at the time," he continued in a reference to his sex life, "was between the sheets." Cox, 27.

42. Cox, 23–34.

43. Cox's next lines allude to the limits of support for the Black Panthers and their tactics within African American communities: "No one I knew seemed to have heard of them, and what's more, they thought they must be crazy." Cox, 35.

44. Cox, 35.

45. Cox, 37.

46. Cox, 38.

47. Thirty-three Black people died in the riots along with ten white people. Thompson, *Whose Detroit?*, 46–47.

48. Cox, *Just Another*, 40.

49. Cox, 41.

50. Cox, 42.

51. Cox, 46.

52. Cox, 47.

53. Cox, 48.

54. Bloom and Martin, *Black against Empire*, 99–114; Rhodes, *Framing the Black Panthers*, 116–33.

55. Cox, *Just Another*, 49–54; Jim Herron Zemora, "1967–1971: A Bloody Period for S.F. Police," *SF Gate*, Officer Down Memorial Page, Officer Herman L. George, https://www.odmp.org/officer/5381-officer-herman-l-george. It turns out that Cox had also been the person responsible for hiding the pistol Huey Newton had used to shoot Officer Frey. Oakland Panther leader David Hilliard had driven to San Francisco immediately after the shootout to make arrangements for hiding the weapon. Both the identities of the Hunters Point police attackers and the whereabouts of Newton's gun remained a mystery until the posthumous publication of Cox's memoir.

56. Rhodes, *Framing the Black Panthers*, 100–104; O'Reilly, "*Racial Matters*," 295. For a participant-observer account highly critical of Cleaver's role in the BPP, see Thelwell, introduction to *Rage*, xxix–xxxii.

57. Bloom and Martin, *Black against Empire*, 2.

58. Presley quoted in Spencer, *The Revolution Has Come*, 94–95.

59. Spencer, 89. Spencer estimates the Panthers' peak membership as 1,200. Others have suggested the membership was significantly higher without providing substantial evidence. Spencer's figure is roughly corroborated by the Nixon administration's June 1970 Huston Plan document, which stated: "Despite its relatively small number of hard-core members—approximately 800 in 40 chapters nationwide—the BPP is in the forefront of black extremist activity today." Interagency Committee on Intelligence (Ad Hoc), "Special Report," June 1970, Huston Plan, Exhibit 1, 154.

60. Murch, *Living for the City*, 160–64; Bloom and Martin, *Black against Empire*, 146, 148, 155.

61. Lazerow, "A Rebel All His Life," 134. On the need for further exploration of this dynamic in Black Panther historiography, see Street, "The Historiography of the Black Panther Party," 371.

62. Cox, *Just Another*, 70. Donna Murch documented Cleaver's role in Hutton's death before the publication of Cox's memoir, but her research was either overlooked or ignored by Bloom and Martin, who published a partisan account similar to that promoted by Panther leadership at the time, claiming that police killed Hutton in an unprovoked attack. See Murch, *Living for the City*, 163–64; and Bloom and Martin, *Black against Empire*, 118–19.

63. According to Cox, at the end of Cleaver's speech at New York University a pair of nuns in their habits even sang along. Cox, *Just Another*, 74.

64. Bloom and Martin, *Black against Empire*, 314–19; Murch, *Living for the City*, 165, 186.

65. Brick and Parker, *A New Insurgency*. The most comprehensive book on SDS history remains Sale, *SDS*.

66. Sale, *SDS*, 315; Hall, *Peace and Freedom*, 121.

67. Sale, *SDS*, 374–79.

68. Senate Committee on Government Operations, *Riots, Civil and Criminal Disorders*, Part 25, 5577; Larabee, *The Wrong Hands*, 67; Sale, *SDS*, 504.

69. *Berkeley Barb*, February 9–15, 1968, quoted in Suri, *Power and Protest*, 171.

70. Perlstein, *Nixonland*, 293–294. The assault resulted in the wounding of twelve other police officers. Four more Black men died during rioting that followed the shootout. Faraj, "Unearthing the Underground," 114.

71. Sale, *SDS*, 503.

72. Perlstein, *Nixonland*, 339.

73. Umoja, "The Black Liberation Army," 227; Faraj, "Unearthing the Underground," 96n71.

74. FBI memo, Moore to Sullivan, September 27, 1968.

75. FBI memo, Director to San Francisco, September 30, 1968, COINTELPRO-Black Extremist, Section 6.

76. Church Committee researchers determined that the BPP was the target of 233 of the 295 COINTELPRO-BNHG operations approved by FBI headquarters. Church Committee, Book III, 188.

77. FBI airtel, Director to SAC San Francisco, May 27, 1969, reprinted in Churchill and Vander Wall, *The COINTELPRO Papers*, 144.

78. Payne, "WACing Off." The FBI began to surveil the Oakland BPP in 1967. In 2012, Seth Rosenfeld used evidence that member Richard Aoki was an FBI informant to publicize his book, *Subversives*, implying Aoki may have been an agent provocateur. But there is no evidence Aoki did anything except provide information. See Trevor Griffey, "When a Celebrated Activist Turns Out to be an FBI Informant," *Truthout*, November 5, 2012.

79. FBI memo, SAC New York to Director, August 8, 1968, COINTELPRO-Black Extremist, Section 3.

80. Austin, *Up against the Wall*, 129–32; Bloom and Martin, *Black against Empire*, 111–14.

81. FBI memo, SAC New York to Director, August 8, 1968.

82. FBI memo, SAC New York to Director, August 7, 1968, COINTELPRO-Black Extremist, Section 3.

83. FBI memo, SAC New York to Director, August 8, 1968.

84. Forman, *The Making of Black Revolutionaries*, 522, 535.

85. FBI memorandum, SAC New York to Director, September 5, 1968, quoted in Churchill and Vander Wall, *The COINTELPRO Papers*, 127–28. Stokely Carmichael recalled his mother's experiences with FBI harassment in his memoir: "The FBI had really been harassing her. Sending in strange Negroes whose names I didn't recognize, all claiming to be 'friends of Stokely's.' Probing for information. 'Heard from Stokely. Where is he going next?'Cars in front of the house. That kind of nonsense.

I didn't like them annoying my mother. But May Charles was unfazed. 'Hey I tell people, now I don't even have to lock up when I go out. J. Edgar Hoover is watching my house, honey.'" Carmichael, *Ready for Revolution*, 640.

86. FBI memo, SAC New York to Director, October 10, 1968, p. 3, COINTELPRO-Black Extremist, Section 4.

87. Rhodes, *Framing the Black Panthers*, 187–88. Seattle BPP chapter captain Aaron Dixon was outside the room where the confrontation happened. He later recalled hearing a loud "BAM!" and Cleaver shouting "motherfucker." Dixon also recalled that Cleaver and Seale were upset that Forman had tried to intimidate them by deploying his "field marshals." Dixon, *My People Are Rising*, 119.

88. Forman, *The Making of Black Revolutionaries*, 522–23. Forman indicated that this was the last time he ever spoke with Cleaver.

89. Rhodes, *Framing the Black Panthers*, 187.

90. Cleaver oral history quote in Carson, *In Struggle*, 342n44. See page 283 for SNCC member Ethel Minor's recollections of Cleaver's consideration of physical attacks on Carmichael and other SNCC leaders.

91. Carmichael, *Ready for Revolution*, 671.

92. The memo stated that the Panthers were keeping the hit on Karenga "in abeyance pending the results of the Huey Newton trial, inasmuch as the BPP wishes to retain as much support from the entire black community as possible." FBI memo, SAC Los Angeles to Director, September 25, 1968, COINTELPRO-Black Extremist, Section 3.

93. Bloom and Martin, *Black against Empire*, 144–45.

94. Bloom and Martin, 145–46.

95. Umoja, "The Black Liberation Army," 227–28.

96. FBI memo, SAC Los Angeles to Director, September 25, 1968, 4, COINTELPRO-Black Extremist, Section 5, 1, 3.

97. FBI memo, Director to SAC Los Angeles, October 31, 1968, COINTELPRO-Black Extremist, Section 6.

98. FBI memo, Director to San Francisco, November 26, 1968, COINTELPRO-Black Extremist, Section 7.

99. FBI memo, SAC New York to Director, December 2, 1968, 2, COINTELPRO-Black Extremist, Section 7.

100. Bloom and Martin, *Black against Empire*, 343.

101. FBI memo, SAC San Francisco to Director, February 2, 1968, COINTELPRO-Black Extremist, Section 7. The name of the gas station holdup suspect is redacted, but it likely referenced Brent.

102. Thomas Poster, "Basie's Wife Tells of Fears of Panthers," *New York Daily News*, September 18, 1968.

103. FBI memo, SAC New York to Director, December 2, 1968, 2.

104. FBI memo, SAC New York to Director, October 10, 1968, 2, COINTELPRO-Black Extremist, Section 4. A copy of the article is attached to the memo.

105. FBI memo, G. C. Moore to W. C. Sullivan, November 3, 1968; FBI memo, Director to Sacramento, November 14, 1968; and "Symposium: Racism in America," Eldridge Cleaver, Sacramento State College, Sacramento, California, October 2, 1968,

attached to FBI memo, "Leroy Eldridge Cleaver," December 11, 1968, COINTELPRO-Black Extremist, Section 5.

106. FBI memo, Moore to Sullivan, November 3, 1968.

107. FBI memo, SAC Chicago to Director, December 4, 1968, COINTELPRO-Black Extremist, Section 5.

108. FBI memo, SAC Chicago to Director, January 13, 1969, COINTELPRO-Black Extremist, Section 6.

109. Church Committee Report, Book III, 188. For more on the FBI's efforts to provoke violence between the Chicago Black Panthers and the Blackstone Rangers, see Church Committee, Book III, 195–98.

110. Bloom and Martin, *Black against Empire*, 228–29.

111. FBI memo, SAC Denver to Director, December 5, 1968, COINTELPRO-Black Extremist, Section 5. For more examples of FBI coordination with local police departments in order to target the Black Panthers, see Church Committee, Book III, 220–23.

112. FBI memo, G. C. Moore to W. C. Sullivan, November 5, 1968, COINTELPRO-Black Extremist, Section 6; Church Committee, Book III, 189–90.

113. FBI memo, Moore to Sullivan, November 5, 1968.

114. FBI memo, SAC Los Angeles to Director, November 29, 1968, COINTELPRO-Black Extremist, Section 7.

115. Church Committee, Book III, 189–98; Austin, *Up against the Wall*, 133; Bloom and Martin, *Black against Empire*, 218–19.

116. Church Committee, Book III, 22; FBI memo, Director to Baltimore, December 12, 1968, COINTELPRO-Black Extremist, Section 7.

117. FBI memo, Director to Baltimore, December 12, 1968.

118. Seale quoted in Bloom and Martin, *Black against Empire*, 344.

119. Cox, *Just Another*, 87.

120. Bloom and Martin, *Black against Empire*, 345–46.

121. Murch, *Living for the City*, 169–74; Bloom and Martin, *Black against Empire*, 176–98. On the Panthers' Peoples' Free Medical Clinics, see Nelson, *Body and Soul*.

122. US members George and Larry Stiner eventually served life sentences for conspiracy to commit murder, but witnesses to the killing claimed that US member Claude Hubert-Gaidi was the shooter and that he was aided by fellow US member Harold Jones-Tawala, both of whom disappeared after the killings and never stood trial. Brown, *Fighting for US*, 96–97; Bloom and Martin, *Black against Empire*, 219–20.

123. Bloom and Martin, *Black against Empire*, 219–20. Seberg later became the target of FBI COINTELPRO operations that spread rumors that a BPP member had fathered her child. Trauma from these operations contributed to her death by suicide. Seberg's experiences with the Panthers and the FBI were dramatized in the 2019 Amazon film *Seberg*, starring Kristen Stewart.

124. Bloom and Martin, 219.

125. For an overview, see Brown, *Fighting for US*, 186n95, which explains how Huey Newton, Ward Churchill, and the memoir of former police informant Louis Tackwood all fueled such conspiracy theories. Bloom and Martin provide a partisan account that echoes such conspiracy theories by emphasizing FBI operations

while portraying the UCLA firefight as a one-way attack by US members: "We still do not know today, to what extent US members were working directly with the FBI or police and whether the killings were planned and implemented under direction of the government." Bloom and Martin, *Black against Empire*, 220.

126. Faraj, "Unearthing the Underground," 133.

127. This killing was part of an ongoing war between US and the LA Panthers that continued for months after the UCLA killings amid ongoing COINTELPRO operations intended to inflame the situation. This included a number of shootings that led to the death of Panther John Savage and the wounding of at least three other Panthers. Church Committee, Book III, 192–93; Davis, *Spying on America*, 109–11.

128. Zimroth, *Perversions of Justice*, 3–7; Kempton, *The Briar Patch*, 1–12. Bloom and Martin provide a partisan account echoing the Panthers' contemporary portrayal of events: *Black against Empire*, 213–14. For the defendants' perspectives, see kioni-sadiki and Meyer, *Look for Me in the Whirlwind*.

129. Zayd Malik-Shakur, "Pig Conspiracy against NY Panther Twenty-One," and Olaywah, "NY Pigs Move to Destroy Panthers," *Black Panther*, April 20, 1969, 10, 11, Bloom Alternative Press Collection.

130. Zimroth, *Perversions of Justice*, 16, 22, 394. Roberts had begun his undercover career in 1964 by spying on Malcolm X for the New York Police Department's political intelligence unit, the Bureau of Special Services and Investigations (BOSSI).

131. A good deal of evidence suggests that many preemptive arrests of alleged terrorists in the United States since 9/11 have involved entrapment. See Aaronson, *The Terror Factory*.

132. Peter L. Zimroth was a federal prosecutor who wrote *Perversions of Justice*, on the New York Twenty-One case, after joining the faculty of New York University's Law School. He argued that New York prosecutors presented solid evidence that several of the defendants had participated in the January 17, 1969, attack on police stations in the Bronx and a school in Queens, but undermined their case by including additional conspiracy charges that were more difficult to prove.

133. Balagoon quoted in Bloom and Martin, *Black against Empire*, 152.

134. Shakur quoted in Bloom and Martin, 152.

135. Police claimed that Baines had kicked a cop in the crotch. Bloom and Martin, 155.

136. Bloom and Martin, 155–59.

137. Umoja, "The Black Liberation Army," 228–29.

138. See lengthy excerpts from this booklet in Zimroth, *Perversions of Justice*, 267–69.

139. Kempton, *The Briar Patch*, 10–11.

140. Zimroth, *Perversions of Justice*, 6.

141. Rudy Johnson, "Joan Bird and Afeni Shakur: Self-Styled Soldiers in the 'Class Struggle,'" *New York Times*, July 19, 1970; Zimroth, *Perversions of Justice*, 6–7, 263–64.

142. Bird quoted in Johnson, "Joan Bird and Afeni Shakur."

143. "Free Joan Bird," digitized clipping from *Liberated Guardian*, 1970, Pinterest, https://www.pinterest.com/pin/443329961472176 3/?lp=true.

144. Bird quoted in "Free Joan Bird." For more of Bird's account of her beating by police, see Zimroth, *Perversions of Justice*, 262–63.

145. Burrough, *Days of Rage*, 182–83.

146. Bloom and Martin, *Black against Empire*, 213.

147. Bass and Rae, *Murder in the Model City*, 3–8, 25–34.

148. Bloom and Martin, *Black against Empire*, 251; Bass and Rae, *Murder in the Model City*, 68.

149. Seale quoted in Bass and Rae, *Murder in the Model City*, 97.

150. Department of Justice document quoted in Bass and Rae, 68–69.

151. Bass and Rae, 164.

152. Bass and Rae, 157–64.

153. This claim began with internal Panther rumors and was spread through Huey Newton's dissertation and the writings of Ward Churchill, whom Bloom and Martin cite in their account of the circumstantial evidence surrounding George Sams: *Black against Empire*, 250–51. Also see Bass and Rae, *Murder in the Model City*, 262–63. Sams and Kimbro each served four-year prison sentences for their roles in the killing.

154. Bass and Rae, 4–5, 8–9.

155. Bass and Rae, 85, 88–91, 102–4.

156. Seale quoted in Johnson, "Joan Bird and Afeni Shakur."

157. *Black Panther*, Vol. 3, No. 6, May 31, 1969, Bloom Alternative Media Collection, Amherst College, box 032, folder: Black Panther (April–June 1969).

158. "Pig Conspiracy against Conn. Panthers," *Black Panther*, Vol. 3, No. 6, 5.

159. Bloom and Martin, *Black against Empire*, 299–302.

160. Cox, *Just Another*, 133.

161. FBI airtel, Director to SAC San Francisco, May 29, 1969, excerpted in Churchill and Vander Wall, *The COINTELPRO Papers*, 145. Bloom and Martin cite this document to make a fallacious argument similar to that of the latter writers: "No aspect of the Black Panther program was of greater concern to the FBI than the Free Breakfast of Children Program, which fostered widespread support for the Panthers' revolutionary politics." *Black against Empire*, 211. The authors base the claim that the BPP was "revolutionary" on a purported reading of Antonio Gramsci, though their analysis is based not on material relationships of power in the United States at the time but on the supposed appeal of Panther rhetoric, which the authors accept at face value without providing evidence: "The Black Panther Party stood out from countless politically insignificant revolutionary cadres because it was creative politically. For a few years, the Party seized the political imagination of a large constituency of young black people. Even more, it articulated this revolutionary movement of young blacks to a broader oppositional movement, drawing allied support from more moderate blacks and opponents of the Vietnam War of every race." Bloom and Martin, 400.

162. This quote's significance has been overstated. A version of this quote first appeared in the Church Committee report, which attributed it to a nonexistent September 1968 *New York Times* article. Bloom and Martin tracked down the quote in a July 15, 1969, United Press International (UPI) story that appeared in the

Oakland Tribune and a half dozen other newspapers of lesser stature. An FBI press release was likely the source of the quote, though such a press release has not been located. Nevertheless, Bloom and Martin printed the quote twice in their book, relegating the discussion of the source to their notes. Bloom and Martin, *Black against Empire*, 3, 210, 444n45.

163. Hilliard quoted in *Berkeley in the Sixties*.

164. The Panthers had originally dug the hole as an escape tunnel to be used in the case of a police attack on the headquarters, but they stopped digging after they hit water. Cox, *Just Another*, 90, 119.

165. Christina Royster-Hemby, "Fighting the Power," *Baltimore Sun*, February 1, 2006; Jean Marbella and Justin Fenton, "Release of Black Panther Leader Renews Decades-Old Debate," *Baltimore Sun*, March 8, 2014.

166. Cox, *Just Another*, 109.

167. Marbella and Fenton, "Release of Black Panther Leader Renews Decades-Old Debate." Baltimore Black Panther leader Marshall "Eddie" Conway spent forty-four years in prison for Sager's murder but maintained his innocence and was released from prison in 2014. Two other Baltimore Panthers were also convicted.

168. Cox, *Just Another*, 139–42. The remaining defendants in the Baltimore case later stood trial under the representation of famed leftist attorney William Kunstler. Prosecutors ended up dropping most of the charges because they could not produce sufficient evidence to tie the accused to Anderson's remains. See Marbella and Fenton, "Release of Black Panther Leader Renews Decades-Old Debate."

169. Church Committee, Book III, 22.

170. Church Committee, Book III, 22. Don Cox drew similar conclusions: "I do not agree with the widespread idea that it was the repression by law enforcement agencies that destroyed the Black Panther Party. We refuse our own history by blaming every negative thing that occurred on COINTELPRO. That is a very convenient way of avoiding analysis. That also gives the pigs much more credit than they merit." *Just Another*, 207.

171. Church Committee, Book III, 188.

Chapter 3

1. Miller interview, 113.

2. Huston interview, 16–17.

3. Gage, "What an Uncensored Letter to M.L.K. Reveals."

4. Sullivan, *The Bureau*, 205–6.

5. Karen Ashley, Bill Ayers, Bernardine Dohrn, John Jacobs, Jeff Jones, Gerry Long, Howie Machtinger, Jim Mellon, Terry Robbins, Mark Rudd, and Steve Tappis, "You Don't Need a Weatherman to Know Which Way the Wind Blows," *New Left Notes*, June 18, 1969, Internet Archive. A brief excerpt of this wordy manifesto is available in Dohrn, Ayers, and Jones, *Sing a Battle Song*, 67–68. For further analysis of this document and the 1969 SDS National Convention, see Varon, *Bringing the War Home*, 49–51; Berger, *Outlaws of America*, 82–89; and Sale, *SDS*, 559–79.

6. Rudd quoted in Bingham, *Witness to the Revolution*, 79.

7. Dohrn quoted in Bingham, 69.

8. Ashley et al., "You Don't Need a Weatherman to Know Which Way the Wind Blows."

9. Varon, *Bringing the War Home*, 118–21.

10. For a sociological analysis of late 1960s' radicals' turn to clandestinity, see Zwerman, Steinhoff, and della Porta, "Disappearing Social Movements." Early twentieth-century anarchist bombers eluded some federal investigations, but they did not form clandestine organizations with sustained guerrilla operations. For an example of a case that confounded federal investigators, including the young J. Edgar Hoover, see the account of the deadly 1920 Wall Street bombing in Gage, *The Day Wall Street Exploded*.

11. FBI memo, R. L. Shackelford to C. D. Brennan, November 5, 1968, COINTELPRO-New Left, Headquarters file, section 1.

12. FBI memo, Shackelford to Brennan, November 5, 1968.

13. FBI memo, SAC Cleveland to Director, August 1, 1969, FBI COINTELPRO-New Left, Cleveland File. Aaron Leonard and Arthur Eckstein brought this document to light, but they also overstated its importance by interpreting it outside the larger context of COINTELPRO-New Left and its sometimes-conflicting dual motives. See Eckstein, *Bad Moon Rising*, 62–63; and Leonard and Gallagher, *Heavy Radicals*. Also see Cunningham, *There's Something Happening Here*, 62–64.

14. Rudd, *Underground*, 149.

15. FBI memo, SAC Cleveland to Director, August 1, 1969, 4.

16. FBI memo, C. D. Brennan to W. C. Sullivan, July 25, 1969, FBI WUO, Roll 5, Section 52.

17. FBI memo, Brennan to Sullivan, July 25, 1969.

18. FBI airtel, SAC Boston to Director, February 26, 1970; FBI memo, SAC Boston to Director, May 15, 1970, COINTELPRO-New Left, sections 2 and 3.

19. Cunningham, *There's Something Happening Here*, 64; Varon, *Bringing the War Home*, 61–62.

20. Varon, *Bringing the War Home*, 61.

21. Wilkerson, *Flying Close to the Sun*, 284.

22. FBI memo, SAC Chicago to Director, March 31, 1970, COINTELPRO-New Left, Chicago File.

23. FBI memo, SAC Cleveland to Director, October 3, 1969, COINTELPRO-New Left, Headquarters File, section 2.

24. SAC Chicago to Director, June 30, 1969, COINTELPRO-New Left, Chicago File.

25. FBI memo, SAC Chicago to Director, June 30, 1969; and FBI airtel, SAC Chicago to Director, September 4, 1969, COINTELPRO-New Left, Chicago File.

26. FBI memo, SAC Chicago to Director, May 19, 1969, in Churchill and Vander Wall, *The COINTELPRO Papers*, 210.

27. FBI memo, Director to SAC Chicago, May 21, 1969, in Churchill and Vander Wall, 211.

28. FBI memo, SAC Cleveland to Director, August 1, 1969, COINTELPRO-New Left, Cleveland File.

29. U.S. General Accounting Office, *FBI Domestic Intelligence Operations*, 133.

30. U.S. General Accounting Office, 133–35.

31. FBI airtel, SAC Chicago to Director, "Top Level Informant Development (TOPLEV)," July 28, 1969, FBI WUO, Roll 5, Section 53.

32. Cunningham, *There's Something Happening Here*, 171–74.

33. Roth quoted in Berger, *Outlaws of America*, 106.

34. FBI airtel, SAC Chicago to Director, August 8, 1969, FBI WUO File, "June Mail" Section.

35. FBI airtel, SAC Chicago to Director, August 8, 1969. The FBI was also unable to spy on SDS from rooms adjoining the National Office because the building housing the office was owned by John Rossen, whom agents described as "a former Communist Party member, and long-time activist in communist front causes" with a known "anti-Bureau attitude."

36. The FBI previously tapped the phones in SDS's Chicago National Office from 1965 to 1966 as part of an investigation of "Communist infiltration" of the organization but terminated its telephone surveillance under orders from the attorney general.

37. FBI teletype, Director to SAC Chicago, September 9, 1969, COINTELPRO-New Left, Chicago File.

38. FBI airtel, SAC Chicago to Director, August 8, 1969.

39. FBI survey, SAC Chicago to Director, November 11, 1969, FBI WUO, Roll 8, "June Mail" section. "Tesur" is an FBI code word for "technical surveillance," otherwise known as telephone surveillance, or electronic wiretapping.

40. Dyson interview, 28 (emphasis in original).

41. FBI memo, SAC Chicago to Director, "Justification for Continuation of Technical or Microphone Surveillance," August 8, 1969, FBI WUO, "June Mail" section.

42. FBI memo, SAC Chicago to Director, "Justification for Continuation of Technical or Microphone Surveillance," August 8, 1969, 5. Chicago police also regularly followed and harassed Weatherman militants throughout the summer and fall of 1969. See Berger, *Outlaws of America*, 106–7; and Varon, *Bringing the War Home*, 153.

43. Varon, *Bringing the War Home*, 74; Rudd, *Underground*, 181.

44. Rudd, *Underground*, ix.

45. Varon, *Bringing the War Home*, 76.

46. FBI memo, SAC Chicago to Director, December 31, 1969, COINTELPRO-New Left, Chicago File.

47. Cunningham, *There's Something Happening Here*, 64; Varon, *Bringing the War Home*, 82; Berger, *Outlaws of America*, 109–12.

48. Lerner, *Swords in the Hands of Children*, 108, 111.

49. *Chicago Tribune* quoted in Varon, *Bringing the War Home*, 83.

50. FBI memo, SAC Chicago to Director, October 13, 1969, COINTELPRO-New Left, Headquarters File part 2.

51. FBI airtel, Director to SAC Albany, October 23, 1969, FBI WUO, Roll 6, Section 57.

52. FBI airtel, Director to SAC Albany, October 23, 1969.

53. FBI memo, C. D. Brennan to W. C. Sullivan, December 19, 1969, FBI WUO, Roll 6, Section 59.

54. FBI memo, Brennan to Sullivan, December 19, 1969.

55. Balto, *Occupied Territory*, 222–23; O'Reilly, *"Racial Matters,"* 310–12; Bloom and Martin, *Black against Empire*, 237–39.

56. Bloom and Martin, *Black against Empire*, 234–36. Chicago police killed nineteen white people during this same period. Chicago's white population was more than twice the size of its Black population.

57. Bloom and Martin, 236–37.

58. Bloom and Martin, 226–28; Balto, *Occupied Territory*, 225; O'Reilly, *"Racial Matters,"* 310–12.

59. Lerner, *Swords in the Hands of Children*, 127–29; Varon, *Bringing the War Home*, 155.

60. Neufeld quoted in Varon, *Bringing the War Home*, 155–56.

61. Lerner, *Swords in the Hands of Children*, 129.

62. Hampton quoted in Bloom and Martin, *Black against Empire*, 230.

63. Seale quoted in Bloom and Martin, 230.

64. Anonymous source, conversation with the author, 2014. For more on Chicago police views toward Hampton, see Balto, *Occupied Territory*, 224–25.

65. Bloom and Martin, *Black against Empire*, 237–39; O'Reilly, *"Racial Matters,"* 311–13. For a more detailed overview of Fred Hampton's assassination and subsequent legal proceedings, see his attorney's account: Haas, *The Assassination of Fred Hampton*. Also see Tayler and Flint, "The Assassination of Fred Hampton: 40 Years Later."

66. The FBI gave O'Neal a $300 bonus after the Hampton-Clark killing, and he remained an informant on the FBI payroll for several more years. Rumors have circulated that O'Neal drugged Hampton the night before the raid. Autopsies later provided conflicting accounts over whether Hampton had secobarbital in his system, and there is no evidence linking O'Neal to the drug. O'Reilly, *"Racial Matters,"* 312.

67. O'Reilly, *"Racial Matters,"* 313–17.

68. Ward Churchill and Jim Vander Wall and others have made this assertion, which has become lore among some on the U.S. Left.

69. Flint Taylor and Jeff Hass, "New Documents Suggest J. Edgar Hoover was Involved in Fred Hampton's Murder," *Truthout*, January 19, 2021, https://truthout.org/articles/new-documents-suggest-j-edgar-hoover-was-involved-in-fred-hamptons-murder/?fbclid=IwAR1dwb8wNzQHLvdHoW9uNkGNUvVPWZfBYBeVAGWOqbn3yOf3folVvOxOWMc. The article features a link to Hoover's December 10, 1960 memo to Special Agent Roy Mitchell. Despite the headline, the article does not provide evidence that Hoover directly ordered Hampton's murder.

70. William O'Neal never imagined that Chicago police would use his sketch in an operation to kill Fred Hampton. Guilt of his involvement in the killings plagued him for two decades. After speaking about his experiences in an interview for the PBS documentary series *Eyes on the Prize*, O'Neal died by suicide. *Eyes on the Prize, America's Civil Rights Movement 1954–1985*, Season 2, Episode 6, *A Nation of Law? 1968–1971*.

71. Varon, *Bringing the War Home*, 156.

72. Gilbert quoted in Varon, 156.

73. Wilkerson, *Flying Close to the Sun*, 314.

74. Varon, *Bringing the War Home*, 159.

75. Dohrn quoted in Varon, 160.

76. Varon, 158–59.

77. WUR, 125–29.

78. FBI memo, C. D. Brennan to W. C. Sullivan, December 20, 1969, FBI WUO, Roll 6, Section 59.

79. FBI memo, R. D. Cotter to W. C. Sullivan, December 31, 1969, FBI WUO, Roll 6, Section 59; FBI correspondence, FBI Director to Attorney General, January 2, 1970, FBI WUO, Roll 6, Section 60; FBI correspondence, FBI Director to Henry Kissinger, January 2, 1970, FBI WUO, Roll 6, Section 60.

80. Nixon, *RN*, 470.

81. Grathwohl, *Bringing Down America*, 119–26. Grathwohl participated in the Days of Rage and dated Weatherwoman Naomi Jaffe.

82. Rudd, *Underground*, 182; Varon, *Bringing the War Home*, 171–72.

83. Rudd, *Underground*, 161.

84. WUR, 38.

85. Burrough, *Days of Rage*, 94–97.

86. Murtagh in Bingham, *Witness to the Revolution*, 294. For the next eighteen months, police kept constant guard at the Murtagh home, and armed guards followed members of the family everywhere they went. Also, from December 1969 to March 6, 1970, Weatherman members carried out additional firebombings in Chicago, Milwaukee, New York, and Cleveland. See Eckstein, *Bad Moon Rising*, 38–42.

87. Burrough, *Days of Rage*, 96.

88. Recent findings suggest that support for civilian casualties was more widespread during Weatherman's early years, including from Bill Ayers and other leaders. See Eckstein, *Bad Moon Rising*, 84–86.

Chapter 4

1. Wilkerson, *Flying Close to the Sun*, 332–44; Rudd, oral history in Bingham, *Witness to the Revolution*, 297–98.

2. Eckstein, *Bad Moon Rising*, 11–12; Varon, *Bringing the War Home*, 173–74; Berger, *Outlaws of America*, 127–29; Wilkerson, *Flying Close to the Sun*, 345–48.

3. Eckstein, *Bad Moon Rising*, 84–85.

4. FBI memo, C. D. Brennan to W. C. Sullivan, April 1, 1970, 1, FBI WUO, Roll 6, Section 6.

5. Richard Nixon, "Presidential Talking Paper," June 5, 1970, Huston Plan, Exhibit 63, 396.

6. Interagency Committee on Intelligence (Ad Hoc), "Special Report," June 1970, Huston Plan, Exhibit 1, 188.

7. An exception is Eckstein, *Bad Moon Rising*, 98–100, 168–73, 239, which offered the first detailed explanation of how Weatherman's townhouse explosion and Nixon's concerns over leftist violence informed the Huston Plan. Hughes, *Chasing Shadows*, 71–73, offers a brief overview of these matters. However, neither of these works analyzes the Huston Plan's role in the development of contemporary U.S.

counterterrorism. For more scholarly work on the history of the Huston Plan, see Theoharis, chapter 1, "The Huston Plan," in *Spying on Americans*; Johnson, chapter 7, "The Huston Plan," in *America's Secret Power*; and Church Committee, Book II, 111–15, and "National Security, Civil Liberties, and the Collection of Intelligence," in Book III, 921–86. For more on how the Huston Plan shaped Nixon and Hoover's bureaucratic conflict, see Gage, "Deep Throat, Watergate, and the Bureaucratic Politics of the FBI," 169–70. For a brief journalistic account of how New Left violence influenced the Huston Plan, see Weiner, *Enemies*, 290–92.

8. FBI memo, "Students for a Democratic Society," March 11, 1970, FBI WUO, Roll 6, Section 60. Grathwohl claimed in his memoir that he recognized in advance that the ignition devices would not work and tipped off the FBI to where the bombs would be placed. The FBI was unable to catch the would-be bombers in the act, however, because Weatherman's leadership reassigned Grathwohl to the Madison collective shortly before the Detroit collective attempted the bombing. See Grathwohl, *Bringing Down America*, 144–45, 151–52, 160–61, 172.

9. FBI teletype, Director to SAC Albany, March 19, 1970, FBI WUO, Roll 6, Section 61.

10. FBI memo, C. D. Brennan to W. C. Sullivan, March 20, 1970, FBI WUO, Roll 6, Section 61.

11. Murray Schumach, "Fewer Bomb Calls Are Made in City," *New York Times*, March 15, 1970.

12. FBI memo, C. D. Brennan to W. C. Sullivan, April 1, 1970, FBI WUO, Roll 6, Section 60.

13. Hoover quoted in FBI memo, Brennan to Sullivan, April 1, 1970, 4.

14. FBI airtel, Director to SAC Boston, March 12, 1970, FBI WUO, Roll 6, Section 60.

15. FBI airtel, Director to SAC Boston, March 12, 1970.

16. FBI airtel, Director to SAC Boston, March 12, 1970.

17. FBI airtel, Director to SAC Boston, March 12, 1970; Swearingen, *FBI Secrets*, 70.

18. FBI airtel, Director to SAC Boston, March 12, 1970.

19. FBI memo, F. S. Putnam to E. S. Miller, March 26, 1973, FBI Vault, Terrorist Photo Album File.

20. FBI airtel, Director to SAC Boston, March 12, 1970.

21. Jeffreys-Jones, *The FBI*, 192–93.

22. FBI memo, SAC Chicago to Director, March 31, 1970, COINTELPRO-New Left, Chicago File.

23. Director to SAC Boston, March 12, 1970; FBI memo, W. C. Sullivan to C. D. Brennan, April 3, 1970, FBI WUO, Roll 6, Section 61.

24. FBI memo, SAC Chicago to Director, March 31, 1970.

25. WUR, 25; Dyson oral history in Bingham, *Witness to the Revolution*, 308–9.

26. FBI memo, C. D. Brennan to W. C. Sullivan, April 3, 1970, FBI WUO, Roll 6, Section 61.

27. FBI memo, Brennan to Sullivan, April 3, 1970. The Justice Department never charged Weatherman members under the Smith Act, probably because the Supreme Court ruled in its 1957 *Yates v. United States* decision that much of the law

was unconstitutional because it violated the First Amendment's freedom of speech protections.

28. WUR, 131. The April 2, 1970, Chicago indictments built on two earlier ones. On December 19, 1969, a Cook County grand jury indicted sixty-four Weather Underground defendants for alleged violations of Illinois law stemming from the Days of Rage. The first federal indictments against Weather Underground guerrillas came on March 17, 1970, when a Cook County judge issued Unlawful Flight to Avoid Prosecution warrants for Kathy Boudin, Cathy Wilkerson, Bernardine Dohrn, and three other Weatherwomen who failed to show up for court hearings stemming from the Days of Rage. Brennan to Sullivan, March 20, 1970; FBI memo, A. Jones to Mr. Bishop, April 7, 1970, FBI WUO, Roll 6, Section 61. These charges were similar to those Attorney General Mitchell lodged against the Chicago Eight a year earlier, on March 20, 1969, for their involvement in the August 1968 demonstrations against the Chicago Democratic National Convention.

29. Berger, *Outlaws of America*, 128–29; Varon, *Bringing the War Home*, 179.

30. Ayers, *Fugitive Days*, 205.

31. Gilbert, *Love and Struggle*, 157. For another account of Weather Underground members' security precautions, see Jones, *A Radical Line*, 7–13.

32. Brian Flanagan, oral history in Bingham, *Witness to the Revolution*, 425.

33. Bill Ayers, oral history in Bingham, *Witness to the Revolution*, 426–27.

34. Rudd, *Underground*, 213–15; Varon, *Bringing the War Home*, 181–82; Berger, *Outlaws of America*, 130. During this meeting, Dohrn, Jones, and Ayers also demoted Mark Rudd from the organization's leadership circle.

35. Burrough, *Days of Rage*, 94–97, 126–27, 141.

36. FBI letter, Director Hoover to John D. Ehrlichman, March 24, 1970, FBI WUO, Roll 6, Section 60.

37. Grathwohl, *Bringing Down America*, 176.

38. Jones, *A Radical Line*, 13–14.

39. Senate Subcommittee on Investigations, *Hearings on Riots, Civil and Criminal Disorders*, 5577–78.

40. In a 1988 article, SNCC veteran Ekwueme Michael Thelwell briefly recalled Ralph Featherstone's political evolution. Featherstone, affectionately known to his friends as "Feather," was a native of Washington, D.C., who volunteered in the 1964 Mississippi Freedom Project, gaining a great deal of respect among locals and fellow activists for his organizing skills. Within a year, however, increasing police and vigilante violence against the Black freedom movement seemed to have pushed Feather to embrace revolutionary violence. Thelwell recalled a visit to Featherstone's small Washington apartment in 1965: "Before I left he reached under the narrow bed. 'I wanna show you something,' he said with suppressed excitement. The 'something,' he said, was an AK47 attack rifle, ugly, ominous, lethal, cradled like a baby on his lap. I begged my brother to get rid of it. I don't know if he did. Not long after he was blown to pieces by a car bomb in ambiguous circumstances the truth of which has never been satisfactorily explained." Thelwell, "1968"; Oglesby, *Ravens in the Storm*, 289–290.

41. Thelwell, "H. Rap Brown / Jamil Al-Amin," xx, xxii.

42. Director to SAC Boston, March 24, 1970.

43. Brennan to Sullivan, April 1, 1970, 1.

44. Brennan to Sullivan, April 1, 1970, 3.

45. Brennan to Sullivan, April 1, 1970, 2, 4, 6.

46. FBI airtel, Director to all SACs, April 17, 1970, FBI WUO, Roll 6, Section 61.

47. U.S. General Accounting Office, *FBI Domestic Intelligence Operations*, 134.

48. Appy, *American Reckoning*, 186–89; Sale, *SDS*, 636–37; Grace, *Kent State*.

49. Nixon, *RN*, 448.

50. Huston interview, 9.

51. FBI, "Ten Most Wanted Fugitives 50th Anniversary," Internet Archive, 37.

52. U.S. General Accounting Office, *FBI Domestic Intelligence Operations*, iv, 42–43.

53. U.S. General Accounting Office, ix, 133.

54. Swearingen, *FBI Secrets*, 70–71.

55. WUR, 132.

56. Weatherman, "A Declaration of a State of War," May 21, 1970, in Dohrn et al., *Sing a Battle Song*, 149–51.

57. Weatherman, 151; Berger, *Outlaws of America*, 137.

58. Michael Stern, "Mayor Vows 'Relentless' Drive to Track Down Police Bomber," *New York Times*, July 11, 1970.

59. Payne, *Deep Cover*, 16.

60. Nixon, "Presidential Talking Paper," 396.

61. Nixon, 396; Theoharis, *Spying on Americans*, 21.

62. Nixon, "Presidential Talking Paper," 397.

63. Nixon, 397.

64. Nixon, 398–99.

65. Interagency Committee on Intelligence (Ad Hoc), "Special Report," 149–50, 166.

66. Interagency Committee on Intelligence (Ad Hoc), 188.

67. Referring to Sullivan and Brennan, Huston stated in an August 1970 memo to Haldeman that Hoover would have fired the members of his staff who worked on the interagency report if he found out that they "supported the options selected by the President." See Tom Huston memorandum to H. R. Haldeman, "Domestic Intelligence," August 5, 1970, Huston Plan, Exhibit 22, 249. On Sullivan's deception of Hoover, see Sullivan, *The Bureau*, 211–12; and Theoharis, *Spying on Americans*, 26–27.

68. Theoharis, 26.

69. Sullivan, *The Bureau*, 211.

70. Sullivan, 213; Theoharis, *Spying on Americans*, 29.

71. Tom Huston memorandum, "Operational Restraints on Intelligence Collection," Huston Plan, Exhibit 2, 194–96.

72. H. R. Haldeman to Tom Huston, "Domestic Intelligence Review," July 14, 1970, Huston Plan, Exhibit 3, 198.

73. Tom Huston memorandum to Richard Helms, Director, Central Intelligence Agency, "Domestic Intelligence," July 23, 1970, Huston Plan, Exhibit 4, 200.

74. Theoharis, *Spying on Americans*, 33.

75. Nixon quoted in Theoharis, 33.

76. Nixon, *RN*, 475.

77. Nixon, 476. Since President Ronald Reagan signed the Civil Liberties Act of 1988, the consensus among historians has been that America's World War II–era internment of Japanese Americans was racist, unjust, and politically unnecessary.

78. Nixon, 476.

Chapter 5

1. Accounts of the shootout vary, but most indicate that gunfire broke out between police and the revolutionaries as the van approached a roadblock set up by police and San Quentin guards, and as Thomas wrested a gun from one of his captors and began shooting at them inside the van. Those sympathetic with the revolutionaries' causes claimed that police and guards fired into the van indiscriminately under the protocol of San Quentin's "no hostage" policy. Police asserted that McClain fired at the roadblock from the van's passenger seat. Haley died of a blast from a shotgun that the revolutionaries had taped to his head. Gunshot wounds permanently paralyzed Thomas; Magee also endured critical wounds. One of the jurors was injured by gunfire as well. For accounts, see Berger, *Captive Nation*, 122–24; Cummins, *The Rise and Fall of California's Racial Prison Movement*, 182–83; Yee, *The Melancholy History of Soledad Prison*, 157–65. According to Berger, Magee later asserted that the group planned to take over a radio station in "an effort to reach the people and dramatically awaken them to the plight of all prisoners, particularly Blacks," by describing the "torturous prison conditions" endured by California prisoners (122–23).

2. For more on how George Jackson and his incarceration influenced Jonathan Jackson's life and politics, see the former's letters to the latter in Jackson, *Blood in My Eye*, 11–25. For Angela Davis's recollections on this matter, see Davis, *Angela Davis*, 266–67. Also see Berger, *Captive Nation*, 120–21.

3. Chamberlin, *The Global Offensive*, 71–73, 101.

4. Weatherman changed its name to Weatherman Underground in October 1970, then to Weather Underground in December 1970. However, for the sake of simplicity, I use the term Weather Underground from this chapter forward. On Canada's October Crisis, see Hewitt, "Cold War Counter-Terrorism," 1–2.

5. Churchill, *Becoming the Tupamaros*, 50. The Tupamaros accused Mitrione of covertly training Uruguayan police in the use of torture techniques. See page 56 for Churchill's summary of the debate over the validity of these claims. The Mitrione kidnapping became the inspiration for Costa-Gavras's 1973 film, *State of Siege*, which later helped inspire the Symbionese Liberation Army's 1974 kidnapping of newspaper heiress Patricia Hearst. No documentary evidence proves that the Tupamaros directly influenced Jonathan Jackson's raid, but circumstantial evidence, such as the timing of his raid, romanticization of the Tupamaros by many in the militant U.S. Left, and Jackson's extensive readings on guerrilla warfare, suggests that such influence was likely.

6. J. Edgar Hoover to all SACs, August 17, 1970, LPG FBI.

7. Hoover to all SACs, August 17, 1970.

8. J. Edgar Hoover to Richard Nixon, August 17, 1970, LPG FBI.

9. Dyson interview, 25–26.

10. The controversy surrounding Davis at UCLA began in July 1969 after an FBI informant named William Divale outed her as a member of the Communist Party in the university newspaper. See Berger, *Captive Nation*, 108.

11. Berger, *Captive Nation*, 108; Cummins, *The Rise and Fall of California's Radical Prison Movement*, 184–85; Davis, *Angela Davis*, 3–12, 278–79.

12. Bingham, *Witness to the Revolution*, 469–85; Bates, *RADS*, 8–10.

13. Armstrong quoted in Bingham, *Witness to the Revolution*, 470.

14. Science for the People Madison Wisconsin Collective, "The AMRC Papers: An Indictment of the Army Mathematics Research Center," in Schmalzer, Chard, and Botelho, *Science for the People*, 71–73.

15. Armstrong quoted in Bingham, *Witness to the Revolution*, 472.

16. Dyson quoted in Bingham, 478.

17. Tabankin quoted in Bingham, 478–79.

18. Bates, *RADS*, 26.

19. FBI memos quoted in Scott Bauer, "FBI Releases 1970 UW Bombing Documents," *Milwaukee Journal Sentinel*, April 6, 2011.

20. Bingham, *Witness to the Revolution*, 479–80, 484. Fine made his way to Canada as well, but separately from the Armstrong brothers. FBI agents eventually caught up with them. Karl was arrested in 1972 and served seven years in prison. David Fine was captured in 1976 and served a three-year prison term. Dwight Armstrong was captured in 1977 and also served three years. Leo Burt, however, remains at large today. He is rumored to have fought in Latin American guerrilla movements during the 1970s.

21. Bates, *RADS*, 36.

22. Theoharis, *Spying on Americans*, 17–18.

23. Felt and O'Connor, *A G-Man's Life*, xxix–xxxi, 16–65.

24. Hoover to all SACs, August 17, 1970.

25. FBI memo, W. M. Felt to Clyde Tolson, September 2, 1970, Huston Plan, Exhibit 44, 328.

26. Felt to Tolson, September 2, 1970, 328.

27. Felt to Tolson, September 2, 1970, 329.

28. Felt, *The FBI Pyramid from the Inside*, 112. Felt's quote may be fictional, but it nonetheless testifies to his differences with Sullivan.

29. J. Edgar Hoover letter to all Special Agents in Charge, "Assistant to the Director—Investigative," June 10, 1970, and FBI memo, M. A. Jones to Mr. Bishop, "DeLoach Retirement; Sullivan and Brennan Promoted," June 19, 1970, in WCS FBI, Section 7.

30. Tom Charles Huston memo to H. R. Haldeman, "Domestic Intelligence," August 5, 1970, Huston Plan, Exhibit 22, 249.

31. Huston quoted in Gentry, *J. Edgar Hoover*, 658.

32. J. Edgar Hoover, SAC Letter 70-48, September 15, 1970, box 274, folder 20 "Huston Plan," US v. Felt.

33. Funding for the operation came from a group of Leary's supporters called the Brotherhood of Eternal Love. The Weather Underground agreed to the plan because it needed the money and saw it as an opportunity to develop skills in breaking people out of prison while building support among the hippie counterculture. In Algeria, Leary stayed briefly at the Panther embassy in Algiers but left after being physically abused by Eldridge Cleaver. Cleaver was angry that Leary had smuggled 20,000 hits of acid into the country, thereby upsetting the Algerian government. Leary supporter Michael Randall recalled, "We had to provide some money to make it easy for Timothy to go to Switzerland and get out of Eldridge's clutches. It was fucked up." After Switzerland, Leary fled to Afghanistan, where he was turned over to U.S. forces and ended up snitching on the Weather Underground, though by that time the guerrillas had caught wind of Leary's intentions and abandoned the safe houses and vehicles they had used for the escape. Bingham, *Witness to the Revolution*, 486–91; Jones, *A Radical Line*, 222–24.

34. Bernardine Dohrn, "Dr. Timothy Leary," September 15, 1970, in Dohrn et al., *Sing a Battle Song*, 154.

35. Timothy Leary letter quoted in FBI memo, R. L. Shackelford to C. D. Brennan, September 22, 1970, FBI WUO, Roll 6, Section 63.

36. Shackelford to Brennan, September 22, 1970.

37. Andrew F. Blake, "4 Campus 'Radicals' Hunted in Boston Police Slaying," *Washington Post*, September 26, 1970; Arthur Jones, "Blast Rips Newburyport Armory," *Boston Globe*, September 21, 1970; Burton-Rose, "Amazon Underground?"

38. Andrew F. Blake, "Informant Was Talking to FBI Men during Brighton Murder-Robbery," *Boston Globe*, October 6, 1970.

39. Bernardine Dohrn, Jeff Jones, and Bill Ayers, "Fall Offensive," October 8, 1970, in Dohrn et al., *Sing a Battle Song*, 156–57.

40. Dohrn, Jones, and Ayers, 158; Payne, *Deep Cover*, 11.

41. Weatherman, "Criminal Courthouse," October 9, 1970, in Dohrn et al., *Sing a Battle Song*, 160.

42. WUR, 35.

43. *Free Angela Davis and All Political Prisoners*, directed by Shola Lynch; Carroll Kirkpatrick, "Nixon Vows 'Total War' against Crime," *Washington Post*, October 16, 1970.

44. Kirkpatrick, "Nixon Vows 'Total War' against Crime."

45. Berger, *Outlaws of America*, 142–43; Dayo F. Gore, introduction to Gore and Aptheker, *Free Angela Davis and All Political Prisoners!* A jury acquitted Davis of all charges on June 2, 1972.

46. WUR, 35.

47. FBI memo, R. L. Shackelford to C. D. Brennan, "SUBJECT: SPECIALIZED TRAINING OF BUREAU PERSONNEL; NEW LEFT MOVEMENT," September 17, 1970, box 102, folder: Plan to Deal with Weather Underground (2 of 4), US v. Felt.

48. Payne, *Deep Cover*, 12.

49. Payne, 12.

50. FBI teletype, Director to all SACs, October 7, 1970; and FBI coded teletype, Director, FBI to President, Vice President, Secretary of State, Director, CIA, Director, Defense Intelligence Agency, Department of the Army, Department of the Air Force, Naval Investigative Service, U.S. Secret Service, and Attorney General, October 6, 1970, FBI WUO, Roll 6, Section 64.

51. WUR, 36; "Ex-Brandeis Coeds Added to FBI Most Wanted List," *Boston Globe*, October 18, 1970; Pam Lambert, "Alice Doesn't Live Here Anymore," *People* April 1993, 61–62.

52. "More Women on Top Ten," *Hartford Courant*, October 18, 1970; UPI, "Radical Leftists Dot Most Wanted List," *Hartford Courant*, October 21, 1971, 35; U.S. Department of Justice, Federal Bureau of Investigation, "FBI's Ten Most Wanted Fugitives, 1950–2010."

53. FBI memo, A. Rosen to Mr. Sullivan, "SUBJECT: INTERAGENCY STUDY GROUP CONCERNING POLITICALLY INSPIRED KIDNAPPINGS," October 22, 1970, box 102, folder: Plan to Deal with Weather Underground (2 of 4), US v. Felt.

54. FBI bulletin, "Kidnapping and Assaults of United States Government Officials," October 23, 1970, DDRS.

55. FBI airtel, Director to SAC Albany, "Security Investigations of Individuals Who Are Members of the Students for a Democratic Society and Militant New Left Campus Organizations," November 5, 1970, FBI WUO, Roll 6, Section 64.

56. Director to SAC Albany, November 5, 1970.

57. FBI airtel, Director to SAC Albany, "Black Student Groups on College Campuses," November 4, 1970; and FBI memo, Executives Conference to Tolson, "Proposed Intensification of Certain Investigations in the Security Field," October 29, 1970, Huston Plan, Exhibit 42, 323–24, and Exhibit 41, 317–20.

58. FBI memo, Executives Conference to Tolson, "Proposed Intensification of Certain Investigations in the Security Field," October 29, 1970, FBI WUO, Roll 6, Section 64.

59. Church Committee, Book III, 320; FBI memo, C. D. Brennan to W. R. Wannall, March 29, 1971, Huston Plan, Exhibit 30, 270.

60. For example, in September 1970 the FBI noted in a series of bulletins to other police agencies that a recent issue of the *Black Panther* newspaper included a cartoon "showing a Panther leaving a police station, gun in hand, with a dead police officer behind him," and that an informant had indicated that a leader of the New York Panthers expressed support for kidnapping American political leaders in order to negotiate the release of Chairman Bobby Seale from prison. FBI bulletin, "Racial Summary, Week of September 21–27, 1970," September 29, 1970, and FBI bulletin, "Racial Summary, Week of September 14–20, 1970," September 22, 1970, DDRS.

61. Brennan to Wannall, March 29, 1971, 270–71; Church Committee, Book III, 319–20; O'Reilly, *"Racial Matters,"* 340–41. The FBI also maintained telephone surveillance of the offices of the Junta of Military Organizations (a "black extremist organization") in Tampa, the Communist Party USA headquarters in New York, and the anticommunist right-wing nationalist Jewish Defense League headquarters in New York.

62. Church Committee, Book III, 298–303.

63. FBI memo, R. L. Shackelford to C. D. Brennan, October 16, 1970, FBI WUO File, Roll 6, Section 64 (emphasis added).

64. FBI memo, SAC New York to Director, SUBJECT: SDS (WEATHERMAN) EXPLOSIONS, April 17, 1970, and FBI memo, SAC New York to Director, SUBJECT: JEFFERY CARL JONES, May 4, 1970, box 285, folder "Shackelford," US v. Gray.

65. Kearney interview, 1–3.

66. See documents in box 107, folder: G91-JEH reinst. bag jobs 241A-L, US v. Felt, including on the SNCC break-in, FBI memo, G. C. Moore to W. C. Sullivan, "FOREIGN INFLUENCE IN RACIAL MATTERS," June 17, 1968. The memo reports on a letter from an official in an African country to SNCC director James Forman. Though the names of the official and the country are redacted, this was likely an official in the government of newly independent Guinea's socialist president Ahmed Sékou Touré. In 1969, SNCC leader Stokely Carmichael moved to Guinea and served as an advisor to Touré.

67. FBI memo, "Squad 47," undated (ca. 1977), US v. Felt.

68. U.S. District Court for the Southern District of New York, U.S. v. John J. Kearney, grand jury indictment, April 7, 1977, Freedom Archives online, COINTELPRO Collection.

69. U.S. District Court for the Southern District of New York, U.S. v. John J. Kearney.

70. Swearingen, *FBI Secrets*, 72–73.

71. FBI memo, Lee Colwell to Director, "U.S. v. W. Mark Felt, et al.; Discovery Procedures," September 5, 1979, 1222537-0 - 62-118045 - Section 8 Serial 1, LPG FBI.

72. Francis J. Martin to Paul V. Daly, "[Redacted] Bag Job," November 3, 1978, 1222537-0 - 62-118045 - Section 8 Serial 1, LPG FBI.

73. FBI airtel, SAC Phoenix to Director (Attn: FBI Laboratory), "WEATHFUG," April 24, 1972.

74. FBI report, "Phoenix Review," September 10, 1976, 1222537-0 - 62-118045 - Section 8 Serial 1, LPG FBI.

75. Swearingen, *FBI Secrets*, 77–78.

76. FBI, August 24, 1976, untitled summary of interview with anonymous (name redacted) Detroit special agent, File Number 1222537-0-62-118045, Section 8, Serial 1, LPG FBI.

77. Sullivan quoted in Eckstein, *Bad Moon Rising*, 162.

78. LaPrade quoted in Myra MacPherson, "The Judgement of the FBI," *Washington Post*, May 16, 1978. The Justice Department later dropped its indictments of Kearney and LaPrade to focus attention on Gray, Felt, and Miller.

79. Eckstein, *Bad Moon Rising*, 159–63.

80. Swearingen, *FBI Secrets*, 78.

81. Kearney interview, 6.

82. U.S. Department of Justice, Federal Bureau of Investigation, Annual Report for Fiscal Year 1971, October 26, 1971, 21.

83. Bloom and Martin, *Black against Empire*, 358–62.

84. U.S. Department of Justice, Federal Bureau of Investigation, Annual Report for 1971, 24–25.

Chapter 6

1. J. Edgar Hoover testimony, Subcommittee of the Committee on Appropriations, "Supplemental Appropriations for Fiscal Year 1971," November 27, 1970, 1100.

2. Hoover testimony, 1101.

3. Jackson, "Kissinger's Kidnapper," 97–98.

4. Hoover testimony, Subcommittee of the Committee on Appropriations, "Supplemental Appropriations for Fiscal Year 1971," November 27, 1970, 1101.

5. Hoover testimony, 1079.

6. Hoover testimony, 1084–87.

7. Hoover testimony, 1098.

8. Hoover testimony, 1096. See note 7 in my introduction for further discussion of bombing statistics.

9. Medsger, *The Burglary*, 31.

10. Jackson, "Kissinger's Kidnapper," 97–98.

11. Fred P. Graham, "Hoover Pressed on Plot Charges," *New York Times*, December 1, 1970; "War Foes Deny Hoover's Charges," *Washington Post*, December 1, 1970.

12. Kunstler quoted in Marvin Olasky, "Kunstler Predicts More 'Repression,'" *Boston Globe*, December 3, 1970.

13. Richard L. Lyons, "Rep. Anderson Assails Hoover for Accusations against Berrigans," *Washington Post*, December 11, 1970.

14. Graham, "Hoover Pressed on Plot Charges."

15. Lyons, "Rep. Anderson Assails Hoover for Accusations against Berrigans." Also see Medsger, *The Burglary*, 35–37.

16. Jack Anderson, "Bugging Expose Is Causing Jitters," *Washington Post*, December 5, 1970; "Bayh Criticizes Hoover Attacks," *Boston Globe*, November 29, 1970.

17. "Bayh Criticizes Hoover Attacks."

18. Felt, *The FBI Pyramid from the Inside*, 89; Sullivan, *The Bureau*, 154–55.

19. Jackson, "Kissinger's Kidnapper," 98–102. A jury eventually acquitted the defendants of most charges on April 2, 1972.

20. "McGovern Calls Hoover Vindictive," *Washington Post*, February 1, 1971.

21. See, for example, Judge Lawrence G. Brooks, "It's Time for J. Edgar Hoover to Retire," *Boston Globe*, January 1, 1971.

22. John Dean memo to John Mitchell, September 18, 1970, Huston Plan, 249.

23. FBI memo, Director to Assistant Attorney General Internal Security Division, "Intelligence Evaluation Committee," February 3, 1971, Huston Plan, Exhibit 26, 261.

24. Theoharis, *Spying on Americans*, 37.

25. Haldeman, *The Haldeman Diaries*, 243.

26. "Boggs Attacks FBI Tactics, Urges Hoover's Dismissal," *Boston Globe*, April 6, 1971; Jack Nelson and Ronald J. Ostrow, "Kennedy: FBI Chief Should Quit," *Boston Globe*, April 8, 1971; Marquis Childs, "FBI Seen Lagging in Bombing Cases," *Washington Post*, March 22, 1971.

27. John W. Finney, "Bomb in Capitol Causes Wide Damage," *New York Times*, March 2, 1971; UPI, "No New Clues Found in Capital Blast," *Boston Globe*, March 3, 1971; Dohrn et al., *Sing a Battle Song*, 169–70.

28. Nixon quoted in Finney, "Bomb in Capitol Causes Wide Damage."

29. Quotes in Finney, "Bomb in Capitol Causes Wide Damage."

30. McGovern quoted in Finney, "Bomb in Capitol Causes Wide Damage."

31. Bernardine Dohrn, "New Morning—Changing Weather," in Dohrn et al., *Sing a Battle Song*, 161–69.

32. FBI memo, R. L. Shackelford to C. D. Brennan, January 5, 1971, FBI WUO, Roll 6, Section 64.

33. "Report Hints of Break in Hill Bombing," *Washington Post*, March 19, 1971.

34. Sikes quoted in Eckstein, *Bad Moon Rising*, 186.

35. "Report Hints of Break in Hill Bombing"; Eckstein, *Bad Moon Rising*, 182.

36. Eckstein, *Bad Moon Rising*, 186–87; Gilbert, *Love and Struggle*, 171–76; Jones, *A Radical Line*, 225–27.

37. Medsger, *The Burglary*, 6–7.

38. Medsger, 184.

39. Medsger, 177–79. The first story to appear was Betty Medsger and Ken Clawson, "Stolen Documents Describe FBI Surveillance Activities," *Washington Post*, March 24, 1971.

40. *WIN* magazine, special issue, "The Complete Collection of Political Documents Ripped-Off from the F.B.I. Office in Media, PA, March 8, 1971" (March 1972). Thank you to Trevor Griffey for providing me with a copy of this magazine. The special issue did not publish all of the documents stolen in Media, just those the burglars sent to journalists after determining them to be newsworthy examples of political surveillance with no relation to criminal or national security investigations.

41. Felt, *The FBI Pyramid from the Inside*, 92.

42. Medsger, *The Burglary*, 129.

43. Medsger, 135–41, 159, 161.

44. Betty Medsger, "Breaking 43 Years of Silence, the Last FBI Burglar Tells the Story of Her Life in the Underground," *Nation*, October 6, 2014.

45. FBI airtel, Director to SAC Albany, April 28, 1971, quoted in Theoharis, *Spying on Americans*, 150.

46. Medsger, *The Burglary*, 329–41.

47. Bloom and Martin, *Black against Empire*, 372–74.

48. Medsger, *The Burglary*, 184–86.

49. "Congress and the FBI," *Washington Post*, March 25, 1971; Medsger, *The Burglary*, 184.

50. Medsger, *The Burglary*, 187.

51. Holland, *Leak*, 13.

52. William C. Sullivan to J. Edgar Hoover, April 5, 1971, WCS FBI, Section 7.

53. J. Edgar Hoover to William C. Sullivan, April 7, 1971, WCS FBI, Section 7.

54. Medsger, *The Burglary*, 332–33, 498–99.

55. "Policies of Paranoia," *New York Times*, March 29, 1971; "What Is the FBI Up To?," *Washington Post*, March 25, 1971; Medsger, *The Burglary*, 184–86.

56. Medsger, *The Burglary*, 141–43, 186.

57. Betty Medsger and Ken Clawson, "Thieves Got Over 1,000 Papers," *Washington Post*, March 25, 1971.

58. Medsger and Clawson, "Thieves Got Over 1,000 Papers."

59. Medsger and Clawson.

60. Rosen informed me in an email that none of the reviews of her book discussed this chapter. I am reinterpreting her findings in the broader context of the FBI's war on leftist insurgency.

61. Rosen, *The World Split Open*, 240–45.

62. Burton-Rose, "Amazon Underground?"; Rosen, *The World Split Open*, 249. L. Patrick Gray hired the first two women FBI special agents in 1972: Susan Lynn Roley, a former Marine from Long Beach, California, and Joanne Pierce, a former nun from upstate New York.

63. Rosen, *The World Split Open*, 244–45, 260.

64. Rosen, 253, 238–39.

65. Rosen, 259–60. I came to similar conclusions while researching the FBI's file on Science for the People, an organization of radical American scientists. From 1969 to 1973, the FBI monitored the group extensively to preempt violence and civil disorder but did not target the group with covert operations because it determined that the organization was not involved in guerrilla violence. See Chard, "Teaching with the FBI's Science for the People File"; and Schmalzer, Chard, and Botelho, *Science for the People*, 39–40, 56–59, 64–67.

Chapter 7

1. Tanenbaum and Rosenberg, *Badge of the Assassin*, 1–2.

2. BLA communiqué quoted in Tanenbaum and Rosenberg, 22–23.

3. Nixon White House Tapes, Conversation 253-23, May 26, 1971, 4:11–5:20 P.M., Executive Office Building.

4. Hinton, *From the War on Poverty to the War on Crime*, 134–38.

5. Thompson, *Blood in the Water*, 199–200.

6. Scahill, *Dirty Wars*, 521; Zulaika, *Terrorism: The Self-Fulfilling Prophecy*.

7. The BLA carried out four earlier unclaimed attacks in California: an October 1970 bombing of a slain police officer's funeral, two January 1971 police shootings, and an attempted bombing in March 1971. Muntaqim, *On the Black Liberation Army*, 5; Tanenbaum and Rosenberg, *Badge of the Assassin*, 9–10.

8. Quoted in Tanenbaum and Rosenberg, *Badge of the Assassin*, 11. The communiqué's reference of the Vietnamese Liberation Army was likely a mistaken reference to South Vietnam's Communist National Liberation Front.

9. Kiernan quoted in Tanenbaum and Rosenberg, 9–10.

10. Williams, *Inadmissible Evidence*, 74. This figure comes from the memoir of an attorney who defended Assata Shakur and other BLA defendants in the 1970s and does not include a citation. However, this figure seems reliable given data collected by the *Guardian*'s The Counted project, which documented 2,239 deaths at the hands of police officers in 2015 and 2016, including 573 Black people. See

Katherine Viner, Lee Glendinning, and Matt Sullivan, "The Counted: People Killed by Police in the U.S.," *Guardian*, https://www.theguardian.com/us-news/ng-interactive /2015/jun/01/the-counted-police-killings-us-database (accessed February 15, 2021). For an explanation of the BLA's activities in the context of these police killings, see Umoja, "The Black Liberation Army and the Radical Legacy of the Black Panther Party," 235.

11. FBI NITEL, Director to New York, May 25, 1971, Moore FBI File, box 19, folder 4, KORM. Hoover also asked agents to consider the possibility that the attacks were acts of "revenge taken against NYC police by the Black Panther Party" for the arrest of the Panther Twenty-One in April 1969.

12. FBI memo, J. Edgar Hoover to Tolson, Sullivan, Bishop, Brennan, Gale, Rosen, and Casper, May 26, 1971, 5:34 P.M., Tolson File, box 25, folder 2, KORM.

13. FBI memo, SAC Joseph K. Ponder to SAC (157-6689), May 27, 1971, 1, box 106, folder 230A-R G54, M27 Nixon/AG, US v. Felt.

14. FBI memo, Ponder to SAC, May 27, 1971.

15. Nixon White House Tapes, Conversation 003-145, May 26, 1971.

16. Nixon White House Tapes, Conversation 003-145.

17. Nixon White House Tapes, Conversation 003-145.

18. J. Edgar Hoover, memo to Tolson, Sullivan, Bishop, Brennan, Casper, Cale, and Rosen, 9:30 A.M., May 27, 1971, box 60, folder 230A-R G54, M27 Nixon/AG, US v. Felt. In a second memo issued at 9:52 A.M. (available in the same folder cited above), Hoover reemphasized, "At the meeting yesterday the President was very determined and very positive that something be done and last night when he called me at home he told me to go all out irrespective in intelligence gathering."

19. Nixon White House Tapes, Conversation 003-169, May 28, 1971. Nixon started the call by validating Hoover's reluctance to involve the FBI in most police murder investigations, affirming his opposition to a bill Senator Richard Schweiker (R-PA) proposed after the New York police ambushes that would have mandated FBI involvement in all police killings. Hoover agreed that the FBI should not participate in this form of what he called "national policing," noting that in over 96 percent of police murder cases, local law enforcement agencies successfully apprehended suspects within thirty days.

20. Nixon White House Tapes, Conversation 003-169.

21. FBI memo, Ponder to SAC, May 27, 1971, 2.

22. Al Baker, "Nearly 5 Decades Later, Man Who Killed New York Officers Wins Parole," *New York Times*, March 14, 2018. See Tanenbaum and Rosenberg, *Badge of the Assassin*, for an example of Bell and his codefendants being portrayed as one-dimensional villains. On Bell's volunteer work, see Anonymous Contributor, "Update on Elderly Black Liberation Prisoner Herman Bell's Upcoming Parole Hearing," It's Going Down, November 15, 2017, https://itsgoingdown.org/update -elderly-black-liberation-prisoner-herman-bells-upcoming-parole-hearing/. During the 1990s and early 2000s, Herman Bell also worked with a group of white working-class anarchist farmers in Maine to organize the Victory Gardens Project, which brought together a multiracial network of community organizers in Athens, Maine; Philadelphia; New York; Boston; East Orange, New Jersey; Portland, Maine, and other

locales to grow and distribute organic vegetables while working to free U.S. political prisoners.

23. Shakur, *Assata*, 243. Shakur's statement aligns with sociologists' argument that many 1970s' leftist radicals adopted clandestine armed struggle for "affective" rather than purely ideological reasons. In other words, Shakur may have joined the BLA out of a commitment to her comrades. See Zwerman, Steinhoff, and della Porta, "Disappearing Social Movements," 89.

24. Quotes in Berger, *Outlaws of America*, 147; and Umoja, "The Black Liberation Army," 232. Also see Varon, *Bringing the War Home*, 184–87. The New York Twenty-One's letter to the Weather Underground first appeared in New York's *Village Voice* and was then picked up by a number of leftist underground newspapers. In addition to praising the Weather Underground, the Panther Twenty-One also heavily critiqued the group for dialing back its emphasis on violent revolution and for appealing to the white youth counterculture.

25. Umoja, "The Black Liberation Army," 232–33.

26. FBI COINTELPRO-BNHG memos quoted in O'Reilly, *"Racial Matters,"* 319.

27. FBI COINTELPRO-BNHG memos quoted in O'Reilly, *"Racial Matters,"* 319; Bloom and Martin, *Black against Empire*, 363–64.

28. New York Panthers and BLA members Dhoruba bin Wahad, Michael Hill, Eddie Jamal Joseph, and Irving Mason later stood trial for the murder, and after a hung jury, pleaded guilty to the lower charge of attempted manslaughter. Bloom and Martin, *Black against Empire*, 363. Seattle BPP chapter captain Aaron Dixon later remembered both Webb and Napier as being highly dedicated rank-and-file Panthers. Dixon, *My People Are Rising*, 214.

29. Umoja, "The Black Liberation Army," 227, 235; Burrough, *Days of Rage*, 200; Bloom and Martin, *Black against Empire*, 358–62.

30. Burrough, *Days of Rage*, 196; Bloom and Martin, *Black against Empire*, 369. Support for the paper came from the Independent Caucus of SDS at the State University of New York.

31. Cleaver quoted in Bloom and Martin, *Black against Empire*, 370.

32. Cleaver quoted in Edward S. Miller, "Introductory Statement for Urban Guerilla Seminar," November 29–30, 1971, box 60, folder 230A-R G54, M27 Nixon/AG, US v. Felt. Miller had taken Cleaver's words from a recent issue of the New York Panthers' *Right On!* newspaper.

33. "Spring Came Early This Year (A Message to the Third World from the Black Liberation Army)," undated BLA paper, ca. January 1972, BLA FBI, Section 1.3. Indeed, the BLA planned its first publicized attack—the May 19, 1971, ambush of Officers Curry and Binetti—after an April 19 shootout between police and Cleaver-faction Panthers that resulted in the death of twenty-one-year-old Panther Harold Russell and the wounding of two other Panthers and two police officers.

34. Burrough, *Days of Rage*, 193–94

35. BLA, "Spring Came Early This Year."

36. Umoja, "The Black Liberation Army," 235.

37. Joseph, *Panther Baby*, 197.

38. Joseph, 196.

39. McCoy, *The Politics of Heroin*.

40. English, *The Savage City*, 325–30; Joseph, *Panther Baby*, 210–12.

41. "Black Panther Here Is Charged in the Shooting of 2 Policemen," *New York Times*, July 31, 1971.

42. Audio and transcripts from excerpts of Nixon and Rockefeller's post-Attica conversations are available online at "40 Years after Attica Rebellion, New Tapes Reveal Nixon, Rockefeller Praised Deadly Crackdown," Democracy Now!, September 16, 2011, http://www.democracynow.org/2011/9/16/40_years_after_attica_rebellion_new. Also see Sam Roberts, "Rockefeller on the Attica Raid, from Boastful to Subdued," *New York Times*, September 12, 2011.

43. New York police also frequently labeled other robberies or police shootings carried out by Black men as BLA actions. Reverby, *Co-conspirator for Justice*, 94.

44. Ronald Butkiewicz interview, 11. Butkiewicz investigated the Puerto Rican nationalist Fuerzas Armadas de Liberación Nacional during the second half of the 1970s before moving on to investigate other clandestine violence in the 1980s and 1990s, including the Unabomber.

45. Burrough, *Days of Rage*, 201.

46. Tanenbaum and Rosenberg, *Badge of the Assassin*, 37–45; Burrough, *Days of Rage*, 202–3. The FBI and NYPD also traced two New York City bank robberies in July and August 1971 to the BLA.

47. Tanenbaum and Rosenberg, *Badge of the Assassin*, 84–89. The other suspects were brothers Gabriel and Francisco Torres, both of whom had loose ties to the BPP. In 2020, Jalil Muntaqim was released from prison in New York State, where he was incarcerated for his role in the Jones-Piagentini killings. Albert Nuh Washington died in prison on April 28, 2000.

48. Hoover memos to Ehrlichman, September 8, September 18, September 28, and November 5, 1971, FBI NEWKILL.

49. The facts surrounding Jackson's death remain disputed. For an overview, see Berger, *Captive Nation*, 135–38, 152. Rebelling prisoners, led by Jackson, killed three guards and two fellow prisoners. Guards retaliated by severely beating dozens of prisoners they suspected of participating in the uprising. Six prisoners, who came to be known as the "San Quentin Six," were later convicted for their role in the killings.

50. Baldwin quoted in Jackson, *Soledad Brother*, x. For more on how Baldwin and others on the left responded to Jackson's death, see Berger, *Captive Nation*, 152–65.

51. Berger, *Captive Nation*, 145.

52. Weather Underground, "George Jackson," August 30, 1971, in Dohrn et al., *Sing a Battle Song*, 175.

53. Weather Underground, 177.

54. BLA communiqué quoted in Mann, *Comrade George*, 135.

55. "Declaration to the People of America by the Inmates at Attica," People's Law Office, September 9, 1971, https://peopleslawoffice.com/declaration-and-5-demands-of-attica/.

56. For a comprehensive account of the Attica uprising and massacre, as well as its background and aftermath, see Thompson, *Blood in the Water*.

57. Weather Underground, "Attica," September 17, 1971, in Dohrn et al., *Sing a Battle Song*, 180.

58. Democracy Now!, "40 Years after Attica Rebellion."

59. FBI airtel, Director to SAC, San Francisco, October 5, 1971, and FBI report, "UNKNOWN SUBJECTS-GUARDS, San Quentin Prison, San Quentin (Marin County), GEORGE LESTER JACKSON-VICTIM," October 15, 1971, George Lester Jackson FBI File, Part 4, FBI Vault.

60. FBI report, "UNKNOWN SUBJECTS-GUARDS," October 15, 1971.

61. Thompson, *Blood in the Water*, 561.

62. Ronald Reagan, "We Will All Become Prisoners," *New York Times*, October 7, 1971. In his rise to power as governor of California, Reagan had received a great deal of assistance from J. Edgar Hoover and the FBI. See Rosenfeld, *Subversives*.

63. FBI airtel, Director to SACs Charlotte, Cincinnati, Detroit, Los Angeles, New York, Philadelphia, San Francisco, "Black Panther Party—Clever Faction, Extremist Matters," September 24, 1971, Moore FBI File, box 19, folder 4, KORM.

64. FBI airtel, Director to SACs Charlotte, September 24, 1971.

65. FBI airtel, Director to SACs Charlotte, September 24, 1971.

66. The document is a list of FBI memos declassified during the legal battles of Felt, Miller, and Gray that the National Archives and Records Administration removed from a public access list of withdrawn FBI documents, box 133, folder F(r) Black Panther, US v. Felt.

67. Shakur quoted in Burrough, *Days of Rage*, 196.

68. Historian David Garrow dug up these figures in FBI documents declassified by the Trump administration in 2017 and included them in a long-winded, sensational essay on the FBI and Martin Luther King's sex life published in a conservative British magazine. Garrow, "The Troubling Legacy of Martin Luther King." For a critical response to this article, see Chard, "When the FBI Targeted the Poor Peoples' Campaign."

69. Two additional police officers were badly wounded, one of them paralyzed. Burrough, *Days of Rage*, 205–17; FBI, "1971: A Time of Terror?," 7, box 102, folder 4, US v. Felt. It is unclear if Brown was part of the BLA, but the word on the street was that the robbery for which he was arrested was one of several BLA-style robberies targeting drug dealers that he had participated in while underground. Thelwell, "H. Rap Brown / Jamil Al-Amin," xxiv–xxv.

70. BLA, "Spring Came Early this Year," 1–2, 24.

71. FBI memo, E. S. Miller to A. Rosen, SUBJECT: NEWKILL, November 23, 1971, FBI NEWKILL.

72. Nixon White House Tapes, Conversation 15-106, November 22, 1971.

73. Nixon White House Tapes, Conversation 15-106.

Chapter 8

1. Hoover quoted from Felt's memory in Felt, *The FBI Pyramid from the Inside*, 133.

2. Felt, 133.

3. Ellsberg, *Secrets*, 422.

4. Felt, *The FBI Pyramid from the Inside*, 131; Nixon, *RN*, 513; Powers, *Secrecy and Power*, 469; Weiner, *Enemies*, 296.

5. Felt, *The FBI Pyramid from the Inside*, 131.

6. Felt, 133–34.

7. Bernstein and Woodward, *All the President's Men*, 243; Felt and O'Connor, *A G-Man's Life*.

8. Felt, *The FBI Pyramid from the Inside*, 133.

9. Felt, 208. Nixon informed Gray that he would decide on a permanent replacement for Hoover after the November election. Tolson retired shortly after Hoover's death.

10. In his memoir, Nixon wrote that unnamed sources informed him that a friend of Ellsberg's who was a "former Defense Department employee" and "Fellow at the Brookings Institution" had taken secret documents from the Pentagon pertaining to President Lyndon B. Johnson's late-1968 halt of the U.S. air war in Vietnam. Nixon recalled that he wanted Johnson's bombing halt documents as election year "ammunition against the antiwar critics, many of whom were the same men who, under Kennedy and Johnson, had led us into the Vietnam morass in the first place." Nixon, *RN*, 512, 515–16.

11. Nixon White House Tapes, Conversation 534-2(3), July 1, 1971. Nixon wrote in his memoir that he first verbally expressed approval for a break-in at the Brookings Institution during a meeting on June 17, 1971, with Kissinger, Haldeman, and Ehrlichman. "I saw absolutely no reason for [the bombing halt] report to be at Brookings, and I said I wanted it back right now—even if it meant having to get it surreptitiously," he recalled. Nixon, *RN*, 512.

12. Miller interview, 123.

13. Nixon White House tapes, conversation number 6-84, July 1, 1971.

14. Nixon White House tapes, conversation number 6-84. Hoover cautioned the president that "the enemies of the administration" were "trying to bait" him into taking a stand against freedom of the press that would divert negative attention away from Kennedy and Johnson's Vietnam policies toward Nixon's war efforts, which the *Pentagon Papers* did not cover.

15. Nixon White House tapes, conversation number 6-84.

16. Nixon quoted in Weiner, *Enemies*, 297.

17. Nixon, *RN*, 513.

18. Nixon, 414; Genovese, *The Watergate Crisis*, 16; Kutler, *The Wars of Watergate*, 113.

19. Genovese, *The Watergate Crisis*, 16.

20. Genovese, *The Watergate Crisis*, 16; Kutler, *Wars of Watergate*, 115. Dr. Fielding's filing cabinet today sits at the Smithsonian National Museum of American History.

21. UPI newswire, October 1970, attached to FBI memo, W. C. Sullivan to Mr. Tolson, October 13, 1970, WCS FBI, Section 7.

22. Hoover handwritten note on FBI memo, Sullivan to Tolson, October 13, 1970. The portions italicized here were underlined in Hoover's original note. Felt recalled this incident in *The FBI Pyramid from the Inside*, 130.

23. Felt, *The FBI Pyramid from the Inside*, 130.

24. Felt, 131; Weiner, *Enemies*, 296.

25. Felt, *The FBI Pyramid from the Inside*, 138.

26. Gray, *In Nixon's Web*, 164.

27. Felt, *The FBI Pyramid from the Inside*, 141–42.

28. Weiner, *Enemies*, 298; Nixon, *RN*, 596.

29. Nixon, *RN*, 598.

30. Nixon, 598–99.

31. Powers, *Secrecy and Power*, 475–76; Felt, *The FBI Pyramid from the Inside*, 165–67.

32. Felt, *The FBI Pyramid from the Inside*, 167.

33. Felt, 167–74.

34. Powers, *Secrecy and Power*, 146.

35. Felt, *The FBI Pyramid from the Inside*, 174.

36. Felt, 208.

37. Richard Nixon, "Eulogy Delivered at Funeral Services for J. Edgar Hoover," May 4, 1972, American Presidency Project.

38. Nixon, "Eulogy Delivered at Funeral Services for J. Edgar Hoover."

39. Miller interview, 139.

40. Miller, 32, 80–81.

41. In this capacity, Miller had carried out three inspections of the Domestic Security Division, experience that Felt believed strengthened his qualifications for leadership of the Domestic Security Division. Felt, *The FBI Pyramid from the Inside*, 139.

42. FBI memo, T. J. Smith to E. S. Miller, Urban Guerrilla Warfare Seminar, November 23,1971, and Edward S. Miller, "Introductory Statement for Urban Guerilla Seminar," November 29–30, 1971, box 60, folder 230A-R G54, M27 Nixon/AG, US v. Felt.

43. Miller, "Introductory Statement for Urban Guerilla Seminar," 1.

44. Miller, 1.

45. Miller, 6. Riddell had fled during the Chicago trial and was sentenced in absentia to ten years in prison. UPI, "10 Get Jail Terms in Chicago Draft Office," *New York Times*, June 10, 1970.

46. FBI report, "Profile of Urban Guerrilla Activity: Groups, Leaders, Incidents," November 22, 1971, box 60, folder 230A-R G54, M27 Nixon/AG, US v. Felt.

47. Miller, "Introductory Statement for Urban Guerilla Seminar," 12.

48. Miller, 12.

49. FBI memo, E. S. Miller to Mr. Rosen, December 6, 1971, box 251, folder Bu. II, US v. Felt.

50. Miller to Rosen, December 6, 1971. Miller followed up with a more detailed proposal on January 14, 1972, which included a list of suspected aboveground Weather Underground supporters as targets. See "Argument for Use of Anonymous Source—Black Bag Technique—Weatherman Investigations," box 251, folder Bu. II, US v. Felt.

51. FBI airtel, Director to SAC New York, March 27, 1972, box 251, folder Dohrn II (ESM), US v. Felt. Also see Eckstein, *Bad Moon Rising*, 162.

52. Ehrlichman, Memorandum for the President, May 3, 1972, quoted in Gage, "Deep Throat, Watergate, and the Bureaucratic Politics of the FBI," 171.

53. Gray, *In Nixon's Web*, 33.

54. Gray actually stated in his memoir that the FBI had not yet captured any Weather Underground fugitives, but in reality, agents had captured Judy Clark in February 1970 and Linda Evans and Dianne Donghi in April 1970. Gray, *In Nixon's Web*, 120; Felt, *The FBI Pyramid from the Inside*, 326.

55. Quoted in Greenberg, *The Dangers of Dissent*, 78.

56. Gray, *In Nixon's Web*, 56. Gray also acknowledged that "people both inside the Bureau and from other agencies . . . urged me to reinstate the capability for [the FBI's black-bag job] use in nondomestic operations" (115).

57. Miller interview, 159–60.

58. Felt, *The FBI Pyramid from the Inside*, 324.

59. FBI, August 24, 1976, untitled summary of interview with anonymous (name redacted) Detroit special agent, Gray FBI File, File Number 1222537-0-62-118045, Section 8, Serial 1, LPG FBI; Gray, *In Nixon's Web*, 114–15; Miller interview, 161.

60. Weather Underground, "The Bombing of the Pentagon," May 19, 1972, in Dohrn et al., *Sing a Battle Song*, 181. The guerrillas intentionally carried out their bombing on May 19, 1972, Ho Chi Minh's birthday.

61. Weather Underground, 181. Nixon's intensified bombings, calculated as a means to force the Vietnamese to accept U.S. terms to a peace deal, included bombardment of Hanoi and critical civilian infrastructure such as ports and dikes.

62. Bart Barnes, "Bombing Fails to Disrupt Pentagon," *Washington Post*, May 20, 1971.

63. Betty Medsger and B. D. Coien, "Who Are Weather People?—Ask FBI," *Washington Post*, May 20, 1972. The article did not cite any recent FBI sources.

64. Chamberlin, *The Global Offensive*, 153.

65. Chamberlin, 153. Five other passengers were wounded and Israeli forces captured two guerrillas.

66. Chamberlin, 154–56. Seventeen of the dead were Puerto Ricans on pilgrimage to the Holy Land. Two of the Japanese Red Army guerrillas also died in the attack, while the third, Kozo Okamoto, was badly wounded and arrested.

67. Gray, *In Nixon's Web*, 116.

68. Gray, 56.

69. Miller especially wanted surveillance on Vietnam Veterans Against the War (VVAW), which over the past year had become a top domestic surveillance target under the "Internal Security—Revolutionary Activities" category, designated for groups the bureau deemed prone to violence. Gray, 57. According to a 1975 FBI letter to the Church Committee, the FBI opened its investigation of VVAW in August 1971 in order to "determine the extent of control over VVAW by subversive groups and/or violence-prone elements in the antiwar movement." Church Committee, Book III, 239n33.

70. Payne, *Deep Cover*, 44. Gray wrote in his memoir that Miller identified the VVAW as "very anti-government and terroristic," and one of many leftist organizations secretly "sheltering terrorists and revolutionaries." He also recalled that

Assistant Attorney General Henry Petersen's recommendation to avoid the legal problems involved in warrantless wiretaps "helped reinforce my own preference for increased live informant and undercover special agent activity in the domestic terrorism arena." Contemporary FBI documents, however, did not frequently use the term "terrorist" in referring to VVAW and its members. More typically, the FBI identified VVAW members as "violence prone" and "extremists." Gray, *In Nixon's Web*, 57.

71. FBI memo, R. L. Shackelford to E. S. Miller, July 21, 1972, 2, box 48, folder: Dir Memo re Bureau priority in re Weatherman, US v. Felt.

72. FBI teletype printed in Payne, *Deep Cover*, 76.

73. Gray, *In Nixon's Web*, 121. Many would consider encouraging his agents to engage in sex through deception to be sanctioning rape.

74. Payne, *Deep Cover*, 141.

75. Payne, 141.

76. FBI surveillance of VVAW went beyond the purported aim of preventing violence—if anything, the bureau was complicit in promoting violence. Evidence from oral histories, contemporary newspaper articles, and sworn testimonies indicates that the bureau thoroughly infiltrated VVAW chapters throughout the country with paid informants, some of whom acted—either independently or at the urging of their handlers—as agent provocateurs, attempting to persuade others in the group to partake in acts of revolutionary violence. VVAW members also endured regular surveillance by plainclothes officers and arrests by local police on questionable pretexts. Hunt, *The Turning*, 149–51. The fact that VVAW members declined Fernandez's weapons offer seems to confirm an account from Cril Payne, one of the Los Angeles "deep cover" agents who infiltrated the group during its cross-country caravan to the Miami Republican Convention. Payne contended that contrary to FBI officials' claims, VVAW members were not violence prone. When joining the caravan with other undercover agents who had already infiltrated the group, Payne was skeptical of their claim that VVAW members were not prone to violence, but he came to agree with their assessment. "After eating, sleeping, rapping, and traveling with these veterans, what was my colleagues' collective impression? It was not what I expected," Payne recalled. "According to the agents, whose opinions I highly respected, the VVAW members they had traveled with had no intention of promoting violent confrontations. My friends had reached the conclusion, based on their personal experiences, that the Bureau was totally wrong in its assessment of this group." Payne, *Deep Cover*, 84.

77. The VVAW FBI files are currently available electronically on a website maintained by opponents of VVAW and its former member John Kerry: http://www.wintersoldier.com/staticpages/index.php?page=20040518192545112. Among other things, more information is needed on the relationship between the FBI's investigation and operations carried out by local police, CREEP, and other federal intelligence agencies.

78. FBI liaison, L. Patrick Gray to H. R. Haldeman, May 31, 1972, LBG FBI, File No. 1222537-0-62-118045, Section 1, Serial 1.

79. The bureau hid the existence of its top-secret undercover operations against VVAW by referring to its undercover agents as informants within its memos.

80. FBI airtel, Acting Director to SAC New York, May 22, 1972, box 251, folder Dohrn II (ESM), US v. Felt.

81. Acting Director to SAC New York, May 22, 1972.

82. Felt, *The FBI Pyramid from the Inside*, 324, 326.

83. FBI letterhead memorandum for Mr. Felt, Subject: Weatherman, July 18, 1972, box 48, folder: Dir Memo re Bureau priority in re Weatherman, US v. Felt.

84. Felt, *The FBI Pyramid from the Inside*, 326.

85. Miller interview, 160–61.

86. Anonymous FBI memo, "Desired Recommendations Which May Result from Weatherman Conference, June 22, 1972," box 48, folder: Dir Memo re Bureau priority in re Weatherman, US v. Felt.

87. "Desired Recommendations Which May Result from Weatherman Conference."

88. FBI memo, R. L. Shackelford to E. S. Miller, July 21, 1972, box 48, folder: Dir Memo re Bureau priority in re Weatherman, US v. Felt.

89. United States v. U.S. District Court (also known as the *Keith* case), 407 U.S. 297 (1972). The court unanimously rebuked Attorney General Mitchell's argument that warrantless FBI taps on Plamondon's phone were legal under the Omnibus Crime Bill of 1968 on the grounds that the surveillance "gather[ed] intelligence information deemed necessary to protect the nation from attempts of domestic organizations to attack and subvert the existing form of Government."

90. Gray, *In Nixon's Web*, 62.

91. Anonymous untitled FBI memo, attached to Anonymous FBI memo, "Desired Recommendations Which May Result from Weatherman Conference, June 22, 1972," box 48, folder: Dir Memo re Bureau priority in re Weatherman, US v. Felt.

92. FBI, August 24, 1976, untitled summary of interview with anonymous (name redacted) Detroit special agent. FBI agents gathered Knapp's testimony in 1976 as the Justice Department prepared indictments against Gray, Felt, Miller, and other bureau officials and agents involved in break-ins and other illegal surveillance tactics during the Weather Underground investigation. Knapp's name is redacted in the latter memo, but it appears in another: Untitled FBI memo, summary of interview of Robert Knapp by SA Michael M. Walters, March 24, 1976, box 115, folder: #351, Knapp, 302, US v. Felt.

93. Holland, *Leak*, 23.

94. Sanford J. Ungar, "Nixon Moves Quickly to Get Control of FBI," *Washington Post*, May 5, 1972.

95. Gray quoted in Ungar, "Nixon Moves Quickly to Get Control of FBI."

96. Felt, *The FBI Pyramid from the Inside*, 12.

97. L. Patrick Gray, FBI Memorandum 4-27, "Memorandum to All Special Agents in Charge," June 7, 1972, LPG FBI, No. 1222537-0-62-118045, Section 1, Serial 1.

98. "The Governance of the FBI," *Washington Post*, May 15, 1972.

99. Ungar, "Nixon Moves Quickly to Get Control of FBI."

100. Felt, *The FBI Pyramid from the Inside*, 12.

101. In particular, the Plumbers worried that O'Brien knew of a loan that business tycoon Howard Hughes made to Nixon's good friend Bebe Rebozo. Genovese, *The Watergate Crisis*, 27.

102. Genovese, 20–21.

103. Gray, *In Nixon's Web*, 60.

104. Holland, *Leak*, 29–30; Bob Woodward and E. J. Bachinski, "White House Consultant Tied to Bugging Figure," *Washington Post*, June 20, 1972.

105. Holland, *Leak*, 32–35, 37–38.

106. Holland, 45–47.

107. Holland, 50–52.

108. Holland, 36–37; Gray, *In Nixon's Web*, 138–39.

109. Woodward, *The Secret Man*, 214. Also see Gage, "Deep Throat, Watergate, and the Bureaucratic Politics of the FBI," 175–76.

110. W. Mark Felt interview, *Face the Nation*, CBS, August 29, 1976, C-SPAN Digital Video Library, http://www.c-span.org/video/?187059-1/w-mark-felt-interview.

111. Nixon quoted in Holland, *Leak*, 63.

112. (Sandy Smith), "Watergate, Contd.," *Time*, August 14, 1972 (published August 7), 21–22. Time magazine published Smith's article without attribution, but I am citing him as the author in parenthesis. Time also typically published its magazines before the official publication date, so this is reflected in my citation as well. For further discussion, see Holland, *Leak*, 70.

113. (Sandy Smith), "The Watergate Issue," *Time*, August 28, 1972 (published August 21), 20; Holland, *Leak*, 70.

Chapter 9

1. The rescue attempt occurred at the Munich Airport, where West German police transported the Black September militants and their hostages in a helicopter with a promise to deliver them by airliner to an unspecified Arab country. West German police captured the three surviving Black September militants in the siege but released them on October 29, 1972, after Palestinian militants hijacked Lufthansa Flight 615 from Damascus to Frankfurt and threatened to blow up the plane. Chamberlin, *The Global Offensive*, 142–43, 161–67. Also see *One Day in September*.

2. Chamberlin, *The Global Offensive*, 142–43, 161–74; McAlister, *Epic Encounters*, 178–81; Stampnitzky, *Disciplining Terror*, 21–27; Naftali, *Blind Spot*, 54–55.

3. Yaqub, *Imperfect Strangers*, 89; Pennock, *The Rise of the Arab American Left*, 143.

4. Stampnitzky, *Disciplining Terror*, 27–28; Naftali, *Blind Spot*, 59–61. Also see the CCCT's founding document: White House memorandum, Nixon to Kissinger, "Action to Combat Terrorism," September 25, 1972, Digital National Security Archive.

5. The committee itself convened only a few times, but its working group met regularly from 1972 to 1977, providing the White House with antiterrorism policy advice, sponsoring a number of conferences on terrorism, and funding several research projects.

6. Gray, *In Nixon's Web*, 117.

7. Gray, 117.

8. Nicholas M. Horrock, "New Senate Panel May Study F.B.I. Drive on Arab Terrorism," *New York Times*, February 13, 1975; Gray, *In Nixon's Web*, 114; FBI memo,

E. S. Miller to Mr. Felt, "Al Fatah; Internal Security—Middle East," September 7, 1972, LPG FBI, File No. 1222537-0-62-118045, Section 8, Serial 1.

9. Yaqub, *Imperfect Strangers*, 87–110; Pennock, *The Rise of the Arab American Left*, 147–53.

10. Miller to Felt, "Al Fatah; Internal Security—Middle East," September 7, 1972. Gray explains Felt and Miller's communication and filing arrangement in *In Nixon's Web* (121); Miller offered additional explanation in his oral history interview (161, 163). This communication and filing procedure was similar to what the FBI used while conducting break-ins targeting alleged Communists in the 1950s and early 1960s.

11. Miller to Felt, "Al Fatah; Internal Security—Middle East," September 7, 1972.

12. Chamberlin, *The Global Offensive*, 149.

13. Miller to Felt, "Al Fatah; Internal Security—Middle East," September 7, 1972.

14. Felt, *The FBI Pyramid from Inside*, 326; Miller interview, 160.

15. There are a few reasons for this. For one, officials considered break-ins at the Arab Information Center to be targeting a "foreign" source (as opposed to the domestic Weather Underground), so from a legal standpoint, indictments for these activities would have been more difficult to prosecute. In addition, Justice Department officials may have taken at face value the FBI's claim that its operation successfully preempted a violent Munich-style attack in the United States. If they did question the FBI, Attorney General Griffin Bell and his staff may have chosen to focus on the Weather Underground break-in indictments because prosecuting the Arab Information Center break-in would have required difficult discovery hearings involving classified intelligence reports on "foreign terrorists" and could have risked greater public backlash. Racist anti-Arab fears may have also played into the Justice Department's decision. As a consequence, most surviving documents on the FBI's investigation of an alleged Palestinian nationalist terrorist plot remain classified.

16. W. Mark Felt interview, *Face the Nation*, CBS, August 29, 1976, C-SPAN Digital Video Library. Felt did not specifically name the target of the FBI's break-ins at the time.

17. Felt, *The FBI Pyramid from Inside*, 325–26. The FBI redacted the names and location of its targets, but I have included them here based on corroborating documentation from Gray, Felt, and Miller's legal proceedings.

18. Gray, *In Nixon's Web*, 114–15.

19. Gray claimed that Felt called him in Seattle "within days" of the Munich attack with urgent intelligence that the Israeli embassy had shared with the CIA. The Israelis supposedly had "info that Al Fatah will try an attack on an eastern airport in the U.S." He claimed that the Israeli tip had been corroborated by a Black Panther informant in Los Angeles, who had passed along information originating with Eldridge Cleaver in Algeria. Gray also wrote that Edward Miller approached him in mid-September with another dire warning: "Dozens of Al Fatah assassins were already here planning to send letter bombs to the home addresses of Israeli diplomats and their families living in the United States and Canada." According to Gray, this is what compelled him to authorize FBI break-ins. Numerous sources contradict Gray's claims, however. First, Felt and Gray authorized the first Dallas break-in

on the day of the Munich attack, not two weeks later. Second, FBI documents in Gray's Director's File, though heavily redacted, reveal that the unnamed LA Panther informant's warnings, which spoke of a possible kidnapping attack in the United States, "were totally unrelated" to the Munich siege. Third, documents from the FBI's Black September File indicate that agents investigated a Black September plot to bomb an airliner, but that this investigation occurred two weeks after the Munich attack and was based on a rumor. It could be that the rumor originated with Israeli intelligence, but the FBI quickly determined that the threat was a false alarm. Fourth, there is no evidence that Al Fatah militants in the United States planned to send letter bombs to Israeli diplomats. However, individuals sent letter bombs from Amsterdam to Israeli targets in the United States, Canada, and Europe on September 20, 1972. Gray, *In Nixon's Web*, 111, 114; U.S. Government Memorandum, Francis J. Martin to Paul V. Daly, "Los Angeles Informant," March 5, 1979, LPG FBI, 1222537-0-62-118045-Section 6 Serial 1; FBI Black September File, September 1972, FBI Vault; Lawrence Van Gelder, "Bombs Mailed to Many Israeli Officials," *New York Times*, September 21, 1972.

20. Pennock, *The Rise of the Arab American Left*, 144, 22–24.

21. Ford quoted in Pennock, 140, 145.

22. Pennock, 146–47.

23. FBI monograph, "The Fedayeen Terrorist: A Profile," June 1970, Government Attic, quoted in Pennock, *The Rise of the Arab American Left*, 144.

24. Felt, *The FBI Pyramid from Inside*, 325. Felt's account of the Arab Information Center operation, despite explaining the motives behind the Dallas field office's break-in request, contains an important inaccuracy. Felt contended that a lower-level Domestic Security Division official at FBI headquarters authorized the Dallas supervisor's request, and that he, Miller, and Gray only learned of the operation after it was a "fait accompli." Miller's memo to Felt on September 7, 1972, belies this claim, however, demonstrating that both men authorized the Dallas field office request. Felt likely made this claim in his memoir in order to resist the Justice Department's efforts to convict him for his role in authorizing the Weather Underground break-ins.

25. FBI memorandum, "RE: Alleged Illegal Activities," attached to FBI memo, Acting Director to Archibald Cox, July 3, 1973, box: 132, folder: F(g) Watergate Special Prosecutor, US v. Felt.

26. FBI memorandum, "RE: Alleged Illegal Activities"; Horrock, "New Senate Panel May Study F.B.I. Drive on Arab Terrorism."

27. Horrock, "New Senate Panel May Study F.B.I. Drive on Arab Terrorism"; Gray, *In Nixon's Web*, 111.

28. Nixon White House Tapes, Tape 784-7, September 21, 1972; Naftali, *Blind Spot*, 59.

29. Lawrence Van Gelder, "Bombs Mailed to Many Israeli Officials," *New York Times*, September 21, 1972.

30. Naftali, *Blind Spot*, 57.

31. Gray, *In Nixon's Web*, 117; White House memorandum, Nixon to Kissinger, "Action to Combat Terrorism," September 25, 1972.

32. No author indicated, "Conference, Special Agents in Charge, Washington D.C., September 25-26, 1972," LPG FBI, 1222537-0-62-118045 EBF 212x1, Section 1, Serial 1; Miller interview, 162.

33. Felt, *The FBI Pyramid from the Inside*, 326. Felt also recalled that in a separate one-on-one conversation, Gray specifically gave Miller permission to authorize black-bag jobs against Weather Underground targets.

34. L. Patrick Gray, "Memorandum to E. S. Miller, RE: Contingency Plans for Handling Terrorist Attacks," undated (ca. January 1973), LPG FBI, 1222537-0-62-118045 EBF 212x1 - Section 1 Serial 1.

35. For more on how U.S. imperialism shaped American policing at home, see Schrader, *Badges without Borders*.

36. Medsger, *The Burglary*, 332–33.

37. "SOP for Responding to International Terrorist Acts Occurring within the United States," no author or date indicated (ca. September 1972), Nixon Presidential Materials Project, White House Special Files, Staff Member and Office Files, Richard C. Tufaro, Subject Files, box 1, Secret Attachments [folder #1], Richard Nixon Presidential Library.

38. U.S. General Accounting Office, *FBI Domestic Intelligence Operations*, 133–35. The GAO report published changes in the percentage of the FBI's domestic security investigations and use of informants but did not publish the actual number of the FBI's investigations. Despite a reduction in the number of the FBI's "extremist" investigations from their peak in FY 1971, when extremist investigations were 161 percent higher than in 1965, "extremist" investigations in FY 1973 remained 122 percent higher than in 1965. The number of domestic security informants utilized by the FBI under Gray's tenure likely exceeded 2,000 and payments to informants likely cost over $6 million. According to the FBI, during Gray's tenure the FBI increased its focus on the American Indian Movement, which carried out a number of high-profile disruptive protests during late 1972 and early 1973, while at the same time decreasing its focus on the disintegrating Black Panther Party.

39. U.S. General Accounting Office, *FBI Domestic Intelligence Operations*, 133–35; FBI report, anonymous author, "Changes in Operation of Intelligence Division since May 3, 1972," March 12, 1973, LPG FBI, 1222537-0-62-118045 EBF 212x1 - Section 1 Serial 1; Jack Ryan interview.

40. U.S. General Accounting Office, *FBI Domestic Intelligence Operations*, 134; FBI report, "Changes in Operation of Intelligence Division since May 3, 1972."

41. Felt, *The FBI Pyramid from the Inside*, 325–26; Gray, *In Nixon's Web*, 114–15.

42. Yaqub, *Imperfect Strangers*, 97–99; Pennock, *The Rise of the Arab American Left*, 147–53. Operation Boulder's existence became known to the public as a result of Abdeen Jabara's lawsuits.

43. For further discussion, see Yaqub, *Imperfect Strangers*, 87–89; and Pennock, *The Rise of the Arab American Left*, 10–12.

44. Azzah quoted in Yaqub, *Imperfect Strangers*, 99. Also see Pennock, *The Rise of the Arab American Left*, 151.

45. Yaqub, *Imperfect Strangers*, 99

46. Pennock, *The Rise of the Arab American Left*, 151.

47. Pennock, 150–51.

48. Pennock, 151. AACC refers to the American Arab Coordinating Committee, Red Crescent is a Syrian affiliate of the International Red Cross, and UHLF is the United Holy Land Foundation.

49. FBI teletype, SAC Baltimore to Acting Director and SAC Newark, "Threat by Alleged Black September Group on September Twelve, Seventy-Two to Bomb Jumbo Jet at East Coast Airport in Next Few Days," September 13, 1972, Black September File, FBI Vault. The FBI documents do not list Israel as the source of the intelligence, but Gray indicated in his memoir that Felt notified him that the threat had been relayed from the Israeli embassy via the CIA. Gray, *In Nixon's Web*, 111.

50. FBI teletype, New York to Acting Director, Atlanta, Newark, and San Juan, "Threat by Alleged Black September Group to Bomb Jumbo Jet at East Coast Airport in Next Few Days," September 14, 1972, 11:45 P.M., Black September File, FBI Vault.

51. William P. Rogers, "Memorandum for the President," December 27, 1972, 2, Nixon Presidential Materials Project, White House Special Files, Staff Member and Office Files, Richard C. Tufaro, Subject Files, box 1, CCCT Working Group [1], Richard Nixon Presidential Library.

52. FBI airtel, Acting Director to All SACS, "Contingency Plan for Handling Terrorist Attacks," January 9, 1973, LPG FBI, 1222537-0-62-118045 EBF 212x1 - Section 1 Serial 1.

53. Gray, *In Nixon's Web*, 111.

54. Horrock, "New Senate Panel May Study F.B.I. Drive on Arab Terrorism."

55. FBI memorandum, "RE: Alleged Illegal Activities," attached to FBI memo, Acting Director to Archibald Cox, July 3, 1973, box: 132, folder: F(g) Watergate Special Prosecutor, US v. Felt. According to this document, the FBI targeted Wadi because he had contacted an FBI source embedded in a "White Hate Group" in Jackson, Mississippi, and was concocting a plan to get Fatah to pay white supremacists to "participate in terrorist acts against Jews in the South." I have seen no other documentation to corroborate this claim, however, and neither Felt nor Gray mentions such a conspiracy in their memoirs. It is possible that FBI domestic security officials concocted this story to justify their illegal break-ins to Special Prosecutor Archibald Cox as he conducted his investigation of events related to the Watergate scandal. However, a memo from CCCT working group member Armin H. Meyer of the State Department on December 7, 1972, corroborates Wadi's New York City arrest and deportation. Meyer wrote, "As a result of FBI deft action, the ringleader of Fatah in the United States, who cleverly by-passed Operation Boulder, was apprehended and persuaded to leave the United States voluntarily on December 6." See Department of State memo, Armin H. Meyer to Members of the Working Group Cabinet Committee to Combat Terrorism, "Minutes of the Tenth Meeting of the Working Group," December 6, 1972, 3, Nixon Presidential Materials Project, White House Special Files, Staff Member and Office Files, Richard C. Tufaro, Subject Files, box 1, CCCT Working Group [1], Richard Nixon Presidential Library. Wadi went on to take a position as the United Arab Emirates' chargé d'affaires in Libya; see Horrock, "New Senate Panel May Study F.B.I. Drive on Arab Terrorism."

56. State Department memo, Armin H. Meyer to Members of the Working Group Cabinet Committee to Combat Terrorism, December 7, 1972.

57. Lisa Belkin, "For Many Arab-Americans, F.B.I. Scrutiny Renews Fears," *New York Times*, January 12, 1991.

58. Horrock, "New Senate Panel May Study F.B.I. Drive on Arab Terrorism."

59. Weiner, *Enemies*, 321–22. Al-Jawary and his accomplices fled the country after the botched attack, but he was arrested in Rome in 1991 and extradited to the United States, where he served a sixteen-year prison term before being released in Sudan in March 2009.

60. Adam Goldman, "I Wrote to Carlos the Jackal, and an Israeli's Assassination Case Was Revived," *New York Times*, January 8, 2017; "FBI Reopens Case of 1973 Assassination of Israeli Diplomat," *Times of Israel*, January 10, 2017.

61. "FBI Reopens Case of 1973 Assassination of Israeli Diplomat."

62. Goldman, "I Wrote to Carlos the Jackal"; "Former P.L.O. Aide in Paris Killed Leaving Bookstore," *New York Times*, January 4, 1977.

63. L. Patrick Gray, Address before the National Symposium on Terrorism, FBI Academy, Quantico, Virginia, January 16, 1976, 4, LPG FBI, 1222537-0-62-118045 EBF 212x1.

64. Stampnitzky, *Disciplining Terror*, 187.

65. Gray, Address before the National Symposium on Terrorism, 9.

66. Stampnitzky, *Disciplining Terror*, 187.

67. Naftali, *Blind Spot*, 19–20, 23, 66–68.

Chapter 10

1. Gray, *In Nixon's Web*, 33.

2. Kutler, *The Wars of Watergate*, 189.

3. Kutler, 253–58; Holland, *Leak*, 117.

4. Nixon White House Tapes, February 16, 1973, Tape 858, Conversation No. 2 (also recorded as Conversation 858-3); Gray, *In Nixon's Web*, 156.

5. Nixon White House Tapes, February 16, 1973, Tape 858; Gray, *In Nixon's Web*, 158, 163.

6. Nixon White House Tapes, February 16, 1973, Tape 858; Gray, *In Nixon's Web*, 166–67.

7. Nixon White House Tapes, February 16, 1973, National Archives transcript, 28. Gray conspicuously omitted this comment from the lengthy account of this conversation in his memoir. Gray, *In Nixon's Web*, 176.

8. Holland, *Leak*, 7.

9. Nixon quoted in Holland, *Leak*, 117.

10. Carl Bernstein and Bob Woodward, "FBI Finds Nixon Aides Sabotaged Democrats," *Washington Post*, October 10, 1972, A1; Holland, *Leak*, 71, 94–95. The article focused on the activities of Donald Segretti, who carried out a number of dirty tricks for the Nixon administration in order to facilitate the president's re-election. As outlined in the article, this included sending a letter to the top newspa-

per in New Hampshire alleging that Democratic presidential candidate Senator Edward Muskie of Maine had used racial slurs to disparage Americans of French Canadian descent. The so-called Canuk letter played an important role in undermining Muskie's presidential bid.

11. Kutler, *Wars of Watergate*, 192, 226.

12. Holland, *Leak*, 98–99.

13. Nixon White House Tapes, October 19, 1972, Conversation No. 370-9, Segment 1, National Security Archive transcript, 2; Richard A. Moss, "Nixon and the FBI: The White House Tapes," National Security Archive; Gray, *In Nixon's Web*, 130; Holland, *Leak*, 99.

14. Felt quoted in Gray, *In Nixon's Web*, 129; Felt, *The FBI Pyramid from the Inside*, 225–26.

15. Gray, *In Nixon's Web*, 134.

16. Dean quoted in Holland, *Leak*, 118.

17. (Sandy Smith), "Questions about Gray," *Time*, March 5, 1973 (published February 26), 14–15; Holland, *Leak*, 123. The article alleged that Gray terminated the wiretaps after the Supreme Court's *Keith* decision ruled that domestic wiretaps required a court order. Smith did not use the term "Kissinger Wiretaps" in his story, as Kissinger's role in the affair had not yet been uncovered.

18. Gray, *In Nixon's Web*, 257–59, 267; Holland, *Leak*, 123–24.

19. For a sympathetic overview of AIM, see Smith and Warrior, *Like a Hurricane*.

20. Gray, *In Nixon's Web*, 198.

21. Gray, 204; Felt, *The FBI Pyramid from the Inside*, 268; "Army Tested Secret Civil Disturbance Plan at Wounded Knee, Memos Show," *New York Times*, December 2, 1977. For the perspective of the regional FBI chief in charge of handling the siege, see Trimbach and Trimbach, *American Indian Mafia*.

22. Gray, *In Nixon's Web*, 204–6; Felt, *The FBI Pyramid from the Inside*, 266–67.

23. "Army Tested Secret Civil Disturbance Plan at Wounded Knee."

24. Black civil rights activist Ray Robinson also disappeared from the siege after joining to support AIM. The FBI and his family believe he was murdered by AIM members who thought he was an informant, though his remains have never been found. The siege was followed by several years of conflict on the Pine Ridge Reservation, which included a low-intensity civil war between AIM and Wilson's GOONs. In this context, AIM activist Leonard Peltier was imprisoned for the 1975 killing of two FBI agents at Pine Ridge and remains incarcerated today, though he maintains his innocence and has been supported by an international campaign to win his release from prison. Mi'kmaq activist Anna Mae Aquash was murdered on Pine Ridge in December 1975. Activists long suspected FBI involvement in her death, but in 2003 federal authorities indicted former AIM activists Arlo Looking Cloud and John Graham, who were eventually convicted for the murder. Aquash's murder occurred amid unfounded suspicions—potentially circulated by law enforcement organizations—that she was a police informant.

25. Felt, *The FBI Pyramid from the Inside*, 271.

26. Smith and Warrior, *Like a Hurricane*, 236.

27. Holland, *Leak*, 129–30.

28. Senate, Committee on the Judiciary, *Hearings on the Nomination of Louis Patrick Gray*.

29. Senate, 671.

30. Nixon quoted in Holland, *Leak*, 136. Also see Weiner, *Enemies*, 324.

31. Gray quoted in Kelley and Davis, *Kelley*, 145.

32. Nixon White House Tapes, April 27, 1973, 4:14–4:16 P.M., Conversation 45-34 (White House telephone), National Security Archive transcript, 1.

33. Felt, *The FBI Pyramid from the Inside*, 297–98; Holland, *Leak*, 141. Contrary to Felt's suspicions, during his time at the FBI, Ruckelshaus quickly came to suspect Nixon's involvement in the Watergate cover-up. He shared his thoughts with the new attorney general Elliot Richardson, who was appointed on the same day that Ruckelshaus received his FBI appointment. See Koncewicz, *They Said No to Nixon*, 151–52.

34. Holland, *Leak*, 140–41.

35. Holland, 7, 145–46.

36. Burrough, *Days of Rage*, 233.

37. See Miller to Felt memos in LPG FBI, Number 1222537-0-62-118045, Section 8, Serial 1.

38. Burrough, *Days of Rage*, 233. Jennifer Dohrn, meanwhile, was pregnant and lived in constant fear of the FBI, whose agents at one point in 1972 considered a plan to take her baby from her in hopes of blackmailing her sister Bernardine into surrender, though the plan was never implemented. Dohrn learned of this plan after receiving declassified FBI documents through a Freedom of Information Act lawsuit (she also learned of the FBI's seizure of her underwear). In a 2005 interview, Dohrn recalled her experiences with FBI surveillance: "I was certainly aware of being followed a lot. I . . . assumed that perhaps my phones were tapped, and I had no idea of the level of extent under which I was being surveilled. I had no idea that break-ins were repeatedly happening into my apartments. I remember when I was pregnant with my first born feeling extremely vulnerable because I was being followed a great deal of the time."

In the same interview, journalist Juan Gonzalez, a former leader of the radical Young Lords organization, recalled FBI agents interrogating him about the Weather Underground in 1972 after he was arrested for violating Selective Service laws and refusing to fight in Vietnam: "I was questioned for about eight hours at F.B.I. headquarters before I was arraigned, and virtually all of the questions that the F.B.I. agents asked me were not about the Young Lords, not about the selective service, but were: When was the last time you saw Bernardine Dohrn? When was the last time that you saw Robbie Roth? When was the last time you saw Mark Rudd? They were obsessed with finding the Weathermen." "Exclusive . . . Jennifer Dohrn, I Was the Target of Illegal FBI Break-Ins Ordered by Mark Felt aka 'Deep Throat,'" *Democracy Now!*, June 2, 2005, https://www.democracynow.org/2005/6/2/exclusive _jennifer_dohrn_i_was_the.

39. Burrough, *Days of Rage*, 218–19, 230.

40. Appy, *American Reckoning*, 214.

41. The Paris Peace Accords were originally proposed by the Provisional Revolutionary Government of South Vietnam. See Weather Underground, "Bombing of the Pentagon," in Dohrn et al., *Sing a Battle Song*, 184.

42. Weather Underground, "Clifford Glover 103rd Precinct," in Dohrn et al., 197–99.

43. FBI memo, R. L. Shackelford to E. S. Miller, September 25, 1973, NARA College Park, box 99, folder "10/2/78—Gray 20—Squad 47," US v. Felt; Eckstein, *Bad Moon Rising*, 159, 180–81, 253.

44. Kunstler quoted in "Howard Norton Machtinger: Weatherman Fugitive," addendum to Shackelford to Miller, September 25, 1973, NARA College Park, Felt-Miller Papers, box 99, folder "10/2/78—Gray 20—Squad 47"; Eckstein, *Bad Moon Rising*, 254.

45. Dohrn et al., *Sing a Battle Song*, 209–10.

46. Varon, *Bringing the War Home*, 296–97; Eckstein, *Bad Moon Rising*, 229–30.

47. Burrough, *Days of Rage*, 236–37.

48. O'Reilly, *"Racial Matters,"* 322.

49. Baker interview, 15; Williams, *Inadmissible Evidence*, 3; "Joint Terrorism Task Forces," FBI, https://www.fbi.gov/investigate/terrorism/joint-terrorism-task-forces (accessed February 15, 2021).

50. UPI, "10 Die in New Orleans Sniper Fire; Gunman Is Slain by Police in Helicopter," *New York Times*, January 9, 1973; "Attorney General Plans to Consider Terrorist Charge," *New York Times*, January 9, 1973; Andrew H. Malcolm, "Sniper Is Remembered as Quiet Youth Who Grew to Hate Whites in the Navy," *New York Times*, January 10, 1973. These articles are among a collection of clippings on the New Orleans sniper incident available in Raymond Luc Levasseur Papers, MS 971, box 9, folder 1 (Black Liberation Army), Special Collections, University of Massachusetts Amherst.

51. L. Patrick Gray, Address before the National Symposium on Terrorism, FBI Academy, Quantico, Virginia, January 16, 1973, 4, LPG FBI, 1222537-0-62-118045 EBF 212x1.

52. Burrough, *Days of Rage*, 241–43.

53. Shakur later stood trial on various charges related to alleged BLA bank robberies but was convicted only for her role in the Foerster killing, even though medical examination of her arm wound found that it would have been impossible for her to fire the gun. Reverby, *Co-conspirator for Justice*, 95; Burrough, *Days of Rage*, 238, 246–48; Umoja, "The Black Liberation Army," 236.

54. Tanenbaum and Rosenberg, *Badge of the Assassin*, 130–35, 140–59; "FBI Places Myers on Most Wanted List," *New York Times*, September 30, 1973.

55. Burrough, *Days of Rage*, 249. According to Burrough, as of 2015 the informant was still alive and in her sixties. In September 1973, operating on a tip from another source, New York police also arrested BLA member Robert "Seth" Hayes, wanted for the assassination of a New York City transit officer. Burrough, 251–52.

56. Burrough, 253–54.

57. Cawley quoted in Umoja, "The Black Liberation Army," 237.

58. Kelley and Davis, *Kelley*, 45–51, 62. During this period, Kelley also worked at FBI offices in Huntington, Pittsburgh, Altoona, Johnstown, and Washington, D.C.

59. Statement of Hon. Thomas F. Eagleton, U.S. Senate, Committee on the Judiciary, *Nomination of Clarence M. Kelley*, 2, 7; Ungar, *FBI*, 582, 585. While chief of police, Kelley increased recruitment of African American officers and used federal Law Enforcement Assistance Administration dollars to introduce helicopter patrols and computer technology into the force, distinguishing the Kansas City Police Department as one of the nation's most cutting-edge departments. Kelley had also been the nemesis of Kansas City Black Panther leader Pete O'Neal, who had become politicized during the April 1968 riots and confronted Kelley along with other Panthers on several occasions. In 1970, facing four years in prison for charges of illegally transporting a shotgun across state lines (a practice that was common in Kansas City, which is on Missouri's state line with Kansas), O'Neal fled the country with his young wife Charlotte, eventually landing in Tanzania, where in 1991 the couple founded the United African Alliance Community Center and school, which serves local families and children. See Donald Bradley, "Pardon Window Is Closing on Pete O'Neal, KC's Black Panther in Africa," *Kansas City Star*, January 15, 2017.

60. Kelley quoted in Carroll Kilpatrick, "Nixon Hails 'New Era' at Home in Talk for Kelley Swearing-In," *Washington Post*, July 10, 1973.

61. Kelley and Davis, *Kelley*, 125.

62. Ungar, *FBI*, 591.

63. Kelley and Davis, *Kelley*, 125.

64. Stern sought more information on documents stolen from the FBI office in Media, Pennsylvania, in March 1971, and the formerly classified FBI documents he received were the first ever to be released through a Freedom of Information Act lawsuit. Kelley and Davis, 177; Medsger, *The Burglary*, 331–34; Laurence Stern, "Hoover War on New Left Bared," *Washington Post*, December 7, 1973; Margaret Gentry, "FBI Bares Hoover's Campaign against New Left," *Boston Globe*, December 7, 1973.

65. Kelley and Davis, *Kelley*, 124–30; Koncewicz, *They Said No to Nixon*, 165–69.

66. Kelley and Davis, *Kelley*, 129.

67. Kelley and Davis, 130–38.

68. Kelley and Davis, 146–48.

69. For a detailed account of the kidnapping, see Toobin, *American Heiress*, 1–4.

70. Nixon quoted in Kilpatrick, "Nixon Hails 'New Era' at Home in Talk for Kelley Swearing-In."

71. Monte A. Hall interview, 18.

72. Graebner, *Patty's Got a Gun*, 1, 11; Cummins, *The Rise and Fall of California's Radical Prison Movement*, 239–41. DeFreeze escaped from Soledad Prison, where he had recently been transferred.

73. Symbionese Liberation Army Western Regional Youth Unit, "Communiqué No. 1," in Pearsall, *The Symbionese Liberation Army*, 39; McLellon and Avery, *The Voices of Guns*, 132, 145; Kelley and Davis, *Kelley*, 193; Payne and Findley, *The Life and Death of the SLA*, 51. The SLA also critically wounded Foster's assistant Robert Blackburn in the attack, which did prompt some police reprisal in Oakland's African

American community. Police raided the Black Panthers' headquarters after the killing, arresting then later releasing several occupants.

74. Kelley and Davis, *Kelley*, 195–97.

75. Kelley and Davis, 196–97.

76. Kelley and Davis, 153, 196; Greenberg, *The Dangers of Dissent*, 85–93. On the Revolutionary Union, a Maoist organization, see Leonard and Gallagher, *Heavy Radicals*.

77. Hall interview, 3–4, 17–18; Kelley and Davis, *Kelley*, 199–200, 215; Cummins, *The Rise and Fall of California's Radical Prison Movement*, 185.

78. Kelley and Davis, *Kelley*, 199–200.

79. Graebner, *Patty's Got a Gun*, 1.

80. "Patricia Hearst's SLA Testament," in Pearsall, *The Symbionese Liberation Army*, 90, 92.

81. Graebner, *Patty's Got a Gun*, 16–20.

82. Kelley and Davis, *Kelley*, 200.

83. Kelley and Davis, *Kelley*, 220–21.

84. Hall interview, 7, 18.

85. McLellon and Avery, *The Voices of Guns*, 412.

86. Botting, *Bullets, Bombs, and Fast Talk*, 25.

87. Kelley and Davis, *Kelley*, 206–7.

88. Clarence M. Kelley, "The FBI's Role in Protecting America," address at the University of Kansas, Lawrence, Kansas, March 29, 1974, 4, CMK FBI, section 9, disk 1.

89. Kelley, "The FBI's Role in Protecting America," 5, 7–8, 12.

90. Hall interview, 9; Kelley and Davis, *Kelley*, 212–13; McLellon and Avery, *The Voices of Guns*, 349; Graebner, *Patty's Got a Gun*, 27–28; Botting, *Bullets, Bombs, and Fast Talk*, 28.

91. Police alleged that the fire started after a bullet struck a gasoline can inside the house. In addition to Donald DeFreeze, the other guerrillas killed were Nancy Ling Perry, Patricia Soltysik, Angela Atwood, William Wolfe, and Camilla Hall. Graebner, *Patty's Got a Gun*, 29. For more on the raid, see Kelley and Davis, *Kelley*, 213; McLellon and Avery, *The Voices of Guns*, 363; Payne and Findley, *The Life and Death of the SLA*, 289.

92. Kelley and Davis, *Kelley*, 210.

93. Kelley and Davis, 211.

94. Austin Scott, "Hearst Case 'Stumps' FBI," *Washington Post*, May 10, 1974.

95. Castiglia, *Bound and Determined*, 96–99.

96. Kelley and Davis, *Kelley*, 219.

97. "Patricia Hearst Conciliates," transcript of SLA recording, February 16, 1974, in Pearsall, *The Symbionese Liberation Army*, 66–67. Parts of Hearst's statement are also quoted in Kelley and Davis, *Kelley*, 200.

98. "Patricia Hearst's SLA Testament," transcript of SLA recording, March 9, 1974, in Pearsall, *The Symbionese Liberation Army*, 89, 93; Kelley and Davis, *Kelley*, 205.

99. McLellon and Avery, *The Voices of Guns*, 330–31; Graebner, *Patty's Got a Gun*, 29–30. Graebner quotes Hearst's memoir, in which she recalled her response

to the LA siege after watching it on television: "I sat there on the floor in a stupor. I was a soldier, an urban guerrilla, in the people's army. It was a role I had accepted in exchange for my very life. There was no turning back. The police or FBI would shoot me on sight, just as they had killed my comrades." FBI agents initially arrived on the scene of the siege, but Kelley ordered them to withdraw. Kelley explained in his memoir that because of their ample numbers and arms, he believed "the matter could and should be handled by the Los Angeles Police Department." It is also possible that Kelley wanted to avoid further damaging the bureau's image by associating it with the gun battle that he and his agents predicted was "almost certainly" about to occur. See Kelley and Davis, *Kelley*, 213–14.

100. Kelley and Davis, *Kelley*, 205.

101. Felt, *The FBI Pyramid from the Inside*, 345.

102. Kelley and Davis, *Kelley*, 153.

103. Kelley and Davis, *Kelley*, 177. Also see Ungar, *FBI*, 567. Kelley issued this memo on December 5, 1973, the day before the Justice Department released the first COINTELPRO documents to journalist Carl Stern. In another move, early in 1974, Kelley commissioned Brandeis University political scientist John T. Elliff to conduct an independent study of FBI domestic security operations under the auspices of the nonprofit Police Foundation. Kelley also made adjustments to the bureau hierarchy, pushing several powerful Hoover loyalists into retirement. See Elliff, *The Reform of FBI Intelligence Operations*, ix; and Ungar, *FBI*, 593–95.

104. Kelley and Davis, *Kelley*, 153.

105. Felt, *The FBI Pyramid from the Inside*, 345–47.

106. Payne and Findley, *The Life and Death of the SLA*, 173.

107. UPI, "SLA Leader Faces Informer Claims," *Hartford Courant*, May 12, 1974; Burton-Rose, *Guerrilla USA*, 286n14.

108. He later apologized. Koncewicz, *They Said No to Nixon*, 137.

109. Kutler, *Wars of Watergate*, 320.

110. Varon, *Bringing the War Home*, 291–98.

111. "Aide in Pentagon Papers Inquiry Quits the National Security Council Staff," *New York Times*, May 3, 1973; Seymour H. Hersh, "Nixon's Active Role in Plumbers: His Talks with Leaders Recalled," *New York Times*, December 10, 1973.

112. Stampnitzky, *Disciplining Terror*, 28.

Epilogue

1. Clarence M. Kelley, "The FBI's Role in Protecting America," address at the University of Kansas, Lawrence, Kansas, March 29, 1974, 5, CMK FBI, section 9, disk 1.

2. Kelley, 4.

3. Senate Internal Security Subcommittee, *Hearings on Terroristic Activity*, Parts 1–9. The Los Angeles Police Department's anticommunist squad underwent a similar transformation into a counterterrorism unit during this period. See Felker-Kantor, *Policing Los Angeles*, 157–60.

4. Theoharis, *The FBI and American Democracy*, 146, 158.

5. Lost on most Americans was the fact that the Iranian student revolutionaries were acting in response to President Carter's decision to shelter deposed Iranian monarch Shah Reza Pehlavi, a brutal tyrant who had been installed in a 1953 CIA-backed coup that overthrew the country's democratically elected prime minister, Mohammad Mossadegh. Appy, *American Reckoning*, 233.

6. Reagan quoted in Wills, *The First War on Terrorism*, 1.

7. Laurie Johnston and Robert Mcg. Thomas, "Notes on People; Congratulations and Champagne from Nixon," *New York Times*, April 30, 1981.

8. Ronald Reagan, "Reagan Statement about the Pardons," *New York Times*, April 16, 1981.

9. Stampnitzky, *Disciplining Terror*, 122–27.

10. Francis, "The Intelligence Community," 903–53.

11. Francis, 940.

12. Senate Subcommittee on Security and Terrorism, *Hearing on Attorney General's Guidelines for Domestic Security Investigations (Smith Guidelines)*.

13. Theoharis, *The FBI and American Democracy*, 163.

14. The heist was pulled off as a joint operation of what remained of the BLA and the May 19 Communist Organization, composed of white anti-imperialists including former Weatherman Judy Clark, who recruited Gilbert and Boudin to participate in the mission. On the state response, see Senate Subcommittee on Security and Terrorism, *Hearing on Attorney General's Guidelines for Domestic Security Investigations*, 4; Zwerman, "Domestic Counterterrorism," 44–45. For an overview of the Nyack incident with a focus on the guerrillas, see Reverby, *Co-conspirator for Justice*, 108–14.

15. William Webster testimony, Senate Subcommittee on Security and Terrorism, *Hearings on the Domestic Security Guidelines*, 25–26.

16. William E. Dyson interview, 66; Richard Connolly, "Task Force Had Role in Halting Holdup," *Boston Globe*, May 20, 1984.

17. Mamdani, *Good Muslim, Bad Muslim*, 12–13.

18. Mamdani, 120, 126, 132.

19. Johnson, *Blowback*; Appy, *American Reckoning*, 321–22.

20. Baker quoted in Miller, *U.S. National Security, Intelligence, and Democracy*, 2.

21. Clancy quoted in Miller, 2. At the time Clancy made this quote, police had overestimated the number of casualties, which turned out to be just under 3,000.

22. The United Freedom Front was an offshoot of the Sam Melville–Jonathan Jackson Unit, a group founded by white working-class Vietnam veterans and ex-convicts from Maine and Massachusetts.

23. Mueller quoted in Theoharis, *The FBI and American Democracy*, 159.

24. George W. Bush, "Address to a Joint Session of Congress and the American People," September 20, 2001, in Meyerowitz, *History and September 11th*, 241. For more on Bush's ahistorical framing, see McAlister, *Epic Encounters*, 278–79; and Stampnitzky, *Disciplining Terror*, 165–68. Intelligence officials did not unilaterally cooperate with President Bush. In March 2004, in a showdown reminiscent of Hoover and Nixon's dispute over the Huston Plan, FBI director Mueller threatened Bush with his resignation if the president required him to continue the FBI's role in

Stellar Wind, an electronic mass surveillance program conducted in coordination with the NSA and opposed by Assistant Attorney General James Comey. The NSA later expanded the program, details of which were leaked by NSA whistle-blower Edward Snowden in 2013. On Mueller and Bush, see Weiner, *Enemies*, 432–39.

25. Theoharis, *The FBI and American Democracy*, 158–59.

26. "Joint Terrorism Task Forces," FBI, http://www.fbi.gov/about-us/investigate /terrorism/terrorism_jttfs (accessed on June 1, 2016).

27. Peace activist Phil Berrigan also endured such treatment, as did Yu Kikumura, a prisoner accused of membership in the Japanese Red Army. Anne-Marie Cusac, "You're in the Hole: A Crackdown on Dissident Prisoners," *Progressive*, December 2001; Nora K. Wallace, "Inmate Questions Post-Sept. 11 Treatment: Richard Williams, at Lompoc for 10 Years, Has Been Segregated since Attacks," *Santa Barbara News-Press*, July 1, 2002, reprinted in Interfaith Prisoners of Conscience Project, *They Never Crushed His Spirit*, 48–56, 57–59; J. Soffiyah Elijah, "Political Prisoners and 9/11: The Reality of Political Prisoners in the United States: What September 11 Taught Us about Defending Them," *Harvard BlackLetter Law Journal* 18 (2002), reprinted in Meyer, *Let Freedom Ring*, 675.

28. "National Security: Prevention of Acts of Violence and Terrorism," 66 Fed. Reg. 55062 (October 31, 2001), https://federalregister.gov/a/01-27472. These rules were last updated in September 2004 and remain in place today. They have been assailed by a number of legal rights organizations, including the National Lawyers Guild, the Center for Constitutional Rights, and Amnesty International. See Interfaith Prisoners of Conscience Project, *They Never Crushed His Spirit*, 50–51.

29. "US: Terrorism Prosecutions Often an Illusion: Investigations, Trials of American Muslims Rife with Abuse," Human Rights Watch, July 21, 2014, https:// www.hrw.org/news/2014/07/21/us-terrorism-prosecutions-often-illusion.

30. New America, "Terrorism in America after 9/11," part IV.

31. Mamdani, *Good Muslim, Bad Muslim*, 258.

32. For recent discussion of the pitfalls of "sixties nostalgia," see Johnson, "The Panthers Can't Save Us Now" and "Who's Afraid of Left Populism?"

33. On recent FBI surveillance, see German, *Disrupt, Discredit, and Divide*; and Gibbons, "Still Spying on Dissent." I disagree with the latter report's framing of FBI surveillance as a historically continuous, nonchanging problem motivated by an interest in repressing freedom of speech, but it nevertheless provides a good overview of recent surveillance and repression of American leftists and Muslims, much of it in the name of preempting terrorism.

34. For further discussion, see Husain, "Terror and Abolition"; and Lindahl, "A CTS Model of Counterterrorism."

Bibliography

Archives

Amherst College Archives and Special Collections, Amherst, MA
    Bloom (AC 1966) Alternative Press Collection
Freedom Archives, San Francisco, CA
National Archives and Records Administration, College Park, MD
    Record Group 60, Department of Justice Case 177-16-13
        (U.S. v. Gray, Felt, Miller)
Raynor Memorial Libraries, Special Collections, Marquette University,
    Milwaukee, WI
    FBI Records, Kenneth O'Reilly Research Materials, 1922–1991
        Detroit Riots, 1967, FBI File
        Moore, Dhoruba, FBI File
        Tolson, Clyde, FBI Personnel File
Richard Nixon Presidential Library, Yorba Linda, CA
    John W. Dean Papers
    Richard C. Tufaro Papers
    David R. Young Jr. Papers
Special Collections and University Archives, University of Massachusetts,
    Amherst, MA
    Raymond Luc Levasseur Papers

Digital Archives and Databases

American Presidency Project. http://www.presidency.ucsb.edu/
C-SPAN Digital Video Library. http://www.c-span.org/about/videoLibrary/
Digital National Security Archive. http://nsarchive.chadwyck.com
Famous Trials, University of Missouri Kansas City School of Law. www.famous
    -trials.com
FBI NEWKILL documents. Free Jalil website. http://www.freejalil.com
    /newkilldocuments.html
FBI Vault. https://vault.fbi.gov
    Black September File
    COINTELPRO-Black Extremist Files
    COINTELPRO-New Left Files
    COINTELPRO-Puerto Rican Groups Files
    George Lester Jackson File
    Terrorist Photo Album File

Freedom Archives. http://freedomarchives.org/
   Black Liberation Collection
   COINTELPRO Collection
   Independent Collections
Gale Cengage Learning, Archives Unbound Digital Database
   The Black Liberation Army and the Program of Armed Struggle, 1970–1983
Gale Cengage Learning, Declassified Documents Reference System. http://gdc
         .gale.com/products/declassified-documents-reference-system/
Government Attic. https://www.governmentattic.org/
Internet Archive. archive.org
   Ernie Lazar FOIA Collection
      William C. Sullivan FBI Personnel File
Miller Center. millercenter.org
   Richard Nixon White House Recordings
National Security Archive. https://nsarchive.gwu.edu/
Nixontapes.org
Richard Nixon Presidential Library Online Archive. https://www.nixonlibrary
         .gov/
   Textual Materials
   White House Tapes Collections

Newspapers, Periodicals, and Digital News Sources

Baltimore Sun	*Nation*
Boston Globe	*New York Daily News*
Chicago Sun	*New York Times*
Chicago Tribune	*People*
Democracy NOW!	*Scanlan's*
Greeley (CO) *Daily Tribune*	*SF Gate*
Hartford Courant	*Truthout*
Kansas City Star	*Washington Post*
Lodi (CO) *News-Sentinel*	*WIN*
Milwaukee Journal Sentinel	

Freedom of Information Act Acquisitions

FBI, L. Patrick Gray, Director's File
FBI, Clarence R. Kelley, Director's File

Government Publications

National Advisory Committee on Criminal Justice Standards and Goals. *Report of the Task Force on Disorders and Terrorism.* Washington, DC: Government Printing Office, 1976.

Organization of American States. "Convention to Prevent and Punish the Acts of Terrorism Taking the Form of Crimes against Persons and Related Extortion That Are of International Significance." Washington, DC, February 2, 1971. http://www.oas.org/juridico/english/treaties/a-49.html.

U.S. Congress, House, Select Committee on Crime. *Reform of Our Correctional Systems: A Report by the Select Committee on Crime.* H.R. Rep. No. 93-329 (1973).

U.S. Congress, Senate, Committee on Appropriations. *Hearings on H.R. 19928: An Act Making Supplemental Appropriations for the Fiscal Year Ending June 30, 1971, and for Other Purposes.* 91st Cong., 2d Sess., November 21–27, 1970.

U.S. Congress, Senate, Committee on Government Operations, Permanent Subcommittee on Investigations. *Riots, Civil, and Criminal Disorders: Hearings before the Permanent Subcommittee on Investigations.* Part 25. 91st Cong., 2d Sess., July 31, August 4, 5, 6, 1970.

U.S. Congress, Senate, Committee on the Judiciary. *Hearings on the Nomination of Louis Patrick Gray III of Connecticut to Be the Director of the Federal Bureau of Investigation.* 93d Cong., 1st Sess., February 28, March 1, 6, 7, 8, 9, 12, 20, 21, 22, 1973.

——. *Nomination of Clarence M. Kelley, of Missouri, to Be Director of the Federal Bureau of Investigation.* 93d Cong., 1st Sess., June 19, 20, 25, 1973.

U.S. Congress, Senate, Committee on the Judiciary, Internal Security Subcommittee. *Hearings on Terroristic Activity.* Parts 1–9. 93d Cong., 2nd Sess.–95th Cong., 2d Sess., September 1974–September 1976.

U.S. Congress, Senate, Committee on the Judiciary, Subcommittee on Security and Terrorism. *Hearing on Attorney General's Guidelines for Domestic Security Investigations (Smith Guidelines).* 98th Cong., 1st Sess., March 25, 1983.

——. *Hearings on the Domestic Security Guidelines.* 97th Cong., 2d Sess., June 24, 25; August 11, 12, 1982.

U.S. Congress, Senate, Select Committee to Study Governmental Operations with Respect to Intelligence Activities. Final Report, Book II. *Intelligence Activities and the Rights of Americans.* 94th Cong., 2d Sess., 1976.

——. Final Report, Book III. *Supplementary Detailed Staff Reports on Intelligence Activities and the Rights of Americans.* 94th Cong., 2d Sess., 1976.

——. *Hearings on Intelligence Activities.* Vol. 2. *The Huston Plan.* 94th Cong., 1st Sess., 1975.

U.S. Congress, Senate, Subcommittee to Investigate the Administration of the Internal Security Act and Other Internal Security Laws. Annual Report. 94th Cong., 2d Sess., February 29, 1976.

——. *Hearings on Terroristic Activity.* Parts 1–9. 93d Cong., 2d Sess.–95th Cong., 2d Sess., September 1974–September 1976.

——. *Weather Underground: Report of the Subcommittee to Investigate the Administration of the Internal Security Act and Other Internal Security Laws.* 94th Cong., 1st Sess. Washington, DC: U.S. Government Printing Office, 1975.

U.S. Department of Justice. *United States Attorneys Bulletin* 17, no. 9. February 28, 1969.

U.S. Department of Justice, Federal Bureau of Investigation. Annual Report for Fiscal Year 1971. October 26, 1971.

———. "FBI's Ten Most Wanted Fugitives, 1950–2010." FBI: 2010. http://www.fbi.gov/stats-services/publications/ten-most-wanted-fugitives-60th-anniversary-1950-2010/ten-most-wanted-fugitives-60th-anniversary-1950-2010-pdf.

U.S. General Accounting Office. *FBI Domestic Intelligence Operations—Their Purpose and Scope: Issues That Need to Be Resolved: Report to the House Judiciary Committee by the Comptroller General of the United States.* Washington, DC, February 24, 1976.

U.S. State Department. "A Report to the National Security Council—NSC 68," April 12, 1950. U.S. State Department Office of the Historian website, https://history.state.gov/milestones/1945-1952/NSC68.

Interviews

Author Interview

Jack Ryan, former FBI special agent, telephone, June 2, 2014.

Nixon Presidential Library Online Archive, https://www.nixonlibrary.gov/

Thomas Charles Huston, by Timothy Naftali, April 30, 2008.

Society of Former Special Agents of the FBI, Inc., FBI Oral Histories, http://www.nleomf.org/museum/the-collection/oral-histories/

Baker, William M., by Michael N. Boone, February 23, 2006.

Butkiewicz, Ronald, by Brian R. Hollstein, March 23, 2009.

Dyson, William E., by Stanley A. Pimentel, January 15, 2008.

Hall, Monte A., by Donald "Max" Noel, May 1, 2008.

Kearney, John J., by Jack O'Flaherty, January 25, 2006.

Miller, Edward S., by Stanley A. Pimentel, May 8, 2008.

Memoirs, Document Collections, and Other Published Primary Sources

Ayers, Bill. *Fugitive Days: Memoirs of an Antiwar Activist.* 2nd ed. Boston: Beacon Press, 2009.

Botting, James. *Bullets, Bombs, and Fast Talk: Twenty-Five Years of FBI War Stories.* Lincoln, NE: Potomac Books, 2008.

Carmichael, Stokely. *Ready for Revolution: The Life and Struggles of Stokely Carmichael (Kwame Ture).* With Ekwueme Michael Thelwell. New York: Scribner, 2003.

Castiglia, Christopher. *Bound and Determined: Captivity, Culture-Crossing, and White Womanhood from Mary Rowlandson to Patty Hearst.* Chicago: University of Chicago Press, 1990.

Cleaver, Eldridge. *Soul on Ice.* 3rd ed. New York: Delta Trade Paperbacks, 1999.

Cox, Don. *Just Another Nigger: My Life in the Black Panther Party.* Berkeley: Heyday, 2019.

Davis, Angela. *Angela Davis: An Autobiography.* 3rd ed. New York: International Publishers, 1998.

Debray, Régis. *Strategy for Revolution: Essays on Latin America*. New York: Monthly Review Press, 1971.

——. *Revolution in the Revolution?* New York: Grove Press, 1967.

Dixon, Aaron. *My People Are Rising: Memoir of a Black Panther Party Captain*. Chicago: Haymarket Books, 2012.

Dohrn, Bernardine, Bill Ayers, and Jeff Jones, eds. *Sing a Battle Song: The Revolutionary Poetry, Statements, and Communiqués of the Weather Underground, 1970–1974*. New York: Seven Stories Press, 2006.

Dyson, William E. *Terrorism: An Investigator's Handbook*. 4th ed. Waltham, MA: Anderson Publishing, 2014.

Ehrlichman, John. *Witness to Power: The Nixon Years*. New York: Simon & Schuster, 1982.

Elliff, John T. *The Reform of FBI Intelligence Operations*. Princeton, NJ: Princeton University Press, 1979.

Ellsberg, Daniel. *Secrets: A Memoir of Vietnam and the Pentagon Papers*. New York: Penguin, 2002.

Federal Bureau of Investigation. *FBI File on Students for a Democratic Society and the Weather Underground Organization*. Wilmington, DE: Scholarly Resources, 1991. Microfilm.

Felt, W. Mark. *The FBI Pyramid from the Inside*. New York: Putnam, 1979.

Felt, W. Mark, and John O'Connor. *A G-Man's Life: The FBI, Being 'Deep Throat,' and the Struggle for Honor in Washington*. New York: Public Affairs, 2006.

Forman, James. *The Making of Black Revolutionaries*. New York: Macmillan, 1972.

Francis, Samuel T. "The Intelligence Community." In *Mandate for Leadership: Policy Management in a Conservative Administration*, edited by Charles L. Heatherly, 903–53. Washington, DC: Heritage Foundation, 1981.

Gilbert, David. *Love and Struggle: My Life in SDS, the Weather Underground, and Beyond*. Oakland, CA: PM Press, 2011.

Gore, Dayo F., and Bettina Aptheker, eds. *Free Angela Davis and All Political Prisoners! A Transnational Campaign for Liberation*. Alexandria, VA: Alexander Street Press, 2014. E-book.

Gosse, Van. *The Movements of the New Left, 1950–1975: A Brief History with Documents*. New York: Bedford/St. Martins, 2005.

Grathwohl, Larry. *Bringing Down America: An FBI Informer with the Weathermen*. As told to Frank Reagan. New Rochelle, NY: Arlington House Publishers, 1976.

Gray, L. Patrick, III. *In Nixon's Web: A Year in the Crosshairs of Watergate*. With Ed Gray. New York: Times Books, 2008.

Guevara, Ché. *Guerrilla Warfare*. Edited by Brian Loveman and Thomas M. Davies Jr. 3rd ed. Wilmington, DE: SR Books, 1997.

Haldeman, H. R. *The Haldeman Diaries: Inside the Nixon White House*. New York: G. P. Putnam's, 1994.

Hayden, Tom, and Students for a Democratic Society. "The Port Huron Statement of Students for a Democratic Society." June 15, 1962. H-Net. http://www.h-net.org/~hst306/documents/huron.html.

Hilliard, David. *This Side of Glory: The Autobiography of David Hilliard and the Story of the Black Panther Party.* Boston: Little, Brown, 1993.

Interfaith Prisoners of Conscience Project. *They Never Crushed His Spirit: A Tribute to Richard Williams.* Montreal: Kersplebedeb, 2006.

Jackson, George. *Blood in My Eye.* 2nd ed. Baltimore: Black Classic Press, 1990.

———. *Soledad Brother.* 2nd ed. Chicago: Lawrence Hill Books, 1994.

Joseph, Jamal. *Panther Baby: A Life of Rebellion and Reinvention.* Chapel Hill, NC: Algonquin Books, 2012.

Kelley, Clarence M., and James Kirkpatrick Davis. *Kelley: The Story of an FBI Director.* Kansas City, MS: Andrews, McMeel & Parker, 1987.

King, Martin Luther, Jr. "Why I Am Opposed to the War in Vietnam." Sermon at the Ebeneezer Baptist Church, Atlanta, Georgia, April 30, 1967. Real News Network. http://therealnews.com/t2/index.php?option=com_content&task=view&id=31&Itemid=74&jumival=4731.

kioni-sadiki, déqui, and Matt Meyers, eds. *Look for Me in the Whirlwind: From the Panther 21 to 21st Century Revolutions.* Oakland, CA: PM Press, 2017.

Lerner, Jonathan. *Swords in the Hands of Children: Reflections of an American Revolutionary.* New York: O/R Books, 2017.

Levasseur, Raymond Luc. "Trouble Coming Every Day." Unpublished memoir, 2015.

Linder, Douglas O., ed. Famous Trials online exhibit and database. University of Missouri - Kansas City School of Law. http://law2.umkc.edu/faculty/projects/ftrials.html.

Malcolm X. *Malcolm X Speaks: Selected Speeches and Statements.* Edited by George Breitman. New York: Grove Press, 1966.

Marighella, Carlos. "Minimanual of the Urban Guerrilla." In *Terror and Urban Guerrillas: A Study of Tactics and Documents*, edited by Jay Mallin, 70–115. Coral Gables: University of Florida Press, 1982.

Meyer, Matt, ed. *Let Freedom Ring: A Collection of Documents from the Movements to Free U.S. Political Prisoners.* Oakland, CA: PM Press, 2008.

New America. "Terrorism in America after 9/11." Accessed February 15, 2021, https://www.newamerica.org/in-depth/terrorism-in-america/what-threat-united-states-today/.

Newton, Huey. "On the Correct Handling of a Revolution." 1967. Verso, October 15, 2016. https://www.versobooks.com/blogs/2865-the-correct-handling-of-a-revolution-by-huey-p-newton.

Nixon, Richard. "Failure of Leadership." 1968 television election ad. YouTube video. 4:03. https://www.youtube.com/watch?v=Te_a2RxqXIo.

———. Inaugural address, January 20, 1969. Miller Center website. https://millercenter.org/the-presidency/presidential-speeches/january-20-1969-first-inaugural-address.

———. *RN: The Memoirs of Richard Nixon.* 2nd ed. New York: Simon & Schuster, 1990.

Oglesby, Carl. *Ravens in the Storm: A Personal History of the 1960s Anti-war Movement.* New York: Simon & Schuster, 2008.

Payne, Cril. *Deep Cover: An FBI Agent Infiltrates the Radical Underground.* New York: Newsweek Books, 1979.

Pearsall, Robert Brainard. *The Symbionese Liberation Army: Documents and Communications.* Amsterdam: Rodopi, 1974.

Plamondon, Lawrence Robert "Pun," and Anne Larabee. "Interview with Lawrence Robert 'Pun' Plamondon." *Journal for the Study of Radicalism* 1, no. 1 (2007): 117.

Rudd, Mark. *Underground: My Life with SDS and the Weathermen.* New York: Harper Collins, 2009.

Seale, Bobby. *Seize the Time: The Story of the Black Panther Party and Huey P. Newton.* New York: Random House, 1970.

Shakur, Assata. *Assata: An Autobiography.* 2nd ed. Chicago: Lawrence Hill Books, 2001.

Shih, Bryan, and Yohuru Williams, eds. *The Black Panthers: Portraits from an Unfinished Revolution.* New York: Nation Books, 2016.

Stern, Susan. *With the Weathermen: The Personal Journal of a Revolutionary Woman.* New York: Doubleday, 1975.

Sullivan, William C. *The Bureau: My Thirty Years in Hoover's FBI.* With Bill Brown. New York: W. W. Norton, 1979.

Swearingen, M. Wesley. *FBI Secrets: An Agent's Exposé.* Boston: South End Press, 1995.

Trimbach, Joseph H., and John M. Trimbach. *American Indian Mafia: An FBI Agent's True Story about Wounded Knee, Leonard Peltier, and the American Indian Movement.* Denver, CO: Outskirts Press, 2007.

Wilkerson, Cathy. *Flying Close to the Sun: My Life and Times as a Weatherman.* New York: Seven Stories Press, 2007.

Williams, Evelyn A. *Inadmissible Evidence: The Story of the African-American Trial Lawyer who Defended the Black Liberation Army.* 2nd ed. Lincoln, NE: iUniverse .com, 2000.

Secondary Source Books, Articles, and Dissertations

Aaronson, Trevor. *The Terror Factory: Inside the FBI's Manufactured War on Terrorism.* New York: Ig Publishing, 2013.

Alexander, Michelle. *The New Jim Crow: Mass Incarceration in the Age of Colorblindness.* New York: New Press, 2010.

Alkebulan, Paul. *Survival Pending Revolution: The History of the Black Panther Party.* Tuscaloosa: University of Alabama Press, 2007.

Appy, Christian G. *American Reckoning: The Vietnam War and Our American Identity.* New York: Viking, 2015.

Austin, Curtis. *Up against the Wall: Violence and the Making and Unmaking of the Black Panther Party.* Fayetteville: University of Arkansas Press, 2006.

Aya, Rod. *Rethinking Revolutions and Collective Violence: Studies on Concept, Theory, and Method.* Amsterdam: Het Spinhuis, 1990.

Bacevich, Andrew J. *America's War for the Greater Middle East: A Military History.* New York: Random House, 2016.

———, ed. *The Long War: A New History of U.S. National Security Policy since World War II.* New York: Columbia University Press, 2007.

Bailey, Beth, and David Farber, eds. *America in the 1970s.* Lawrence: University Press of Kansas, 2004.

Balto, Simon. *Occupied Territory: Policing Black Chicago from Red Summer to Black Power.* Chapel Hill: University of North Carolina Press, 2019.

Barak-Erez, Daphne. "Israeli Anti-terrorism Law: Past, Present, and Future." In *Global Anti-terrorism Law and Policy*, 2nd ed., edited by Victor V. Ramraj, Michael Hor, Kent Roach, and George Williams, 597–620. Cambridge: Cambridge University Press, 2012.

Bass, Paul, and Douglas W. Rae. *Murder in the Model City: The Black Panthers, Yale, and the Redemption of a Killer.* New York: Basic Books, 2006.

Bates, Tom. *RADS.* New York: HarperCollins, 1992.

Batvinis, Raymond J. *Hoover's Secret War against Axis Spies: FBI Counterespionage during World War II.* Lawrence: University Press of Kansas, 2014.

———. *The Origins of FBI Counterintelligence.* Lawrence: University Press of Kansas, 2007.

Belew, Kathleen. *Bring the War Home: The White Power Movement and Paramilitary America.* Cambridge, MA: Harvard University Press, 2018.

Berger, Dan. *Captive Nation: Prison Organizing in the Civil Rights Era.* Chapel Hill: University of North Carolina Press, 2014.

———, ed. *The Hidden 1970s: Histories of Radicalism.* New Brunswick, NJ: Rutgers University Press, 2010.

———. *Outlaws of America: The Weather Underground and the Politics of Solidarity.* Oakland, CA: AK Press, 2006.

Bernstein, Carl, and Bob Woodward. *All the President's Men.* New York: Simon & Schuster, 1974.

Bernstein, Lee. *America Is the Prison: Arts and Politics in Prisons in the 1970s.* Chapel Hill: University of North Carolina Press, 2010.

Bingham, Clara. *Witness to the Revolution: Radicals, Resisters, Vets, Hippies, and the Year America Lost Its Mind and Found Its Soul.* New York: Random House, 2016.

Blackstock, Nelson. *COINTELPRO: The FBI's Secret War on Political Freedom.* 2nd ed. New York: Pathfinder Press, 1988.

Blakely, Ruth. "Constructing State Terrorism." In *Constructions of Terrorism: An Interdisciplinary Approach to Research and Policy*, edited by Michael Stohl, Richard Burchill, and Scott Englund, 53–66. Berkeley: University of California Press, 2017.

Bloom, Joshua, and Waldo E. Martin Jr. *Black against Empire: The History and Politics of the Black Panther Party.* Berkeley: University of California Press, 2013.

Blumenau, Bernhard. *The United Nations and Terrorism: Germany, Multilateralism, and Antiterrorism Efforts in the 1970s.* Basingtoke: Palgrave Macmillan, 2014.

Brick, Howard, and Gregory Parker, eds. *A New Insurgency: The "Port Huron Statement" and Its Times.* Ann Arbor: Michigan Publishing, 2015.

Brown, Scot. *Fighting for US: Maulana Karenga, the US Organization, and Black Cultural Nationalism*. New York: New York University Press, 2003.

Burrough, Bryan. *Days of Rage: America's Radical Underground, the FBI, and the Forgotten Age of Revolutionary Violence*. New York: Penguin Press, 2015.

Burton-Rose, Daniel. "Amazon Underground? Female Antiwar Fugitives and Fissures of Solidarity in the Women's Community." Unpublished paper, May 2009.

———. *Guerrilla USA: The George Jackson Brigade and the Anticapitalist Underground of the 1970s*. Berkeley: University of California Press, 2010.

Carson, Clayborne. *In Struggle: SNCC and the Black Awakening of the 1960s*. 2nd ed. Cambridge, MA: Harvard University Press, 1995.

Cecil, Matthew. *Branding Hoover's FBI: How the Boss's PR Men Sold the Bureau to America*. Lawrence: University Press of Kansas, 2016.

———. *Hoover's FBI and the Fourth Estate: The Campaign to Control the Press and the Bureau's Image*. Lawrence: University of Kansas Press, 2014.

Chalmers, David Mark. *Backfire: How the Ku Klux Klan Helped the Civil Rights Movement*. Lanham, MD: Rowman and Littlefield, 2005.

Chamberlin, Paul Thomas. *The Global Offensive: The United States, the Palestine Liberation Organization, and the Making of the Post-Cold War Order*. New York: Oxford University Press, 2012.

Chard, Daniel S. "Rallying for Repression: Police Terror, Law-and-Order Politics, and the Decline of Maine's Prisoners' Rights Movement." *The Sixties: A Journal of History Politics and Culture* 5, no. 1 (2012): 47–73.

———. Review of *Bad Moon Rising: How the Weather Underground Beat the FBI and Lost the Revolution*, by Arthur M. Eckstein. *Journal of American History* 104, no. 3 (2017): 817–18.

———. "*SCAR'd TIMES*: Maine's Prisoners' Rights Movement, 1971–1976." MA thesis, University of Massachusetts Amherst, 2011.

———. "Teaching with the FBI's Science for the People File." *Radical History Review* 127 (2017): 180–85.

———. "When the FBI Targeted the Poor Peoples' Campaign." *Jacobin*, August 12, 2019. https://jacobinmag.com/2019/08/mlk-martin-luther-king-fbi-disclosures-david-garrow.

Charles, Doug. *Hoover's War on Gays: Exposing the FBI's 'Sex Deviates' Program*. Lawrence: University Press of Kansas, 2015.

———. *J. Edgar Hoover and the Anti-interventionists: FBI Political Surveillance and the Rise of the Domestic Security State, 1939–1945*. Columbus: Ohio State University Press, 2007.

Charles, Doug, ed. *The Federal Bureau of Investigation: Histories, Powers, and Controversies of the FBI*. 2 vols. Forthcoming, Santa Barbara: ABC/CLIO.

Churchill, Lindsey. *Becoming the Tupamaros: Solidarity and Transnational Revolutionaries in Uruguay and the United States*. Nashville, TN: Vanderbilt University Press, 2014.

Churchill, Ward, and Jim Vander Wall. *Agents of Repression: The FBI's Secret Wars against the Black Panther Party and the American Indian Movement*. 3rd ed. Cambridge, MA: South End Press, 2002.

——. *The COINTELPRO Papers: Documents from the FBI's Secret War on Dissent.* 2nd ed. Boston: South End Press, 2002.

Clegg, John, and Adaner Usmani. "The Economic Origins of Mass Incarceration." *Catalyst* 3, no. 3 (2019): 9–53.

Cobb, Charles E., Jr. *This Nonviolent Stuff'll Get You Killed: How Guns Made the Civil Rights Movement Possible.* Durham, NC: Duke University Press, 2015.

Cohen, Jonathan. "1967 Terrorism Act, No. 83 of 1967." South African History Online, July 6, 2012. http://www.sahistory.org.za/topic/1967-terrorism-act-no-83-1967.

Crespino, Joe. *Strom Thurmond's America.* New York: Hill and Wang, 2012.

Cummins, Eric. *The Rise and Fall of California's Radical Prison Movement.* Stanford, CA: Stanford University Press, 1994.

Cunningham, David. *Klansville, U.S.A.: The Rise and Fall of the Civil Rights-Era Ku Klux Klan.* New York: Oxford University Press, 2013.

——. *There's Something Happening Here: The New Left, the Klan, and FBI Counterintelligence.* Berkeley: University of California Press, 2004.

Davis, James Kirkpatrick. *Assault on the Left: The FBI and the Sixties Antiwar Movement.* Westport, CT: Praeger, 1997.

——. *Spying on America: The FBI's Domestic Counterintelligence Program.* New York: Praeger, 1992.

della Porta, Donna. *Clandestine Political Violence.* New York: Cambridge University Press, 2013.

——. *Social Movements, Political Violence, and the State: A Comparative Analysis of Italy and Germany.* New York: Cambridge University Press, 1995.

Donner, Frank J. *Age of Surveillance: The Aims and Methods of America's Political Intelligence System.* New York: Alfred A. Knopf, 1980.

——. *Protectors of Privilege: Red Squads and Police Repression in Urban America.* Berkeley: University of California Press, 1990.

Eckstein, Aurthur M. *Bad Moon Rising: How the Weather Underground Beat the FBI and Lost the Revolution.* New Haven: Yale University Press, 2016.

Emerson, Gloria. *Winners & Losers: Battles, Retreats, Gains, Losses and Ruins from the Vietnam War.* 5th ed. New York: Harcourt Brace Jovanovich, 1976.

English, T. J. *The Savage City: Race, Murder, and a Generation on the Edge.* New York: William Morrow, 2011.

Faraj, Gaidi. "Unearthing the Underground: A Study of Radical Activism in the Black Panther Party and Black Liberation Army." PhD diss., University of California Berkeley, 2007.

Farber, David. *Chicago '68.* Chicago: University of Chicago Press, 1997.

——. *Taken Hostage: The Iran Hostage Crisis and America's First Encounter with Radical Islam.* Princeton, NJ: Princeton University Press, 2005.

Farrell, John A. "When a Candidate Conspired with a Foreign Power to Win an Election." *Politico*, August 6, 2017. https://www.politico.com/magazine/story/2017/08/06/nixon-vietnam-candidate-conspired-with-foreign-power-win-election-215461.

Felker-Kantor, Max. *Policing Los Angeles: Race, Resistance, and the Rise of the LAPD*. Chapel Hill: University of North Carolina Press, 2018.

Fellman, Michael. *In the Name of God and Country: Reconsidering Terrorism in American History*. New Haven, CT: Yale University Press, 2010.

Fernández, Johanna. *The Young Lords: A Radical History*. Chapel Hill: University of North Carolina Press, 2020.

Flamm, Michael. *Law and Order: Street Crime, Civil Unrest, and the Crisis of Liberalism in the 1960s*. New York: Columbia University Press, 2005.

Francis, Samuel T. "The Intelligence Community." In *Mandate for Leadership: Policy Management in a Conservative Administration*, edited by Charles L. Heatherly, 903–53. Washington, DC: Heritage Foundation, 1981.

Fronc, Jennifer. *New York Undercover: Private Surveillance in the Progressive Era*. Chicago: University of Chicago Press, 2009.

Gage, Beverly. *The Day Wall Street Exploded: A Story of America in Its First Age of Terror*. New York: Oxford University Press, 2009.

———. "Deep Throat, Watergate, and the Bureaucratic Politics of the FBI." *Journal of Policy History* 24, no. 2 (2012): 157–83.

———. "Terrorism and the American Experience: A State of the Field." *Journal of American History* 98, no. 2 (June 2011): 73–94.

———. "What an Uncensored Letter to M.L.K. Reveals." *New York Times Magazine*, November 11, 2014.

Garrow, David. "The Troubling Legacy of Martin Luther King." *Standpoint*, May 30, 2019: 30–37.

Genovese, Michael A. *The Watergate Crisis*. Westport, CT: Greenwood Press, 1989.

Gentry, Curt. *J. Edgar Hoover: The Man and the Secrets*. New York: W. W. Norton, 1991.

Georgakas, Dan. "Armed Struggle—1960s and 1970s." In *Encyclopedia of the American Left*, edited by Mary Jo Buhle, Paul Buhle, and Dan Goergakas, 57–63. New York: Oxford University Press, 1998.

German, Mike. *Disrupt, Discredit, and Divide: How the New FBI Damages Democracy*. New York: New Press, 2019.

Gibbons, Chip. *Still Spying on Dissent: The Enduring Problem of FBI First Amendment Abuse*. Washington, DC: Defending Rights and Dissent, 2019.

Gilmore, Ruth Wilson. *Golden Gulag: Prisons, Surplus, Crisis, and Opposition in Globalizing California*. Berkeley: University of California Press, 2007.

Gitlin, Todd. *The Sixties: Days of Hope and Rage*. 2nd ed. New York: Bantham Books, 1993.

Goldstein, Robert Justin. *Political Repression in Modern America: From 1870 to the Present*. Boston: G. K. Hall, 1978.

Grace, Thomas M. *Kent State: Death and Dissent in the Long Sixties*. Amherst: University of Massachusetts Press, 2016.

Graebner, William. *Patty's Got a Gun: Patricia Hearst in 1970s America*. Chicago: University of Chicago Press, 2008.

Graham, Hugh Davis, and Ted Robert Gurr, eds. *Violence in America: Historical and Comparative Perspectives: A Report to the National Commission on the Causes and Prevention of Violence*. New York: New American Library, 1969.

Green, James. *Death in the Haymarket: A Story of Chicago, the First Labor Movement, and the Bombing That Divided Gilded Age America*. New York: Random House, 2006.

Greenberg, Ivan. *The Dangers of Dissent: The FBI and Civil Liberties since 1965*. Lanham, MD: Lexington Books, 2010.

Greenberg, Karen J. *Rogue Justice: The Making of the Security State*. New York: Crown Publishing, 2016.

Haas, Jeffrey. *The Assassination of Fred Hampton: How the FBI and the Chicago Police Murdered a Black Panther*. Chicago: Lawrence Hill Books, 2010.

Haines, Gerald K., and David A. Langbart. *Unlocking the Files of the FBI: A Guide to Its Records and Classification System*. Wilmington, DE: Scholarly Resources, 1993.

Hall, Simon. *Peace and Freedom: The Civil Rights and Antiwar Movements in the 1960s*. Philadelphia: University of Pennsylvania Press, 2005.

Herman, Edward S., and Gerry O'Sullivan. *The "Terrorism" Industry: The Experts and Institutions That Shape Our View of Terror*. New York: Pantheon Books, 1989.

Hernandez, Kelly Lytle, Khalil Gibran Muhammad, and Heather Ann Thompson, eds. "Historians and the Carceral State." Special issue, *Journal of American History* 102, no. 1 (2015).

Hewitt, Steve. *The British War on Terror: Terrorism and Counterterrorism on the Home Front since 9/11*. London: Bloomsbury Publishing, 2007.

———. "Cold War Counter-Terrorism: The Evolution of International Counter-Terrorism in the RCMP Security Service, 1972–1984." *Intelligence and National Security* 33, no. 1 (2018): 1–17.

Hinton, Elizabeth. *From the War on Poverty to the War on Crime: The Making of Mass Incarceration in America*. Cambridge, MA: Harvard University Press, 2016.

Hinton, Elizabeth, and DeAnza Cook. "The Mass Criminalization of Black Americans: A Historical Overview." *Annual Review of Criminology* 4, no. 1 (2020): 2.1–2.26.

Hoecker, Robin E. "The Black and White behind the Blue and White: A History of Black Student Protest at Penn State." Bachelor's thesis, Pennsylvania State University, 2002.

Hoffman, Bruce. *Inside Terrorism*. New York: Columbia University Press, 2006.

Holland, Max. *Leak: Why Mark Felt Became Deep Throat*. Lawrence: University Press of Kansas, 2012.

Hughes, Ken. *Chasing Shadows: The Nixon Tapes, the Chennault Affair, and the Origins of Watergate*. Charlottesville: University of Virginia Press, 2014.

Human Rights Watch. "U.S.: Terrorism Prosecutions Often an Illusion: Investigations, Trials of American Muslims Rife with Abuse." July 21, 2014. https://www.hrw.org/news/2014/07/21/us-terrorism-prosecutions-often-illusion.

Hunt, Andrew E. *The Turning: A History of Vietnam Veterans against the War.* New York: New York University Press, 1999.

Husain, Atiya. "Deracialization, Dissent, and Terrorism in the FBI's Most Wanted Program." *Sociology of Race and Ethnicity*, June 2, 2020.

———. "Terror and Abolition." *Boston Review*, June 11, 2020. https://bostonreview .net/race/atiya-husain-terror-and-abolition.

Isserman, Maurice, and Michael Kazin. *America Divided: The Civil War of the 1960s.* 4th ed. New York: Oxford University Press, 2012.

Jackson, Justin. "Kissinger's Kidnapper: Eqbal Ahmad, the U.S. New Left, and the Transnational Romance of Revolutionary War." *Journal for the Study of Radicalism* 4, no. 1 (2010): 75–119.

Jackson, Richard. "Knowledge, Power and Politics in the Study of Political Terrorism." In *Critical Terrorism Studies: A New Research Agenda*, edited by Richard Jackson, Marie Breen Smyth, and Jeroen Gunning, 49–65. New York: Routledge, 2009.

Jackson, Richard, Marie Breen Smyth, and Jeroen Gunning. "Critical Terrorism Studies: Framing a New Research Agenda." In *Critical Terrorism Studies: A New Research Agenda*, edited by Richard Jackson, Marie Breen Smyth, and Jeroen Gunning, 216–36. New York: Routledge, 2009.

Jacobs, Ron. *The Way the Wind Blew: A History of the Weather Underground.* New York: Verso, 1997.

Jeffreys-Jones, Rhodri. *The FBI: A History.* New Haven, CT: Yale University Press, 2007.

Jensen, Richard Bach. *The Battle against Anarchist Terrorism: An International History, 1878–1934.* New York: Cambridge University Press, 2014.

———. "The United States, International Policing, and the War against Anarchist Terrorism." *Terrorism and Political Violence* 13, no. 1 (2001): 15–46.

Johnson, Cedric. "Panther Nostalgia as History." Review of *Black against Empire: The History and Politics of the Black Panther Party*, by Joshua Bloom and Waldo E. Martin Jr. *New Labor Forum* 23, no. 2 (2014): 112–15.

———. "The Panthers Can't Save Us Now." *Catalyst* 1, no. 1 (2017): 57–86.

———. "Who's Afraid of Left Populism?" *New Politics* 17, no. 2 (2019). https:// newpol.org/issue_post/whos-afraid-of-left-populism/.

Johnson, Chalmers. *Blowback: The Costs and Consequences of American Empire.* 2nd ed. New York: Henry Holt, 2004.

Johnson, Loch K. *America's Secret Power: The CIA in a Democratic Society.* New York: Oxford University Press, 1989.

———. *A Season of Inquiry Revisited: The Church Committee Confronts America's Spy Agencies.* Lawrence: University Press of Kansas, 2015.

Jones, Thai. *A Radical Line: From the Labor Movement to the Weather Underground: One Family's Century of Conscience.* New York: Free Press, 2004.

Katsiaficas, George. *The Imagination of the New Left: A Global Analysis of 1968.* Boston: Beacon Press, 1987.

Kempton, Murray. *The Briar Patch: The People of the State of New York v. Lumumba Shakur Et Al.* New York: E. P. Dutton, 1973.

Koncewicz, Michael. *They Said No to Nixon: Republicans Who Stood Up to the President's Abuses of Power*. Oakland: University of California Press, 2018.

Kornweibel, Theodore, Jr."*Seeing Red*": *Federal Campaigns against Black Militancy*. Bloomington: Indiana University Press, 1998.

Kumamoto, Robert. *The Historical Origins of Terrorism in America*. London: Routledge, 2014.

Kutler, Stanley. *The Wars of Watergate: The Last Crisis of Richard Nixon*. New York: Alfred A. Knopf, 1990.

Kutler, Stanley, and Richard Nixon. *Abuse of Power: The New Nixon Tapes*. New York: Free Press, 1997.

Laqueur, Walter. *A History of Terrorism*. 7th ed. New Brunswick, NJ: Transaction Publishers, 2012.

Larabee, Ann. "Why Historians Should Use Caution When Using the Word 'Terrorism.'" *Journal of American History* 98, no. 1 (2011): 106–10.

———. *The Wrong Hands: Popular Weapons Manuals and Their Historic Challenges to a Democratic Society*. New York: Oxford University Press, 2015.

Law, Randall D., ed. *The Routledge History of Terrorism*. New York: Routledge, 2015.

———. *Terrorism: A History*. Malden, MA: Polity Press, 2009.

Lazerow, Jama. "'A Rebel All His Life': The Unexpected Story of Frank 'Parky' Grace." In *In Search of the Black Panther Party: New Perspectives on a Revolutionary Movement*, edited by Jama Lazerow and Yohuru Williams, 104–57. Durham, NC: Duke University Press, 2006.

Leonard, Aaron, and Conor A. Gallagher. *Heavy Radicals: The FBI's Secret War on America's Maoists*. London: Zero Books, 2015.

———. *A Threat of First Magnitude: FBI Counterintelligence and Infiltration from the Communist Party to the Revolutionary Union, 1962–1974*. London: Repeater Books, 2017.

Lindahl, Sondre. "A CTS Model of Counterterrorism." *Critical Studies on Terrorism* 10, no. 2 (2017): 1–19.

Mamdani, Mahmood. *Good Muslim, Bad Muslim: America, the Cold War, and the Roots of Terror*. New York: Pantheon, 2005.

Mann, Eric. *Comrade George: An Investigation into the Life, Political Thought, and Assassination of George Jackson*. New York: Harper & Row, 1974.

Marable, Manning. *Malcolm X: A Life of Reinvention*. New York: Viking, 2011.

Marx, Karl. "The Eighteenth Brumaire of Louis Bonaparte." In *The Marx-Engels Reader*, 2nd ed., edited by Robert C. Tucker, 594–617. New York: W. W. Norton, 1978.

Mayer, Jane. *The Dark Side: The Inside Story of How the War on Terrorism Turned into a War on American Ideals*. New York: Anchor Books, 2009.

McAlister, Melani. *Epic Encounters: Culture, Media, and U.S. Interests in the Middle East since 1945*. Berkeley: University of California Press, 2005.

McCoy, Alfred. *The Politics of Heroin: CIA Complicity in the Global Drug Trade*. 2nd ed. Chicago: Lawrence Hill Books, 2003.

McLellon, Vin, and Paul Avery. *The Voices of Guns*. New York: Penguin, 1977.

Medsger, Betty. *The Burglary: The Discovery of J. Edgar Hoover's Secret FBI.* New York: Alfred A. Knopf, 2014.

Messer-Kruse, Timothy. *The Trial of the Haymarket Anarchists: Terrorism and Justice in the Gilded Age.* New York: Palgrave Macmillan, 2011.

Meyerowitz, Joanne, ed. *History and September 11th.* Philadelphia: Temple University Press, 2003.

Miller, Martin A. *The Foundations of Modern Terrorism: State, Society, and the Dynamics of Political Violence.* Cambridge: Cambridge University Press, 2013.

Miller, Russell A., ed. *U.S. National Security, Intelligence, and Democracy: From the Church Committee to the War on Terror.* New York: Routledge, 2008.

Mueller, John, and Mark G. Stewart. *Chasing Ghosts: The Policing of Terrorism.* New York: Oxford University Press, 2016.

Mulloy, D. J. "Is There a 'Field'? And If There Isn't, Should We Be Worried about It?" *Journal of American History* 98, no. 1 (2011): 111–14.

Mumford, Kevin. *Newark: A History of Race, Riots, and Rights in America.* New York: New York University Press, 2007.

Muntaqim, Jalil. *On the Black Liberation Army.* Montreal: Arm the Spirit / Solidarity, 2002.

Murch, Donna Jean. *Living for the City: Migration, Education, and the Rise of the Black Panther Party in Oakland, California.* Chapel Hill: University of North Carolina Press, 2010.

Naftali, Timothy. *Blind Spot: The Secret History of American Counterterrorism.* New York: Basic Books, 2005.

National Advisory Commission on Civil Disorders. *The Kerner Report: The 1968 Report of the National Commission on Civil Disorders.* 2nd ed. New York: Pantheon, 1988.

Nelson, Alonrda. *Body and Soul: The Black Panther Party and the Fight against Medical Discrimination.* Minneapolis: University of Minnesota Press, 2013.

Newton, Huey P. "War against the Panthers: A Study of Repression in America." PhD diss., University of California Santa Cruz, 1980.

Olmsted, Kathryn. *Challenging the Secret Government: The Post-Watergate Investigations of the CIA and FBI.* Chapel Hill: University of North Carolina Press, 1996.

O'Reilly, Kenneth. *Black Americans: The FBI Files.* Edited by David Gallen. New York: Carroll & Graf, 1994.

——. *"Racial Matters": The FBI's File on Black America, 1960–1972.* New York: Free Press, 1989.

Payne, Les, and Tim Findley. *The Life and Death of the SLA: A True Story of Revolutionary Terror.* New York: Ballantine Books, 1976.

Payne, Roz. "WACing Off: Gossip, Sex, Race, and Politics in the World of FBI Special Case Agent William A. Cohendet." In *In Search of the Black Panther Party: New Perspectives on a Revolutionary Movement*, edited by Jama Lazerow and Yohuru Williams, 158–80. Durham, NC: Duke University Press, 2006.

Pearson, Hugh. *Shadow of the Panther: Huey Newton and the Price of Black Power in America.* Cambridge, MA: Perseus, 1995.

Pennock, Pamela E. *The Rise of the Arab American Left: Activists, Allies, and Their Fight against Imperialism and Racism, 1960s–1980s*. Chapel Hill: University of North Carolina Press, 2017.

Perlstein, Rick. *Nixonland: The Rise of a President and the Fracturing of America*. New York: Scribner, 2008.

Pliley, Jessica. *Policing Sexuality: The Mann Act and the Making of the FBI*. Cambridge, MA: Harvard University Press, 2014.

Poveda, Tony. *The FBI in Transition: Lawlessness and Reform*. Pacific Grove, CA: Brooks/Cole Publishing, 1990.

Powers, Richard Gid. *Broken: The Troubled Past and Uncertain Future of the FBI*. New York: Free Press, 2004.

——. *Secrecy and Power: The Life of J. Edgar Hoover*. New York: Free Press, 1987.

Prados, John. *The Family Jewels: The CIA, Secrecy, and Presidential Power*. Austin: University of Texas Press, 2013.

Prashad, Vijay. *The Darker Nations: A Peoples History of the Third World*. New York: New Press, 2007.

Priest, Dana, and William M. Arkin. *Top Secret America: The Rise of the New Security State*. New York: Little, Brown, 2011.

Rafael, Sam. "In the Service of Power: Terrorism Studies and U.S. Intervention in the Global South." In *Critical Terrorism Studies: A New Research Agenda*, edited by Richard Jackson, Marie Breen Smyth, and Jeroen Gunning, 34–48. New York: Routledge, 2009.

Rapoport, David C. "The Four Waves of Modern Terrorism." In *Attacking Terrorism: Elements of a Grand Strategy*, edited by Audrey Kurth Cronin and James M. Ludes, 46–73. Washington, DC: Georgetown University Press, 2004.

Reverby, Susan. *Co-conspirator for Justice: The Revolutionary Life of Dr. Alan Berkman*. Chapel Hill: University of North Carolina Press, 2020.

Rhodes, Jane. *Framing the Black Panthers: The Spectacular Rise of a Black Power Icon*. New York: New Press, 2007.

Rosen, Ruth. *The World Split Open: How the Modern Women's Movement Changed America*. New York: Penguin, 2000.

Rosenau, William. "'Our Backs Are against the Wall': The Black Liberation Army and Domestic Terrorism in 1970s America." *Studies in Conflict & Terrorism* 36, no. 2 (2013): 176–92.

Rosenfeld, Seth. *Subversives: The FBI's War on Student Radicals and Reagan's Rise to Power*. New York: Picador, 2013.

Sale, Kirkpatrick. *SDS*. New York: Random House, 1973.

Scahill, Jeremy. *Dirty Wars: The World Is a Battlefield*. New York: Nation Books, 2013.

Schaller, Michael. *Right Turn: American Life in the Reagan-Bush Era, 1980–1992*. New York: Oxford University Press, 2007.

Schmalzer, Sigrid, Daniel S. Chard, and Alyssa Botelho, eds. *Science for the People: Documents from America's Movement of Radical Scientists*. Amherst: University of Massachusetts Press, 2018.

Schmidt, Regin. *Red Scare: FBI and the Origins of Anticommunism in the United States*. Copenhagen: Museum Tusculanum Press, 2000.

Schrader, Stuart. *Badges without Borders: How Global Counterinsurgency Transformed American Policing.* Oakland: University of California Press, 2019.

Schrecker, Ellen. *Many Are the Crimes: McCarthyism in America.* New York: Little, Brown, 1998.

Seligman, Amanda I. "'But Burn—No': The Rest of the Crowd in Three Civil Disorders in 1960s Chicago." *Journal of Urban History* 37, no. 2 (2011): 230–55.

Smith, Paul Chaat, and Robert Allen Warrior. *Like a Hurricane: The Indian Movement from Alcatraz to Wounded Knee.* New York: New Press, 1999.

Spencer, Robyn C. *The Revolution Has Come: Black Power, Gender, and the Black Panther Party in Oakland.* Durham, NC: Duke University Press, 2016.

Stampnitzky, Lisa. "Can Terrorism Be Defined?" In *Constructions of Terrorism: An Interdisciplinary Approach to Research and Policy,* edited by Michael Stohl, Richard Burchill, and Scott Englund, 11–20. Berkeley: University of California Press, 2017.

———. *Disciplining Terror: How the Experts Invented "Terrorism."* New York: Cambridge University Press, 2013.

Stone, Geoffrey R. *Perilous Times: Free Speech in Wartime from the Sedition Act of 1798 to the War on Terrorism.* New York: W. W. Norton, 2004.

Storrs, Landon R.Y. *The Second Red Scare and the Unmaking of the New Deal Left.* Princeton, NJ: Princeton University Press, 2013.

Street, Joe. "The Historiography of the Black Panther Party." *Journal of American Studies* 44, no. 2 (2010): 351–75.

Summers, Anthony. *Official and Confidential: The Secret Life of J. Edgar Hoover.* New York: G. P. Putnam's Sons, 1993.

Suri, Jeremi. *Power and Protest: Global Revolution and the Rise of Détente.* 2nd ed. Cambridge, MA: Harvard University Press, 2005.

Tanenbaum, Robert, and Philip Rosenberg. *Badge of the Assassin.* New York: E. P. Dutton, 1979.

Tayler, G. Flint, and Ben H. Elson. "The Assassination of Fred Hampton: 40 Years Later." *Police Misconduct and Civil Rights Law Report* 9, no. 12 (November/December 2009).

Thelwell, Ekwueme Michael. "H. Rap Brown / Jamil Al-Amin: A Profoundly American Story." Foreword to *Die Nigger Die! A Political Autobiography,* by H. Rap Brown (Jamil Abdullah Al-Amin), 1–18. 2nd ed. Chicago: Lawrence Hill, 2002.

———. Introduction to *Rage,* by Gilbert Moore. 2nd ed. New York: Carroll and Graf, 1993.

———. "1968: A Score-Settling, Ass-Kicking, Head-Whipping, Dues-Taking, Hypocrisy-Exposing, Innocence-Destroying, Delusion-Ending Year." *VOICE Magazine,* March 1988.

Theoharis, Athan G. *The FBI and American Democracy: A Brief Critical History.* Lawrence: University Press of Kansas, 2004.

———. *Spying on Americans: Political Surveillance from Hoover to the Huston Plan.* Philadelphia: Temple University Press, 1978.

Theoharis, Athan, and John Stuart Cox. *The Boss: J. Edgar Hoover and the Great American Inquisition.* Philadelphia: Temple University Press, 1988.

Thompson, Heather Ann. *Blood in the Water: The Attica Uprising of 1971 and Its Legacy.* New York: Pantheon, 2016

———. *Whose Detroit? Politics, Labor, and Race in the Modern American City.* Ithaca, NY: Cornell University Press, 2001.

———. "Why Mass Incarceration Matters: Rethinking Crisis, Decline, and Transformation in Postwar American History." *Journal of American History* 97, no. 3 (2011): 703–34.

Thompson, Heather Ann, and Donna Murch. "Rethinking Urban America through the Lens of the Carceral State." *Journal of Urban History* 41, no. 5 (2015): 751–55.

Thorup, Mikkel. *An Intellectual History of Terror: War Violence, and the State.* New York: Routledge, 2010.

Toobin, Jeffrey. *American Heiress: The Wild Saga of the Kidnapping, Crimes, and Trial of Patty Hearst.* New York: Doubleday, 2016.

Townshend, Charles. "'Methods Which All Civilized Opinion Must Condemn': The League of Nations and International Action against Terrorism." In *An International History of Terrorism: Western and Non-Western Perspectives,* edited by Jussi M. Hanhimäki and Bernhard Blumenau, 34–50. London: Routledge, 2013.

Tyson, Timothy B. *Radio Free Dixie: Robert F. Williams and the Roots of Black Power.* Chapel Hill: University of North Carolina Press, 1999.

Umoja, Akinyele O. "The Black Liberation Army and the Radical Legacy of the Black Panther Party." In *Black Power in the Belly of the Beast,* edited by Judson L. Jeffries, 224–51. Chicago: University of Illinois Press, 2006.

———. *We Will Shoot Back: Armed Resistance in the Mississippi Freedom Movement.* New York: New York University Press, 2013.

Ungar, Sanford J. *FBI.* Boston: Little, Brown, 1976.

Varon, Jeremy. *Bringing the War Home: The Weather Underground, the Red Army Faction, and Revolutionary Violence in the Sixties and Seventies.* Berkeley: University of California Press, 2004.

———. "Dumbing Down the Underground." Review of *Days of Rage: America's Radical Underground, the FBI, and the Forgotten Age of Revolutionary Violence,* by Bryan Burrough. *Los Angeles Review of Books,* April 29, 2015. https://lareviewofbooks.org/article/dumbing-down-the-underground/#!.

———. "A History of Violence and the Myth of American Exceptionalism." *Journal of American History* 98, no. 1 (2011): 121–24.

Weiner, Tim. *Enemies: A History of the FBI.* New York: Random House, 2012.

Wickham-Crowley, Timothy B. *Guerrillas and Revolution in Latin America: A Comparative Study of Insurgents and Regimes since 1956.* Princeton, NJ: Princeton University Press, 1992.

Wills, David C. *The First War on Terrorism: Counter-Terrorism Policy during the Reagan Administration.* Lanham, MD: Rowman and Littlefield, 2003.

Winkler, Carol K. *In the Name of Terrorism: Presidents on Political Violence in the Post-World War II Era.* Albany: State University of New York Press, 2006.

Woodward, Bob. *The Secret Man: The Story of Watergate's Deep Throat.* New York: Simon & Schuster, 2005.

Yaqub, Salim. *Imperfect Strangers: Americans, Arabs, and U.S.-Middle East Relations in the 1970s.* Ithaca, NY: Cornell University Press, 2016.

Yee, Min S. *The Melancholy History of Soledad Prison.* New York: Harper's Magazine Press, 1973.

Zimroth, Peter L. *Perversions of Justice: The Prosecution and Acquittal of the Panther 21.* New York: Viking, 1972.

Zulaika, Joseba. *Terrorism: The Self-Fulfilling Prophecy.* Chicago: University of Chicago Press, 2009.

Zwerman, Gilda. "Domestic Counterterrorism: U.S. Government Responses to Political Violence on the Left in the Reagan Era." *Social Justice* 16, no. 2 (1989): 31–63.

———. "Mothering on the Lam: Politics, Gender Fantasies, and Maternal Thinking in Women Associated with Armed Clandestine Organizations in the United States." *Feminist Review* 47 (1994): 33–56.

Zwerman, Gilda, Patricia G. Steinhoff, and Donatella della Porta. "Disappearing Social Movements: Clandestinity in the Cycle of New Left Protest in the U.S., Japan, Germany, and Italy." *Mobilization: An International Journal* 5, no. 1 (2000): 85–104.

Video Recordings

1971. Directed by Johanna Hamilton. Maximum Pictures and Fork Films, 2014.

Berkeley in the Sixties. Directed by Mark Kitchell. California Newsreel, 1990.

COINTELPRO 101. Freedom Archives, 2010.

Eyes on the Prize, America's Civil Rights Movement, 1954–1985. Directed by Henry Hampton. Films Media Group, 1994.

Free Angela Davis and All Political Prisoners. Directed by Shola Lynch. Codeblack Films/Lionsgate, 2013.

One Day in September. Directed by Kevin McDonald. Passion Pictures, 1999.

Weather Underground. Directed by Sam Green and Bill Siegel. The Free History Project, 2002.

Why We Fight. Directed by Eugene Jarecki. Sony Pictures Classics, 2006

Index

Note: Page numbers in italics signify graphics.

Citizens' Commission to Investigate the FBI, 151–53

Clancy, Tom, 264

clandestinity, 4, 81, 104, 276n8. *See also* underground infrastructures

Clark, Judy, 242, 263, 320n54, 335n14

Clark, Mark, 91, 93–94

Clark, Ramsey, 27, 33, 126, 146

Clawson, Ken, 156

Cleaver, Eldridge, 16, 31, 41, 58, 59, 61, 65, 308n33; antipolice rhetoric of, 53, 172; background of, 50; as BLA spokesperson, 171–72, 173; and BPP split with Newton, 52, 59, 141, 170–71; expelled from Algeria, 243; flees to Algeria, 36, 52; as presidential candidate, 51–52; Reagan challenged to duel by, 50, 60; and SNCC, 56, 57

Cleaver, Kathleen, 52, 59, 63, 171–72

Clutchette, John, 120

Cohendet, William, 54

COINTELPRO–Black Nationalist-Hate Groups (COINTELPRO-BNHG), 8, 28–29, 30, 38–39, 40, 54–62, 63–64, 75–76, 296n127; BPP factionalism and split encouraged by, 39, 153, 170–71; breakfast for children program targeted by, 72–73, 297n161; establishment of, 28–29

COINTELPRO-CPUSA, 25–26, 286–87n51

COINTELPRO–New Left, 29–30, 153, 220; description of, 82–89

COINTELPRO Papers, The (Churchill and Vander Wall), 7, 279n26

COINTELPROs, 6–8, 26, 28–29, 252–53, 287n54; exposure of, 153, 220, 247; formal ending of, 153, 163, 253; launching of, 246

COINTELPRO–White Hate Groups, 28

Collins, Patrick, 207

Colson, Charles W., 206, 234

Columbia University student strike (1968), 29, 30, 53

Comey, James, 336n24

Committee to Reelect the President (CREEP), 201, 209, 229, 233

communes, 104–5, 107

Communism, 9

Communist Party USA (CPUSA): FBI targeting of, 25–26, 34, 138, 190, 286–87n51, 309n61; and New Left, 82–83

Congress for Racial Equality (CORE), 28–29, 47

conspiracy theories: and BPP, 63, 64, 65, 295–96n125; and Nixon, 188–89; and Weather Underground, 178

Convention on the Prevention and Punishment of Terrorism (1937), 10

Conway, Marshall "Eddie," 298n167

Cooke, Gordon, 51, 66–67

Coolidge, Calvin, 286n43

counterterrorism: vs. BLA, 2, 76, 175; in Bush administration, 2, 8, 102, 228, 259, 264, 265–66; CCCT as first agency devoted to, 12, 212, 216, 218–19, 225, 226, 236, 258, 259, 323n5; as concept, 258–59; FBI and development of, 8, 141, 183, 202–4, 211–13, 219–21, 232, 239–40, 260, 265; and Felt, 221, 232, 239–40; and Gray, 8, 211–12, 219–20, 227, 232, 239–40; and guerrilla insurgencies, 3, 258; and Huston Plan, 12, 101–2, 118–19; informal, 132–40, 141; institutionalizing domestic, 218–21; and Joint Terrorism Task Forces, 243, 263, 265; Miller's efforts to develop, 194–95, 202–3; and Munich Olympics attack, 211–12; and PATRIOT Act, 2, 12, 102, 264–65; and preemption, 1–2, 8, 66, 102, 105, 157, 211, 212–13, 217–18, 223–25, 252, 256, 258; in Reagan administration, 259, 261–62; as term, 1–2; and Thurmond, 21, 260, 262; and Watergate scandal, 12–13; and wiretaps, 11–12, 265–66. *See also* terrorism

Federal Bureau of Investigation (FBI): and African American communities, 26–27; and AIM, 249, 326n38; approach to urban guerrilla warfare by, 97–98, 109–10, 163, 193–96, 220, 258; Arabs and Arab Americans as targets of, 212–18, 221–27, 324n15, 327n55; and BLA, 163, 164, 169, 175, 176–77, 181, 220, 243–45, 331n55; and BPP, 7–8, 38–39, 53, 54–62, 63, 71, 73, 170–71, 182, 294n92; break-ins by, 13–14, 121–22, 123–24, 126, 137–40, 159–60, 181, 196–97, 202, 213–18, 240–41, 324n15, 324n19, 325n24; and Capitol bombing, 150–51; Church Committee investigation of, 63, 75–76, 155, 217, 220, 277–78n16; and civil liberties, 6, 31, 34, 119, 155–56, 160, 205, 229; and Communist Party, 25–26, 34, 138, 190, 286–87n51, 309n61; and Congress, 145–46, 153–54, 205; and counterterrorism, 8, 141, 183, 202–4, 211–13, 219–21, 232, 239–40, 260, 265; Domestic Security Division of, 26, 29, 77, 182, 190, 196, 203, 227, 249–50; Domestic Security Guidelines of, 262; and George Jackson death, 180; and Hampton-Clark killings, 94–95, 301n66; and Hearst kidnapping/SLA, 248, 249–56, 258; Hoover battle with Nixon over, 13–14, 31–34, 91, 103–4, 148–49, 184, 186, 231; and hostage crises, 8, 216; illegal surveillance practices of, 8, 27, 88, 121–22, 123–24, 126, 133, 136–39, 159–60, 183, 196, 197–98; indexes of, 25, 221; informants used by, 71, 103, 104–5, 121, 126, 127, 128, 133–34, 135, 156, 182, 221, 245, 321n76, 326n38, 331n55; internal bureaucratic conflicts within, 112–13; Kelley tenure as director of, 246–48, 255, 259; and killings of police, 163, 164, 168–69, 175, 177, 243, 314n19; and Ku Klux Klan, 7, 28, 34, 179; mass surveillance

activities of, 1, 14, 24–25, 26–27, 86–87, 133, 135–36, 141, 143, 154–60, 193, 199, 213, 246, 250; and Media burglary, 151–54; and ML King, 24, 26, 28, 29, 78, 287n55, 317n68; morale within, 13, 187, 203, 246, 255; Nixon's attempt to control, 191–92, 197, 229; and Palestinian nationalists, 212, 213, 214; paranoia and conspiracy theories about, 7, 63, 151–52, 158–59, 295n124; and police brutality, 30, 40, 179–80; policy reforms by, 205; public image of, 6, 14, 27, 31, 143, 146, 148–49, 153–54, 205, 206, 220, 231, 246; resources requested by, 22, 143–44, 220; Ruckelshaus tenure as head of, 231, 238–39, 247; SAC responsibilities in, 123–24; scholarship on, 277n16; and Science for the People, 313n65; and Stokely Carmichael, 29, 284n10, 293–94n85; Ten Most Wanted list of, 17–18, 23, 34, 112, 133, *134*, 244–45, 285n40; and "terrorism" term, 100–101, 109–11, 194–96; undercover agents of, 8, 200, 209, 240, 258; and VVAW, 199–200, 201, 237, 249–50, 320–21nn69–70, 321n76; and Watergate scandal, 207–8, 220, 282–83n47; Weather Underground investigation by, 4–5, 83–90, 96–98, 103–6, 108–9, 112–13, 197–98, 202–3, 220, 240–41, 242; and women's movement, 157–59; and Wounded Knee occupation, 235–36. *See also* COINTELPROs; Gray, L. Patrick; Hoover, J. Edgar

Federal Sabotage Act of 1918, 23, 285n38

Feingold, Judi, 152–53

Felt, W. Mark, *186*; and Arab Information Center break-in, 213, 214, 217, 218, 324–25n19, 325n24; background of, 126–27; and FBI counterterrorism, 221, 232, 239–40; felony conviction of, 14; forced resignation of, 231, 239; and Gray, 198, 201, 202, 205, 206,

234–35; and Hoover, 127, 152, 184, 186; illegal surveillance and break-ins advocated by, 13–14, 126, 127, 128, 129, 135, 137, 185–86, 187–88, 194, 204, 209, 211–12, 213, 214–15, 219, 240, 255–56; indictment of, 214; and Miller, 185, 187–88; and Nixon, 187, 208, 230; Reagan pardon of, 261; and Sullivan, 127–28, 129, 146, 190–91; as Watergate "Deep Throat," 13–14, 126, 185, 204, 206–7, 208, 230, 231, 233; and Wounded Knee occupation, 235–36

Fernandez, Pablo Manuel, 201

Finch, Bob, 114

Fine, David, 125, 307n20

Flanagan, Brian, 89, 107

Fliegelman, Ronald, 93, 103

Flint War Council, 95–96, 98

Foco theory, 4, 45, 81–82, 170, 249, 291n22; explained, 45

Foerster, Werner, 244, 331n53

Ford, Gerald, 216

Ford, Joudon, 67

Fordi, Peter, 145

Foreign Intelligence Surveillance Act of 1978, 261

Forman, James, 47, 55, 56, 57

Fort, Jeff, 60–61

Foster, Marcus, 248–49, 256, 332n73

Francis, Samuel T., 262

Frappier, Nancy, 136

Freedom of Information Act, 155

French Revolution, 280–82n28

Frey, John, 49, 292n55

Friedan, Betty, 158, 159

Froines, John, 17

Front de liberation du Quebec (FLQ), 134

Fuerst, John, 112–13

Fuerzas Armadas de Liberación Nacional (FALN), 260

Gage, Beverly, 282–83n47

Gayler, Noel, 114

George, Herman L., 49–50, 292n55

George Jackson Brigade, 260

Ghetto Informant Program (GIP), 26–27

Gilbert, David, 95, 107, 263, 335n14

Gilday, William, 130

Goebel, Linda, 15, 35, 285n40

Gold, Ted, 99

Gonzalez, Juan, 330n38

Gonzalez, Vergilio, 206

Goodman, Andrew, 179

Graham, John, 329n24

Grathwohl, Larry, 97, 103, 108, 303n8

Gray, L. Patrick, 194, 214, 237; and BLA, 243–44; and counterterrorism, 8, 211–12, 219–20, 232, 239–40; domestic surveillance reduced by, 221; and Felt, 198, 201, 202, 205, 206, 234–35; forced resignation of, 231, 238; and illegal surveillance activities, 137, 197, 198, 200, 201–2, 204, 214–15; on international terrorism, 199, 219–20, 227; and Kissinger wiretaps, 234–35, 329n17; named by Nixon to replace Hoover, 13, 187, 192, 208–9, 232–33, 318n9; as Nixon loyalist, 230–31; nominated as permanent FBI director, 229, 234; Senate confirmation hearings of, 219–30, 231, 234–35, 237–38; targeting of Arabs and Arab Americans by, 214–15, 221, 324–25n19; and Watergate, 206, 207–8, 228, 257

Green, Woody, 244

Greenwich Village townhouse explosion (1970), 98, 99–101

Guatemala coup (1954), 9

guerrilla warfare, 10, 42, 44–45. *See also* urban guerrilla warfare

Guevara, Ernesto Ché, 4, 81, 82, 170; "Message to the Tricontinental" by, 44–45

Haig, Alexander, 247

Haldeman, H. R., 33; and Hoover, 148, 189; and Huston Plan, 114, 117, 128–29; and Watergate, 207, 233, 257

Huston Plan: drafting of, 20, 113–18; as first counterterrorism attempt, 12, 101–2, 118–19; and Hoover, 11, 13, 102, 116–17, 118, 120–21, 148, 305n67; Huston's effort to reinstate, 128–29; scholarship on, 302–3n7
Hutton, Bobby, 51, 292n62

illegal surveillance practices: and "black bag jobs," 25, 286n48; against Communist Party, 25; and counterterrorism, 8, 11–12, 183; Felt advocacy of, 13–14, 126, 127, 128, 129, 135, 137, 185–86, 187–88, 194, 204, 209, 211–12, 213, 214–15, 219, 240, 255–56; and Gray, 137, 197, 198, 200, 201–2, 204, 214–15; Hoover authorization of, 1, 121, 133, 135–36, 140, 159–60, 190–91, 196–97; Hoover reluctance to use, 6, 27–28, 90, 121, 168–69; mail tracking and opening, 122, 136–37, 138, 159–60; Miller advocacy of, 13, 137, 187–88, 194, 196, 197–98, 209, 211–12, 240; Nixon support for, 188–89, 193, 318n11; by Squad 19, 139–40; by Squad 47, 137–39, 140, 194, 196–97, 202, 240–41; Sullivan advocacy of, 90, 135, 139, 188; Supreme Court on, 203–4, 322n89; warrantless wiretaps, 25, 33, 102, 121–22, 136, 138–39, 197–98, 203–4, 230, 256, 264–65, 322n89. *See also* break-ins
informants, 132–33; in BLA, 245, 331n55; in BPP, 71, 182; in KKK, 28; reduction in number of, 221, 326n38; underage, 121, 126, 127, 128, 135, 156; in VVAW, 321n76; undercover agents differentiated from, 7; in Weatherman, 103, 104–5
Institute for Policy Studies, 249
Intelligence Evaluation Committee (IEC), 148
Interagency Committee on Intelligence (Ad Hoc), 115–16

Interdivisional Information Unit (IDIU), 33
Internal Revenue Service (IRS), 31, 284n12
International Association of Chiefs of Police, 148–49, 166, 169
International Telephone and Telegraph (ITT), 242
Iran coup (1953), 9
Iran hostage crisis, 261, 335n5
Irish Republican Army, 11
Israel, 10, 199, 218–19
ITT–Dita Beard controversy, 192, 205, 237

Jabara, Abdeen, 216, 222, 223
Jackson, Andrew, 245
Jackson, George, 120, 180, 316n49; killing of, 175, 177–78, 180
Jackson, Jesse, 92
Jackson, Jonathan, 8, 120–21, 122, 126, 306n1; and Angela Davis, 124, 307n10
Jackson State College, 111
Jacobs, Jamal, 174
Jacobs, John, 97, 98, 107
Japanese Red Army, 199, 320n66
Al-Jawary, Khalid Duhhan, 225–26
Jaworski, Leon, 248
Jewish Defense League (JDL), 135, 276n9, 309n61
Johnson, Cedric, 276n11
Johnson, Chalmers, 264
Johnson, Deborah, 91
Johnson, Lyndon B., 9, 21, 22, 105, 179; and Hoover, 24, 26, 27, 28, 287n63; and Vietnam, 184, 241, 318n10
Johnson, Marlin C., 86, 88, 94–95, 106
Johnson, Matthew, 49
Johnson, Raymond, 41
Joint Terrorism Task Forces (JTTFs), 243, 263, 265
Jones, Jeff, 83, 97, 107, 137; FBI manhunt for, 100, 150–51, 241
Jones, Joe Lee, 245
Jones, LeRoi, 47

Seale, Bobby, 36, 43, 56, 63, 71, 76, 145; antipolice rhetoric of, 70, 73, 172; BPP membership frozen by, 62, 283n5; and Chicago Eight, 17, 65, 194, 284n10; and survival programs, 72, 93

Seberg, Jean, 63, 295n123

Segretti, Donald, 328n10

Senate Internal Security Committee, 21, 25

Shackelford, Robert L., 82–83, 130, 136–37, 150, 197

Shakur, Afeni, 66

Shakur, Assata, 170, 243, 244, 315n23, 331n53

Shakur, Lumumba, 182

Shakur, Mutulu, 263

Shakur, Zayd Malik, 244

Shaw, Jack, 146

Sierakowski, Stanley, 75

Sikes, Robert L. F., 150

Sirhan, Sirhan Bishara, 216

Sirica, John, 229

Smith, Sandy, 207, 209, 233, 234–35

Smith, William French, 262

Smith Act of 1940, 106, 303–4n27

Snowden, Edward, 336n24

Socialist Workers Party (SWP), 26, 34, 249–50

Soledad Brothers, 120

solitary confinement, 265, 336n27

Soltysik, Patrica, 248, 333n91

Somoza Debayle, Anastasio, 263

South Africa: Terrorism Act of 1967, 10

Southern Christian Leadership Conference (SCLC), 28–29

Special Target Informant Development Program (SPECTAR), 200, 209

Squad 19 (Los Angeles), 139–40

Squad 47 (New York), 137–39, 140, 194, 196–97, 202, 240–41

Stalin, Joseph: *The Foundations of Leninism*, 74

Stampnitzky, Lisa, 227

Stanford, Maxwell, 26

State of Siege (Costa-Gavras), 306n5

"States of emergency," 23, 285n38

Stein, Anne, 108

Steinem, Gloria, 158

Stellar Wind, 335–36n24

Stern, Carl, 220, 247, 334n103

Stiner, George and Larry, 295n122

St. Louis, MO, 109, 131, 182, 195

Stone, Harlan Fiske, 286n43

Student Nonviolent Coordinating Committee (SNCC), 29, 52, 138; and BPP, 55–57

Students for a Democratic Society (SDS), 15, 136; 1969 national convention of, 79–81, 86; and armed guerrilla struggle, 52, 53; COINTELPRO operations against, 29, 83–84, 87, 88; disintegration of, 140

Sturgis, Frank, 206

Subcommittee on Terrorism and Security, 262

"suicide bugs," 204

Sullivan, William C., 79, 90–91, 97; background of, 77, 78; and Felt, 127–28, 129, 146, 190–91, 239; and Hoover, 78, 89, 90, 128, 146, 154, 184, 185, 187, 189–90; and Huston Plan, 11, 78–79, 114, 115, 116–17; illegal surveillance advocated by, 90, 135, 139, 188; and Kissinger wiretaps, 190–91; poison-pen letter to King by, 78, 287n55; and "terrorism," 100, 101, 110; and Weatherman, 84, 96

suspect communities, 26–27, 213, 258

Swearingen, M. Wesley, 139, 140; *FBI Secrets*, 112–13

Symbionese Liberation Army (SLA), 248–56; about, 248; assassination of Marcus Foster by, 248–49, 256, 332n73; attack on Los Angeles hideout of, 252, 253–54, 255, 333n91; blows to FBI by, 256, 258; Hearst in captivity of, 250–51; Hearst joining of, 251, 254; kidnapping of Hearst by, 232, 248, 249, 306n5